MW01595953

The Orphan in Fiction and Comics since the 19th Century

The Orphan in Fiction and Comics since the 19th Century

By

Marion Gymnich,
Barbara Puschmann-Nalenz,
Gerold Sedlmayr
and Dirk Vanderbeke

Cambridge
Scholars
Publishing

The Orphan in Fiction and Comics since the 19th Century

By Marion Gymnich, Barbara Puschmann-Nalenz, Gerold Sedlmayr
and Dirk Vanderbeke

This book first published 2018

Cambridge Scholars Publishing

Lady Stephenson Library, Newcastle upon Tyne, NE6 2PA, UK

British Library Cataloguing in Publication Data
A catalogue record for this book is available from the British Library

Copyright © 2018 by Marion Gymnich, Barbara Puschmann-Nalenz,
Gerold Sedlmayr and Dirk Vanderbeke

All rights for this book reserved. No part of this book may be reproduced,
stored in a retrieval system, or transmitted, in any form or by any means,
electronic, mechanical, photocopying, recording or otherwise, without
the prior permission of the copyright owner.

ISBN (10): 1-5275-0926-5
ISBN (13): 978-1-5275-0926-9

CONTENTS

Introduction

The Orphan in Fiction and Comics since the 19th Century

Marion Gymnich, Barbara Puschmann-Nalenz, Gerold Sedlmayr, Dirk Vanderbeke

The present study investigates the vast and diverse appearances of the orphan in fictional narratives. It analyses the ways in which this figure has been represented and given expression in literature from the beginning of the 19th century to the present. Literature is a privileged space in which key concepts pertaining to the way in which we have fashioned our societies and ourselves are discussed, negotiated, and formed. By tracing the development the representation of the orphan character has undergone in the past 200 years, it is possible to shed light on the evolution of other important concepts, like childhood, family, the status of the parental legacy, individualism, charity, etc. Of course, a study like ours cannot deal with the orphan motif exhaustively. In the first four of our chapters, we will focus on British literature, with the occasional look across the Atlantic and at Postcolonial Anglophone literatures. In contrast, the last chapter—dealing with the orphan in comics—will concentrate primarily on US-American texts, simply because the US has always been the prime market for comic books.

Orphans in the Victorian Novel

In the first chapter, Marion Gymnich discusses the figure of the orphan in the Victorian period, a time that is often considered to be "the most famous age of orphan stories" (Reynolds 2009, 273), having brought forth some of the best-known literary orphans, including Charles Dickens's Oliver Twist, Charlotte Brontë's Jane Eyre and Thomas Hardy's Jude

Fawley. In the Victorian period the term "orphan" was generally used somewhat more broadly than today, referring to children who had lost both of their parents as well as to those who still had a father or a mother, i.e., half-orphans (cf. Peters 2000, 1). While one may assume that, due to factors such as the death of many women in childbirth, Victorian children were indeed much more likely to lose at least one of their parents than children today, this historical fact alone is hardly sufficient to explain why the orphan was such an immensely popular figure in Victorian literature.

As the examples mentioned above already suggest, Victorian literary orphans tend to be younger and often more innocent than their predecessors in 18th-century and early-19th-century literature (König 2014). While the emotional intensity with which depictions of (suffering) orphans are often endowed in the Victorian novel may partially be accounted for by the use of the orphan as a supposedly universal embodiment of loneliness, Victorian representations of orphans are also informed by the sociocultural coordinates and ideologies of the period. The concept of childhood as a time of innocence, which burgeoned in Romanticism and developed into a fully-fledged idealisation of childhood in the course of the Victorian period, rendered an exploration of the orphaned child more interesting for Victorian writers and readers alike. Similarly, the "ideology of the 'proper' family", which was conceived of as "a refuge from the world" (Alston 2008, 17), resonates in Victorian images of orphanhood in various ways. In the light of idealised notions of the social unit of the (nuclear) family, the adopted child could become an intruder (*Jane Eyre*) or the agent who makes bliss in a family-like unit possible in the first place (Eppie in George Eliot's *Silas Marner*). In any case, the situation of the Victorian orphan is by definition a precarious one. In a society that knew neither adoption laws nor reliable security networks for parentless children, the (young) orphan is dependent on others' goodwill as well as on his or her own resilience and ingenuity.

While it would be intriguing to examine a wider range of representations of orphans in Victorian literature, including both dramatic texts and popular narratives (e.g. street ballads), the chapter will primarily discuss texts that have become classics. The main reason for the decision to choose novels by well-known authors is that these are the texts that have proved to be enormously influential as far as the history of the literary orphan is concerned. Though they were shunned by Modernist writers as relics of outdated stories of self-improvement and maudlin sentimentality, figures such as Oliver Twist, Pip Pirrip and Jane Eyre serve as "prototypical orphans" to the present day, providing templates for postcolonial rewritings as well as for children's literature and for images of orphanhood circulating in today's popular culture. Yet, a closer look at some of the orphans roaming the Victorian novel soon shows that authors like Dickens, the Brontë sisters, George Eliot and Thackeray do not simply reproduce the same kind of character again and again. Instead, orphans turn out to be enormously versatile figures in terms of their characteristics, their fictional life trajectories and in terms of the issues that are addressed via this particular literary figure.

The proliferation of orphans in Victorian literature mainly results from the fact that this figure lent itself like no other to negotiating a range of different social problems and anxieties. Political discourses in the Victorian period even identified the orphans themselves as a social problem. After all, public interest in the orphan was fuelled by

> the anxiety Victorians felt when trying to cope with the large number of orphans and street children in their own time. Newspaper articles and novels attempted to focus on successful management of orphans from all classes, and, in most cases, these children were seen as threats to maintaining a successful, productive society because they did not have any solid, secure moral influences or, in many cases, a verifiable history (Reynolds 2009, 278).

Several emigration schemes were put into effect during the period in order to send orphans abroad, where they were supposed to help populate the British colonies and, ideally, make their fortunes. The chapter on orphans in the Victorian novel suggests a basic distinction between three different (proto)types of orphans: the pathetic orphan, the orphan as a figure of hope, and the orphan as adventurer. Each of these three types fulfils (multiple) distinct functions and relates to Victorian discourses in specific ways. The pathetic orphan for instance served as a potent vehicle for social criticism targeting institutions such as the workhouse and practices such as baby farming as well as the widespread callousness of individuals in the face of the plight of parentless children. While a number of writers utilise the figure of the pathetic orphan to intensify social critique, there are also novels that use this trope ironically, for instance as a device to reveal a character's hypocrisy. The orphan as a figure of hope embodies widespread notions of self-improvement. Thus, it does not come as a particular surprise that this type of orphan can be found quite often in the genre of the *bildungsroman,* whose protagonists frequently embody the notion that success is based primarily on the individual's intellectual and moral resources. Towards the end of the 19th century, the trope of the orphan as a figure of hope is increasingly discredited, giving way to a bleaker outlook on an orphan's chance of achieving (worldly) success and finding happiness. A considerable amount of optimism survives in adventure novels, which often feature orphans as protagonists. Here, even very young orphans like Kipling's Mowgli continue to display an outstanding gift for surviving and even thriving in the most adverse circumstances. This also turns the orphaned protagonists of the adventure novel, which is typically set in colonies or regions that could be colonised, into representatives of imperialist thinking.

The Orphan in 20th- and 21st-Century British Fiction

For a considerable time, Nina Auerbach's article "Incarnations of the Orphan" (1975) remained the solitary investigation of the literary orphan figure. It stood alone in the evaluation of a motif that was extremely popular in 18th- and 19th-century fiction in Britain, but had received little critical attention that could be called systematic or theoretically well-founded. In addition, Auerbach's initiative, whose temporal frame extended beyond the 19th century, abstained from seriously considering the orphan in narratives of her own era. While Eva König's book-length study (2014) is proof enough that the lacuna remains a rewarding field for scholarship, it is restricted to the orphan in the Early Modern novel. In her two chapters, Barbara Puschmann-Nalenz compensates for this omission.

Auerbach's reticence to engage with 20th-century fiction may have had two reasons. In the Edwardian era, the popularity of the orphan character had shifted to children's literature, as David Floyd's recent research shows. Moreover, the rise of fantasy literature, which began in Britain in the last half of the 19th century thanks to George MacDonald and William Morris, but gathered steam in the first half of the 20th century with J.R.R. Tolkien and C.S. Lewis, exhibited a different use of the orphan trope, which equally persisted in romance and crime fiction or thrillers. Amazingly, however, the motif was all but abandoned for mainstream fiction, even in narratives thematising war or other catastrophic events. This striking development—the second possible reason for criticism's disregard of the orphan character—is disclosed in the chapter "The Gap or, the Dying Orphan", which also addresses the perplexing link between the interval in orphan narratives and the generational blank in British social history caused by the original catastrophe of the 20th century, the First World War. When Auerbach declares Stephen Dedalus, hero of *A Portrait of the Artist as a Young Man* (1916), the paradigmatic orphan figure for 20th-century narrative fiction (Auerbach 1975, 416-17), her clarification of the ways and purposes in which Joyce uses the "orphan" character remains problematic, particularly because it is only in the last lines that

Stephen makes himself an orphan by exile to become an artist, imploring the "old artificer" (Joyce [1916] 1973, 253) to be his (god)father. Towards the end of the century, Julia Kristeva's socio-political analysis of the foreigner (Kristeva 1991, 1-2, 21-23) depicts this figure as self-orphaned much like Auerbach's portrayal of Stephen. Auerbach claims that Joyce plays with the orphan myth, only to debunk it in *Ulysses* in the figure of Stephen (Auerbach 1975, 416). Her second example, *The Horse's Mouth* (1957) by Joyce Cary, appears in a very incongruent combination with *A Portrait of the Artist*—an incomparability that is ignored by the critic. While Stephen imaginatively represents the orphaned exile as self-made man, Cary's protagonist Jimson, according to Auerbach, stands for "perpetual incoherence and loss" (Auerbach 1975, 418), thereby heralding a new beginning of the literary motif.

The chapter "The Gap" in this volume is dedicated—partly on account of the discrepancies in Auerbach's concluding evaluations—to the analysis of rare examples of narratives from the first half of the 20th century, where the central character is orphaned as a child or young person. When Auerbach prefers to address the orphan figure of the modernist period "as a picaresque artist" (Auerbach 1975, 416) she points to an important innovative element of the trope that first emerges in Joyce's *Portrait*, but which the reader also encounters in several mainstream novels of lesser renown: the orphaned artist figure that foretells an interconnection with the orphaned protagonist of fantasy fiction. "Picaresque", however, is an attribute atypical of the characters in the narratives at hand. Their melancholia, isolation and premature disappearance indicate a gloomy or disconcerted mood. The historical hiatus making itself felt in British society as well as in the literary history of the English orphan narrative and its criticism demanded a return to origins or the laying of new foundations, or both. "The Gap" is thus an ambiguous key-word with regard to the literary orphan figure in the English novel, since such a blank space also opens up in and is constitutive for the orphan's life narrative and (self-) image.

While up to the 1980s the orphan remains a rarity in literary fiction despite the historical reality of two world wars that produced a great number of orphaned children, Anglophone narratives of the past twenty years show an overwhelmingly frequent use of the character (cf. also Puschmann-Nalenz 2014). In the chapter "Some Things Remain Broken Forever"—a quotation from Kazuo Ishiguro's novel *When We Were Orphans*—the range of novelistic employments of the orphan, with an emphasis on post-millennial works, is explored. The orphan as *picaro* can be found in a few narratives and thus continues a tradition which criticism has observed from Defoe to Joyce. Yet tragedy, bereavement and absence also play a greater part in the fictions published from the 1980s onwards, with the disappearance of the mother as a strikingly common motif. Socio-cultural theories by Julia Kristeva and feminist postulations by Luce Irigaray are called on to explain this literary particularity in an age when the death of mothers of young children—compared to the 18th and 19th centuries—is uncommon. The wide range of orphan figures appears even more diverse when, apart from the biological, also functional and cultural orphans, increasingly narrativised in the last fifteen years, expand the compass of the motif and its concomitant themes.

As a consequence of the multiplicity of circumstances considered relevant for orphanhood today, the question of parental substitution receives high priority in fictions; hence, in-laws, foster-mothers or -fathers and institutions such as orphanages take centre stage in part 3 of the chapter "Some Things Remain Broken Forever". In a number of cases, the evaluation of fictional surrogates reveals them as poor-to-wicked replacements because of their incapacity and unwillingness to offer affection, thus recalling the *topos* of the fairy-tale stepmother. This seems all the more noteworthy since in the social reality of recent decades the institutionalised substitution of parental care and educational functions has become a favourite topic for public discussion and political agendas. In the literary narratives, the family, a much-debated phenomenon, still emerges to be as fundamental for an individual as it remains problematic. Successful emotional substitution of a parent turns out to be a scarcity in the sample of about twenty British and postcolonial novels.

The orphan as a person of unknown or unrevealed origins, but endowed with graces that render him/her a communal benefit or a blessing for others is a rare but lately re-surfacing figure that also ostentatiously refers back to the ancient mythology of the foundling. In this type, surrealistic elements can mingle with mythic ones. With a renewed myth as a component of contemporary fiction, the orphan becomes a polysemiotic sign. In the middle of the second decade of the 21st century the trope of the literary orphan proves to be an increasingly colourful and fascinating device.

The chapter closes with a brief reflection on a topic that emerges several times in the novels, because of its close link to the orphan figure: "home" is assessed as a subject of narrative attention.

Orphans in Fantasy

In the penultimate chapter, Gerold Sedlmayr looks at fantasy literature. Rather than offering a broad overview, he aims at a detailed consideration of the orphan motif in three of the most successful and influential fantasy narratives of recent times, namely J.K. Rowling's *Harry Potter* septology (1997-2007), Philip Pullman's *His Dark Materials* trilogy (1995-2000), and George R.R. Martin's *A Song of Ice and Fire* series (1996ff.), which will comprise a projected seven volumes at its completion; at the time of writing, five volumes have been published, the last being *A Dance with Dragons* (2011). No doubt, orphans have prominently featured in fantasy tales for a long time: Peter Pan and his Lost Boys are orphans, just like Frodo in Tolkien's *The Lord of the Rings*, the eponymous Prince Caspian in the fourth novel of C.S. Lewis' *The Chronicles of Narnia*, Ged in Ursula Le Guin's *Earthsea* tales, or the child protagonists in Lemony Snicket's *A Series of Unfortunate Events* series. Apart from these "true" orphans, there are many characters that Maria Nikolajeva terms "functional orphans" (Nikolajeva 2002, 172), i.e. individuals that grow up as if they did not have any parents, although these may still be alive. This is the case, for example, with Lucy, Edmund, Susan and Peter, the central protagonists in many of Lewis' *Narnia* stories.

It is strange, therefore, that hardly any critical work has been done in this field. James Michael Curtis, who, in 2016, submitted his PhD thesis *In Absentia Parentis: The Orphan Figure in Latter Twentieth Century Anglo-American Children's Fantasy*, claims that "[t]he vast majority of sustained critical work on orphans in literature—works written for children and for adults—focus predominantly on realist texts from the nineteenth century, leaving both the entirety of the twentieth century and the fantasy genre virtually ignored" (2016, 7). While this bespeaks the implicit prioritisation of "realist" literature over fantastic and fantasy tales in traditional canon formation, Curtis also proposes that, at least regarding the study of children's literature, scholars "have passed over these types of characters as mere recurrent tropes, devoid of any real substance beyond their being narrative fixtures or staples of nineteenth-century social reform" (2016, 1). Quite obviously, as Curtis demonstrates in his thesis, such scholarly disregard is undeserved. Even if the orphan were nothing but a "narrative fixture" (which is not the case, as the present volume seeks to demonstrate), its on-going use would not necessarily indicate that an archetypal universalist meaning was attached to the motif. On the contrary, since it is reused in, and hence cannot help being adapted to different contexts, it rather reveals its protean nature and becomes itself expressive of the respective culturally specific mind-sets.

Accordingly, while it may be true that many literary orphan characters function as a "manifestation of loneliness" but at the same time "represent the possibility for humans to reinvent themselves", as Melanie A. Kimball (1999, 559) argues in her examination of the orphan motif in fifty folktales from different cultures, the implied consequences still differ widely. For instance, in C.S. Lewis' *The Horse and His Boy*, the third instalment in the *Narnia* series, the functional orphanhood of Shasta, who ultimately is able to discover his parents, his true name, and hence his "roots", is more than a nice narrative commonplace. Rather, it quite explicitly functions as the vehicle of a problematic, ideologically biased "Orientalist" narrative meant to reveal the moral, spiritual and intellectual "superiority" or "paternity" of Northern European cultures. Of course, depending on the critic's own take, the evaluation of a text's historical situatedness may lead to different results. Hence, to take another example, Lauren Byler very specifically regards *Harry Potter* as symptomatic of the prevailing neoliberal climate in the late 20th and 21st centuries in which concepts of "self-improvement and self-sufficiency" (2016, 115) are propagated at the expense of communal cohesion: "the overarching message of the series is that extreme individualism epitomizes the most admirable and valuable type of personhood" (120). The present contribution argues otherwise: namely that Voldemort's extreme individualism, which in turn is a consequence of his own orphan status, has catastrophic effects, which can only be countered by the community of which Harry, another orphan, becomes an integral part; whenever Harry isolates himself and so follows in the footsteps of Voldemort, he comes close to failure. Be that as it may, Byler's intriguing article is representative of much critical work on fantasy in that she mentions Harry's all-too-obvious status as orphan only in passing, without taking into account the possible relevance of the trope for her argument. In fact, when she suggests that, by letting go of the powerful Elder Wand at the end of the series, Harry "effectively concludes his makeover from a self-estranged orphan to a self-possessed hero" (Byler 2016, 137), she does not even consider whether the neoliberal individual might be synonymous with (postmodern) orphanhood. Byler's article hence is indicative of the fact that while there is hardly any critical work that focuses specifically on the orphan motif, there are numerous contributions that—if ever so slightly—touch upon topics which are relevant for an evaluation of the orphan heroes in fantasy tales: in the case of Harry Potter, for example, there are articles on Harry's relationship to his parents, on all kinds of surrogate parents, on friendship, etc. The same goes for *His Dark Materials* and *A Song of Ice and Fire*.

In this sense, Curtis' PhD thesis—which exclusively focuses on children's literature, though—most certainly fills a gap. His approach is strictly psychoanalytical, arguing that

> children's fantasy orphan narratives [...] externaliz[e] inner psychological processes and [allow] the orphan protagonists [...] the opportunity to process psycho-developmental struggles in the absence of the parental influence that child developmental theorists claim is vital to the normalizing trajectory towards successful psychological progression to adulthood. (Curtis 2016, 16)

In contrast, the present study is not so much interested in the psychological development of the protagonists, but in the connection between the orphan motif, the influence and status of myth, and generic implications of fantasy. Starting from both Brian Attebery's assumption that "fantasy, as a literary form, is a way of reconnecting to traditional myths and the worlds they generate" (2014, 9) and Jacques Derrida's observations on the link in Plato's work between *mythos*, writing, and the orphan, of which Laura Peters also avails herself in her study on the Victorian orphan, it will be asked in which ways the orphan figure in fantasy functions both as a strategic device to negotiate Western metaphysical traditions and a means to "write oneself" in any meaningful way. In *Harry Potter*, this negotiation happens on the basis of the juxtaposition of Harry and Voldemort, both of whom must come to grips with their own orphan background in order to find their place in the world but choose different ways to do so: while Voldemort attempts to set himself up as wholly original, Harry realises that his own story can only be of consequence if he accepts its being entwined with the stories of others—which in turn carry equal significance and worth. Similarly, the functional orphan Lyra, the main protagonist in Pullman's decidedly intertextual trilogy, probes the truth claims of her parents as soon as she realises who they are, and ultimately understands that while each conscious being carries their own true story, such truth is never essential in the Platonic sense, but always material, dynamic and tied to a living here and now. In Pullman's cosmos, there is no capital-lettered Truth, no paternal *Logos*, which would be binding in any absolute sense; no destiny written in advance. Martin's *A Song of Ice and Fire* may eventually turn out to be more conventional than Rowling's and Pullman's narratives, depending, amongst other things, on whether Dany, the central orphan character, will be successful by the end of the series. After all, judged by our standards, she is driven by the outdated belief that she has the dynastic right to be queen of Westeros, a right that has come down to her from her parents via "blood". However, while the fantasy genre commonly returns to bygone ways of placing the self in the world (for example through "blood right") and so, on the metalevel, also to older (parental) modes of storytelling—what Northrop Frye refers to as "mythic", "romantic" and "high mimetic" modes—*A Song of Ice and Fire* demonstrates that it necessarily does so by way of moving through the "low mimetic" and "ironic" modes as well. This, though, is part of their *ratio*: the fantasy stories discussed here are innovative precisely because they creatively refer back to older myths and stories, but without being able to or even wanting to ultimately insist on their binding powers.

Orphans in Comics

In the volume's last chapter, Dirk Vanderbeke widens the scope and looks at a medium situated between literature and the graphic/visual arts. If orphans are no longer a central motif in mainstream 20th-century literature until the 1980s, this is decidedly not the case in the comics where ever since the end of the 19th century orphans seem to be the norm rather than the exception. Depending on the different genres—funnies and gag-a-day-strips, comic books, superhero comics, underground comix, and autobiographical comics—orphans appear in very diverse contexts, even if specific patterns are, of course, clearly noticeable. Sometimes the motif serves the generic requirements, or traditional narrative types are resurrected, but then the orphan occasionally also seems to serve commercial interests. In the face of their near ubiquity, however, orphans in comics have not been systematically researched. Of course, in the discussion of single works like *Gasoline Alley* or subgenres like the superhero comics the motif could not have escaped notice, but no thorough investigation has yet been published, an omission which this chapter intends to remedy.

When sequential pictorial narratives started to appear in American newspapers and Sunday supplements, the stories were short and consisted of only a few pictures. These minimal stories, usually culminating in a joke, lent themselves to the depiction of humorous pranks and mischief and thus also to juvenile protagonists, and as the format did not allow for any development of background or extended characterisation, it is occasionally difficult or impossible to determine whether the youngsters are orphans or functional orphans, or whether parents simply do not make an appearance. Thus, we learn only after quite some time that the Yellow Kid is, indeed, an orphan while most of the other urchins seem to have parents who are, however, usually absent from the stories.

When the artists began to organise the strips into longer narrations which were still published in the original format of daily strips, this also had an impact on the orphan motif. Unlike novels, which can speed up the narration and omit unwelcome aspects of the story but also include elements that were not considered suitable for the innocent entertainment of the funnies, the comic strips published on a day-to-day-basis were at the same time more and less realistic. They were less realistic as the time is frequently frozen and no real development takes place, but they are also more realistic as temporal gaps are very rare, if they exist at all. In addition, the series, which often ran on for many years—some are still around today—were not completely planned out, and experimental changes could be introduced quickly; in this they are similar to serialised novels of the 19th century, which could also accommodate reader's responses for higher circulation and commercial success. If a new feature or figure seemed promising to the comic artist or the publisher, it could be included immediately, but if it did not meet the approval of the audience, it could easily be dropped again equally quickly. Famously, the publisher of *Gasoline Alley* wanted to increase the appeal and reach a female audience and thus demanded to have a child added to the strip. But as courtship, marriage, and pregnancy would take up considerable time and also include elements that were not acceptable in the funnies, the child was delivered as an orphan to the doorstep of the main character and, being very successful, stayed with him ever after. Similarly, Huey, Dewey and Louie were dropped off at Donald's house by his sister and simply never picked up again—in consequence, most readers assume that they must be orphans, even though strictly speaking they are on a very long visit to their uncle.

In such cases, orphanhood is not linked to any loss, grief, or suffering, but once orphans are presented outside of a safe environment like the peer group in the Yellow Kid comics or the home of the foster parent in *Gasoline Alley*, more traditional plot elements or clichés à la *Oliver Twist* appear. In *Little Orphan Annie*, the orphanage where the young heroine grows up is a dismal place with little warmth or affection, and the danger of being returned there remains a constant threat throughout the series. In other stories, in particular in early detective and superhero comics, orphans and orphanages are occasionally introduced as potential victims of corrupt and criminal officials and administrators; they will eventually be saved by the respective hero who originally, and particularly in the era of the New Deal, frequently followed a social agenda.

With the rise of the superhero comics, the motif of the orphan undergoes a radical change. As in 20th-century fantasy, the heroes and, less often, heroines are to some extent constructed on the patterns of the mythological hero and follow modified variants of the heroic journey described in the Campbellian monomyth, and thus they are quite regularly orphans. In addition, some of them witness the violent death of one or both parents which may trigger the decision to fight crime. But then those heroes are also haunted by the return of the trauma and occasionally more or less justified feelings of guilt. Over the decades, such stories of origin are usually embellished and extended, and in some storylines the heroic orphans have become neurotic or even psychotic.

With the turn to underground comix, graphic novels and life writing, orphans become less frequent. Autobiographical plot elements and more mature topics shift the works towards the real living conditions of the 20th century in which orphanhood is no longer a common phenomenon. The loss of parents happens at later stages of life, and the actual moment of loss is often embedded in the routines or mechanics of modern life; in consequence, the experience is numbed and the protagonists have to come to terms with their seeming indifference and failure at "authentic" grief. These works may still show the graphic eccentricities and an occasionally bizarre imagery that mark some subgenres of comics and graphic novels, but they are ultimately quite close to the narratives in mainstream literature which explore emotional responses to tragedy in our world, a world that is marked by alienation, inhibitions, fragmentation, and isolation.

In comics journalism or documentary comics, the focus is often on catastrophes like war or natural disasters, and here orphans or functional orphans may become important again. The orphan appears as the emblematic consequence of failed politics, aggression and violence, inhumanity, or simply social incompetence and indifference in our urban landscapes.

Works Cited

Alston, Ann. 2008. *The Family in English Children's Literature*. New York and London: Routledge.

Attebery, Brian. 2014. *Stories about Stories: Fantasy and the Remaking of Myth*. Oxford: Oxford University Press.

Auerbach, Nina. 1975. "Incarnations of the Orphan." *English Literary History* 42: 395-419.

Byler, Lauren. 2016. "Makeovers, Individualism, and Vanishing Community in the *Harry Potter* Series." *Children's Literature* 44: 115-46.

Cunningham, Hugh. 2005. *Children and Childhood in Western Society since 1500*. 2nd edn. Harlow: Pearson.

Curtis, James Michael. 2016. *In Absentia Parentis: The Orphan Figure in Latter Twentieth Century Anglo-American Children's Fantasy*. Dissertation thesis. The University of Southern Mississippi.

Floyd, David. 2014. *Street Urchins, Sociopaths and Degenerates: Orphans of Late-Victorian and Edwardian Fiction*. Cardiff: University of Wales Press.

Joyce, James. (1916) 1973. *A Portrait of the Artist as a Young Man*. New York: Viking.

Kimball, Melanie A. 1999. "From Folktales to Fiction: Orphan Characters in Children's Literature." *Library Trends* 47 (3): 558-78.

König. Eva. 2014. *The Orphan in Eighteenth-Century Fiction: The Vicissitudes of the Eighteenth-Century Subject*. Houndmills: Palgrave Macmillan.

Kristeva, Julia. 1991. *Strangers to Ourselves*. Translated by Leon S. Roudiez. New York: Harvester Wheatsheaf. [French original: 1988].

Nikolajeva, Maria. 2002. *The Rhetoric of Character in Children's Literature*. Lanham: Scarecrow Press.

Peters, Laura. 2000. *Orphan Texts: Victorian Orphans, Culture and Empire*. Manchester: Manchester University Press.

Puschmann-Nalenz, Barbara. 2014. "The Figure of the Orphan in Contemporary Fiction." In *Narrating Loss: Representations of Mourning, Nostalgia and Melancholia in Contemporary Anglophone Fictions*, edited by Brigitte Johanna Glaser and Barbara Puschmann-Nalenz, 179-202. Trier: WVT.

Reynolds, Susan. 2009. "Dumbledore in the Watchtower: *Harry Potter* as a Neo-Victorian Narrative." In *Harry Potter's World Wide Influence*, edited by Diana Patterson, 271-92. Newcastle-upon-Tyne: Cambridge Scholars.

CHAPTER ONE

THE ORPHAN IN THE VICTORIAN NOVEL

MARION GYMNICH

Even though 18th-century literature already features a remarkable number of orphans, as Eva König has shown in her study *The Orphan in Eighteenth-Century Fiction* (2014), characters who have lost their parents appear to become even more prominent as literary figures in the course of the 19th century, which "might also be called 'the century of the orphan'" (Floyd 2014, 1). Victorian literature is replete with male and female orphans of varying ages and different social classes, some of whom fail in their endeavours or even die, while others prosper and are granted a happy ending, yet often only after having endured a considerable amount of hardship. "One can hardly open a novel by Dickens, the Brontë sisters, or George Eliot without stumbling over at least one orphan", as Laura Peters puts it in *Orphan Texts* (2000, 1). Thus, it should come as no particular surprise that many of the most memorable characters in 19th-century literature turn out to be orphans: Oliver Twist, David Copperfield, Pip Pirrip, Jane Eyre, Heathcliff, Catherine Earnshaw, Jude Fawley and Kim are just some of the many well-known literary characters in Victorian novels who are shown to grow up without parents. As these examples already illustrate, orphans often appear as main characters in Victorian novels, which additionally stresses the pivotal role the situation of parentless individuals played in literature from that era. Moreover, Victorian writers frequently juxtapose several orphans in one and the same text, which renders the motif even more visible and invites comparison. Sometimes two or more orphans share the status of main characters, for example in Emily Brontë's *Wuthering Heights* (1847) and in Elizabeth Gaskell's *Wives and Daughters*, which was first published as a serial from 1864 to 1866. There may also be further orphans in the background, appearing as minor characters or being mentioned in passing at some point or other in the course of a text. In Charles Dickens's *David Copperfield* (1849-50), for instance, there is a veritable host of orphans, including the title character, his mother Clara, Little Em'ly, Ham Peggotty, James Steerforth, Tommy Traddles, the angelic Agnes Wickfield as well as the bitter and passionate Rosa Dartle, and even a young servant girl from the workhouse who is simply known as "the Orfling".

In the Victorian period, the designation "orphan" was not restricted to children who had lost both of their parents; instead, the term was also used to refer to those boys and girls who still had one parent (cf. Peters 2000, 1). As will be shown below, it may make a huge difference whether the remaining parent is the mother or the father. Generally, literary texts tend to suggest that children who still have a father are better off than those whose remaining parent is their mother. At first sight, this general observation may appear to be at odds with "Victorian ideology [which] would seem to suggest that mothers were idealized figures who commanded worship" (Vallone 2000, 219), but the advantage of still having a father can in fact be accounted for quite easily by the period's highly gendered economy, which ensured that men on the whole stood a much better chance of making a living and providing for children than women, whose options on the job market were extremely limited. Widows were thus much more likely to become destitute or dependent on the goodwill of others than widowers. This gender imbalance is echoed in Victorian literature. In Elizabeth Gaskell's industrial novel *North and South* (1854-55), for instance, the working-class widower Nicholas Higgins manages to provide for his own children and even supports the widow and children of his co-worker Boucher after the latter's suicide. Gaskell's *Wives and Daughters*, by contrast, alludes to the fact that typical women's occupations in the Victorian period, such as governess and domestic servant, made it extremely difficult for a widow to spend time with her own child, since employers were more than likely to force a woman to separate from her child.

Another variable that was bound to have an impact on the fate of an orphan was his/her social class (cf. Peters 2000, 7), as many novels are apt to remind us. While orphans from the working class typically faced the danger of becoming destitute and thus ending up in the notorious institution of the workhouse, upper-class orphans were more likely to lead a financially secure and relatively comfortable life, even if they were deprived of affection. The title character in Oscar Wilde's *The Picture of Dorian Gray* (1891) is a case in point. Middle-class orphans, by contrast, were in danger of losing their social position and descending into the working class or even becoming destitute. This is the threat that appears to hang over the protagonist in Charlotte Brontë's novel *Jane Eyre* (1847), whose mother belonged to the upper class but was cast off by her wealthy family upon marrying a poor clergyman. When Jane's parents died, they could not leave her any money, which made her totally dependent on her relatives' goodwill.

As the examples mentioned so far already show, the term "orphan" does not refer to a clear-cut social category in Victorian literature; instead, it served as an umbrella term encompassing a wide range of different life trajectories, whose variability countless novels sought to explore. Even if one has to concede that the likelihood of becoming an orphan was significantly higher in the 19th century than it is today—due to factors such as "[t]he indisputable facts of shorter life-spans for adults, maternal death, widespread disease" (Vallone 2000, 220)—the omnipresence of parentless children in Victorian novels arguably cannot simply be accounted for by means of demographic figures. In the following, I will discuss various factors that may help to explain the popularity of literary orphans in the Victorian period.

First and foremost, the Victorian preoccupation with orphans is closely linked with changing attitudes towards childhood. What sets the many orphans populating Victorian fiction apart from the majority of their 18th- and early-19th-century predecessors is the tendency of Victorian novelists to introduce orphans as children, more often than not providing memorable scenes that depict the ways in which their parentless state has shaped their childhood as well as their personality. 18th-century literature, on the whole, "rarely deals with the orphan's formative childhood experiences" (König 2014, 2) and usually focusses on parentless individuals who have already reached a marriageable age. This changes drastically in Victorian novels. The interest in orphaned children is particularly intriguing in a period that cherished childhood as a very special stage in human life (a fact that also accounts for the late 19th century becoming the beginning of the first "golden age" of children's literature) and that tended to idealise the institution of the family,[1] while simultaneously tolerating child labour[2] and sending large numbers of orphans into the colonies in the context of so-called emigration schemes.[3]

According to Jenny Keating, "[i]n the early decades of the nineteenth century, children had still been viewed as younger adults, responsible for their actions and their conditions. By the end of the century a sentimental view was taking hold" (2009, 18). The notion of childhood as a distinct and particularly important stage of human life, which contributes to "nineteenth-century authors' fondness for using child characters" (Nelson 2014, 78), provides a vital key to understanding the striking preoccupation with young orphans in Victorian literature. As Lewis C. Roberts puts it, "[f]or many Victorians, childhood was an idealized life quite apart from the corruptions of adulthood, and for that very reason, childhood and children represented an ideal to strive for, and to protect" (Roberts 2005, 354). The Victorian notion of childhood as a stage of life that deserves to be protected can be traced back to concepts of human development which emerged earlier, in particular in the late 18th century and in the context of Romanticism, which is associated with the idea of seeing "children as close to nature and in some sense uncorrupted and pure" (Clarke 2004, 8). Although the exalted and sentimental Victorian concept of childhood is the outcome of developments that started at the very latest in the 18th century,[4] 19th-century literature does more than just perpetuate existing notions, as Claudia Nelson stresses:

> even while we concede that the Victorians inherited from older generations their interest in childhood, and some of their ideas about it, we may legitimately contend that Victorian conceptions of childrearing, of the state of being a child, and of the emotional importance of children to a society dominated by adults took on such weight as to represent something new in Western history. Never before had childhood become an obsession within the culture at large—yet in this case "obsession" is not too strong a word. (Nelson 2014, 69)[5]

In the course of the 19th century, the idealisation of children gave rise to a decidedly nostalgic approach to childhood among people from the middle class, for whom "[c]hildhood […] became the repository of good feelings and happy memories which could help the adult to live through the stickier patches of later life" (Cunningham 1991, 151). This preoccupation with childhood explains why orphans in Victorian literature are often significantly younger than their 18th-century predecessors, for instance those orphans who appear as "damsels in distress" in 18th-century Gothic novels. Last but not least, the tendency to idealise childhood as a time of innocence in the Victorian period also accounts for the appearance of famously incorruptible orphan characters such as Oliver Twist in Dickens's eponymous novel, who seems to be miraculously immune to any kind of temptation and corruption.[6]

A wide range of literary texts from the Victorian period include interesting portrayals of childhood, which are part of a "cult of the child that emerged in the nineteenth century" (Wagner 2008, 203). If these children happen to be orphans, the notion of childhood as an idealised stage of life deserving protection more often than not appears to be compromised, however, since orphans are frequently shown to be exposed to a harsh reality at a very early age. Instead of being sheltered and nurtured by parents or other caretakers, orphans in Victorian literature are typically presented in situations where they can expect little sympathy, let alone affection. There are comparatively few stories about orphans who are lucky and find caring and loving foster parents right from the start, but these stories do exist. Sometimes caretakers who make it possible for an orphan to experience a happy, largely carefree childhood are found in quite unlikely places in Victorian literature. In George Eliot's *Silas Marner* (1861), for example, it is an aging bachelor who turns out to be a loving foster father for a little girl, while a pack of wolves, a panther and a bear prove to be excellent caretakers for a toddler in Rudyard Kipling's Mowgli stories.

The overwhelming interest in orphans is a feature that Victorian novels share with the fairy tale (cf. Kimball 1999, 561), a genre that became extremely popular in the course of the 19th century and that may in fact have contributed to the overall fascination with orphans as literary figures throughout the period.[7] While the fairy tale was still considered inappropriate reading for middle-class children in the late 18th and early 19th centuries, having been "equated [...] with all that was ignorant and coarse" (Avery 1994, 123), the tales were at least "kept alive by chapbooks aimed at the cottage home" (123). In the course of the 19th century, however, the stories "were rediscovered, and gentrified and put out in up-market editions" (123). In addition to English fairy tales, the French tales by Charles Perrault and *The Arabian Nights*, which had already been available in English translations in the 18th century, were widely read. Since 1823, selected tales by the Grimms had been translated into English, and the first complete translation (by Margaret Hunt) was published in 1884 (Briggs 1991, 302). The hypothesis that the frequent occurrence of orphans in the Victorian novel is at least partially due to the popularity of the fairy tale can be supported by widespread intertextual references to this genre.[8]

According to Melanie Kimball, one may assume that the literary figure of the orphan has a certain universal appeal. Kimball, who derives her conclusions from a comparative analysis of 50 folktales originating in different cultural contexts, argues that the prominent role played by orphan heroes and heroines in fairy tales—and other types of literature—is a consequence of the fact that they are from the start singled out as exceptional characters: "orphans are clearly marked as being different from the rest of society. They are the eternal Other" (Kimball 1999, 559). Choosing an orphan as protagonist thus seems to be an ideal strategy in the realist novel for making sure that this character is likely to be perceived as unique without having to endow said character with any unusual qualities that would undermine the reality effect. The exceptional position ascribed to an orphan tends to be especially striking in those cases where the literary motif of the orphan overlaps with another one, that of the foundling. The latter has been used since antiquity to stress the uniqueness of characters. The motif of the foundling has frequently been embedded in mythological or religious frameworks which serve to lend the orphan special importance, singling her or (more often) him out as the one predestined (by gods, supernatural beings, or fate) to achieve great things, as Rachel Bowlby points out in her sketch of what one might refer to as the "foundling plot":

> A baby is abandoned by parents who cannot or will not give it a life; by good fortune it is rescued; eventually, it goes on to achieve great things. In some such sequence, this foundling story has been powerful and perennial, all the more so in that it is so far from likely reality in cultures in which, for whatever reasons, the abandonment of infants has been common. [...] Two famous ancient foundling stories being those of Moses and Oedipus. Each involves a rescued baby boy who later becomes a great man (Bowlby 2013, 87).

The trope of the foundling being saved "by good fortune" and growing up "to achieve great things" sometimes also informs the representation of children in Victorian literature, a case in point being the "man's cub" Mowgli in Kipling's *The Jungle Book* (1894). Mowgli's fate is of course reminiscent of that of two of the most famous foundlings in antiquity: Romulus and Remus.

Strictly speaking, not all foundlings are necessarily orphans. Sometimes characters who appear to be parentless at first sight turn out to have been deserted or given up by their mother, their father, or even both of their parents. Miss Havisham's adopted daughter Estella, who is not aware of the fact that her parents are criminals and are in fact still alive, in *Great Expectations* is a case in point. Stories involving children who have been given up by their parents constitute what is perhaps the darkest facet of the representation of parentless individuals in Victorian literature, since they allude to various factors that may have caused parents to desert their children in the first place, including crime and destitution. Often such stories are based on the fact that women gave up their children (or were forced to do so) in order to avoid the shame of being an unmarried mother. In fact, as Tamara Wagner reminds us, in the 19th century orphanhood served as "a common euphemism for illegitimacy" (2008, 204). Ultimately, the idea of deserting a child also entails the disconcerting question of whether the love for one's child, which we tend to consider as "normal", really comes quite as natural as one would perhaps like to believe.

One explanation for the popularity of orphan characters holds that parentless children are likely to provoke a strong emotional response among readers. This intense reaction derives from the pity orphan characters are almost bound to trigger, coupled with the possibility of "[o]rphan characters in folktales and literature symboliz[ing] our isolation from one another and from society" (Kimball 1999, 559). In other words, the figure of the orphan may manifest deep-seated human fears: "Orphans are a tangible reflection of the fear of abandonment that all humans experience. [...] Orphans are a reminder that the possibility of utter undesired solitude exists for any human being" (559).[9] By exploring what loneliness may feel like (and how one may try to cope with this emotion), representations of orphan characters invite the readers to feel empathy, i.e., "to imagine what it is like to live the life of another person who might, given changes in circumstance, be oneself" (Nussbaum 1995, 5). In this way, representations of parentless children may achieve what Martha Nussbaum considers one of the prime functions of literature, namely arousing empathy and being "disturbing in a way that history and social science writing frequently are not. Because it [literature] summons powerful emotions, it disconcerts and puzzles" (5). This function of literary orphans is visible in the (numerous) novels from the Victorian period that depict orphans whose suffering is caused by hard-hearted individuals, inhumane institutions or a combination of both.

Despite a potentially universal emotional response to the loneliness embodied by the literary figure of the orphan, one still has to assume that there is a considerable degree of cultural and historical variation with respect to representations and interpretations of orphan characters. In other words, the orphan is hardly a timeless trope; instead, it is a literary figure that responds in manifold ways to preoccupations, anxieties and hopes that are characteristic of its time. In this vein, Nina Auerbach argues that the figure of the orphan in Victorian literature was informed by the uncertainties Victorians had to face in a world that was undergoing radical change due to the far-reaching impact of industrialisation, urbanisation, new scientific developments, and a growing religious unease:

> When we think of the Victorian orphan, we think first of all of the lost boys wandering through Dickens' London, embodying in their pathos all the Victorians' self-pity and terror in the mazes of the new world the nineteenth century has inaugurated. Industrialism, religious conflict, and scientific discoveries had orphaned the Victorian age of its sense of its

past; the other side of the orphan's freedom was his fear, his need of guidance in a world without maps. (Auerbach 1975, 410)

As Auerbach points out, the literary orphan in Victorian literature can be interpreted as the embodiment of a feeling of loss and rootlessness that was arguably typical of its time, which appears to have been an "orphaned age" in some respects.

Yet at least early- and mid-Victorian culture was also informed by a strong belief in progress—a notion that is likewise reflected in many literary orphans. There are numerous parentless characters in Victorian novels who end up being successful despite their very humble beginnings in life. After periods of hardship, many a fictional orphan ultimately reaches a very respectable and secure social position. This approach to the literary figure of the orphan supports the Victorian ideal of self-improvement and the hope that prosperity could be achieved by means of one's own efforts, which was for instance promoted by Samuel Smiles's *Self-Help* (1859).[10] What literary figure could be better suited for furthering a belief in the human potential for shaping one's own fate than an individual who starts his or her life in the most adverse circumstances, being more often than not dispossessed in financial terms in addition to being deprived of emotional nurturing? While other characters could hope to benefit from their parents' financial, emotional and/or moral support, the orphan frequently was left to his or her own devices. Although orphans in Victorian literature are not universally presented as being poor, this at least appears to have been a widespread pattern. Thus, the orphan is also the ideal protagonist for the "from rags to riches"-story, which became increasingly popular in the 19th century in Great Britain as well as in the United States. By showing "the resilience of the natural victim, always managing to survive" (Auerbach 1975, 395), male orphans are apt to exemplify the ideal of the self-made man. The manufacturer Mr Thornton in Gaskell's *North and South* is depicted as a self-made man who had to support his mother and sister after his father's suicide, when he was still very young.[11] Heathcliff in Emily Brontë's *Wuthering Heights*, who at first does not call any worldly possessions his own, at one point disappears for a while only to return with a remarkable fortune and the manners of a gentleman (though admittedly not the attitude of one). There are many orphans in Victorian literature who ultimately cannot be kept down by specific obstacles or a hostile environment, no matter how precarious their situation is at times: David Copperfield manages to change his life for the better at the age of ten, and Oliver Twist as well as Jane Eyre are close to starvation at certain points in their lives, but end up in affluent positions.

Both Jane and Oliver are not entirely "self-made" characters, however, since they are ultimately saved by family members; Oliver is reunited with parts of his family, and Jane is first saved from destitution by her cousins and then inherits money from an uncle who made his fortune in Madeira. This positive impact of family members on the individual's fate supports the Victorian idealisation of the family. Still, the loss of one's parents generally seems to create much less emotional turmoil and suffering for Victorian literary orphans than for many of their 20th- and 21st-century counterparts (see the chapter "Some Things Remain Broken Forever" by Barbara Puschmann-Nalenz in this volume). While this at times surprising lack of mourning appears to be at odds with the powerful Victorian "myth of the loving nuclear family" (Alston 2008, 9), the comparative ease with which the loss of their parents is accepted by many literary orphans in 19th-century novels confirms the strong belief in individual progress, which fosters an orientation towards the future rather than the past.[12] Unlike many orphans in recent literature, including J.K. Rowling's Harry Potter (see the chapter by Gerold Sedlmayr in this volume), Victorian literary orphans typically do not go to great lengths to gather information about their parents and may thus, from today's perspective at least, even display a certain callousness.

In her comparative analysis of fairy tales, Kimball notes significant differences in terms of how societies deal with orphans. While there are cultures that tend to "cut them off from society at large" (Kimball 1999, 559), there are others in which "orphans are regarded as special people who must be protected and cared for at all costs" (559). In Victorian culture and literature both of these attitudes appear to coexist; while many officials argued that orphans should be taken care of because they held enormous promise for the future, literary texts from the period time and again focus on orphans being bullied by their peers, maltreated by caretakers and expelled from family circles that might include them. In numerous Victorian novels, orphans have to undergo considerable hardship before they find an environment in which they are cherished and protected, if they happen to find such an environment at all. To a certain extent, the fictional orphans' life trajectories reflect Victorian discourses about how society should deal with parentless children as well as the institutions that were established as a consequence of these discourses. Throughout the 19th century, there was no legislation which regulated adoption; instead, "[b]efore the Adoption of Children Act of 1926, which established a legal framework for full adoption, adoptions in England most often took the form of ad hoc arrangements, usually but not always within families" (Bowlby 2013, 139).[13] This seems to suggest that liberalism, which shaped the Victorian economy, also had an impact on family politics.

As the examples mentioned above already suggest, any study of representations of orphans in Victorian literature is also bound to address the depiction of caretakers, including widowed fathers and mothers, grandparents, aunts, uncles, brothers and sisters, stepfathers and stepmothers, foster mothers and fathers, guardians and mentors as well as people working in various institutions whose purpose was taking care of and educating orphans. The way caretakers are presented turns out to be crucial for what is arguably one of the main functions of orphan stories, i.e., the didactic goal of inviting readers to take an interest in the fate of orphans and to contribute to social reform movements. In Charlotte Brontë's *Jane Eyre*, for instance, the infamous Lowood School is transformed into a truly charitable institution once the public has recognised the despicable way in which said institution was run by the hypocritical Mr Brocklehurst. The depiction of deficits in institutions and allusions to possible improvements alike were apt to encourage Victorian readers to get interested in charitable work, or at least that is what some writers may have hoped for.

The figure of the orphan is situated at the intersection of various discourses that preoccupied Victorian society. It was, for instance, intimately connected with notions of individual progress. After all, what could be better evidence of the possibility of achieving something in one's life than a "poor and friendless" orphan eventually turning out to be successful against all odds? The impact of the cultural master narrative of self-improvement, which was informed by Puritan work ethics, even caused the authorities to increase the number of orphans by turning children of the poor into "orphans", as Peters points out:

> the state was actively encouraged to make orphans of the children of the poor. By mid-century, following evidence submitted by Mr Hickson, the Committee of the House of Commons was advocating the removal of children from "unworthy" parents (unworthy in this sense means poor and in need of relief) (Peters 2000, 13).

This policy, which is, for instance, applied in Dickens's *Great Expectations* when Jaggers "creates" an orphan by taking Estella away from her mother (cf. Gordon 2002, 215), went hand in hand with a custom practised in the notorious institution of the workhouse, which routinely separated children from their parents.[14] Destitute men and women were widely regarded as unfit for parenting. Simultaneously, the idealisation of the family and the growing significance of the "home" in the 19th century are two of the concepts that are often negotiated and problematised by means of focussing on orphans. Laura Peters claims "that the prevalence of the orphan figure can be explained by the central role which the family played at the time" (Peters 2000, 1). In the Victorian period, even "[t]he Queen herself seemed to offer a model of perfect domesticity in her large family, middle-class values, and reliance on her husband" (Vallone 2000, 217).

For an orphan, "home" often turns out to be a highly ambivalent concept. On the one hand, "home" may be an object of intense desire for a parentless child, which more often than not remains elusive. When Oliver Twist meets Mr Brownlow, the prospect of finding a good home seems to be within his reach—only to give way to cruel disappointment when Fagin and his gang force him to come back with them. Nina Auerbach argues that "[t]he figure of the wandering orphan, searching through an alien world for his home, has fascinated generations of novelists" (1975, 395). On the other hand, "home" may turn into a negative concept from the point of view of an orphan, becoming a prison due to the hostility or downright cruelty of caretakers, as Jane Eyre's experience at Gateshead exemplifies; or it may simply mark a void, perhaps never to be filled completely. Finally, orphans were also embedded in the discourses and practices of imperial expansion. After all, in the official discourse of the time, "the orphan embodies a surplus excess to be expelled to the colonies" (Peters 2000, 19), a notion which is reflected in the emigration schemes.

As will be shown below in more detail, orphans turn out to be highly versatile figures appearing in a wide range of literary texts in different genres and fulfilling diverse functions in Victorian literature. The figure of the orphan appears to be ideally suited for addressing a number of discourses, issues and problems that are characteristic of the Victorian period. Although critics sometimes use the umbrella term "orphan novel" to pay tribute to the amazing popularity of orphans, it is worthwhile noting that orphans are not typical of a specific genre *per se*. Instead, they appear in various different genres, which is further evidence of the versatility of this figure. Still, one may identify some genres where orphans can be found particularly frequently—and this may even serve as a clue to some of the functions the literary figure of the orphan may fulfil. To a certain extent, the genres in which fictional orphans are especially prominent tend to correlate with three basic types of orphans that can be identified in Victorian literature and that will be discussed in the following sections of this chapter: (1) the *pathetic orphan*, who is particularly prominent in the social problem novel; (2) the *orphan as a figure of hope*, who occurs most often in novels of development; and (3) the *orphan as adventurer*, who is, of course, primarily to be found in adventure stories.

The Orphan as Pathetic Figure

Despite the Victorian inclination to idealise childhood, this stage of life is usually not presented in a very positive manner in literary texts from this period; instead, the predominant impression of childhood one is likely to derive from literature is that of "an intensely frustrating time, shaped by loneliness, boredom, abuse or neglect" (Nelson 2014, 78). The remarkable number of orphaned children in Victorian literature has certainly contributed very much to this overall effect. Rachel Bowlby claims that the "study of the emotions of childhood" in Dickens's novels focuses more on "terror and impotence than Romantic wonder" (2013, 116). By and large, this could also be said about novels by a number of other Victorian writers. What many of the orphans in Victorian literature who come to mind most readily—e.g. Oliver Twist, David Copperfield, Philip (Pip) Pirrip, Esther Summerson and Jane Eyre—have in common is that they serve as figures who are apt to inspire pity, which is in particular triggered by scenes set during their childhood. The figure of the parentless child as a powerful "manifestation of loneliness" (Kimball 1999, 559) is likely to generate sympathy because the orphans' "outcast state is not caused by any actions of their own but because of their difference from the 'normal' pattern established by society" (559) For most literary orphans, their parentless state correlates with loneliness and a lack of affection, which the children are often painfully aware of and which is usually portrayed vividly, in an emotionally intense way.

In Dickens's *Bleak House* (1852-53), for instance, the loneliness experienced by the orphan Esther Summerson is expressed by informing the reader that her doll, which is still fondly remembered by the grown-up narrator when she is talking about her childhood, was the little girl's only confidante and her sole object of affection:

> My dear old doll! I was such a shy little thing that I seldom dared to open my lips, and never dared to open my heart, to anybody else. It almost makes me cry to think what a relief it used to be to me, when I came home from school of a day, to run upstairs to my room, and say, "O you dear faithful Dolly, I knew you would be expecting me!" and then to sit down on the floor, leaning on the elbow of her great chair, and tell her all I had noticed since we parted. (Dickens [1852-53] 2001, 14)

By emphasising that the doll, i.e., an inanimate object, provides the sole outlet for Esther's desire to talk about her day, while her aunt is invariably cold and stern in her interactions with the girl, the novel turns the orphan into a target for the readers' sympathy. Esther Summerson is not the only orphan character in Victorian literature who uses a "doll to control her sense of loss" (Maynard 2005, 293). For Jane Eyre, a doll, which is described as being "shabby as a miniature scarecrow" (Ch. Brontë [1847] 1985, 61), constitutes the only object she can love. This is bound to evoke pity since, as the narrator reasons in retrospect, "human beings must love something, and, in the dearth of worthier objects of affection, I contrived to find a pleasure in loving and cherishing a faded graven image" (61). The ways in which the narrators Jane Eyre and Esther Summerson express the loneliness and lack of affection they experienced during their childhood is characteristic of what one might describe as a "rhetoric of orphanhood", which one encounters in many Victorian novels. Time and again, orphans are described as small, frightened and shy ("shy little thing") to stress their vulnerability and their need of protection in a melodramatic way. Moreover, the presentation of the orphan's plight is typically informed by emotional intensity, which may be expressed directly ("It almost makes me cry to think") or by means of exclamations ("My dear old doll!"; "'O you dear faithful Dolly, I knew you would be expecting me!'").

In addition to suffering from loneliness and a lack of affection, orphans are often exposed to physical maltreatment in Victorian novels, being deprived of sufficient food or exposed to various forms of punishment and hardship. It is in particular this facet of the representation of orphans in Victorian literature that is reminiscent of the genre of the fairy tale, where "[t]he majority of the orphans [...] is mistreated" (Kimball 1999, 562). This emphasis on suffering intensifies the predicament orphan characters are in, as Kimball observes with respect to the fairy tale: "It is not enough that the character be an orphan; his or her isolation must further be defined by hostility" (562). In the fairy tale, relatives—most often stepmothers, (step)brothers and (step)sisters—tend to be the ones who display hostility, whereas Victorian novels also show orphans exposed to hostile guardians, teachers and other representatives of institutions that were supposed to take care of and educate orphans. The depiction of the miserable situation of parentless children within institutions (charity schools, orphanages, workhouses, etc.) is one of the features that sets the Victorian representations of orphans apart from fairy tales, but also from earlier novels about parentless individuals. In other words, the orphan in the Victorian novel is often situated at the intersection of the private and the public/institutional sphere. This also implies that orphaned children, who should be associated with the private sphere due to their age, were often perceived as being transgressive due to their visibility in the public sphere, roaming the streets as beggars or petty criminals like Fagin's boys in *Oliver Twist* (often othered as "street Arabs"), for instance.[15] In Dickens's *Bleak House*, the poor orphan Jo, who "sweeps his crossing all day long" ([1852-53] 2001, 189), is visible in the public space due to his work.

While fairy-tale characters typically lack psychological depth, complexity and ambiguity, one might perhaps expect Victorian novels to provide a more intense study of the various *reasons* for the way orphans are treated. Yet, quite often, the information about the motivation behind a character's hostility towards an orphan remains superficial or obscure. While jealousy, greed and, quite simply, hard-heartedness are time and again alluded to as relevant factors (just like in the fairy tale), Victorian novels typically deny the readers a detailed insight into the mind of the character(s) neglecting an orphan. This lack of information proves to be conducive to increasing the pity readers are likely to feel with the orphan. If the readers were given reasons for the way Mrs Reed treats her niece Jane Eyre or if they were confronted with a subtle psychological exploration of the jealousy causing Hindley Earnshaw to treat Heathcliff in a cruel fashion, the readers might begin to understand the characters' motivation for disliking a particular orphan, which would perhaps distract from the desired focus on the orphan's suffering. What is instead reiterated throughout Victorian novels in the hostile characters' reactions to the orphans they neglect, punish or mistreat is a set of assumptions and a concomitant terminology that is indicative of pre-Romantic and specifically Hobbesian attitudes towards children, which still circulated widely in the Victorian period. Mistrust of and an aversion to children's supposedly innate badness are expressed by some of the most unpleasant characters in Victorian literature, including Mr Murdstone and his sister Jane in *David Copperfield* as well as Mrs Reed and Mr Brocklehurst in *Jane Eyre*. The portrayal of the friendless orphan's suffering and especially of his/her thoughts and emotions typically corrects views expressed by characters like the ones mentioned above. The insight into the children's minds usually shows the reader beyond doubt that their behaviour is informed by helplessness and despair rather than by bad instincts or "sinfulness". This is for instance the case when David Copperfield bites his stepfather Mr Murdstone or when Jane Eyre hits her cousin John Reed; both orphans clearly are desperate and just try to defend themselves. The callousness of caretakers like the ones mentioned above, who are more interested in keeping the cost of taking care of an orphan as low as possible than in the parentless child's wellbeing, is generally made very clear. The hypocrite Mr Brocklehurst, who preaches humility to the orphaned girls at Lowood while treating his family to nice and expensive clothes, is a well-known example of this stance.

The most common approach to establishing an orphan as a pathetic figure is introducing the character in a miserable situation that is typical of his or her largely unhappy childhood. This strategy is for example pursued by Charlotte Brontë in *Jane Eyre*, where the title character is introduced as a girl who is likely to evoke the readers' pity right from the start. One of the very first images in the novel is that of the ten-year-old orphan being excluded from an apparently blissful family scene consisting of Jane's cousins "clustered round their mamma in the drawing-room: she lay reclined on a sofa by the fireside, and with her darlings about her (for the time neither quarrelling nor crying) looked perfectly happy" (Ch. Brontë [1847] 1985, 39). From the beginning it is made very clear that Aunt Reed feels neither sympathy nor affection for her niece, but regards her as an intruder, a nuisance and a burden. While the aunt seems to be all but blind to the shortcomings and flaws of her own son and daughters—though these are blatantly obvious to the readers—she is always ready to find fault with Jane. This is the reason why John Reed is not scolded for bullying his cousin, although his behaviour causes the girl to live in a permanent state of fear: "He bullied and punished me; not two or three times in the week, nor once or twice in a day, but continually: every nerve I had feared him, and every morsel of flesh on my bones shrank when he came near" (42). This emphatic description of Jane's anguish is likely to evoke sympathy. The servants, who do not dare to antagonise their employer, are loath to help Jane and even readily join in scolding and punishing the girl. The young orphan thus seems to be entirely isolated, friendless, and at the mercy of her relatives' moods and whims.

Moreover, Jane's situation is a socially precarious one, as her largely hostile environment repeatedly lets her know. Having neither money nor legal rights, she is entirely dependent on her relatives' goodwill, respectively on her aunt's willingness to continue to honour the promise she gave her late husband on his deathbed. Fourteen-year-old John Reed regards his cousin Jane as an intruder who is not part of the family, as he tells her very bluntly:

> "You have no business to take our books; you are a dependant, mamma says; you have no money; your father left you none; you ought to beg, and not to live here with gentlemen's children like us, and eat the same meals we do, and wear clothes at our mamma's expense." (42)

The servant Bessie joins the chorus of characters threatening Jane with the possibility of becoming destitute: "'You ought to be aware, miss, that you are under obligations to Mrs Reed; she keeps you; if she were to turn you off you would have to go to the poorhouse'" (44). Her dependence on the goodwill of Mrs Reed increases Jane's overall sense of insecurity.

Her miserable situation is also picked up by way of a *mise en abyme* in a scene in which Bessie sings a ballad that constructs a pitiful image of the loneliness of an orphan:

> My feet they are sore, and my limbs they are weary;
> Long is the way, and the mountains are wild;
> Soon will the twilight close moonless and dreary
> Over the path of the poor orphan child.
> Why did they send me so far and so lonely,
> Up where the moors spread and gray rocks are piled?
> Men are hard-hearted, and kind angels only
> Watch o'er the steps of a poor orphan child.
> […]
> There is a thought that for strength should avail me;
> Though both of shelter and kindred despoiled;
> Heaven is a home, and a rest will not fail me;
> God is a friend to the poor orphan child. (54)

The song is reminiscent of poems like William Blake's "The Chimney Sweeper" from *Songs of Innocence* in suggesting that the child can only hope for a better future in the afterlife. The song, which "laments the exile of the friendless orphan even as it allegorizes every Christian soul's journey to an eternal end" (Corbett 2008, 251), presumably serves to make Jane even more acutely aware of her situation and causes her to cry. Bessie, who already displays a good deal of emotional obtuseness by choosing this particular ballad to sing to an orphan in the first place, admonishes Jane not to cry and thus again reveals a striking lack of empathy. Given the fact that Jane generally portrays Bessie as a comparatively friendly inhabitant of Gateshead, the overall lack of pity the child is confronted with is made even more obvious. The inclusion of a ballad with religious overtones that conjures up images of an orphan in a bleak and hostile landscape who does not expect any help from people and regards God and his angels as the only friends reiterates the rhetoric of the pathetic orphan and simultaneously suggests that this figure was a recognisable trope in Victorian culture.

The scenes in which Jane is introduced as a friendless, lonely orphan bear a number of similarities with the beginning of Charles Dickens's *Great Expectations* (1861). Here, the protagonist Philip Pirrip (Pip) is initially presented to the readers as a small boy, feeling cold and being all alone in the graveyard where his parents and siblings have been buried. In retrospect, the narrating I describes himself as a "small bundle of shivers growing afraid of it all and beginning to cry" (Dickens [1861] 1994, 6). The expression "small bundle of shivers" highlights the pathetic role of the orphan. No sooner has Pip started to cry than he is threatened by an escaped convict, who is described as a "fearful man, all in coarse grey, with a great iron on his leg" (6) saying in "a terrible voice" (6): "'Keep still, you little devil, or I'll cut your throat!'" (6). The scene in which the small, frightened boy is intimidated by a supposedly violent convict is another memorable tableau from Victorian literature that is likely to generate pity for an orphaned protagonist. In *Great Expectations*, Dickens right from the start "evokes the feelings of a child who is powerless in the face of an assortment of tyrannical adults, from Magwitch, who appears in the opening chapter, to the frightening Miss Havisham who orders him to 'Play', to the affectionless, much older sister who is bringing him up" (Bowlby 2013, 115). One of the few exceptions in Pip's otherwise hostile environment is the good-natured blacksmith Joe Gargery, his brother-in-law, who is situated in-between the role of a peer and that of an affectionate father figure throughout the novel. Due to the fact that Joe never forsakes Pip, even when the latter feels embarrassed by the unrefined manners of the simple blacksmith, one could in fact argue that Pip is never quite as forlorn as Jane.

In a number of Victorian novels, including the ones mentioned above, the readers' tendency to feel pity with the orphan protagonist is enhanced by the fact that the orphans are allowed to tell their own story in retrospect. In doing so they implicitly or explicitly make the readers aware of the limits implied by a child's perception and understanding of the world and of his/her situation as an orphan, which tends to make them appear more endearing, innocent and helpless at the same time. In *David Copperfield*, for example, the readers repeatedly observe how the naïve little boy is cheated by characters who are physically superior to him, ranging from the "friendly waiter", whom he meets on his way to school, to the "young man with the donkey", who steals everything David possesses when the latter is about to flee from London to search for his aunt. In a similar fashion, Pip's musings about his parents, whom he cannot remember, are a token of his childish view of the world:

> The shape of the letters on my father's [tombstone], gave me an odd idea that he was a square, stout, dark man, with curly black hair. From the character and turn of the inscription, "*Also Georgiana Wife of the Above*", I

drew a childish conclusion that my mother was freckled and sickly. (Dickens [1861] 1994, 5)

This portrayal of orphans echoes the interest in children's idiosyncratic perception of the world that can already be observed in Romantic poems such as Wordsworth's ballad "We Are Seven", where the lyrical I wonders at a little girl's obstinate refusal to distinguish between her dead siblings and her living ones. The representation of children in novels like those mentioned above consequently continues an approach that was already pursued in Romantic literature.

An interesting variation on the pattern of introducing the orphan in a miserable situation can be found in Emily Brontë's *Wuthering Heights*. Here, the ghost of the late Catherine Linton appears to Lockwood in the guise of a little girl imploring him to let her enter the house. In this scene, the depiction of the orphan as an object of pity is combined with a strong emphasis on the uncanny: Lockwood tries to remove a branch that appears to be knocking against the window of the room that he is supposed to sleep in during his visit at Wuthering Heights; but, to his utter dismay, when he reaches out, his hand does not touch a branch, "instead of which, my fingers closed on the fingers of a little, ice-cold hand" (E. Brontë [1847] 1985, 67). The uncanny, which causes Lockwood to experience "[t]he intense horror of nightmare" (67), prevents the character from feeling pity. While the readers may certainly understand this reaction on the part of the character, the description of "a most melancholy voice sobb[ing], 'Let me in—let me in!'" (67) and explaining "shiveringly [...] 'I'm come home, I'd lost my way on the moor!'" (67) is likely to give rise to pity with the miserable (ghost) child, who wants to come home, but is denied entrance. Paula Krebs argues that Emily Brontë makes use of the banshee motif in her depiction of Cathy's ghost, modifying the motif in order to highlight the intense loneliness felt by the ghost:

> The ghost of Catherine bears at least a strong family resemblance to an Irish banshee, although Brontë's banshee does not wail for members of old Irish families. Nor does she wail for the death of a Wuthering Heights family member. Instead, she is a female ghost who wails for herself, for her own isolation and death. (Krebs 1998, 46)

The trope of the child who has been lost on the moor provides another link to images of children one encounters in Romantic poetry, for example in Wordsworth's "Lucy Gray".[16] The inclination to feel a certain amount of sympathy with the wailing girl might be increased by Lockwood's subsequent behaviour, which can be accounted for by fear and panic, but which is also undeniably cruel, as he admits himself:

> I discerned, obscurely, a child's face looking through the window—terror made me cruel; and, finding it useless to attempt shaking the creature off, I pulled its wrist on to the broken pane, and rubbed it to and fro till the blood ran down and soaked the bedclothes: still it wailed, "Let me in!" and maintained its tenacious gripe, almost maddening me with fear. (E. Brontë [1847] 1985, 67)

While the bleeding ghost has been read as an allusion to female sexuality (cf. Krebs 1998, 47), the cruel treatment of the child is also reminiscent of the physical mistreatment undergone by many orphans in Victorian novels. The choice to introduce Catherine as a child revenant is an intriguing one. After all, according to the internal chronology of the story, Catherine has been dead for some time when Lockwood visits Wuthering Heights. Moreover, she was a married woman who had given birth to a daughter when she died. Drawing upon the trope of the pitiful orphan in the introduction of one of the central characters arguably invites the readers to feel more sympathy with her than they might otherwise do.

The introduction of Catherine is rendered even more complex by the fact that Lockwood read some of her makeshift diary entries shortly before he encounters her ghost. These traces of the thoughts and emotions Catherine felt during her childhood indicate that she was not the typical helpless orphan, and certainly not a shy or naïve one. She characterises herself as a rebel, refers to her elder brother Hindley as "detestable" and as a "tyrant" and completes her account with a caricature of the puritanical servant Joseph (E. Brontë [1847] 1985, 62-63). The fact that her notes are described as having been written in the margins of printed books and even religious texts—thus presumably "defiling" texts from the point of view of many Victorians—reinforces the impression that Catherine Earnshaw was anything but a meek child. By including elements of rebellion and combining the stereotype of the friendless, pathetic orphan with the image of the uncanny (ghost) child Emily Brontë provides an interesting version of the literary orphan.

In addition to presenting orphans in miserable situations during their childhood, the trope of the pathetic orphan sometimes serves as a kind of shorthand for stressing the fragility, vulnerability and helplessness of female characters who are still young, but clearly grown up.[17] A case in point is David Copperfield's mother, Clara, who is an orphan and worked as a nursery governess before getting married to David's father (Dickens [1849-50] 1992, 11). When the latter dies before David is even born, Clara is helpless and still immature. Thus, the young widow is an easy victim for Mr Murdstone, who becomes her second husband and expects Clara to be submissive and obedient. Even though she realises that Murdstone and his sister Jane, who lives with the couple, dislike David and treat him in a very harsh way, she does not dare to defend her own son, watching in tears when he is accused unfairly, punished and sent away to school. Clara's untimely death seems to confirm her fragility. There are also many orphans among the female characters in Victorian novels who end up as "fallen women": Hetty Sorrel in George Eliot's *Adam Bede* (1859), the title character in Elizabeth Gaskell's novel *Ruth* (1853) and Little Em'ly in *David Copperfield* are cases in point. These characters can be read as a 19th-century counterpart of the 18th-century "damsel in distress". While the latter was typically rescued by the hero at the very last moment, their Victorian successors are usually not saved; instead, they are fooled and ruined by the false promises of a man from a higher social class.

Yet the overall impression of adult female orphans in the Victorian novel is not limited to that of a weak and helpless person. Instead, writers often establish a contrast between the female orphan as *femme fragile*, whose lack of protection is likely to cause her ruin, and orphaned women who show a remarkable degree of energy, determination, and resilience. In *Adam Bede* the "fallen woman" Hetty Sorrel is juxtaposed with her orphaned cousin Dinah Morris, a virtuous and charismatic lay preacher. In a similar fashion, the frail and guileless orphan Laura Fairlie in Wilkie Collins's sensation novel *The Woman in White* (1859-60), who becomes a victim of the evil plans hatched by Sir Percival Glyde and Count Fosco, is contrasted with her energetic and resourceful half-sister Marian Halcombe, who tries to come to Laura's rescue. A similar contrast between two female orphans is established in Bram Stoker's *Dracula* (1897). Both of Dracula's female victims—Lucy Westenra and Mina Harker née Murray—are orphans. While Dracula was already stalking Lucy when her mother was still alive, it is only after the latter's death that the young woman is finally turned into a vampire, which seems to stress once more the orphan's special vulnerability. In her case, just as with Hetty Sorrel, a certain helplessness is combined with a pronounced flirtatiousness, which indicates a lack of morals from a Victorian point of view and renders the characters more likely to become victims of seduction. Mina, by contrast, proves to be anything but an easy victim for Dracula and finally plays a crucial role in bringing about his defeat.

One of the main functions of the pathetic orphan in Victorian literature, and in particular in early- to mid-Victorian novels, was to serve as a vehicle for social criticism. This particular function is intimately linked to the concept of childhood as a time of innocence, which makes sure that the young orphan is almost automatically perceived as a victim when shown to be exposed to maltreatment or presented in a dismal situation, as Peters claims: "A legacy from the Romantic conceptualization of the child invested the child with an innocence; in this particular case the poor child was innocent of the causes of his or her poverty" (Peters 2000, 8). Due to their supposed innocence and helplessness, orphaned children are generally more likely to trigger pity than adults, which is why they appear frequently in the social problem novel, a genre that routinely sought to evoke pity in order to make readers aware of inhumane working conditions in factories, of the dismal slum districts in industrial cities, of the misery experienced by people in the workhouse and a range of other deficits in Victorian society.

Institutions that were in charge of taking care of parentless children constitute one of the main targets of criticism in social problem novels. While workhouses and charity schools were supposed to provide parentless children with a better prospect in life, Victorian orphan narratives tend to offer a very bleak picture of these institutions. The descriptions of workhouses and charity schools in social problem novels are often quite drastic. Instead of being provided with a good start in life, insufficient food combined with a lack of respect and affection is what awaits the workhouse orphan. In *Oliver Twist*, the heterodiegetic narrator leaves the reader in no doubt regarding the kind of future a baby born in the workhouse can expect, informing us already on the very first page that the protagonist has just entered a "world of sorrow and trouble" (Dickens [1837-39] 1985, 45):

> he was badged and ticketed, and fell into his place at once—a parish child—the orphan of a workhouse—the humble half-starved drudge—to be cuffed and buffeted through the world,—despised by all, and pitied by none. (Dickens [1837-39] 1985, 47)

These predictions concerning Oliver's future oppose the political discourse of the time that was based on the assumption that orphans were given the chance to "better themselves" if the state took care of them. Yet, notwithstanding the high hopes that were associated with the upbringing of orphans under the guardianship of the authorities, a sojourn in the workhouse was a social stigma: "despite the claims made about the special care and attention paid to orphan children of the poor, the children—as former inhabitants of the workhouse—were stigmatised within the community at large" (Peters 2000, 15). According to Baruch Hochman and Ilja Wachs, "[n]o other Dickens novel centers so directly on the terrors and threats of the orphan condition" (1999, 32). In the workhouse, Oliver and the other children suffer from malnourishment, since the inmates of the institution have to survive on "small quantities of oatmeal; [...] three meals of thin gruel a day, with an onion twice a week, and half a roll on Sundays" (Dickens [1837-39] 1985, 55).

In addition to the workhouse, the system of "baby farming" is harshly criticised in *Oliver Twist*. Since there is no woman who could breastfeed the baby in the workhouse where he is born, Oliver is "farmed", i.e., "dispatched to a branch-workhouse some three miles off, where twenty or thirty other juvenile offenders against the poor-laws rolled about the floor all day, without the inconvenience of too much food or too much clothing" (48).[18] The woman who is paid for taking care of the orphans tries to keep as much of the money she receives for the children as possible; in other words, "she appropriated the greater part of the weekly stipend to her own use, and consigned the rising parochial generation to even a shorter allowance than was originally provided for them" (48). Oliver stays with the greedy woman up to the age of nine. The children are "sickened from want and cold", sometimes fall "into the fire from neglect" or are "inadvertently scalded to death when there happened to be a washing" (48-49). As the narrator points out, the parish authorities choose to turn a blind eye and thus tolerate the maltreatment of children they are supposed to help: "the board made periodical pilgrimages to the farm, and always sent the beadle the day before, to say they were going. The children were neat and clean to behold, when *they* went; and what more would the people have?" (49). The prime target of criticism here is, of course, the person who is entrusted with the care of a group of small children and who clearly feels no compassion with or interest in them, being driven solely by greed.[19] Simultaneously, the narrator accuses a system that does nothing to prevent this kind of corruption; ultimately, the supposedly respectable people and the authorities involved in taking care of orphans are not much better than Fagin and his band of thieves, who unabashedly exploit parentless children.

In Charlotte Brontë's *Jane Eyre*, the charity school Lowood, which was partially inspired by The Clergy Daughters' School at Cowan Bridge, where the author's two elder sisters died due to an epidemic (Edwards 1999, 195), is presented in a similarly bleak way. Though Jane leaves her Aunt Reed's house with comparatively high hopes, Lowood School, "an Institution for educating orphans" (Ch Brontë [1847] 1985, 82), confronts the protagonist with new hardships. The girls attending the school are malnourished and their clothes offer hardly any protection from the cold: "Our clothing was insufficient to protect us from the severe cold; we had no boots, the snow got into our shoes, and melted there; our ungloved hands became numbed and covered with chilblains, as were our feet" (92). The lack of food in Lowood causes bullying among the girls of the kind Oliver Twist also encounters in the workhouse: "whenever the famished great girls had an opportunity they would coax or menace the little ones out of their portion" (92). The terrible conditions at the school reach a climax when many of the girls fall ill due to a typhus epidemic and die: "Semi-starvation and neglected colds had predisposed most of the pupils to receive infection: forty-five out of the eighty girls lay ill at one time" (108). Yet the criticism expressed in *Jane Eyre* is not directed at the institution of the charity school as such. What is denounced is rather the hard-heartedness and hypocrisy of individuals who prevent a charitable institution from doing beneficial work. This distinction between the institution on the one hand and the individuals who run it on the other hand is made clear when the school is radically reformed in the wake of the epidemic:

> Inquiry was made into the origin of the scourge, and by degrees various facts came out which excited public indignation in a high degree. The unhealthy nature of the site; the quantity and quality of the children's food; the brackish, fetid water used in its preparation; the pupils' wretched clothing and accommodation—all these things were discovered. (115)

The discovery of the deficits is the starting point for the transformation of Lowood School into "a truly useful and noble institution" (115), where orphaned girls are provided with a sound education, which prepares them for a career as teacher or governess. The reforms have been brought about by making the public aware of the neglect of the parentless girls.

As the discussion above has shown, a criticism of institutions in Victorian orphan narratives ultimately more often than not amounts to a criticism of the individuals who run these institutions. This already suggests that the negative representation of institutions ties in with the depiction of hard-hearted and cruel individuals who fail to be adequate caretakers for an orphan, including Mrs Reed (*Jane Eyre*), Esther Summerson's aunt Miss Barbary (*Bleak House*), Mr Murdstone and his sister (*David Copperfield*), and Joseph (*Wuthering Heights*). The fairy tale very often shows orphans being mistreated by members of their own sex (cf. Kimball 1999, 562)—a pattern that by and large also seems to apply to Victorian novels. In *Jane Eyre*, for instance, "Uncle Reed's early death deprives Jane of the surrogate father in whose goodness she continues to trust long after his demise" (Corbett 2008, 240). Mrs Reed's dislike of her niece is so intense that she even mars the latter's chance of a better future, as she confesses to Jane shortly before her death: "'for you to be adopted by your uncle [in Madeira], and placed in a state of ease and comfort, was what I could not endure. I wrote to him; I said I was sorry for his disappointment, but Jane Eyre was dead; she had died of typhus fever at Lowood'" (Ch. Brontë [1847] 1985, 267). Even if caretakers do not mistreat the orphan they are in charge of, their ideas of an appropriate education frequently leave something to be wished for. Miss Havisham in *Great Expectations* is presumably one of the worst foster mothers one can imagine. Although she seems to love her adopted daughter Estella after her own fashion, her educational principles are based on the misguided premise of turning the girl into her personal "agent of revenge" (Peters 1995, 191). The upper-class widows Mrs Reed in *Jane Eyre* and Mrs Steerforth in *David Copperfield* are shown to spoil their own children, which proves to be extremely harmful for these children as well as for others. In a moment of remorse, Steerforth even explicitly blames his mother for his lack of moral principles: "'I wish to God I had had a judicious father these last twenty years!' […] 'I wish with all my soul I had been better guided!'" (Dickens [1849-50] 1992, 275). Yet there are also many novels that present individuals who turn out to be good caretakers for an orphaned child (e.g. David Copperfield's eccentric aunt Betsey Trotwood), thus presumably trying to teach their readers a lesson in charity by suggesting that orphans deserve care and protection and by promising that those who offer help will be amply rewarded.

This idea is particularly prominent in George Eliot's novel *Silas Marner* (1861), in which an orphan transforms the protagonist's life completely, changing it in all respects for the better. In contrast to most of the other novels discussed in this chapter, *Silas Marner* places the focus very clearly on the foster father and not on the parentless child. The orphan Eppie is only introduced relatively late in the novel, and she is hardly individualised. The title character has experienced a considerable amount of injustice in his life, having been falsely accused of a crime in his hometown. The false accusation has hardened him and has forced him to leave his past life in the North of England behind. In his new home in the village of Raveloe he has remained an outsider. While he "once loved his fellow with tender love, and trusted in an unseen goodness" (Eliot [1861] 1985, 141), as the narrator puts it, the weaver Silas Marner is now only interested in his work and in the gold he is earning. The narrator describes the man's life as follows:

> year after year, Silas Marner had lived in this solitude, his guineas rising in the iron pot, and his life narrowing and hardening itself more and more into a mere pulsation of desire and satisfaction that had no relation to any other

being. His life had reduced itself to the functions of weaving and hoarding, without any contemplation of an end towards which the functions tended. (68)

The way in which Silas's attitude towards his coins is presented suggests that it borders on an obsession with his treasure: "he would on no account have exchanged those coins, which had become his familiars, for other coins with unknown faces. He handled them, he counted them, till their form and colour were like the satisfaction of a thirst to him" (68). Given this description of his personality, Silas Marner might at first sight seem a singularly bad choice as caretaker for a small child. Yet, when his gold is stolen and he finds a baby girl whose mother has just died on his doorstep, the old bachelor immediately proves that he can indeed be a good foster father. Although he approached the child initially because her golden hair made the near-sighted man believe for a moment he had found his missing gold, he does not hesitate to adopt the helpless child. When one of the villagers suggests taking the girl away from Silas, he insists on keeping her (172). He feels amply compensated for the loss of his gold by the presence of the little girl, whom he grows to love very much.

The child brings about a process of emotional and spiritual reawakening for the weaver that starts the moment she ends up on his doorstep. Far from being disappointed when "instead of hard coin with the familiar resisting outline, his fingers encountered soft warm curls" (167), Silas is spontaneously reminded of his sister, "whom he had carried about in his arms for a year before she died, when he was a small boy without shoes or stockings" (168). As Robert Dunham points out, the child thus "effects the forward-looking movement of Silas' soul first of all by revitalizing his roots in the past" (1976, 651). When the girl wakes up, he instinctively offers her affection as well as food, showing his capacity for nurturing a child:

> Silas pressed it [the child] to him, and almost unconsciously uttered sounds of hushing tenderness, while he bethought himself that some of his porridge, which had got cool by the dying fire, would do to feed the child with if it were only warmed a little. [...] The porridge, sweetened with some dry brown sugar from an old store which he had refrained from using for himself, stopped the cries of the little one, and made her lift her blue eyes with a wide quiet gaze at Silas, as he put the spoon into her mouth. (Eliot [1861] 1985, 168-69).

As the passage quoted above suggests, Marner's emotional reaction is caused by the awareness of the pretty child being in need of help and protection. By means of images like "the little golden head" (166) and "blue eyes [...] veiled by their delicate half-transparent lids" (166), the description of the child time and again emphasises the girl's fragility as well as her beauty and innocence. The effect that the sight of the small child resting peacefully on Silas Marner's lap is likely to have upon an onlooker is even likened to the Romantic notion of the sublime:

> She was perfectly quiet now, but not asleep—only soothed by sweet porridge and warmth into that wide-gazing calm which makes us older human beings, with our inward turmoil, feel a certain awe in the presence of a little child, such as we feel before some quiet majesty or beauty in the earth or sky—before a steady glowing planet, or a full-flowered eglantine, or the bending trees over a silent pathway. (175)

As the narrator points out explicitly, similar to the experience of nature, the sight of the innocent child is apt to inspire awe and thus can have a beneficial effect.

Arguably, this sense of wonder triggered by the girl is also linked to her incipient agency. Despite the girl's undeniable helplessness and fragility, she is shown to take the initiative instinctively when her mother is dead:

> mammy's ear was deaf [...]. Suddenly, as the child rolled downward on its mother's knees, all wet with snow, its eyes were caught by a bright glancing light on the white ground, and, with the ready transition of infancy, it was immediately absorbed in watching the bright living thing running towards it, yet never arriving. That bright living thing must be caught; and in an instant the child had slipped on all fours, and held out one little hand to catch the gleam. [...] the little one, rising on its legs, toddled through the snow, the old grimy shawl in which it was wrapped trailing behind it (165).

The pathetic image of the infant making her way all alone through the snow to Silas Marner's door is certainly apt to evoke sympathy in the reader, but it also seems to express a certain survival instinct. The girl walks right into the weaver's cottage, where she immediately feels at home, "like a new-hatched gosling beginning to find itself comfortable" (166). The initial promise of a new home for the child is fulfilled. Thanks to her foster father, the orphan Eppie experiences a blissful, almost idyllic childhood.

Her upbringing turns out to be quite unusual for the Victorian period, since she is "reared without punishment" (189) by her foster father, who cannot bring himself to punish the little girl he loves so dearly. Thus, Eppie is a rare exception among literary representations of orphanhood in the Victorian period: a child who knows "nothing of frowns and denials" (189). Eppie's upbringing is based on mutual trust and strong affection. The success of this kind of education serves to confirm the Romantic notion of children as innocent beings. Her parents' "disgrace" has had no impact on Eppie's personality; instead, she thrives on the unconditional love she is given by her foster father, which even endows her with "a touch of refinement and fervour which came from no other teaching than that of tenderly-nurtured unvitiated feeling" (206). While many other orphans in Victorian literature learn nothing or next to nothing about their parents, Silas tells Eppie what he knows about the circumstances of her mother's death. This is indicative of a mutual trust between the girl and her foster father, whose relationship is devoid of "painful barrier[s] between their minds" (205). Silas Marner's love for the child and his trust in her are fully reciprocated. From the start, Eppie shows her foster father daughterly affection; as a grown-up, she puts her heartfelt gratitude into the following words: "'If it hadn't been for you, they'd have taken me to the workhouse, and there'd have been nobody to love me'" (226). Beyond being loved by her foster father, Eppie also appears to be a prime example of the redemptive child in more general terms, "stirring the human kindness in all eyes that looked on her" (184).

Silas Marner's life is improved in every respect due to the fact that he decides to care for the orphan; his "adoptive fatherhood is the making of him, the happy turning point in his life" (Bowlby 2013, 142): "Parenthood is the beginning of Silas Marner's 'new self', a rebirth for someone who had been up till then almost totally withdrawn from his local world and who had suffered the loss of the one thing, his accumulated 'gold', to which he was attached" (132). In addition to being rewarded by Eppie's daughterly love, he is also integrated into the community, since "as the weeks grew to months, the child created fresh and fresh links [sic] between his life and the lives from which he had hitherto shrunk continually into narrower isolation" (Eliot [1861] 1985, 184). That the weaver now becomes part of the rural community is due to the fact that "the villagers finally have something they can understand about Marner: his love for a child" (Pond 2013, 701). While his previous preoccupation with his money arrested "his thoughts in an ever-repeated circle, leading to nothing beyond itself" (Eliot [1861] 1985, 184), his love for the child opens up an interest in the future that is entirely new to the weaver. This effect of the presence of a child is already alluded to in the epigraph, a quote from Wordsworth's pastoral poem "Michael", which stresses that Eliot's novel is clearly indebted to Romantic notions of childhood: "A child, more than all other gifts / That earth can offer to declining man, /

Brings hope with it, and forward-looking thoughts" (n.pag.). Moreover, his love for Eppie allows Silas Marner to integrate his past into his identity, which turns him into a more fully developed human being: "As the child's mind was growing into knowledge, his mind was growing into memory: as her life unfolded, his soul, long stupefied in a cold narrow prison, was unfolding too, and trembling gradually into full consciousness" (185). Eventually, Silas Marner achieves "a consciousness of unity between his past and present" (202), which enables him to be at peace with his life, including even the former false accusations.

Silas Marner's impulse to take care of the little girl is contrasted with the total failure in their role as caretakers displayed by the girl's biological parents. Eppie was born into a clandestine marriage. While her working-class mother Molly was addicted to "the demon Opium to whom she was enslaved, body and soul" (164), her upper-class father, Godfrey Cass, the Squire's eldest son, acknowledges neither his wife nor his daughter. On New Year's Eve, Molly decides to go to the Squire's house to disclose the fact that his son is married and has a child. Yet she never reaches her destination since she dies on the way. Godfrey, who is present when his dead wife's body is discovered, is exhilarated at the prospect of being freed from the burden of being married to a "hated wife" (175) and unwilling to acknowledge his fatherhood. As Bowlby points out, "Eliot carefully presents all Godfrey's impulses as tending in the opposite direction from Silas's; the actual father resists and rejects what comes naturally to the man who has no connection with the child" (2013, 137). Only many years later, when Eppie is already a young woman, Godfrey Cass finally admits that he is her father. He musters the courage to tell his wife about his first marriage and his child, and his wife concurs with his plan to adopt Eppie.

When Godfrey reveals his intention to Silas and Eppie, the weaver is shocked, "trembling violently" (Eliot [1861] 1985, 229), but does not want to deny his foster daughter the chance of leading a prosperous life. Eppie, however, rewards his love by insisting on staying with him. Both Eppie and Silas vehemently deny the validity of the claims raised by the biological father:

> Eppie had given a violent start, and turned quite pale. Silas, on the contrary, who had been relieved, by Eppie's answer, from the dread lest his mind should be in opposition to hers, felt the spirit of resistance in him set free, not without a touch of parental fierceness. "Then, sir," he answered, with an accent of bitterness [...]—"then, sir, why didn't you say so sixteen year ago, and claim her before I'd come to love her, i'stead o' coming to take her from me now, when you might as well take the heart out o' my

body? God gave her to me because you turned your back upon her, and He looks upon her as mine: you've no right to her!" (230-31)

In her answer, Eppie reveals the full extent of the love she feels for her foster father:

> "I should have no delight i' life any more if I was forced to go away from my father, and knew he was sitting at home, a-thinking of me and feeling lone. We've been used to be happy together every day, and I can't think o' no happiness without him. [...] And he's took care of me and loved me from the first, and I'll cleave to him as long as he lives, and nobody shall ever come between him and me." (233-34)

The bond that has been forged between the orphan and her foster father turns out to be strong and lasting. Even Eppie's marriage does not separate her from her father, since the young couple decides to live with Silas Marner, and the last words of the novel are addressed to Silas by his foster daughter, confirming once more a vision of domestic bliss: "'O father,' said Eppie, 'what a pretty home ours is! I think nobody could be happier than we are'" (244). The image of an idyllic home, on which the story closes, has been made possible by an aging bachelor taking in an orphan and providing her with unconditional fatherly love. The depiction of the bond between the orphan and her foster father is undeniably highly sentimental, which here serves to stress the positive effects of taking care of a parentless child.

Even if Kristen Pond argues that Silas Marner's "role as the sole caretaker of Eppie [...] sets him apart from the traditional English family model" (2013, 701), it is striking that there are several male characters in Victorian literature who appear to be remarkably devoted fathers. In Dickens's "third and best-selling" (Gitter 1999, 675) Christmas story "The Cricket on the Hearth" (1845), there is a poor widower called Caleb Plummer who strives to give his blind daughter a perfect life by pretending that they live in affluence and that the father is still substantially younger and more vigorous than he really is; in other words, the man reasons that his daughter's blindness "might be almost changed into a blessing, and the girl made happy by these little means" (Dickens [1845] 2006, 189). The father has gone to great lengths to keep up the illusion: "For years and years, he had never once crossed that threshold at his own slow pace, but with a footfall counterfeited for her ear; and never had he, when his heart was heaviest, forgotten the light tread that was to render hers so cheerful and courageous!" (192). Although the story implies that this kind of deception is not wise in the long run, the narrator leaves us in no doubt that the motivation for the father's behaviour is solely his love for his daughter: "Caleb was no sorcerer, but in the only magic art that still remains to us, the magic of devoted, deathless love" (188). Despite her father's attempts to provide her with a happy life, the girl is doubly marginalised, being ultimately "excluded from the Christmas transformations and reconciliations of the more worldly characters" (Gitter 1999, 686) due to her motherless state and her blindness, which reinforces the trope of the pathetic orphan.

While there are many pathetic orphans in Victorian literature, who are often portrayed in a sentimental fashion to inspire pity, there are also some texts that appear to re-examine this image critically. William Makepeace Thackeray's *Vanity Fair* (1847-48) is a case in point. The novel presents an orphaned protagonist who differs in many respects from the orphans discussed so far: Throughout the novel, Rebecca (Becky) Sharp is shown to be a clever and egocentric woman who does not hesitate to manipulate others to reach her goals. Right from the start, it is made clear that she does not conform to 19th-century notions of femininity in terms of temperament, attitudes or behaviour. From a Victorian point of view, some of her utterances appear immoderate and unfeminine, as the following scathing comment on her school exemplifies: "'I hate the whole house,' continued Miss Sharp in a fury. 'I hope I may never set eyes on it again. I wish it were in the bottom of the Thames, I do'" (Thackeray [1847-48] 1994, 7). Fury and hate were certainly not among the attributes deemed appropriate for Victorian girls or women. Even if today's readers are likely to be more lenient in this respect, the fact that Becky never betrays any signs of moral principles or scruples is bound to prevent readers from feeling sympathy with her.

While many Victorian novels contain memorable childhood scenes, as was pointed out above, the readers are granted only short glimpses of Becky's childhood. The protagonist is introduced as a young woman who is just leaving school. Her parents, who are both dead, are not introduced as having been respectable people, at least from the point of view of the Victorian middle class. Her mother is referred to as a French "opera-girl" (9), and her father is portrayed as an artist and art teacher who had "a great propensity for running into debt, and a partiality for the tavern" (9). Moreover, the father is described as having been violent: "When he was drunk, he used to beat his wife and daughter; and the next morning, with a headache, he would rail at the world for its neglect of his genius" (9). This fragmentary information about Becky's childhood might very well have served as a starting point for developing sentimental images of a pathetic childhood shaped by poverty and abuse. Such scenes would, however, presumably have defied the overall purpose of Thackeray's portrayal of

Becky Sharp. In contrast to the novels discussed above, *Vanity Fair* is highly satirical and does not draw upon the image of the pathetic orphan, arguably even seeking to undermine this very trope. Thackeray's flawed orphan Becky challenges the sentimental Victorian stereotype of the battered, rejected, yet almost incorruptible orphan. Her upbringing has endowed her with "the dismal precocity of poverty" (10), as the narrator puts it, and she is certainly no Oliver Twist in terms of attitude or demeanour.

Instead of portraying her as a pathetic orphan, the novel repeatedly shows Becky making strategic use of this sentimental image in order to sway others' opinions in her favour. At one point, she successfully performs the role of the poor orphan who cannot but be grateful for any small token of kindness:

> One day, Amelia [Amelia Sedley; a friend Becky is staying with] had a headache, and could not go upon some party of pleasure to which the two young people were invited: nothing could induce her friend to go without her. "What! you who have shown the poor orphan what happiness and love are for the first time in her life—quit *you*? never!" and the green eyes looked up to Heaven and filled with tears; and Mrs. Sedley could not but own that her daughter's friend had a charming kind heart of her own. (Thackeray [1847-48] 1994, 23)

A similar scene can be found later on when Becky tries to defend herself against the accusation of being ungrateful:

> "Do you think I have no heart? Have you all loved me, and been so kind to the poor orphan—deserted—girl, and am *I* to feel nothing? O my friends! O my benefactors! may [sic] not my love, my life, my duty, try to repay the confidence you have shown me? Do you grudge me even gratitude, Miss Crawley? It is too much—my heart is too full;" and she sank down in a chair so pathetically, that most of the audience present were perfectly melted with her sadness. (136)

Moreover, she refers to herself as a "poor orphan" (146) in a letter in which she seeks to win favour for her clandestine marriage. Whenever it suits her interests, she draws upon the stance of the lonely orphan who is bound to be grateful for acts of kindness and skilfully emulates the melodramatic rhetoric and body language reiterated in many Victorian orphan narratives. Yet it is made quite clear by the narrator that her display of emotions as well as her humility are nothing but pretence. Becky is time and again shown to be entirely unfeeling. This lack of emotions is not excused by her upbringing and by her being an orphan, since there is no attempt to explain the character's behaviour in psychological terms. After all, as was already suggested above, a psychological exploration of the protagonist would presumably defeat the satirical intention of Thackeray's novel. What the text certainly does, however, is confirm the currency of the trope of the pathetic orphan in Victorian literature.

Similar to *Jane Eyre*, *Vanity Fair* includes a song in which the predicament of an orphan is depicted in a highly sentimental fashion as a *mise en abyme*. The similarities to the ballad in Charlotte Brontë's novel, which was discussed above, are striking; in both cases, the orphan in the song is alone in a hostile (natural) environment. The first stanza of the song in *Vanity Fair* reads as follows:

> Ah! bleak and barren was the moor,
> Ah! loud and piercing was the storm,
> The cottage roof was shelter'd sure,
> The cottage hearth was bright and warm—
> An orphan boy the lattice pass'd,
> And, as he mark'd its cheerful glow,
> Felt doubly keen the midnight blast,
> And doubly cold the fallen snow. (Thackeray [1847-48] 1994, 31)

Despite similarities on the textual level, there are crucial differences between the functions of the orphan songs in the two texts. Jane listens to a ballad sung by someone else (Bessie) and is made acutely aware of her own misery as a result; the images constructed in the song reinforce her loneliness and thus affirm the stereotype of the pathetic orphan. In *Vanity Fair*, by contrast, it is the orphan herself who sings the maudlin song in an attempt to render her situation more pitiful for the sake of an audience and in order to reach her goals (first and foremost that of ensnaring a rich husband). Singing with (feigned) emotion and making sure that her voice duly falters at the end of the song, Becky invites her listeners to recognise "the allusion to her departure, and to her hapless orphan state" (32). She thus stages the image of the forsaken orphan in the presence of others, presumably without actually feeling any of the loneliness attributed to the orphan in the song, but with the intention of exploiting the trope's potential to induce sympathy.

Elizabeth Gaskell's last novel *Wives and Daughters* juxtaposes a number of orphan characters; some of these are presented in a way that reiterates the stereotype of the pathetic orphan, while others challenge this trope to a certain extent. The depiction of Osborne Hamley's clandestine marriage obviously draws upon the image of the pathetic orphan. Osborne, the eldest son of Squire Hamley, does not admit to his parents that he is married because his wife Aimée is a French Catholic, used to be a servant and is "a little orphan girl" (Gaskell [1864-66] 2003, 272), having neither family nor fortune. The orphan here is marginalised in terms of class, nationality and religion. Thus, it is only after Osborne's untimely death that Squire Hamley finds out about his son's marriage and his grandchild. He is immediately prepared to take care of and love the orphaned infant, although he is anything but happy about his son's choice of wife and initially even refuses to meet Aimée (Gaskell [1864-66] 2003, 510). This rejection on the part of the father-in-law is juxtaposed with a sentimental portrait of the young widow: "And all this time a little young grey-eyed woman was making her way [...] towards the dead son, whom as yet she believed to be her living husband" (510). Her claim that "[a] woman is never tired with carrying her own child" (511) is corrected by the heterodiegetic narrator in a comment in parentheses, albeit in a fashion that reveals sympathy with the woman: "(which was not true; but there was sufficient truth in it to make it believed by both mistress and servant)" (511). The pathetic image of Aimée is reinforced once more when she finally meets her father-in-law: "At this instant the door softly opened, and right into the midst of them came the little figure in grey, looking ready to fall with the weight of her child" (513). The narrator highlights the fragility of the young woman, her exhaustion and her devotion to her child in a manner that is apt to evoke pity and approval of her demeanour on the part of the readers.

When the protagonist Molly Gibson is introduced, the narrator alludes briefly to the trope of the pathetic orphan ("Poor child! it is true that she had lost her mother", 4), only to undermine any potential sentimental effect immediately by saying, "but that was hardly an event in the sense referred to; and besides, she had been too young to be conscious of it at the time" (4). In other words, Molly, whose mother died when the girl was only three years old, is introduced in a fashion that departs from the trope of the pathetic orphan. Moreover, Molly's close and loving relationship with her father, a country doctor, seems to have compensated her for the early loss of her mother. She has neither been deprived of parental affection nor has her orphaned state led to financial straits. Unlike many orphans in Dickens's novels, Molly has been able to lead a quite comfortable life so far and, all in all, has "a very happy childhood" (31). A further strategy used to undermine a potential sentimental effect is the brief and matter-of-fact reference to the mother's death, which avoids details that would be apt to portray this death in a pathetic light:

> Mr Gibson did not speak much about the grief at the loss of his wife, which
> it was supposed that he felt. Indeed, he avoided all demonstrations of

sympathy, and got up hastily, and left the room when Miss Phoebe Browning first saw him after his loss, and burst into an uncontrollable flood of tears, which threatened to end in hysterics. (Gaskell [1864-66] 2003, 27)

Mr Gibson is presented as a very pragmatic man who has "rather a contempt for demonstrative people, arising from his medical insight into the consequences to health of uncontrolled feeling" (28). The tendency to depart from a sentimental approach towards the depiction of orphanhood is also apparent when the narrator mentions more or less in passing that Molly's mother was an orphan herself. The heterodiegetic narrator appears to emulate the stance adopted by Mr Gibson upon the death of his wife by providing merely what Joellen Masters calls a "thumbnail biography" (2004, 9) of the wife. The narrator only informs the readers that she kept her granduncle "company in his old age; he, the woman-contemning [sic] old bachelor, became thankful for the cheerful presence of the pretty, bonny Mary Pearson, who was good and sensible, and nothing more" (Gaskell [1864-66] 2003, 27). Eventually, she ended up marrying her uncle's successor, Mr Gibson.

When the widower Mr Gibson decides to remarry at the age of 43, his prime motivation is protecting his daughter, who is at this point admired by one of his apprentices: "'It's a very awkward position for a motherless girl like her to be at the head of a household with two young men in it'" (70). In other words, the doctor's decision is very much informed by what he considers to be appropriate due to social conventions. While the life led by him and his daughter has been harmonious, Mr Gibson deems it right to forestall rumours by procuring a stepmother for his daughter, though there are some hints in the text that suggest that Mr Gibson's decision to remarry is not entirely dependent on his wish to ensure female supervision for Molly: "Yesterday he had looked upon her more as a possible stepmother for Molly; today he thought more of her as a wife for himself" (93). Although the country doctor is not immune to Mrs Kirkpatrick's charms, he does not get to enjoy a harmonious married life. Very soon, it becomes clear that the two are not a very good match as far as their temperaments, attitudes and opinions are concerned.

The marriage also introduces Molly to another orphan: her new stepsister Cynthia Kirkpatrick. Cynthia has led a life that is very different from Molly's and that has a good deal more in common with the literary orphans one encounters in most of the Victorian novels mentioned so far. In Cynthia's case it was the girl's father who died early, leaving a wife and a young daughter behind. Since the widow was not provided for financially, she had to return to her profession as governess. As a consequence, Cynthia has grown up largely separated from her mother. It is made clear, however, that this was only partially due to the fact that the governess could not bring her daughter with her. Even when the girl was still very young she was forced to spend her holidays at school, since her mother preferred visiting rich people—a situation that is criticised by other characters, including even some of the people the mother stays with: "'The only thing that makes me uneasy now is the way in which she seems to send her daughter away from her so much; we never can persuade her to bring Cynthia with her when she comes to see us'" (82). In addition, the readers are informed that Mrs Kirkpatrick does not want her daughter to be present at her wedding because she feels "how disagreeable it would be to her to have her young daughter flashing out her beauty by the side of the faded bride, her mother" (109). Cynthia explicitly expresses criticism of the lack of affection she has experienced her entire life: "'Somehow, I cannot forgive her for her neglect of me as a child, when I would have clung to her. Besides, I hardly ever heard from her when I was at school'" (200). In contrast to a character like Aimée, Mrs Kirkpatrick is neither a motherly woman nor a very affectionate one. Nevertheless, she does not turn into the proverbial "evil stepmother" when she marries Mr Gibson. In comparison to other characters in Victorian literature who fail as caretakers, such as Mrs Reed in *Jane Eyre* or Pip's sister in *Great Expectations*, Mrs Kirkpatrick arguably is a less threatening character.

The Orphan as a Figure of Hope

Although the figure of the pathetic orphan constitutes perhaps the most memorable image of parentless children in Victorian novels, orphans were also frequently stylised as figures who embody hope. In fact, the pathetic orphan sometimes turns into a figure of hope in the course of the story, as some of the examples discussed so far already show, which means that the two images are far from being mutually exclusive. To a certain extent, this kind of transformation can be seen as a further parallel to the genre of the fairy tale. Marina Warner claims that fairy tales "typically offer hope of release from poverty, maltreatment, and subjection" (2014, xxii), and something very similar could be said about many orphan narratives, especially early- and mid-Victorian ones. This attitude towards orphans was based on the way parentless children were seen in socio-political discourses of the time.[20] The association with hope and happy endings is certainly one of the features that have turned the orphan into a particularly attractive figure for readers, both in the 19th century and today. An improvement of the situation of the orphan was sometimes brought about by drawing upon "the classic narrative of the orphan's fortuitous inheritance" (Wagner 2008, 209)—a tradition that can, for instance, be seen in Dickens's *Oliver Twist*.[21] While the discovery of (affluent) family members or an inheritance help to bring about a happy ending in a number of orphan narratives, many Victorian novels rather stress the parentless characters' agency and their potential to change their situation by means of relying on their own resources, displaying a sometimes inordinate amount of resilience, pluck, and determination to change their life. In the case of Jane Eyre, finding family members and inheriting a considerable sum from her uncle in Madeira certainly makes it easier for the protagonist to become independent, but her personality has already been shaped by other developments at this point, especially by her repeatedly taking the initiative—by agreeing wholeheartedly to being sent to Lowood, by studying to become a teacher, by advertising for a new teaching position, by refusing to become Mr Rochester's mistress, etc.

A novel that exemplifies the importance often attributed to the orphan's agency particularly well is Charles Dickens's fictional autobiography *David Copperfield*. David's father already died before his son was born, and his mother marries Mr Murdstone, who turns out to be the proverbial evil stepfather. His mother's death leaves David feeling miserable and lonely, "an orphan in the wide world" (Dickens [1849-50] 1992, 109). At first, his fortune changes for the worse when his stepfather sends the boy to work in a warehouse at the age of ten instead of allowing him to continue his education at school. David is desperate and feels doomed to a life as an uneducated labourer, but he still works hard in order to gain respect: "I know that I worked from morning until night, with common men and boys, a shabby child. [...] I knew from the first, that, if I could not do my work as well as any of the rest, I could not hold myself above slight and contempt" (142). Quite soon, the protagonist decides to run away from London in order to find his aunt in Dover instead of simply accepting his fate. His plan works out, his aunt is willing to help him, and David can go back to school. When the protagonist is older, he still has to work hard for his success, as he tells the reader repeatedly, for instance in the following passages, in which he describes his struggle with stenography:

> I did not allow my resolution [..] to cool. It was one of the irons I began to heat immediately, and one of the irons I kept hot, and hammered at with a perseverance I may honestly admire. I bought an approved scheme of the noble art and mystery of stenography (which cost me ten and sixpence); and plunged into a sea of perplexity that brought me in a few weeks to the confines of distraction. (465)

> There was nothing for it but to turn back and begin all over again. It was very hard, but I turned back, though with a heavy heart, and began laboriously and methodically to plod over the same tedious ground at a snail's pace; stopping to examine minutely every speck in the way, on all sides, and making the most desperate efforts to know these elusive characters by sight wherever I met them. I was always punctual at the office [...] and I really did work, as the common expression is, like a cart-horse. (466-67)

The imagery used in the passages above reinforces the idea that the path of self-improvement requires considerable exertion. Perseverance is singled out as one of the key qualities necessary for success given the fact that the individual typically has to prove his or her stamina when faced with setbacks. When his financial security is once more gone due to his aunt having lost her money, David shows himself to be both resolute and grateful for what she has done for him up to this point; he is ready to assume responsibility for himself and for others:

> I was not dispirited now. [...] What I had to do was to show my aunt that her past goodness to me had not been thrown away on an insensible, ungrateful object. What I had to do was to turn the painful discipline of my younger days to account, by going to work with a resolute and steady heart. What I had to do was to take my woodman's axe in my hand, and clear my own way through the forest of difficulty (443).

Again, an image from the domain of physical labour is drawn upon to highlight the sustained effort that is required on the part of the character. What is also noteworthy is that David now considers his previous experiences, specifically the hardships he has gone through due to his parentless state, as an asset helping him overcome the new obstacles he meets. In other words, his having had to work at the age of ten in retrospect is seen by him as having had a character-building effect.

Self-improvement is regarded as an ongoing process in *David Copperfield*; i.e., David uses his achievements as stepping stones for moving on and achieving something even better. At the age of 21, he has secured "a respectable income" (533) for himself and is "in high repute" (533) due to his self-taught command of stenography, which serves him well for "reporting the debates in Parliament for a Morning Newspaper" (533). Still, he is aiming at a higher goal, having his first literary works published. Finally, at the end of the story, the narrating I is looking back upon his life with evident satisfaction: "I had advanced in fame and fortune, my domestic joy was perfect, I had been married ten happy years" (735). Professional success coupled with domestic bliss here are the goals of the orphan's life trajectory and the reward for his determination. By focusing on the individual's potential to shape his or her own destiny, orphan narratives appear to be informed by Victorian ideas of self-improvement, made popular by texts such as Samuel Smiles's *Self-Help*, which propagates the idea that "[t]he spirit of self-help is the root of all genuine growth in the individual" (17). In this vein, Annette Federico argues that "Dickens's engagement with timely questions about what the pursuit of happiness means, morally and ideologically, in Victorian culture—and what happiness means subjectively, to individuals—links *David Copperfield* to the liberal goals of self-determination, equality, and fair opportunity" (2003, 70).

David Copperfield is one of the prime examples of the *bildungsroman* or novel of development, which is among the most prominent genres of Victorian literature and often features orphans as protagonists. The *bildungsroman* became popular in the aftermath of the translation of Goethe's *Wilhelm Meister* (1795-96) into English by Thomas Carlyle in 1824 (cf. Nelson 2014, 78). One of the essential characteristics of this genre is the high degree of self-reflexivity displayed by the protagonist—a feature that is emphasised in fictional autobiographies, which typically make use of the temporal and cognitive distance between the narrating I and the experiencing I to stress the protagonist's self-reflexivity. The traditional *bildungsroman* traces the development of an individual from his/her childhood to a stage of life when the grown-up protagonist has achieved a stable position in society.

There are several reasons for presenting orphans as protagonists in the *bildungsroman*. One of these is that parentless characters are often forced to become independent at an earlier age than children growing up with their parents. When David Copperfield has found his aunt and returns to school after having been forced to work in the warehouse and to walk all the way from London to Dover at the age of ten, he is aware of being set apart from the other boys by what he has already gone through:

> It seemed to me so long, however, since I had been among such boys, or among any companions of my own age [...] that I felt as strange as ever I have done in all my life. I was so conscious of having passed through scenes of which they could have no knowledge, and of having acquired experiences foreign to my age, appearance, and condition as one of them, that I half believed it was an imposture to come there as an ordinary little schoolboy. (Dickens [1849-50] 1992, 197)

Orphans are frequently shown to be more mature than other children their age. As John Maynard points out, the genre of the *bildungsroman* typically focusses on "the relation between the individual and her society and the nature of the individual's psychology" (2005, 287). Both the individual's position in society and his/her psychology are likely to be fraught with specific problems and tensions in the case of an orphaned protagonist, since "they have no connection to the familial structure which helps define the individual" (Kimball 1999, 559) under ordinary circumstances. The *bildungsroman* frequently traces an individual's development from integration via disillusionment (coupled with separation) to experience and, finally, to re-integration. For orphans, the first step of this development (from integration to disillusionment and separation) is typically non-existent; instead, separation is often their basic condition in life given the fact that they have no family to separate from. While there are no parents to shape the orphan's character, there are potentially manifold other influences, including mentors of very different kinds. David Copperfield, for instance, is reinforced in his belief in perseverance by his aunt. When the latter loses her money, she refuses to give up and tells her nephew "with an aspect more triumphant than dejected: 'We must meet reverses boldly, and not suffer them to frighten us [...]. We must live misfortune down'" (Dickens [1849-50] 1992, 425). The traditional target of the *bildungsroman* is a (re-)integration of the individual into society. More often than not, an orphan has to struggle particularly hard if he/she wants to gain a respectable place in society. Choosing an orphan as main character also invites reflections on one of the crucial themes of this type of novel: "To the extent that the bildungsroman is seen as about the integration of the individual into society it will focus on the issue of how much the individual is a product and creature of society and, more specifically, on the ways in which he or she should be read as an allegory of the society's condition" (Maynard 2005, 287). For all of the reasons mentioned above, orphans arguably constitute particularly interesting protagonists for novels of development.

Many of the protagonists of the *bildungsroman* essentially embody the Victorian ideal of self-help, i.e., the maxim that "[h]elp from without is often enfeebling in its effects, but help from within invariably invigorates" (Smiles 2002, 17), or at least they learn to appreciate the importance of working hard for their progress, as the example of Pip in *Great Expectations* shows. At first, he relies primarily on external (financial) help that is given to him, without even trying to find out who his benefactor is, and, on the whole, "fits comfortably into the European novel tradition of the young man from the provinces setting out for the city where he will acquire urban sophistication and life experience" (Wirth-Nesher 1986, 260). Simultaneously, he fails to recognise what the blacksmith Joe Gargery, who is a foster father/brother/companion for Pip, has done for him and even feels embarrassed when the simple, but good-hearted and honest man comes to visit him in London. It is only when the identity of Pip's benefactor is revealed and the protagonist finds himself in a moral dilemma that he learns to rely on his own resources and starts to work hard instead of acting the part of the young gentleman: "Many a year went round, before I was a partner in the House; but, I lived happily with Herbert and his wife, and lived frugally, and paid my debts, and maintained a constant correspondence with Biddy and Jo" (Dickens [1861] 1994, 439).

The image of the orphan success story "from rags to riches" was a very influential template on both sides of the Atlantic.[22] Yet there were also novels that criticised this plot pattern to a certain extent. A case in point is the depiction of the character of Josiah Bounderby in Dickens's social problem novel *Hard Times* (1854). Bounderby himself routinely draws upon both the image of the pathetic orphan and the success story of the disadvantaged child in order to render his biography more impressive. He is introduced to the readers as "a rich man: banker, merchant, manufacturer, and what not" (Dickens [1854] 1994, 12) who is always eager to "vaunt himself a self-made man" (12). In order to stress his personal achievement Bounderby never tires of enumerating the hardships he allegedly had to endure during his childhood. He thus portrays himself to his interlocutors as a man who once was "one of the most miserable little wretches ever seen" (13), a child who "was always moaning and groaning" and "ragged and dirty" (13). To complete the list of his miseries, Bounderby also talks about his mother having deserted him and having left him in the care of his grandmother, whom he characterises as "the wickedest and the worst old woman that ever lived. If I got a little pair of shoes by any chance, she would take 'em off and sell 'em for drink" (14). Bounderby supposedly had to rely on his own resources and even make do without any kind of formal education. While his listeners tend to be duly impressed by this account of his early life, it is ultimately revealed that Bounderby's "model biography" emulating (and exaggerating) the stereotype of the orphan's progress from rags to riches is nothing but a lie. His mother did not desert him, there was no wicked grandmother, and he came "of parents that loved him as dear as the best could, and never thought it hardship on themselves to pinch a bit that he might write and cipher beautiful" (234). Though Bounderby's father did indeed die when Josiah was eight, the mother was still able to provide for her son. The revelation that Bounderby actually had a very decent chance to attend school may serve to undermine the "from rags to riches"-story, perhaps even raise the question of how likely such a development really was in Victorian society, especially at a time when primary education was not yet obligatory. Beyond that, the false stories Bounderby tells about his early life contribute to his depiction as a hypocrite, who condemns those who do not get by on their own without really knowing what it is like to be poor.

The juxtaposition of different orphans in Emily Brontë's *Wuthering Heights* arguably serves to put the Victorian orphan success narrative into perspective as well. In some respects, Heathcliff appears to embody the typical success story. He starts out as a foundling, who is picked up by Mr Earnshaw in Liverpool and whose parents remain unknown throughout the story. During his childhood, Heathcliff experiences primarily rejection, hardship and maltreatment: "Doubly orphaned, first by his abandonment on the streets of that city [Liverpool], and then by Mr Earnshaw's death, Heathcliff then suffers torments from Hindley" (Banerjee 1996, 58). Still, he somehow acquires considerable wealth and a "manner [that] was even dignified" (E. Brontë [1847] 1985, 135) over the course of merely three years, which is a quite impressive achievement given the fact that he apparently had no external help. The mystery of how Heathcliff manages to become rich and educated is never resolved; Nelly merely speculates that "[h]is upright carriage suggested the idea of his having been in the army" (135) and that he may have made the money by criminal activities, but there is no evidence to support any of this. In other words, a part of the plot that is usually paid much attention to in the novel of development is left out. In this way *Wuthering Heights* eschews the imperative of identifying specific values, patterns of behaviour or other factors as conducive to (financial and social) success. The implicit criticism of the usual success stories one may see in this strategy is reinforced by the fact that Heathcliff's "from rags to riches" story does not end well; his actions destroy or at least seriously impair the happiness of others, and wealth, education and a higher social status do not ensure his own happiness. Apparently, the only brief spells of happiness Heathcliff experiences in his life are the times he spends with Catherine on the moors, in a world that is removed from the impact of society's notions of appropriate behaviour and rigid class distinctions. Heathcliff's story thus appears to undermine the prevalent narrative of worldly success.

Heathcliff's failure is largely due to his position as an outsider, which he never manages to overcome. The foundling is marked as an outcast in several respects, being described as "a dirty, ragged, black-haired child" (77), "as dark almost as if it came from the devil" (77) and speaking "some gibberish that nobody could understand" (77). A number of critics have considered the references to Heathcliff's dark features as an allusion to the transatlantic slave trade. Maja Lisa von Sneidern, for instance, observes: "The English city with the most spirited commerce in slaves was Liverpool. [...] [B]y the interbellum period (1763-1776) she had eclipsed her competitors and was the premier slaving port in Britain" (Von Sneidern 1995, 171-72). The reference to Heathcliff having been found in Liverpool thus raises the possibility of a postcolonial reading of the character as "an irregular black, a mongrel, a source of great anxiety for the mid-nineteenth-century Victorian" (172). Other critics, including Terry Eagleton, have argued that the parentless boy might be associated with immigration from Ireland in the context of the Famine. Despite his "otherness", the foundling quickly becomes Mr Earnshaw's favourite. But while some orphan narratives suggest that showing affection for a parentless child leads to a positive outcome, Mr Earnshaw's interest in Heathcliff has destructive results. Most members of the Earnshaw household dislike Heathcliff and show this very clearly, as the narrator Nelly Dean recalls: "Hindley hated him, and to say the truth I did the same; and we plagued and went on with him shamefully, for I wasn't reasonable enough to feel my injustice, and the mistress never put in a word on his behalf, when she saw him wronged" (E. Brontë [1847] 1985, 78-79). Here, the orphan functions as an intruder, as someone who "disturbs the family narrative" (Peters 2000, 31). Upon Mr Earnshaw's death, Hindley "had learnt to regard his father as an oppressor rather than a friend, and Heathcliff as a usurper of his parent's affections, and his privileges, and he grew bitter with brooding over these injuries" (E. Brontë [1847] 1985, 79). Consequently, Heathcliff becomes a victim, but also learns to retaliate with hatred and malice, showing no consideration for others' well-being. To a certain extent, Heathcliff thus anticipates the type of the "rebellious orphan" with his "immoderate levels of narcissism, seeking only to serve him or herself without any aspirations to assimilation", which David Floyd (2014, 9) considers to be characteristic of late Victorian literature.[23]

Neither Heathcliff nor the elder Catherine can be read as figures of hope despite their "measurable" success in conventional terms (wealth, education, high rank, marriage with an upper-class wife/husband); in Emily Brontë's novel, this kind of success is not what counts. In spiritual and emotional terms, both fail and suffer. It is only the younger generation portrayed in *Wuthering Heights* that eventually is more successful; at least the younger Catherine and Hareton can be seen as figures of hope. The younger Catherine is born prematurely and loses her mother only two hours after her birth, beginning her life as "a puny, seven months' child"

(E. Brontë [1847] 1985, 201). At first, she is "[a]n unwelcomed infant" (201), but this changes soon: "It might have wailed out of life, and nobody cared a morsel, during those first hours of existence. We redeemed the neglect afterwards; but its beginning was [...] friendless" (201). Right from the start, the infant apparently displays a resilience that ensures her survival, and that again seems to come to the surface later in life, when she is once more friendless and is forced by Heathcliff to marry her sickly and egocentric cousin Linton. Catherine's fate is not that of a typical protagonist of a novel of development, since she stays at home and in the immediate surroundings of Thrushcross Grange.[24] She is educated by her father, who apparently is quite lenient regarding his educational principles, but "curiosity and a quick intellect urged her into an apt scholar; she learnt rapidly and eagerly" (E. Brontë [1847] 1985, 224). Her upbringing seems to have fostered her capacity to resist ill treatment. Hareton is raised in ignorance by Heathcliff, remaining even illiterate. While the latter has acted as an employer and not as a foster father in his relation to Hindley's son, he still has "not treated him physically ill; thanks to his fearless nature, which offered no temptation to that course of oppression; it had none of the timid susceptibility that would have given zest to ill-treatment, in Heathcliff's judgment" (231). Both Catherine and Hareton ultimately overcome obstacles by being brave, while Linton, who lives in a permanent state of fear and displays a "sickly peevishness" (235), is despised by his own father and dies at a young age. The idea that "spirit", resilience and courage will be rewarded, whereas an individual does not benefit from a timid behaviour resonates throughout Victorian orphan narratives. When Catherine and Hareton eventually discover their affection for each other, they happily remain in an idyllic state of reclusiveness. The garden that the younger Catherine and Hareton plant at Wuthering Heights can be read as "a straightforward symbol of renewal and growth; an external sign of their youth, love, and re-born hope" (Marsh 1999, 100).

While mid-Victorian novels on the whole seem to cherish the notion of the orphan as a figure of hope, late Victorian narratives increasingly undermine this optimism, as Thomas Hardy's anti-*bildungsroman Jude the Obscure* (1896) exemplifies. The title character is an orphan who seeks to improve his life by learning, apparently following in the footsteps of characters like David Copperfield. Initially, the text appears to reiterate the image of the pathetic orphan to a certain extent. The protagonist Jude Fawley has lost both of his parents and is living with his unmarried aunt Drusilla, who does not seem to bestow many tokens of affection on the boy. Jude, who is referred to as slender, is introduced carrying heavy buckets of water, while overhearing his aunt say to some of her neighbours: "'It would ha' been a blessing if Goddy-mighty had took thee too, wi' thy mother and father, poor useless boy! But I've got him here to stay with me till I can see what's to be done with un, though I am obliged to let him earn any penny he can'" (Hardy [1896] 1974, 37). Although this introduction to Jude's relation with his aunt does not seem to bode particularly well, Aunt Drusilla turns out to be a far cry from caretakers such as Jane Eyre's aunt Mrs Reed. Apparently, she is not a particularly affectionate person but she does not mistreat her nephew, who is described as "physically comfortable" (53). The trope of the pathetic orphan is evoked even more strongly when Jude decides to quit the task of scaring away birds from a farmer's field due to his sympathy with the hungry creatures:

> at length his heart grew sympathetic with the birds' thwarted desires. They seemed, like himself, to be living in a world which did not want them. Why should he frighten them away? They took upon them more and more the aspect of gentle friends and pensioners—the only friends he could claim as being in the least degree interested in him, for his aunt had often told him that she was not. […] A magic thread of fellow-feeling united his own life with theirs. Puny and sorry as those lives were, they much resembled his own. (39)

Similar to other orphans in Victorian novels, Jude is aware of his loneliness, and this causes him to develop a strong feeling of empathy with others, which is to become one of his prominent character traits.

His other main character trait is a wish to learn, to improve his prospects in life. Predictably, his path to education is anything but smooth. Inspired by a teacher, Jude becomes an autodidact. Similar to David Copperfield, Jude Fawley is cheated by adults, most prominently by the "itinerant quack-doctor" (51) Vilbert, who promises to procure Latin and Greek grammar books for Jude in exchange for "names and addresses of the cottagers who were willing to test the virtues of the world-renowned pills and salve" (53) sold by the quack-doctor. While the young boy honours his part of the deal, Vilbert does not, which causes Jude to be downcast and disillusioned:

> He was an unsophisticated boy, but the gift of sudden insight which is sometimes vouchsafed to children showed him all at once what shoddy humanity the quack was made of. There was to be no intellectual light from this source. The leaves cropped from his imaginary crown of laurel; he turned to a gate, leant against it, and cried bitterly. (53)

Yet, after a while, he comes up with the idea of contacting his former teacher and asking him to send him some books. When this second attempt at getting hold of books proves successful, Jude dedicates much of his time to reading and learning classical languages. What he completely lacks during the many years of studying is a mentor, who could offer guidance. Eventually, Jude is deterred from his path of studying by Arabella, who seduces him and tricks him into marriage. When the marriage fails and his wife leaves for Australia with her parents, the hope of pursuing an academic career is briefly rekindled in Jude, only to come to an end once more when he realises that he will not be able to afford the fees for higher education. Ultimately, his "lofty aspirations to study at Christminster are frustrated by his orphanhood, which decrees his station as stonemason" (Floyd 2014, 5). Unlike many earlier fictional orphans, Jude is not able to overcome the limitations in terms of class and income. The protagonist's thwarted dreams of rising socially are exacerbated by his failure as far as finding domestic happiness is concerned.

Jude's empathy, which has grown from his recognition of his loneliness, is one of the reasons why he does not hesitate to take in Arabella's son, whose existence he was not aware of and whose parentage seems initially somewhat doubtful, although he is said to resemble Jude. Strictly speaking, this boy is no orphan, of course, but he has essentially led the life of a parentless child, a "functional orphan" (Nikolajeva 2002, 172), up to this point, having been left behind by his mother to live with his grandparents in Australia, who have now apparently grown tired of taking care of the child. It is made clear that the boy does not know who his parents are, which means that he must have felt like an orphan. When Jude hears from Arabella that she does not want her son to stay with her, he does not hesitate to take care of the boy. His reasoning upon this occasion suggests that the question of paternity is of minor importance to him:

> "What a view of life he must have, mine or not mine!" he said. "[…] The beggarly question of parentage—what is it, after all? What does it matter, when you come to think of it, whether a child is yours by blood or not? All the little ones of our time are collectively the children of us adults of the time, and entitled to our general care." (Hardy [1896] 1974, 288)

This attitude recalls the reaction of Silas Marner upon seeing Eppie, but in the case of Jude, acting upon an altruistic impulse does not pay off in the long run. In fact, his decision to take in the child eventually leads to disastrous consequences for himself as well as for Sue, whom he is living with at the time.

The description of the boy who has so far lived the life of an orphan echoes the trope of the pathetic orphan:

> In the down train that was timed to reach Aldbrickham station about ten o'clock the next evening, a small, pale child's face could be seen in the gloom of a third-class carriage. He had large, frightened eyes [...]. [...] He was Age masquerading as Juvenility, and doing it so badly that his real self showed through crevices. (289)

The boy is alone, appears to have been unwanted and has presumably experienced things unknown to other children his age. Both Jude and Sue do their best to offer him a good home, taking care of the child with a "tender interest of an ennobling and unselfish kind" (301), as the narrator puts it. Still, it seems to be impossible to cheer up the boy, to make him laugh und to help him overcome a state that is "singularly deficient in all the usual hopes of childhood" (301). While one might conjecture that this hopelessness points to a background of maltreatment, abuse or other traumatic experiences, the readers are never told what happened in the boy's past, which remains entirely enigmatic. In the presentation of Jude's childhood, the heterodiegetic narrator characterised the boy as someone who is "an ancient man in some phases of thought, much younger than his years in others" (51). In the boy arriving from Australia the notion of being "too old" in some respects, yet immature in others seems to be taken to an extreme: He entirely lacks youthful optimism, apparently seeing life in the bleakest terms possible, but he also misinterprets situations in a "childish" fashion. This combination, which is presented as endearing in other literary orphans (including the young Jude), ultimately proves fatal in this case, since it culminates in the boy killing both himself as well as his two younger half-siblings, confronting Jude and Sue with an awful spectacle (345).

Jude and Sue assume that this terrible deed is the result of "a fit of aggravated despondency that the events and information of the evening before had induced in his morbid temperament" (345). This assumption is reinforced by a piece of paper on which the boy has written "'Done because we are too menny'" (345). The horror of this scene is subsequently embedded in more general conclusions that Jude hears from a doctor:

> "The doctor says there are such boys springing up amongst us—boys of a sort unknown in the last generation—the outcome of new views of life. They seem to see all its terrors before they are old enough to have staying power to resist them. He says it is the beginning of the coming universal wish not to live." (346)

In other words, the orphan here becomes an emblem of universal despair and despondency or, to use Wagner's terms, an expression of "a more general sense of dislocation and disorientation" (2008, 204), exceeding a personal situation.[25] While parentless individuals in early- to mid-Victorian novels, similar to orphans in fairy tales, often "embody the hope that whatever the present situation, it can change for the better" (Kimball 1999, 559), this optimism increasingly vanishes in orphan narratives from the late Victorian period.

Jude the Obscure undermines patterns informing earlier Victorian success stories in more senses than one. In addition to challenging the (Romantic) notion of the innocent child, the novel also criticises the idea that the colonies—and specifically Australia—promise hope and a new beginning, which fuelled the orphan emigration schemes in the period. In *David Copperfield*, Australia offers a fresh start for the "fallen women" Little Em'ly and Martha, and it is the place where the Micawber family finally is successful after having failed time and again in Britain. Similarly, in *Great Expectations*, Magwitch makes his fortune in Australia. In *Jude the Obscure*, by contrast, a child who has grown up in Australia arrives in the "mother country" in a deeply disturbed state and ends up killing his half-siblings due to a profound depression and hopelessness. The depiction of the orphan turned child-murderer also has to be seen in the wider context of the "waning of sentimental portrayals of childhood" (Floyd 2014, 7) towards the end of the 19th century and, more specifically, a general shift from the "sentimentalized child" to the "sensationalized child" (Wagner 2008, 202).

The Orphan as Adventurer

While the optimism that was still associated with the figure of the orphan in many early- and mid-Victorian novels is more and more challenged in late-Victorian literature, it survives in particular in the genre of the adventure novel, where orphans frequently appear as protagonists. The conventions of the adventure novel require the (usually male) protagonists to break free from their homes and familiar surroundings. This task is arguably easier for orphans, who may even be forced to leave their homes or who may not have a home in the first place. The figure of the orphan as adventurer shares some features with the *picaro*, but at least young orphans such as Kipling's Kim and Mowgli or Stevenson's Jim Hawkins also lack characteristics of the prototypical picaresque anti-hero, since they for instance very much support the Victorian notion of self-improvement rather than relying purely on their luck. Moreover, the figure of the (male) orphan as adventurer has to be seen in the context of the emergence of a large number of boys aiming at "a redefinition of manliness over the second half of the nineteenth century, a movement away from emotionalism and androgynous virtue and toward a more hard-bitten, stoic, and physical ideal" (Nelson 2014, 77). The lack of a home and parents, who could provide shelter and a sense of security, typically forces the child in adventure stories to develop already at a comparatively early age exactly the (supposedly masculine) qualities listed by Nelson. The British adventure story in the late 19th century, with its imperialist emphasis on "exploration, acquisition and colonization" (Floyd 2014, 126) is thus, first and foremost, a masculine story.

A particularly striking example of an orphan who shows a very adventurous spirit right from the start is Mowgli in Rudyard Kipling's *The Jungle Books*. In contrast to the pathetic orphan, he is neither timid nor shy. Even the very first description of Mowgli in *The Jungle Books*, which shows him turning up unexpectedly at the entrance of the cave of the wolves, suggests that he is a little boy who is singularly unafraid:

> Directly in front of him, holding on by a low branch, stood a naked brown baby who could just walk—as soft and as dimpled a little atom as ever came to a wolf's cave at night. He looked up into Father Wolf's face, and laughed. (Kipling [1894-95] 1994, 14)

This scene, in which Mowgli is introduced to the readers, turns out to be programmatic for the boy's life in the jungle. He does not miss his parents and readily accepts the wolves as his surrogate family. What is more, Mowgli's behaviour suggests that he feels like a *primus inter pares*, "pushing his way between the cubs to get close to the warm hide" (14) of mother wolf. The latter's characterisation of the boy as "bold" (14) seems entirely apt; he demonstrates very clearly that he can hold his own in the proverbial and literal fight for the survival of the fittest in the jungle. To make the readers aware of the exceptional quality of Mowgli's demeanour, they are reminded that the wolves could easily kill the baby; Father Wolf knows that he "could kill him with a touch of [his] foot" (14). Yet, the wolves are not inclined to do so; instead, they are prepared to defend Mowgli against the tiger Shere Khan, even if this means "fight[ing] to the death" (16-17).

When the tiger turns up, the readers learn that the foundling is not really an orphan, but has apparently been left behind by his parents when the tiger attacked their camp: "'Its parents have run off'" (15). The text thus reiterates the Victorian idea that one's biological parents are not necessarily the ideal family. In other words, the fate of the functional orphan Mowgli echoes Victorian family politics, which considered the act of taking children away from their parents legitimate and even desirable under certain circumstances. The wolves, who are ready to fight for their "adoptive son", are presented as better caretakers than the boy's biological parents, who deserted him in a life-threatening situation. Moreover, Mowgli's bold demeanour indicates that he is not his parents' son, but rather belongs among the wolf pack. Mother Wolf's predictions for the boy support the idea that orphans can expect a bright future, provided they are allowed to grow up in the right environment: "'The man's cub is mine [...]—mine to me! He shall not be killed. He shall live to run with the pack and to hunt with the pack; and in the end, look you, hunter of little naked cubs—frog-eater—fish-killer—he shall hunt *thee*'" (15). Mowgli also shows that he is in the right place when he manages to win the favour of the wolf pack. During his presentation at the wolf council he sits contentedly among the predators, "laughing and playing with some pebbles" (17). Fearlessness is the key to Mowgli being accepted by the wolves, and it is also the quality that ultimately helps him defeat Shere Khan. The notion that bold, fearless behaviour of a child is rewarded proves to be one of the recurring ideas in Victorian depictions of orphans: Hareton is not physically mistreated by Heathcliff due to his "fearless nature" (E. Brontë [1847] 1985, 231), Eppie is rewarded for resolutely making her way to Silas Marner's house, and, when looking back on her childhood, the grown-up narrator Jane Eyre believes that a bolder demeanour would have improved her standing in Gateshead: "I know that had I been a sanguine, brilliant, careless, exacting, handsome, romping child—though equally dependent and friendless—Mrs Reed would have endured my presence more complacently; her children would have entertained for me more of the cordiality of fellow-feeling" (Ch. Brontë [1847] 1985, 47).

In addition to the wolf pack, the panther Bagheera and the bear Baloo play an important role as mentors in Mowgli's education; they teach him how to get along in the jungle. Mowgli's surrogate family and his mentors endow him with great self-confidence; he is always sure that they will also support him in the confrontation with his archenemy, the tiger: "And Mowgli would laugh and answer: 'I have the pack and I have thee [Bagheera]; and Baloo, though he is so lazy, might strike a blow or two for my sake. Why should I be afraid?'" (Kipling [1894-95] 1994, 21). Bagheera and Baloo come to Mowgli's rescue when the boy has been abducted by the Bandar-log, the Monkey-People, and the wolf Akela and one of Mowgli's wolf-brothers eventually help him defeat Shere Khan.

When Mowgli has to leave the wolf pack, his surrogate family continues to support him, as they promise when he takes his leave from the jungle: "'Ye will not forget me?' said Mowgli. 'Never while we can follow a trail,' said the cubs. 'Come to the foot of the hill when thou art a man, and we will talk to thee; and we will come into the croplands to play with thee by night'" (29). Even when he is rejected first by the wolf pack and then by the inhabitants of the human village, Bagheera, Baloo and his wolf family stay loyal and keep him company. Contrary to many other literary orphans, Mowgli thus hardly ever feels lonely, although he has to cope with the challenge of living in between two worlds.

Kim in Kipling's eponymous novel (1901) is another striking example of the orphan as adventurer. The way the protagonist is introduced in the very first sentences of the novel almost reads like a reversal of introductory scenes in novels such as *Great Expectations* and *Jane Eyre*, which feature frightened, subdued, bullied orphans: Kim sits boldly astride a canon in the Indian city of Lahore, "in defiance of municipal orders" (Kipling [1901] 1987, 49). His position already exudes a good deal of self-confidence; beyond that, the symbolism implied in this scene is made transparent when the heterodiegetic narrator explains: "Who hold Zam-Zammah, that 'fire-breathing dragon', hold the Punjab, for the great green-bronze piece is always first of the conqueror's loot" (49). The narrator even situates Kim's role as "conqueror" explicitly within an imperial dichotomy: "There was some justification for Kim—he had kicked Lala Dinanath's boy off the trunnions—since the English held the Punjab and Kim was English" (49). While Oliver Twist appears to be lost in a labyrinthine Victorian London, Kim O'Hara feels entirely at home in the city of Lahore. He knows how to get along with Indians of various castes and creeds. In contrast to Oliver Twist, who is constantly hungry and is punished when he eventually dares to ask for "more" in the workhouse, Kim knows exactly how to procure tasty food for himself as well as for the lama, whom he accompanies for a while; he tells the holy man: "'Give me the bowl. I know the people of this city—all who are charitable. Give, and I will bring it back filled'" (61). Instead of needing someone who takes care of him, it is the (orphaned) child who helps the grown-up in this case. When he decides to join the lama on the latter's quest, Kim calls himself the disciple of the holy man (cf. 64). Yet it seems doubtful whether he intends to learn anything from the lama; his main intention appears to be looking after him.[26] He is aware of the fact that the holy man, who appears quite helpless and unworldly in comparison to Kim, needs the boy's support in order to achieve his goals. Instead of presenting the protagonist as a pathetic orphan, he is shown to adopt this role occasionally on purpose, in order to get what he wants, using lines like "'I am very poor. My father is dead—my mother is dead'" (78) to induce others to help him. What is more, the narrator informs us that Kim enjoys the role-playing and performance required for successful begging (67), which makes the task look like a game and prevents the reader from feeling pity with the boy. It is noteworthy that Kim does not resort to illegal means in order to survive, unlike Fagin's boys in *Oliver Twist*. What he does regularly, however, is lie (71); still, we are told that there are some people, such as Mahbub Ali, he does not lie to (cf. 71), which suggests that he has essentially a good character, although he certainly does not come across as being innocent.

Kim does not have a particularly promising start in life, being the son of an Irish nurse-maid (cf. 49, 60) and "Kimball O'Hara, a young colour-sergeant of the Mavericks, an Irish regiment" (49). What increases the impression that Kim belongs to the group of children who were likely to be taken away from their parents in the Victorian period is the information that his father "fell to drink and loafing up and down the line with the keen-eyed three-year-old baby" (49) and even became addicted to opium after his wife's death. Moreover, the boy was looked after by a half-caste woman smoking opium (cf. 49).[27] Although the orphan Kim is white, which privileges him in the imperial dichotomy, he is "a poor white of the very poorest" (49). His father was clearly incapable of providing properly for his son; yet he seems to have cared about the child in his own way. The (somewhat misguided) attempt to secure Kim's future is apparent in the father scrawling on his son's baptismal certificate "with some confused idea that he was doing wonders for his son [...] scores of times '*Look after the boy. Please look after the boy*'" (133). The father cares about his son's future, but does not really know what to do to help him along. Kim, in contrast, turns out to be a boy who knows exactly how to take care of himself.[28]

There are hints that "[s]ocieties and chaplains" (49), i.e., the Church and other institutions, tried to take care of the boy in the past, but he very much prefers staying clear of authorities and enjoys his freedom, similar to one of the most well-known orphans in American literature, Mark Twain's Huckleberry Finn. Kim leads a life that is described in a way that is bound to make it sound appealing to young readers:

> he knew the wonderful walled city of Lahore from the Delhi Gate to the outer Fort Ditch; was hand in glove with men who led lives stranger than anything Haroun al Rashid dreamed of; and he lived in a life wild as that of the Arabian Nights, but missionaries and secretaries of charitable societies could not see the beauty of it. His nickname through the wards was "Little Friend of all the World"; and very often, being lithe and inconspicuous, he

executed commissions by night on the crowded housetops for sleek and shiny young men of fashion. (51)

The freedom to go wherever he wants (even at night) and the explicit intertextual references to the fairy tales of *The Arabian Nights* endow the passage above with a sense of excitement, mystery and glamour—especially for young readers. The fact that Kim is known as "Little Friend of all the World" suggests that he does not feel lonely—unlike many other orphans in Victorian literature. For Kim, being an orphan primarily means being free—at least up to the point when he has to attend school after all. When he was put into an institution before, he ran away because the regulated life at school does not suit him (137).

Finally, however, he cannot avoid being sent to a school any longer. There are two options for him: a school run by the Catholic Church, which would presumably fit Kim's Irish ancestry, and a Military Orphanage. That these alternatives are mentioned in the novel reflects the fact that there was indeed a network of institutions looking after orphans even in the Raj.[29] Kim dislikes being inside one of these immensely; he perceives Western clothes (jacket and trousers) to be "crippling" "for body and mind alike" (154), he can find "no good place to sleep" (159) and is beaten by the other boys (159). In an interesting twist, Kim, who was perfectly able to hold his own in the streets of Lahore among his peers as well as among adults, now becomes a victim of bullying—similar to many orphans in 19th-century novels. Nevertheless, the novel leaves no doubt that attending the school is necessary for Kim. Here, he is prepared for a career in the secret service, the "Great Game."

Kim manages to accumulate a range of male mentors with very different backgrounds, "representing various aspects of a notably diverse culture" (Floyd 2014, 140). In terms of emotional bonding, the lama appears to be the most important character for Kim—a fact that becomes apparent when we are informed that Kim considers the lama to be "his father and mother" (Kipling [1901] 1987, 215). In addition, there is the horse-trader Mahbub Ali, a "big burly Afghan" (66), who uses Kim's talents for his purposes. Colonel Creighton may be thought of as a third mentor for the boy, albeit the one whom he apparently feels the least emotional attachment to. All of these men care about Kim, respect his talents and see something special in him. Colonel Creighton, the representative of the British Empire, seems to be interested in Kim almost despite himself:

It was absurd that a man of his position should take an interest in a little country-bred vagabond; but the Colonel remembered the conversation in the train, and often in the past few months had caught himself thinking of the queer, silent, self-possessed boy. His evasion, of course, was the height of insolence, but it argued some resource and nerve. (176)

The qualities that the three men appreciate in Kim are different and reflect their individual value systems. The lama, for instance, claims: "'I have known many men in my so long life, and disciples not a few. But to none among men, if so be thou art woman-born, has my heart gone out as it has to thee—thoughtful, wise, and courteous; but something of a small imp'" (118). He ascribes several positive qualities to Kim, but also a certain mischievousness ("something of a small imp"). Moreover, both the choice of the word "imp" and the doubts regarding Kim being "woman-born", which suggest supernatural overtones, serve to emphasise how exceptional Kim is from the point of view of the holy man.

All in all, Kim displays great confidence in his actions; there are only few occasions when he is downcast or feels alone. In one of these rare moments he seems to struggle with a feeling of loneliness that culminates in questioning his identity: "'Who is Kim—Kim—Kim?'" (233). Although readers may be inclined to feel sympathy with Kim's situation, and may in fact consider the question raised by him an extremely likely one in an orphan narrative, the narrator downplays the boy's predicament and (quite condescendingly) ascribes his trouble to a combination of immaturity and the "Oriental" influence he has been exposed to throughout his life:

> A very few white people, but many Asiatics, can throw themselves into a mazement [sic] as it were by repeating their own names over and over again to themselves, letting the mind go free upon speculation as to what is called personal identity. When one grows older, the power, usually, departs, but while it lasts it may descend upon a man at any moment. (233)

The lack of sympathy with an orphan who, for once, is not his usual, confident self that is displayed here by the narrator emphasises how consistently the novel departs from the template of the pathetic orphan. Instead of using a moment in which the protagonist feels miserable as a starting point for creating a sentimental effect, the narrator mocks the character's attitude. Later on, there is a similar situation; Kim wonders once more: "'I am Kim. I am Kim. And what is Kim?' His soul repeated it again and again" (331). But this time, the boy is shown to overcome his preoccupation with himself, getting a grip on reality in a way that is implicitly appreciated by the narrator:

He did not want to cry—had never felt less like crying in his life—but of a sudden easy, stupid tears trickled down his nose, and with an almost audible click he felt the wheels of his being lock up anew on the world without. Things that rode meaningless on the eyeball an instant before slid into proper proportion. Roads were meant to be walked upon, houses to be lived in, cattle to be driven, fields to be tilled, and men and women to be talked to. (331)

According to the dichotomy between the "Oriental" and the "Occidental" that informs Kipling's novel, one could argue that this pragmatic, even utilitarian manner of perceiving his environment is meant to suggest that the protagonist is essentially a European, a "Sahib", after all. Overcoming a brief moment of "Oriental" doubt, he has regained his sense of purpose.

Rudyard Kipling is among those authors who "brought to a basically insular and provincial British audience the colour, the glamour and the romance of the British overseas enterprise", as Edward W. Said (1987, 7) puts it. In this context, orphans—Kim as well as Mowgli—played a role that was significantly different from that of the pathetic orphan in the novels discussed above. Orphans who, though still very young, are shown to be completely at ease in an environment that is "exotic" and at times dangerous serve to make imperialism palatable to a predominantly young readership. *Kim* is among the more well-known examples of "a large body of imperial fictional tales which can be called popular orphan adventure narratives" (Peters 2012, 63). What these have in common is an adoption of "deeply masculinist" (65) norms as well as an advocacy of imperialism, which even provides the orphan with a family he is otherwise deprived of.[30]

Robert Louis Stevenson's adventure novels *Treasure Island* (1883) and *Kidnapped* (1886) propagate very similar notions of masculinity and self-confidence. Jim Hawkins, the protagonist of *Treasure Island*, is not an orphan to begin with, but his father only appears very briefly at the beginning of the novel. The father is present when the first pirate arrives at the "Admiral Benbow" inn, but he is incapable of getting rid of the intruder, who immediately becomes a nuisance. Due to the fact that the father falls seriously ill, he fails to embody a strong, patriarchal presence. As he becomes increasingly weaker, Jim and his mother are left in charge of the inn: "it was plain from the first that my poor father was little likely to see the spring. He sank daily, and my mother and I had all the inn upon our hands" (Stevenson [1883] 1999, 9). Jim's mother is not presented as a strong person, either; instead, she sometimes even proves to be a burden for the protagonist, for instance when they have to flee from the approaching pirates:

"My dear," said my mother suddenly, "take the money and run on. I am
going to faint." This was certainly the end for both of us, I thought. How I
cursed the cowardice of the neighbours; how I blamed my poor mother for
her honesty and her greed, for her past foolhardiness and present
weakness! We were just at the little bridge, by good fortune; and I helped
her, tottering as she was, to the edge of the bank, where, sure enough, she
gave a sigh and fell on my shoulder. I do not know how I found the
strength to do it all, and I am afraid it was done roughly; but I managed to
drag her down the bank and a little way under the arch. (24)

The mother here is depicted as an encumbrance, and the novel right from
the start indulges in the fantasy of the boy who can achieve what adults
fail to accomplish. This concept is further elaborated in the course of the
adventure novel, when Jim time and again manages to save the day, for
instance by accidentally overhearing Long John Silver's plans or by
sailing the ship almost entirely on his own. The autodiegetic narrator
leaves the readers in no doubt regarding the importance of his actions.[31]
While both of his parents fail as role models, Jim soon finds a range of
surrogate father figures, all of whom share a natural authority, although
they stand for very different values: Dr Livesey, Squire Trelawney,
Captain Smollett, and the pirate Long John Silver. During the treasure
hunt and the conflict with the pirates, Jim shows that he is competent and,
similar to Kim, wins the respect of all of the surrogate father figures.

David Balfour, the protagonist in Stevenson's *Kidnapped*, does not
appear to be quite as young as the orphan characters in the novels
discussed above, but he is still inexperienced at the beginning of the story,
referring to himself as having been "little more than a child" (Stevenson
[1886] 2014, 29) when he loses both of his parents. His only remaining
relative, a rich uncle, first tries to kill him and then sells him to the crew of
a ship that is heading for the colonies, where he is supposed to work as an
indentured labourer ("in those days of my youth, white men were still sold
into slavery on the plantations, and that was the destiny to which my
wicked uncle had condemned me", 44). On the ship, David Balfour meets
Alan Breck Stewart, with whom he escapes. Although Alan is an outlaw,
the "mercurial Roman Catholic Highlander" (Hunt 2001, 131) serves as a
mentor, who introduces the "sober, inexperienced Protestant lowlander"
(131) David to the Highlands and masters various dangerous situations
with him.

As the examples discussed above have shown, the protagonists in
Victorian adventure stories are often orphaned boys who grow up in a
world where loneliness is overcome quickly, if it occurs at all, and where
male bonding plays a crucial role for defining one's identity:

[N]ot only are we in a masculine world dominated by travel, trade, adventure and intrigue, we are in a celibate world, in which the common romance of fiction and the enduring institution of marriage have been circumvented, avoided, all but ignored. At best, women help things along: they buy you a ticket, they cook, they tend the ill, and … they molest men. (Said 1987, 12)

In other words, presenting orphaned protagonists was also a way of (largely) avoiding female characters in the genre of the adventure story. When Jim Hawkins's mother is mentioned, she is presented primarily as a nuisance and a burden, as was pointed out above. But the stories featuring orphans as adventurers may also be read as childhood fantasies, which evoke a sense of freedom that serves to idealise childhood as a special stage in human life.

The "Afterlives" of the Victorian Orphan from the 20th Century to the Present

Although "the myth of the orphan—which at its high point practically constituted orphan-worship—was losing its efficacy as the [19th] century drew to a close" (Auerbach 1975, 411), the Victorian images of orphanhood have had a lasting impact on Anglophone literature and popular culture. In fact, at the beginning of the 20th century, orphans still seemed to be as popular as ever in Anglophone children's literature. In Frances Hodgson Burnett's children's novels *A Little Princess* (1905) and *The Secret Garden* (1911), for instance, there are very memorable female orphans.[32] The "lost boys" in J.M. Barrie's novel *Peter Pan* (1911) are an Edwardian echo of the tales of neglect that can also be found in many orphan narratives from the Victorian period. In the middle of the 20th century, Enid Blyton's *Adventure* series (1944-55) features the orphans Philip, Dinah, Jack and Lucy-Ann, who master all sorts of dangerous situations on their own, thus following in the footsteps of Kim, Jim Hawkins, and other heroes of adventure stories. All in all, the images of orphans that have been shaped by Victorian writers—the pathetic orphan, the orphan as a figure of hope, and the orphan as adventurer—appear to be firmly embedded in the cultural memory to the present day, having served as a blueprint for many later orphan narratives for children, including J.K. Rowling's *Harry Potter* novels (1997-2007), Sophie in Roald Dahl's *The BFG* (1982), Bod in Neil Gaiman's *The Graveyard Book* (2008) as well as the Baudelaire siblings in Lemony Snicket's *A Series of Unfortunate Events* (1999-2006). As the examples mentioned so far already suggest, traces of Victorian portrayals of orphans can be found in particular in children's literature from the 20th and 21st centuries, where "[t]he absence of parental authority allows the space that the fictive child needs for development and maturity, in order to test (and taste) his independence and to discover the world without adult protection" (Nikolajeva 2009, 230).

Recently, images of Victorian orphanhood have also been revisited by postcolonial writers, especially in revisionist historical fiction. *Remembering Babylon* (1993) by the Australian author David Malouf is a case in point. The novel, which is set in Queensland in the middle of the 19th century, features an English orphan from the working class who used to be exploited on a ship before he was cast overboard and ended up living with an Indigenous clan in the outback for a number of years. When this boy, Gemmy, who has all but lost his ability to speak English in the years he has not used his native language, remembers bits and pieces of his past life, the glimpses that are presented to the readers offer horrible and haunting images of a destitute orphan's life in 19th-century England— images that are in fact quite familiar from Victorian social problems novels and serve to put the sentimental images of parentless children into perspective.

Notes

[1] Cf. Floyd (2014, 28): "by the middle of the Victorian period, the nuclear family acquired an almost mythical status as the proper context in which a child should be raised, and furthermore came to be regarded as the cornerstone of a balanced, moral culture".

[2] Even the introduction of laws that were supposed to protect children certainly did not guarantee a carefree childhood: "Protective labour legislation gradually raised the permitted age for first employment (in 1874 it was made ten in textile factories, extended in 1878 to workshops and non-textile factories; in 1891 it went up to eleven; in 1901 to twelve)" (Davin 1996, 4).

[3] Cf. Peters (2000, 79): "The emigration to the colonies of orphan children of the poor marked both a new phase in the state (parish) provision for such children and a concerted effort to ensure the familial nature of empire by settling the colonies with British children. The two endeavours coincide in the notion that the colonies were the birthright of British children—hence providing a special opportunity to a very special responsibility of the Government, the provision for orphan children of the poor." From the 1850s onward, a huge number of orphaned and destitute children—all in all more than 60,000—were sent to Bermuda, New South Wales and Canada to live there permanently (cf. Peters 2000, 103).

[4] Cf. Roberts (2005, 354): "This focus on childhood is often traced to eighteenth-century concerns over education and the accompanying recognition of childhood

as an ideally separate and unique phase of human life. John Locke and Jean Jacques Rousseau promoted educational philosophies which defined all children as capable of developing into rational, enlightened human beings through a nurturing system of education based on experience and observation rather than rote memorization or harsh, punitive discipline. Seeing the child as a tabula rasa, a blank slate, Locke argued that educators must carefully evoke the desire to learn in each individual child. Rousseau argued that children were born in a state of innate innocence, not original sin, and that social institutions corrupted such childhood virtue."

[5] Cf. also Cunningham (1991, 152): "The idea of childhood as properly a time of happiness had its origins [...] in the first half of the century, but it was only later that it was expressed in its fullest vigour. Childhood began to play a part similar to that which Ruskin had sketched out for women and the home; it was both a place of refuge for those wearied by life's struggles and a source of renewal which would enable the adult to carry on. In effect, that is, childhood was a substitute for religion."

[6] Cf. Peters (2000, 42): "Throughout his trials [...] Oliver does manage to retain his innocence and his inherent faith by refusing to participate either in the official institutional narrative forced on him, or in the criminal narrative that Monks so desperately wants to thrust upon him."

[7] On parallels between fairy-tale orphans and their literary counterparts, cf. König (2014, 1-2).

[8] Cf., for instance, Esther Summerson's comment: "I was brought up, from my earliest remembrance—like some of the princesses in the fairy stories, only I was not charming—by my godmother" (Dickens [1852-53] 2001, 14). In Dickens's *David Copperfield*, the narrator at one point says about his aunt that "[s]he vanished like a discontented fairy" ([1849-50] 1992, 15) and later refers to "Aladdin's palace, roc's egg and all" (29). In *Jane Eyre*, the narrator compares Mr Rochester's house Thornfield Hall to Bluebeard's castle (Ch. Brontë [1847] 1985, 138), and Kipling's *Kim* (1901) contains a reference to the "Arabian Nights" ([1901] 1987, 51). In Elizabeth Gaskell's *North and South*, there are also numerous allusions to fairy tales, including the following ones: "which was recalling to Mr. Hale some of the wonderful stories of subservient genii in the Arabian nights—one moment stretching from earth to sky and filling all the width of the horizon, at the next obediently compressed into a vase small enough to be borne in the hand of a child" ([1854-55] 1982, 81); "'I may be the Cinderella to put on the slipper after all'" (92).

[9] In a similar vein, Hochman and Wachs (1999, 14) argue that "the orphan condition is not essentially the objective state of growing up without one's real parents, or even of being bruised and battered by wicked stepparents and brutal, exploitative institutions. It is, rather, a state of mind that besets the orphan child and the adult whom that child eventually becomes, but that also, ultimately, informs some part of everyone's imagination. Loss is a primary condition of human life; orphanhood is the ultimate reach of our ineluctable sense of loss".

[10] "*Self-Help* was one of the most popular works of nonfiction published in England in the second half of the nineteenth century. It sold 20,000 copies within a year of its appearance and surpassed a quarter of a million by the time of Samuel Smiles's death forty-five years later. [...] Consisting of a series of inspiring biographies of notable figures who rose to prominence through their own endeavours, his book encouraged working- and lower-middle-class men to climb the ladder of social and economic success" (Sinnema 2002, vii).

[11] The character describes his past as follows: "'Sixteen years ago, my father died under very miserable circumstances. I was taken from school, and had to become a man (as well as I could) in a few days. I had such a mother as few are blest with; a woman of strong power, and firm resolve. We went into a small country town, where living was cheaper than in Milton, and where I got employment in a draper's shop (a capital place, by the way, for obtaining a knowledge of goods). Week by week our income came to fifteen shillings, out of which three people had to be kept. My mother managed so that I put by three out of these fifteen shillings regularly. This made the beginning; this taught me self-denial'" (Gaskell [1854-55] 1982, 84-85).

[12] The refusal to dwell on the loss of one's parents, which informs the attitudes of many literary orphans in 19th-century literature, can also be read in the context of the Victorian distrust of powerful emotions (cf. Stedman 2002).

[13] Cf. also Bowlby (2013, 139): "A more formal system of 'placing' children for adoption through the mediation of agencies began to take shape in the 1920s; their work was one of the spurs to the passing of the 1926 Act, but informal adoptions continued to occur in the 1930s and during the war."

[14] Cf. Liza Picard's account of the workhouse: "To enter the workhouse meant giving up all self-respect, and abandoning family ties. It was dreaded with unimaginable fear. The Poor Law Act of 1601, which in its turn had replaced the old monastic charities, had set up parochial Poorhouses. They were suddenly seen by the Establishment to be too lenient. Things had to change. The poor could not be allowed to go on sponging on their richer neighbours. In 1834 the law was drastically altered. Every parish had to provide a workhouse. [...] No longer should an old or disabled person who just needed a bit of help to stay in his or her own house draw 'outdoor relief' from the parish. Spouses who had lived together for decades were to go into the workhouse and be separated into wards for 'male paupers' and 'female paupers'. Their children were taken from them" (Picard 2006, 93).

[15] On the visibility of poor children in the public sphere, cf. Davin (1996, 15): "Children in the urban working class in the last decades of the nineteenth century and the early years of the twentieth were both numerous and noticeable. Unlike their 'betters' they spent much time out in the street. 'Teeming' children figured in almost every depiction of a poor neighbourhood, and the crowd of children in a cramped court was a common photographic subject. 'Ragged urchins' were as clichéd an index of squalor as were blocked gutters, broken windows or washing across the street."

[16] Wordsworth's ballad "Lucy Gray" features a child who lives in isolation (stanza 2: "No Mate, no comrade Lucy knew; / She dwelt on a wild Moor, / The sweetest Thing that ever grew / Beside a human door!"), dies on the moor in a snow storm and is seen as a revenant (stanzas 15-16): "Yet some maintain that to this day / She is a living Child, / That you may see sweet Lucy Gray / Upon the lonesome Wild. // O'er rough and smooth she trips along, / And never looks behind; / And sings a solitary song / That whistles in the wind."

[17] In this context, it is worthwhile noting that the notion of girls being in need of protection for a longer period than boys was even embedded in British legislation: "Sex made a difference: girls were held to need protection for longer. For the Prevention of Cruelty Act (1889) and the LCC's Public Control Committee in 1900, a child was a boy under fourteen or a girl under sixteen. The age of consent (which affected girls only) was raised from twelve to thirteen in 1875, then to sixteen in 1885, though some social purity campaigners argued that eighteen or even twenty-one should be the 'age of female responsibility'" (Davin 1996, 4).

[18] For most of the Victorian period, the future of babies born in the workhouse was indeed anything but secure: "it was not until 1895 that the Boards of Guardians of the workhouses received any instructions for dealing with their infant charges. Until then the care of children was left to the aged female inmates of the workhouse with little supervision" (Pugh 2007, 80).

[19] On the practice of "baby farming" and its abuses in the Victorian period, cf. Keating (2009, 23): "the first major legislation dealing with how children were looked after was the Infant Life Protection Act 1872, which followed major 'baby farming' scandals. 'Baby farming', or 'professional adoption', was the practice whereby the parents (generally unmarried mothers) of children whom they could not afford or manage to look after, paid someone, usually a middle-aged woman, a lump sum to look after the child. There was a tacit assumption that the mother would not be returning to reclaim the child and that the baby farmer would not overly strive to keep it alive. Probably some of those looking after the babies did their best to care for them but naturally the cases which hit the headlines were the scandals".

[20] Cf. Peters (2000, 8): "As the 'child' of the Poor Law Board the figure of the orphan was singularly invested with a special significance. Crucial to this significance was the fact that the orphan, as the responsibility of the Board of Guardians rather than the parents, was considered to be a figure of promise and hope".

[21] In *Oliver Twist*, the author makes use of extremes in order to maximise the emotional impact of Oliver's story, as Michael Wheeler points out: "The early chapters of *Oliver* present the stark realities of the workhouses which were the product of the Poor Law Amendment Act of 1834, but Bumble and the workhouse board are later balanced by the benevolent fairy godfather and godmother figures in the novel: Mr Brownlow and Mrs Maylie" (1985, 26).

[22] In the United States, the "from rags to riches" story is in particular associated with Horatio Alger, who wrote a series of novels about boys who improve their situation by being clever and working hard, beginning with *Ragged Dick* (1867).

The title character of this text is an orphan living on the streets of New York and working as a boot-black. By honesty and hard work he paves his way to becoming an office-boy. The novels by Alger have contributed to disseminating the notion of the "American Dream", propagating the idea that "'in this free country poverty in early life is no bar to a man's advancement'", as one of the characters in *Ragged Dick* (1962, 108) puts it.

[23] Floyd's description of the rebellious orphan in fact very much reads like a characterisation of Heathcliff: "This type [...] pursues self-serving aims without regard for those with whom he or she comes into contact and even exerts a kind of malicious intent, at times causing harm to others. Rather than pursuing inclusion, this type not only rebels against but at times seeks the ruin of the social or family structures from which he or she is exiled" (Floyd 2014, 9).

[24] Cf. *Wuthering Heights*: "Till she reached the age of thirteen, she had not once been beyond the range of the park by herself. [...] she was a perfect recluse; and, apparently perfectly contented" (E. Brontë [1847] 1985, 224).

[25] According to Peter Arnds, the boy "[m]ore than anything or anyone in Hardy's works [...] embodies the deeply felt pessimism of the author with regard to the further course of mankind" (1998, 232).

[26] The role reversal as far as the position of the grown-up and the child is concerned of course echoes imperialist notions: "Kim with the insight and intuition of the born colonialist, recognizes that the lama is a new territory worth annexing and possessing" (Sullivan 1993, 154).

[27] Teresa Hubel, who provides a very illuminating reading of *Kim* through the lens of the category "class", argues that Kim's fate is reminiscent of the widespread practice of taking children away "from what the ruling class whites believed were degrading influences: working-class parents, working-class communities, and working-class places of residence. [...] He [Kipling] was, in fact, only doing what white administrators all over India tried to do to the children of European soldiers, sailors, servants, and railway workers, whether these children were orphaned or not" (2004, 240).

[28] Cf. Floyd's observation that "[u]nlike that of the usual orphan, the consequences of Kim's lack of family are less a crippling hindrance and more an enabling occasion that allows the autonomy he enjoys" (2014, 139). What Floyd fails to take into consideration is the fact that the idea of orphanhood as an "enabling occasion" was far from unusual at the time; after all, it shaped the socio-political discourse about orphans in the Victorian period to a considerable extent.

[29] Cf. Hubel: "In the early decades of the nineteenth century, orphanages and charity schools for the children of 'poor whites' and Eurasians sprang up initially in or near the great imperial cities of the plains, Calcutta, Madras, and Bombay, and later in virtually every town, cantonment, and hill station" (2004, 240).

[30] For a discussion of lesser known popular orphan adventure narratives, cf. the article by Peters (2012).

[31] Cf.: "[F]rom these dozen words I understood that the lives of all honest men aboard depended upon me alone" (Stevenson [1883] 1999, 56); "Then it was that

there came into my head the first of the mad notions that contributed so much to save our lives" (72).

[32] For American children's literature, Joe Sutliff Sanders reaches a similar conclusion: "Although the orphan girl novel came to popularity in the nineteenth century, it was during the opening decades of the twentieth century that orphan girl novels proliferated" (2011, 65).

Works Cited

Alger, Horatio. 1962. *Ragged Dick and Mark, the Match Boy*. New York: Collier.

Alston, Ann. 2008. *The Family in English Children's Literature*. New York and London: Routledge.

Arnds, Peter. 1998. "The Boy with the Old Face: Thomas Hardy's Antibildungsroman *Jude the Obscure* and Wilhelm Raabe's Bildungsroman *Prinzessin Fisch*." *German Studies Review* 21 (2): 221-40.

Auerbach, Nina. 1975. "Incarnations of the Orphan." *English Literary History* 42 (3): 395-419.

Avery, Gillian. 1994. *Behold the Child: American Children and their Books, 1621-1922*. London: The Bodley Head.

Banerjee, Jacqueline. 1996. *Through the Northern Gate: Childhood and Growing Up in British Fiction, 1719-1901*. New York: Peter Lang.

Bowlby, Rachel. 2013. *A Child of One's Own: Parental Stories*. Oxford: Oxford University Press.

Briggs, Katharine M. 1991. "Nachwort." In *Englische Märchen*, edited by Katharine Briggs and Ruth Michaelis-Jena, 299-323. Reinbek bei Hamburg: Rowohlt.

Brontë, Charlotte. (1847) 1985. *Jane Eyre*. Harmondsworth: Penguin.

Brontë, Emily. (1847) 1985. *Wuthering Heights*. Harmondsworth: Penguin.

Clarke, John. 2004. "Histories of Childhood." In *Childhood Studies: An Introduction*, edited by Dominic Wyse, 3-12. Malden et al.: Blackwell.

Corbett, Mary Jean. 2008. "Orphan Stories and Maternal Legacies in Charlotte Brontë." In *Other Mothers: Beyond the Maternal Ideal*, edited by Ellen Bayuk Rosenman and Claudia C. Klaver, 227-47. Columbus, OH: Ohio State University Press.

Cunningham, Hugh. 1991. *The Children of the Poor: Representations of Childhood since the Seventeenth Century*. Oxford: Blackwell.

Davin, Anna. 1996. *Growing Up Poor: Home, School and Street in London 1870-1914*. London: Rivers Oram Press.

Dickens, Charles. (1837-39) 1985. *Oliver Twist*. Harmondsworth: Penguin.
—. (1845) 2006. "The Cricket on the Hearth: A Fairy Tale of Home." In *Charles Dickens. A Christmas Carol and Other Christmas Books*, edited by Robert Douglas-Fairhurst, 163-242. Oxford: Oxford University Press.
—. (1849-50) 1992. *David Copperfield*. Ware, Hertfordshire: Wordsworth.
—. (1852-53) 2001. *Bleak House*. Ware, Hertfordshire: Wordsworth.
—. (1854) 1994. *Hard Times*. London: Penguin.
—. (1861) 1994. *Great Expectations*. Harmondsworth: Penguin.
Dunham, Robert H. 1976. "Silas Marner and the Wordsworthian Child." *Studies in English Literature, 1500-1900* 16 (4): 645-59.
Eagleton, Terry. 1995. *Heathcliff and the Great Hunger*. London: Verso.
Edwards, Mike. 1999. *Charlotte Brontë: The Novels*. Houndmills, Basingstoke: Macmillan.
Eliot, George. (1861) 1985. *Silas Marner: The Weaver of Raveloe*. Harmondsworth: Penguin.
Federico, Annette. 2003. "David Copperfield and the Pursuit of Happiness." *Victorian Studies* 46 (1): 69-95.
Floyd, David. 2014. *Street Urchins, Sociopaths and Degenerates: Orphans of Late-Victorian and Edwardian Fiction*. Cardiff: University of Wales Press.
Gaskell, Elizabeth. (1854-55) 1982. *North and South*. Oxford: Oxford University Press.
—. (1864-66) 2003. *Wives and Daughters*. Ware, Hertfordshire: Wordsworth.
Gitter, Elisabeth G. 1999. "The Blind Daughter in Charles Dickens's 'Cricket on the Hearth'." *Studies in English Literature, 1500-1900* 39 (4): 675-89.
Gordon, Jan B. 2002. "Dickens and the Transformation of Nineteenth-Century Narratives of 'Legitimacy'." *Dickens Studies Annual* 31: 203-65.
Hardy, Thomas. (1896) 1974. *Jude the Obscure*. London: Macmillan.
Hochman, Baruch, and Ilja Wachs. 1999. *Dickens: The Orphan Condition*. Madison: Fairleigh Dickinson University Press.
Hubel, Teresa. 2004. "In Search of the British Indian in British India: White Orphans, Kipling's *Kim*, and Class in Colonial India." *Modern Asian Studies* 38 (1): 227-51.
Hunt, Peter. 2001. *Children's Literature*. Oxford: Blackwell.
Keating, Jenny. 2009. *A Child for Keeps: The History of Adoption in England, 1918-45*. London: Palgrave Macmillan.

Kimball, Melanie A. 1999. "From Folktales to Fiction: Orphan Characters in Children's Literature." *Library Trends* 47 (3): 558-78.

Kipling, Rudyard. (1894-95) 1994. *The Jungle Books*. Harmondsworth: Penguin.

—. (1901) 1987. *Kim*. Harmondsworth: Penguin.

König, Eva. 2014. *The Orphan in Eighteenth-Century Fiction: The Vicissitudes of the Eighteenth-Century Subject*. Houndmills, Basingstoke and New York: Palgrave Macmillan.

Krebs, Paula M. 1998. "Folklore, Fear, and the Feminine: Ghosts and Old Wives' Tales in *Wuthering Heights*." *Victorian Literature and Culture* 26 (1): 41-52.

Marsh, Nicholas. 1999. *Emily Brontë's Wuthering Heights*. Houndmills, Basingstoke: Macmillan.

Masters, Joellen. 2004. "'Nothing More' and 'Nothing Definite': First Wives in Elizabeth Gaskell's *Wives and Daughters* (1866)." *Journal of Narrative Theory* 34 (1): 1-26.

Maynard, John R. 2005. "The Bildungsroman." In *A Companion to the Victorian Novel*, edited by Patrick Brantlinger and William B. Thesing, 279-301. Malden, MA and Oxford: Blackwell.

Nelson, Claudia. 2014. "Growing Up: Childhood." In *A New Companion to Victorian Literature and Culture*, edited by Herbert F. Tucker, 69-81. Chichester: Wiley-Blackwell.

Nikolajeva, Maria. 2002. *The Rhetoric of Character in Children's Literature*. Lanham: Scarecrow Press.

—. 2009. "Harry Potter and the Secrets of Children's Literature." In *Critical Perspectives on Harry Potter*, edited by Elizabeth E. Heilman, 225-41. 2nd edn. London and New York: Routledge.

Nussbaum, Martha C. 1995. *Poetic Justice: The Literary Imagination and Public Life*. Boston: Beacon Press.

Peters, Laura. 1995. "The Histories of Two Self-Tormentors: Orphans and Power in *Little Dorrit*." *The Dickensian* 91 (3): 187-97.

—. 2000. *Orphan Texts: Victorian Orphans, Culture and Empire*. Manchester and New York: Manchester University Press.

—. 2012. "Popular Orphan Adventure Narratives." In *Dickens and Childhood*, edited by Laura Peters, 557-75. Farnham: Ashgate.

Picard, Liza. 2006. *Victorian London: The Life of a City 1840-1870*. London: Phoenix.

Pond, Kristen A. 2013. "Bearing Witness in *Silas Marner*: George Eliot's Experiment in Sympathy." *Victorian Literature and Culture* 41: 691-709.

Pugh, Gillian. 2007. *London's Forgotten Children: Thomas Coram and the Foundling Hospital*. Stroud: The History Press.

Roberts, Lewis C. 2005. "Children's Fiction." In *A Companion to the Victorian Novel*, edited by Patrick Brantlinger and William B. Thesing, 353-69. Malden, MA and Oxford: Blackwell.

Said, Edward W. 1987. "Introduction." In Rudyard Kipling. *Kim*, 7-46. Harmondsworth: Penguin.

Sinnema, Peter W. 2002. "Introduction." In Samuel Smiles. *Self-Help: With Illustrations of Character, Conduct, and Perseverance*, edited by Peter W. Sinnema, vii-xxviii. Oxford: Oxford University Press.

Smiles, Samuel. 2002. *Self-Help: With Illustrations of Character, Conduct, and Perseverance*, edited by Peter W. Sinnema. Oxford: Oxford University Press.

Stedman, Gesa. 2002. *Stemming the Torrent: Expression and Control in the Victorian Discourses on Emotions, 1830-1872*. Aldershot: Ashgate.

Stevenson, Robert Louis. (1883) 1999. *Treasure Island*. London: Penguin.

—. (1886) 2014. *Kidnapped*. Oxford: Oxford University Press.

Sullivan, Zohreh T. 1993. *Narratives of Empire: The Fictions of Rudyard Kipling*. Cambridge: Cambridge University Press.

Sutliff Sanders, Joe. 2011. *Disciplining Girls: Understanding the Origins of the Classic Orphan Girl Story*. Baltimore: The Johns Hopkins University Press.

Thackeray, William Makepeace. (1847-48) 1994. *Vanity Fair*. London: Penguin.

Vallone, Lynne. 2000. "Fertility, Childhood, and Death in the Victorian Family." *Victorian Literature and Culture* 28 (1): 217-26.

Von Sneidern, Maja-Lisa. 1995. "*Wuthering Heights* and the Liverpool Slave Trade." *English Literary History* 62 (1): 171-96.

Wagner, Tamara. 2008. "'We have orphans […] in stock': Crime and the Consumption of Sensational Children." In *The Nineteenth-Century Child and Consumer Culture*, edited by Dennis Denisoff, 201-15. Aldershot: Ashgate.

Warner, Marina. 2014. *Once Upon a Time: A Short History of Fairy Tale*. Oxford: Oxford University Press.

Wheeler, Michael. 1985. *English Fiction of the Victorian Period 1830-1890*. London and New York: Longman.

Wirth-Nesher, Hana. 1986. "The Literary Orphan as National Hero: Huck and Pip." In *Dickens Studies Annual: Essays on Victorian Fiction*. Vol. 15, edited by Michael Timko, Fred Kaplan and Edward Guiliano, 259-27. New York: AMS Press.

Wordsworth, William. (1800) 1965. "Lucy Gray." In *Lyrical Ballads*, edited by R.L. Brett and A.R. Jones, 161-63. London and New York: Methuen.

—. (1800) 1965. "We Are Seven." In *Lyrical Ballads*, edited by R.L. Brett and A.R. Jones, 66-68. London and New York: Methuen.

CHAPTER TWO

THE GAP OR, THE DYING ORPHAN

BARBARA PUSCHMANN-NALENZ

After the fictional orphan had attained a preeminent position in early- and mid-Victorian novels a remarkable alteration in the character's shaping took place during the late Victorian and Edwardian eras. David Floyd (2014, "Introduction") ascribes this change in significance and design to a cultural shift towards disillusionment. According to him, a changing, increasingly troubled and critical view of the family emerged in Britain during the *fin-de-siècle* decades, which also had an effect on the literary motif of the orphan. The title of his book *Street Urchins, Sociopaths and Degenerates* is outspoken in naming the roles orphans assumed in popular and genre fiction during the two last decades of the 19th century.[1] In this era's social imagery the orphan was linked to New Imperialism[2] or the contemporaneous normative public awareness of unacculturated situations such as a state of social neglect in the lower classes, the appearance of the New Woman, or what was considered sexual deviancy. Between 1880 and 1900 popular fiction thematising adventure, crime or sexual ambiguity retained the trope of the orphan, as Floyd demonstrates. In numerous genre novels the orphan was not any longer a child, but an adult (7). Instead of the pitiable young person that evoked reader sympathies, the orphan's mysterious, uncanny and—because of an "aberration" (8)—menacing aspects frequently took centre stage. For the time after the turn to the 20th century Floyd's study focuses on Edwardian children's fantasy literature, where the orphan character still enjoyed great acclaim and surfaced in the most famous juvenile fictions of the time.[3] I contend that research on serious narrative fiction discloses a break in the use of the orphan motif, which opened up soon after the beginning of the 20th century and reached into the 1970s. It interrupts the accumulation of orphaned figures in the tradition of literary narratives, since during the periods before and after this hiatus British novels with representations of orphan characters abound. Since it is obvious that during the 18th and 19th centuries the orphan occupied a prominent place in the social imagery, the abrupt decrease and eventual cessation in the occurrence of this figure in literary prose fiction remains conspicuous.

This chapter focuses on the marked interval of more than 60 years in the history of the fictional orphan's representation under two aspects: first, where and in what way was the motif still operative in British or Anglo-Irish novels? Second, how can the paradox be explained that in the first half of the last century, with two world wars leaving many orphans behind, the interest in the narrativisation of the orphan in mainstream fiction dramatically declined? In briefly addressing the second, more general question before entering into the analysis of several orphan narratives I shall summarily try to account for some of the reasons for this discontinuity, which entailed the temporary near-disappearance of the orphan from British literary fictions. My argument implies that the interruption in the novelistic use of this sign or symbol has to be placed in a wider frame, for which several of Virginia Woolf's essays published in the early 1920s provide a contextual background.[4]

My first hypothesis in explaining the discontinuity of the orphan motif claims that the marked socio-cultural change, which literature reflected and helped to produce, caused a rupture of 19th-century literary conventions, in which the orphan character had partaken. When several years after the beginning of the 20th century the focus of literature shifted to other themes this was linked to a preference for diverse figural representatives—with the orphan no longer among them. The innovative and liberating turn in writing also included the adoption of unaccustomed methods of narrativisation after the end of the Victorian Age, following *fin-de-siècle* anti-Victorian criticism. The challenges of the societal and cultural "threshold", I would like to emphasise, were acknowledged by the new writers as having emerged *prior to* the outbreak of the First World War. Early-20th-century protests against strict conservativism were retrospectively held responsible for having generated a response from modernist art and literature. In the paper to be called "Character in Fiction", read to "The Heretics" in Cambridge in May 1924, Virginia Woolf vividly exemplified the alertness of her generation's intellectual and cultural avant-garde, who had recognised and approved of a widespread change. She claims already for the beginning of the second decade of the 20th century that the moment had come to leave the established ways behind and to venture an optimistic departure with the post-Edwardian generation of writers, since British fiction as well as everyday life were changing: "The Victorian cook lived like a leviathan in the lower depths, formidable, silent, obscure, inscrutable; the Georgian

cook is a creature of sunshine and fresh air; in and out of the drawing-
room, now to borrow the *Daily Herald*, now to ask advice about a hat"
(Woolf [1924] 1966, I, 320). In its printed version, her article "Mr.
Bennett and Mrs. Brown" appeals to the audience to realise that
democratisation, liberalisation and openness for new ideas had already
spread *before* the seminal catastrophe shook European countries.

My argument, which does not want to deny the contradictions of the
topic, holds that the "gap" in the fictionalisation of the orphan is an effect
of the new British writers' engagement with an innovative novelistic
representation of wo/man that basically differed from realism and the
social novel of the 19th century. This shift was put into words clear and
straightforward by Virginia Woolf: "All human relations have shifted—
those between masters and servants, husbands and wives, parents and
children. And when human relations change there is at the same time a
change in religion, conduct, politics, and literature" (321). Precisely
because the narrative literature of the 19th century had abundantly used
the orphan s/he had of late become a literary convention, a stock character.
Woolf points to stereotyped thematic as well as diegetic elements when
she exhibits "the conventions which are commonly observed by the
novelist" and about which she remarked in 1925 that an author "must
discard" them to produce modern art (Woolf [1925] 1966, 107). Early
20th-century writers in Britain—the younger generation whom Woolf
addresses as Georgians—were dedicated to the exploration of individual
and subjective consciousness and abstained from creating orphan figures
in spite of their propensity for representing the disconnected individual.
Orphans, I wish to argue, were part of the Victorian literary symbolic,
notwithstanding their materialisation in the most famous novels of the two
preceding centuries. For the modernist writers the motif had ceased to be
necessary or expressional, and to continue in the same tracks proved
meaningless, so that Woolf metaphorically stated in her essay on the
unimpressive Mrs Brown in the railway carriage: "Meanwhile the train
was rushing to the station where we must all get out" (Woolf [1924] 1966,
333). Time was pressing, Mrs Woolf claimed, to artistically convey the sea
change before it was too late. Tellingly, I contend, the fictional orphan
character nearly vanished into oblivion after 1910.

The innovative push in literature partly resulted from the Freudian
exploration of the conscious and unconscious, which drew attention to the
way the human mind functions: "For the moderns 'that', the point of
interest, lies very likely in the dark places of psychology" (Woolf [1925]
1966, 108). Virginia Woolf regarded a specific date as having had an
enormous impact on every aspect of life in Britain when "in or about

December, 1910, human character changed" (Woolf [1924] 1966, 320), as she further remarked in her provocative speech and essay on the apparent cultural discontinuity. Several events, I conclude, had proved especially influential: the end of the Edwardian era in May 1910; the general elections of December 19, which led to a coalition of Liberals, Irish Nationalists and Labour against the ruling parliamentary group of Conservative MPs; and, lastly and probably most importantly for Woolf, the exhibition "Manet and Post-Impressionism" in London, which opened in December 1910. Several members of the Bloomsbury Group considered this moment a change of paradigm; the *Telegraph* calls it "a Culture Quake" (Hodgkinson 2004), whereas the majority of the exhibition's contemporaneous visitors regarded the paintings as well as the organisers with contempt. Transgressing the "threshold", modernist fiction took novel views of human nature centre stage and wished to explore the fascinating inner life of "an ordinary mind on an ordinary day" (Woolf [1925] 1966, 106). The orphan, on the contrary, is exceptional, not "ordinary". As Auerbach said, the 18th- and 19th-century fictional orphan "stands supreme" (1975, 403). Frequently the orphan character had worked as a kind of catalyst for his or her social environment, thereby demonstrating the power of the weak. Ordinary "Mrs Brown", if anything, is the unprepossessing mousy protagonist Mrs Woolf favours for modern fiction.

A special attraction of the orphan figure lies in the possibility to manipulate his/her (own) biography and circumstances; this opportunity generally turns him/her into a cipher to be filled by creative imagination—including the writer's. The parentless individual, deprived of origins with the concomitant certainties and obligations, enjoys greater freedom than other characters and is supposed to be in a position—precarious though it often seems—to invent him-/herself. Need and distress brought about by the loss of parents generally prevail in the depictions of the literary orphans' lives; yet the sensational and exciting aspects of misery representations also appealed to the mostly middle-class Victorian readership. As Auerbach's argument, worthy of discussion, has pointed out about *A Portrait of the Artist* and its protagonist Stephen Dedalus, the hero's being orphaned offers him the chance of an unlimited distancing from disaffecting traditions and an inadequate environment.[5] James Joyce, being Irish, celebrates the exile, a modern variety of the voluntarily orphaned character, and exposes in him the finally unencumbered self-reflexivity of the artist. It is the artist who subsequently becomes a figure representing exceptionality in fiction (cf. for *The Longest Journey* below).

Surprisingly at first sight, the number of fictional orphans continued to decline in the era of each of the two world wars even in narratives that address war. Hypothetically I deduce from the history of the novel in the early- to mid-20th century that an inverse quantitative relation dialectically connects the occurrence of "real" orphans with the incidence of their fictional counterparts. So far the present argument additionally gathers that if authors aimed at a narrativisation of continuity in a society aware of the ruptures and changes subsequent to the Great War the unbelonging orphan—a being without history, roots or ties—proved thematically less amenable and as an iconic image inappropriate.

Four of the sparse examples from the 20th century between the end of the Victorian Age and the beginning of postmodernism in literature will more closely be inspected here, with the focus on the orphan characters they contain. The crucial question why so few "highbrow" novels and writers—in contrast to SF, adventure novels or popular romance—deal with orphanhood during these decades will emerge again after my readings. Unlike novels of the 19th century, the most famous narratives of the early 20th century abstain from fictionalising the orphaned hero/ine: neither Joseph Conrad's nor D.H. Lawrence's or Virginia Woolf's best-known works take the emblematic figure into account. Mainstream novels between 1945 and 1975 primarily address the thematic priority of class fractions and problems of cultural hegemony. Their focus, I would wish to state, lies on the concern with a balance between continuity and realignment and the individual's place therein. The generation of Alan Sillitoe and Kingsley Amis, or young writers John Wain and William Golding considered particularly challenging topics of socialisation, social mobility and cultural class distinctions. They address the outsider and problems of exclusion, but do not choose the orphan figure to demonstrate them; the emphasis is put on class, society and the bewildered "average" individual.

Rudyard Kipling's novel *Kim* came out in 1901, only a few months after Queen Victoria's death. My first exemplary text *The Longest Journey* (1907), the second novel by E.M. Forster, who already belonged to a new generation, was also published when Edward VII was King of the UK and Emperor of India. Two books from the thirties, George Orwell's *Burmese Days* (1934) and *The Death of the Heart* (1938) by Anglo-Irish writer Elizabeth Bowen, exemplify in very different ways the fiction of the interwar years. Evelyn Waugh's *Brideshead Revisited* (1945) is the last and the only first-person narrative in this investigation. These texts, which thematise orphanhood, are generally not considered the most important novels produced in the course of four decades, nor are they fundamental with regard to narratorial innovation. From different angles they explore the questioning of traditions, the disintegration of the British Empire and the difficult struggle for the individual's assessment in the ranks of society. These interests are generally affine to the well-connected rather than the "untethered" orphaned subject; therefore, considerable weight is put on problems of social integration. Although a hallmark of contemporary narrative fiction today, the orphan figure must be regarded as a rarity outside genre fiction even up to the 1980s.[6]

E.M. Forster makes the orphan Rickie (Frederick) Elliot the central character and anti-hero of his *bildungsroman The Longest Journey*. A third-person omniscient narrator closely and chronologically devises the protagonist's mind and journey through life. It resembles a long and painful quest for the sensitive orphan's artistic true self as distinct from conventions, duties and other people's attitudes. It ends with the sudden death of the protagonist in a fatal accident.[7] Rickie had already experienced the unexpected death of his parents, later of his child and several of his acquaintances. The novel leads to a struggle between two opposed types of men: on the one hand, there is Rickie, who is crippled and physically fragile, but educated and idealistic deep inside. He contrasts with his half-brother Stephen Wonham, who suddenly emerges—a vigorous, handsome and physically strong man, but lacking intellectual capacity, appearing in speech prosaic and of rather coarse manners. In the end he earns Rickie's respect, because as an illegitimate son Stephen proves able to resist and even despise bourgeois conventions including morality and dares to *be* himself (Forster [1907] 1962, 309)—an achievement that has not been reached by the protagonist. Immediately before his death, Rickie ambivalently attains this freedom, after having been tied to the world which is ruled by his wife's family, the aristocratic Pembrokes, whose head Herbert Pembroke is the third figure in the masculine triangle of the novel. Stephen, an energetic man, but blunt in conversation and of irresponsible drinking habits, is in the end saved by Rickie from an approaching train. Rickie dies, deprecatingly dismissed by Pembroke. He sacrifices his life for a man regarded as intellectually as well as socially inferior and is himself given up by those surrounding him. By his act of rescue, the protagonist also shows that he is capable of deeds in spite of his secret passivity and indulgence in elitist debates. Cambridge and philosophical discussions—often about epistemological questions— with Rickie's belligerent intellectual friend Stewart Ansell had been the environment where he spiritually felt at home.[8] To stick to the ideals of humanism in an environment where materialism and shallowness prevail had seemed impossible to Rickie, originally an innocent who developed through experience into an unhappy person.

Choosing an optimistic reading by excluding Rickie's ambiguities and hesitancy one may claim that he has detached his existence from the shame he felt about his mother's adultery and his illegitimate half-brother. He also separates himself from the security of a middle-class position as classics teacher in a second-rate boarding school harshly run by his brother-in-law Herbert. By spatially distancing himself spontaneously from his dominant wife and a failed marriage, instead seeking reconciliation with his brother, he accepts the "offense" against the hegemony of a bourgeois moralistic order. His turning away from the Pembrokes is also evident in the little esteem Rickie has for money and inheritance (Forster [1907] 1962, 214-15)—issues of the highest importance for his wife and brother-in-law (230-32). Agnes and Herbert Pembroke more and more reduce their concerns to material matters and social appearances, whereas Rickie leaves everything literally behind when he goes in search for his brother, who departed after they had quarrelled. The weakness and disappointment, which made him suffer for most of his life, have eventually given way to a courageous determination, for which he pays with his life.

His orphaned condition, together with his enthusiasm for writing poetry, is important for the structure of the novel and the characterisation of Rickie Elliot, because as a solitary individual he stands opposed to the clan-like family of the Pembrokes and their authoritative universe. Early he accepts an invitation to stay in their country house, "because he felt he ought to" (Forster [1907] 1962, 42). A similar dutiful response leads to his marriage proposal, after Agnes's fiancé Gerald has miserably died in an accident during a football match. Rickie, born with a crippled foot, can barely walk. His convictions are revealed as romantic by the narrator; moreover, his quest for "the Holy Grail" (174) of artistic fulfilment and wisdom seems more and more unrealistic. Through his close connection with the Pembrokes, who offer him the teaching position, he subsequently experiences the stifling effect of succumbing to prestige-driven decisions, emptied traditions and the paralysing rules of a particular class that contrasts with his own background, which was marked by the desertion of his father and a miserable childhood. Youth in a public school meant loneliness and torture; as a teacher at Sawston he recognises a repetition of the same tormenting principles (178-80). Cambridge and university life with like-minded companions meant paradise to him, yet he also failed to attain "the Holy Grail" there.

Rickie's increasing willingness to compromise leads to hypocrisy, but eventually he reaches a point where he can affirm the value of sincere emotionality in human relationships. Reluctantly, yet driven by duty, he saves a life marked by the "earthiness" which characterises Stephen, who was an "accident" (Forster [1907] 1962, 320), the result of a respectable woman's passionate love affair: the "natural" son of a farmer and Rickie's mother. In spite of his weakness and hopelessness the protagonist, an existential hero, does not die after a futile existence, as which his brother-in-law wants to consider Rickie's life. Herbert Pembroke's disparaging attitude is only evident through the omniscient narrator when, after the protagonist's death, "in his heart he [Herbert] could not regret that tragedy, already half-forgotten, conventionalized, indistinct. Of course death is a terrible thing. Yet death is merciful when it weeds out a failure" (318). An omniscient narrator also reveals that the dead, this "lame" man, had not totally abandoned his agonised quest for something more authentic and meaningful than conventional life. Only posthumously does he reach his destination to be recognised as a renowned writer.

Like Rickie's infirmity, caused by his poor health and misshaped foot, which is severed together with his other leg in the fatal accident on the railway tracks, his orphaned, severed state is also symbolic. He had missed emotional closeness in his childhood and youth, especially after his mother's death, and grown into surroundings that were equally devoid of warmth and love; but he also shows no zest for life, a quality he can only observe in other men. He even slackened in his enthusiasm for intellectual and "elitist" issues after leaving Cambridge, then wearily fulfilling commonplace duties and expectations. Stephen, unprincipled and rough, the (moral) "accident", but one that "can still walk" (Forster [1907] 1962, 312) in spite of his drunkenness, is saved. The novel concludes with Stephen's reflections, while he is holding his baby daughter. "He was alive and had created life" (320) are the words with which the personalised narrator confronts the reader with this man's amazed and grateful retrospect. He is aware of the gift of life he has been granted and optimistically looks forward to more joy, while he cannot thank his rescuer: "The body was dust, and in what ecstasy of his could it share? The spirit had fled, in agony and loneliness, never to know that it bequeathed him salvation" (320). Rickie's posthumous reputation as a poet even makes Stephen wealthy. The narrative's closure may be considered as brushing sentimentality, but the awe for life which Stephen expresses evokes the phrase of the Edwardian "cult of life" and the novels of D.H. Lawrence a few years later.[9] To celebrate earthbound life and the corporeal as an integral part of human nature stands out at the end as a proposition and—considering Rickie's life-journey—as a warning of the illusionary potential of humanism, which the protagonist realises before the end: "Books and friends were not enough" (312). Humanist ideals and dreams have not sufficed to withstand the pull and urge towards concessions and self-alienation in professional as well as private life. Realising that he would once more submit, "for he knew that the conventions would claim him soon" again (312), he admits his weakness. Before he returns home, however, he is fatally injured when he wearily saves his brother—the social scandal and long-time family secret—, who has gone to sleep on the rails at the level crossing.

The juxtaposition of the two brothers extends to the notion of national identity and fundamental values, which, I contend with reference to the following quotations, are undercut by the narrator's inclination to ironise. At the end of the novel Stephen pensively and with a touch of religious emotion states about his own position and significance: "Though he could not phrase it, he believed that he guided the future of our race, and that, century after century, his thoughts and his passions would triumph in England" (Forster [1907] 1962, 320). Earlier on, Rickie, in rare unison with Herbert Pembroke, is overcome by a differently-based kind of patriotism, when they visit the future school building with adjacent chapel and survey the Jacobean remnants that contrast with the parts restored in the Industrial Age. Their discussion on education and patriotism leads to more garbled talk: "They rejoiced that their country was great, noble, and old. 'Thank God I'm English,' said Rickie suddenly. 'Thank Him indeed,' said Mr. Pembroke, laying a hand on his back" (55). The narrator leaves their conversation more than once to the reader's own discretion.

The relation between the two brothers is constructed in a specific way. Neither does Rickie invite agreement from the characters or the reader, nor does Stephen gain approval. A figural opposition is built which persists throughout the narrative, with the protagonist brushing the Apollonian and Stephen the Dionysian principle—(cf. Vanderbeke, "Comics" in the present volume, 244), yet not without ambiguities. Pembroke defies either of these two by his empty traditionalism and a certain baseness. To harmonise the dualism is the objective of the two brothers' attempts at reconciliation. How to "connect" the contrastive *weltanschauungen* while saving ideals from an expedient and hard-headed pragmatism remains an open question, however. The caption of Wojta's article (2010) rightly describes the course of the novel as "meandering"; the adjective not only applies to Rickie Elliot's development, but equally to the construction of plot, character constellations and the issues that also worried Edwardian society. The "stream" of life (e.g. Forster [1907] 1962, 217), family, conventions, individualism and continuity present conflicting challenges, which cannot leave men unmoved or untroubled. The socially approved norm remembered by Rickie, "'Born an Elliot—born a gentleman.' So the vile phrase ran" (217), is a maxim the protagonist had early learned to obey and come to despise. For a long time, Rickie remained unable to accept another principle: that of common humanity, by which an illegitimate brother had entered the dying-out old family. That he did not come in through the paternal line is a further embarrassment. For Stephen Wonham the epithet "gentleman" does not nearly fit his own self-description (211), so that his nature made him additionally inacceptable. Stephen, "the man he had tried to bury" from his conscience (216), becomes Rickie's *fatum*. In a moment of epiphany he gains the insight that greed and meanness can be opposed even by him, a declining man revealed as weak, irresolute and as a childless orphan personally disconnected from past and future.

In Forster's fourth novel, the canonical *Howards End* (1910), the Schlegel siblings Margaret, Helen and Tibby are orphaned as young adults and inherit a substantial sum of money. They have an aunt who mothers them and a background which enhances the young women's autonomy, so that their orphaned state does not imply exclusion or loneliness. However, the house in London, in which they live and from which they have to part since a developer plans to build an apartment house on the site, has great importance for them as their family home. The significance of the place to which they are tied is realised by Ruth Wilcox at least as much as by Margaret Schlegel. This leads to Mrs Wilcox leaving her house Howards End, for her "the Holy of Holies" (Forster [1910] 1921, 85), to the Schlegel sisters, whose loss of an ancestral home causes her to speak of them as "poor girls" (83). Topics of contrasts and conflicts between characters or classes, of social conventions vs. nature, and of money vs. idealism, are addressed in this novel as they were in *The Longest Journey*.

Of Human Bondage (1915) by William Somerset Maugham is the story in the manner of a *bildungsroman* of the handicapped orphan Philip Carey, whose parents die when he is nine years old. It can to a large extent be autobiographically contextualised and was considered the masterpiece of this one-time very popular writer, even though serious criticism has not really acknowledged it.

George Orwell's John Flory, protagonist of *Burmese Days*, a novel set in the 1920s, is not literally an orphan, but the son of well-meaning parents on the one hand. The author also furnished him with a few autobiographical characteristics: as a very young man he was sent to Burma—then part of India as the British Raj—, there to become a moderately successful timber merchant. Later he is not able to go back to England. On the other hand, he feels estranged from the small European colony at the station, which is peopled by some officials and men in the timber trade, who temporarily stay there and then disappear for weeks in the jungle to oversee the harvesting of trees. Flory harbours "Bolshie" ideas (Orwell [1934] 1977, e.g. 32) and is disgusted by the contemptuous talk and behaviour towards the natives, which his compatriots, who oppose the reforms initiated after World War I, openly display. Insularity already characterises the life of the handful of Britons, who allegedly have come to represent the superiority of European civilisation in rural colonial India, but it is Flory who is the isolated, because desperately lonely, individual in this "island". Life at a small, filthy outpost in a tropical climate follows strict rules, is boring, empty and trite, bearable only with large quantities of alcohol, debauchery and ritualised antagonisms. Flory hates the place and is disaffected by colonial life, because it has spread corruption to his own thinking as well. In spite of his strong ambivalence he considers the colony his home. Actually he is orphaned, not least since European, respectively English culture is unreachable there. The repeated authorial observation about the mildewed books—detective novels at most or "the pink one" (*Financial Times*)—symbolically hints at its remoteness. The phrase "orphaned manliness" in the title of a scholarly article pays tribute to the disconnected masculinity which is due to the split dutifulness in Flory's life. He wants to observe the noble gentleman ideal, which demands fairness and respect towards others, including natives, whereas he appears adverse to, if corrupted by, the behavioural code of Imperial colonialism, to which he also ought to be loyal.[10]

By contrast, the young woman Elizabeth Lackersteen, who freshly arrives from Britain, is a literal orphan (Orwell [1934] 1977, 85). Her orphan state, however, is little more than a narrative device of the plot to bring her to Burma, because her only relatives still alive are a couple living at the station. Moreover, Anglo-India is considered a marriage-market. She shares none of John Flory's ideas which would lead to regarding the Burmese as fully human or to critically think about the exploitation of the country's resources by Europeans (e.g. 112). The men in the small colonial headquarters have to demonstrate their loyalty to the British Raj, yet do not even approve of the liberalising rules, spread after new laws have passed Parliament and been transmitted through the colonial authorities. According to recent regulations, natives who hold an office under colonial rule ought to be admitted to European social clubs— an innovation that is generally considered scandalous by the British at Kyauktada (28, 221). "In any town in India the European Club is the spiritual citadel, the real seat of the British power, the Nirvana for which native officials and millionaires pine in vain" (17). Flory, standing in taciturn opposition to the opinions of the very small European community and befriending the native surgeon, continuously faces arguments over these questions at the Club. In Kyauktada this is a delapidated establishment where the British meet in the evening to socialise, mainly by playing bridge, drinking and gossiping. They like to talk about the socialist danger or the "blacks" as an inferior species, whom, after the end of the Great War, they consider "'almost as bad as the lower classes at home'", since "'there is no doubt that the democratic spirit is creeping in, even here'" (28). "Here", in the British Raj, the members of the Club regard themselves as the outpost of the cultural and civilising elite.

Disfigured by a hideous birthmark, which designates him as exceptional, Flory clumsily tries to win Elizabeth's favour. Thereby he, who is alienated from the other Europeans by his preference for "highbrow" intellectualism (189) and respect for Oriental culture, hopes to change his solitary habits and lonely life at the age of 35. Personalised narration makes his intents explicit (55). Flory is bound to fail in his pursuit, being a bad suitor, and the girl whom he adores does not share any of his thoughts or interests. Elizabeth proves fully immersed in the circumscribed world and limited outlook of the other Britons, which includes the superiority of the white race, the ignorance of and contempt for the foreign culture and—last but not least—the purity of white women. Her persuasions distract her regard and attention from Flory and make him seem dreadful on account of his debauchery in the past and his controversial position in the British community. Instead she favours a young military man, the Honourable Lieutenant Verrall from a distinguished family, who appears as the prime representative of Imperial rule in India. Verrall is heading the military police, who arrive to quash a local revolt of the natives. Yet unexpectedly it is Flory who suddenly becomes something of a local hero, because together with his friend the doctor he courageously saves the members of the Club during a riot. Despite his resulting gain in prestige and notwithstanding his clear-sighted view that "young men of Verrall's stamp do not marry penniless girls met casually in obscure Indian stations" (247) John Flory fails with his marriage proposal after having been publicly disgraced by his former Burmese mistress and subsequently rejected by Elizabeth for good. He commits suicide, upon which the girl marries Mr Macgregor, the leading member of the white community, who nostalgically looks back on undiluted colonial times prior to the Great War. Intrigue, corruption, brutality and evil intentions are generally victorious. Orwell's novel ends on a pessimistic note, thus reflecting the author's views on colonialism and a class-ridden society. It hardly surprises that he was severely attacked for his depiction of British rule in India.

The orphan state of the 22-year-old English girl serves to illustrate a dependence on unquestioned "majority opinions" and her aunt's role model, since Elizabeth has been bereft of every other guide by her orphan condition and her stay in these claustrophobic surroundings. She is portrayed as aspiring to a traditional lifestyle as a white lady married to a colonial official and waited on hand and foot by Oriental servants, towards whom cruelty and contempt are still justified. With bitter sarcasm the omniscient narrator concludes the description of her career with a reassessment of colonialism: "in short, she fills with complete success the position for which Nature had designed her from the first, that of a burra memsahib" (272)—"a (grand) white foreign woman of high social status living in India; especially: the wife of a British official" ("Memsahib").

Apart from socialist ideas and a far-from-disinterested representation of the British Raj the author has more recently also been blamed for misogyny (cf. Seshagiri 2001). His portrayals of Mrs and Elizabeth Lackersteen as superficial, insensitive and "baiting" women provoke such criticism. Their behaviour is seen as prompted by imperialism and an innate racist attitude. As the only difference between Mrs Lackersteen and her niece the critic observes that the first-mentioned becomes hysterical and invites ridicule, whereas the latter raises hopes she cannot fulfil (cf. also Blackstock 2005). Elizabeth is characterised by coldness and her preoccupation with an advantageous match. Native women are, however, not spared in the novelist's devastating representation either. Craving for power over a man, Flory's Burmese mistress as well as the local chief's native wife also extract money or influence from their relationship with an influential man and show themselves as destructive and intriguing as most men. By the narrator, the reader's sympathy is clearly directed away from the female characters.[11] The European Club is a male community, where women can only be present as wives or the dependent relatives of a member. An aberrant man may come under the pressure of assimilation and conformism, but these are indispensable stances for a woman in colonial India. Life in the Raj is disclosed as backward-looking also with regard to gender-roles. The Reforms, hatefully debated in Kyauktada, included the right to vote for women in the Representation of the People Act of 1918.[12]

The Longest Journey and *Burmese Days* show their male protagonists in an orphaned condition as they strive for an autonomy which their social environment is unwilling to grant them. Having started into adult life with intellectual interests and moral values they lose much of their mental alertness under social pressure in middle age. Emotionally unable to communicate their suffering and loneliness they cannot any longer "connect".[13] Interestingly, neither anti-hero finds the relief he had hoped for in a wife or future wife, because each woman, orphaned or not, regularly fails to establish a personal bond. The condition of unbelonging and displacement, which for Flory and Elliot result from the friction with society in combination with their unsuccessful knowledge of other minds, renders isolation and ensuing death inescapable. To be "cut off" from one's origins, from the imagined community of the nation and—in Flory's case—from the collective identity of the colonial station, causes the orphaning of the protagonist in an emotional and spiritual sense. To be severed from the future as well—neither Flory nor Elliot fathers a surviving child—seems to condemn the protagonist to disappearance without a trace left. The orphans in these novels are neither street urchins nor sociopaths, but estranged members of well-respected social ranks. Herbert Pembroke's utterance about "a failure", however, exposed by the narrator as cynical, represents the opinion of the worthy middle classes about one of their set. Only Rickie's poetical work survives. It even makes his disinherited illegitimate half-brother a wealthy man.

In Elizabeth Bowen's novel *The Death of the Heart* (1938), the orphaned protagonist Portia is sixteen years old at the onset of the plot.[14] After having been orphaned, the girl joined her half-brother Thomas Quayne in London. Even though her parents were considered the trespassing outcasts of polite society, she had led a fairly happy albeit restless life with them on the Continent. Thomas runs an advertising company, and his father has bequeathed Portia to him and his snobbish wife Anna. They ought to accept the girl to live there at least for a year after his demise. Portia is also a Quayne, Mr Quayne Sr's daughter by a second, unsuitable marriage. On an individual level, the fictional disappearance of parents by death, separation and estrangement signalises the generally difficult situation of the family, when seen as a sequence of generations: Anna's mother also died when she was a child, Thomas's father left when he was a teenager, and his own marriage remained childless.

The narrator leaves no doubt that—in spite of what other characters believe (Bowen [1938] 1965, 319)—Portia neither feels at home (333) nor does she belong with this affluent, distinguished couple, who inhabit a house on Windsor Terrace adjacent to Regent's Park and are well established in the London society. By contrast, "Portia is unsocialised, a noble savage cast adrift in the *beau monde*" (Ellmann 2011, 136), naïve and good-hearted. Due to the family division she can only keep close to the housekeeper Matchett, from whom she learns about the social undesirability of her own existence on account of her parents' moral

conduct—a piece of information Portia herself hands on to other young
people (Bowen [1938] 1965, 248). By Matchett, who does not share her
sophisticated employers' conservative views and comforts her, she is
called "a good girl" several times. For her relatives Portia, like Major
Brutt, constitutes a "standing, or, better still, undermining reproach"
(314).[15] The major, another unfortunate "innocent" (383), is an unemployed,
formerly approved veteran of the Great War and tried colonial officer in
Malay. He seeks the relation with the Quaynes mainly because he enjoys it
and it has been offered, partly because it might help him find a job. Yet his
experience in life renders him clear-sighted: "he knew he stood where she
[Anna] might not wish him to stand—outside a shut door, a forgotten
messenger for whom there might be an answer and might not" (317).
Major Brutt, "being nicer" (313) than others in the circle of the Quaynes,
extends his friendship to Portia and keeps presenting her with jigsaw
puzzles for her pastime, while he sends Anna flowers he cannot afford in
order to gratefully please her. Anna, for her part, fancies the writer St
Quentin and 23-year-old Eddie as a youthful admirer, thus successfully
competing for him with Portia. The girl believes Eddie's words that he
loves and even wishes to marry her. When she is rejected by the young
man, who spends his time with persons of a doubtful reputation and flirts
with various women, Anna's fate as a young girl repeats itself (cf. 296):
Anna's one-time lover Robert Pidgeon, an acquaintance of Major Brutt's,
deserted her, leaving her with a dead heart.[16]

A sentence pronounced by Portia's suitor Eddie, "I suppose, that I'm I
at all is just a romantic fallacy" (Bowen [1938] 1965, 255) hints at a
passing of modernism's concern with individual consciousness. One
critic's conclusion that Bowen transcends modernist concepts[17] is founded
on her narrativisation of "the end of an inner life" (360), which becomes
the narrative's major theme. In the novel this "death" is linked to the
repeatedly emerging motif of personal betrayal, which Bowen embeds in
the anxieties about an imminent betrayal of family, tradition or status. The
hollowness of a person's centre is symbolised by images especially of
deserted rooms (e.g. 101) and desolate spaces (e.g. 243, 328-29). The
novel, mostly told by a third-person narrator, though often from a shifting
figural point-of-view, presents Portia in several inserted passages as
focaliser and diarist. The diary, which is espied and severely criticised by
the girl's sister-in-law Anna, proves the existence of an inner life that
Portia tries to hold on to. Her entries, however, also testify to the
importance of exteriority, to whose representation the novel pays an
enormous attention. Spaces, objects, movements, rooms and surfaces are
foregrounded as they appear to vision. Apart from the visual also

numerous auditory, haptic and olfactory perceptions are addressed, e.g. the scent of the mutton joint being basted on a Sunday (249).

Rather conventionally, the plotline may seem to lead straight from innocence to experience. However, the unhappy ending as well as the protagonist's "merciless extreme innocence" (cf. Ellmann 2011, 135) contradicts this traditional pattern. The social near-exclusion of Portia by those plotting against her defies the paradigm. First she learns from the double-dealing St Quentin that Anna and Eddie both know her diary, and finally she disappears from the text before the last chapter. For the established Quayne household the orphaned girl presents a burdensome and irritating element, though by no means the only one. Portia's father, who is also Thomas's father, was deemed beyond the pale because he had fathered a child during an extramarital affair and subordinated himself to his lady's order to marry Portia's mother and leave England for good. Having lost his reputation and home he travelled with his second wife and their child on the Continent from place to place until he died. Like Mr Quayne Sr., Major Brutt equally becomes the laughing-stock of Anna, Thomas and Eddie, who consider Brutt a phase-out model dating back to '14/18, whereas he naïvely believes in them as true friends. It is the major, who lives in solitude in a shabby hotel, with whom the girl takes refuge after her devastating departure from Eddie, who told her to go. Even though she thereupon proposes marriage to the middle-aged major, she cannot share his life either (Bowen [1938] 1965, 356-58).

Portia's perceived "orphaned unostentation" (35) can be called her defining characteristic, which makes her appear sweet and childlike to the Quaynes and the men whom she meets in their household, although her existence disturbs their established life. "No presence could be less insistent than hers" (231) is the almost unanimous opinion about Portia.[18] Since she accommodates without trouble and remains conforming in behaviour, she is an absent presence in the house of the Quaynes until she becomes a present absence there as in the narrative itself. In the final chapter "Portia" only supplies a prime topic of conversation for Anna, Thomas, their visitor St Quentin and the domestic servants Matchett and Phyllis. This development, however, shows a circular rather than a teleological course, as the novel's opening chapter presented a dialogue between Anna and St Quentin, with Portia and her diary as subjects of discussion. Before the end Portia has eventually ceased to be an agent in the novel and, on Major Brutt's bed, passively awaits what the Quaynes intend to do with her (359).

Thus the orphan remains only as an empty space. Portia avoids—even in her diary—disclosing her self (275), because it has proved a mistake to do so. Her error results in a silencing of her inner world after she has briefly become more insistent, because during a vacation in Seale-on-Sea, where Portia spends several weeks in a more common environment with smart teenagers, she was aware that having a boyfriend made a difference. She did not feel orphaned any more, and especially other young people did not consider her an orphan any longer (217), since the orphan is a person without close supportive ties. In a pathetic scene with Major Brutt she desperately talks and "connects" for the last time, after which she is excluded from the narrative text. "Not only Windsor Terrace, Eddie, and Major Brutt but the novel itself finally refuses to accommodate her" (Kitagawa 2000, 491).[19]

The motifs of death, dwindling into unostentation, and disappearance of the fictional orphan already form striking developmental details in the rare works where s/he emerges. Even more thought-provoking, however, seems the vanishing of the literary trope "orphan". I wish to argue that a literary discontinuity, like that of the disappearing orphan, forms another response to the cultural faultlines of a period which left many contemporaries distraught. After the General Strike, John Galsworthy, whom Virginia Woolf counted among the "traditionalists" who employ literary conventions gone stale and inadequate, wrote in the preface to one of his novels, a sequel of the *Forsyte Chronicles*:

> The England of 1926 [...] with one foot in the air and the other in a Morris Oxford, is going round and round [...]. Everything now being relative, there is no longer absolute dependence to be placed on God, Free Trade, Marriage, Consols, Coal, or Caste (Galsworthy 1929, vii).

The images of "closing doors" and "seeing off" with their metaphorical connotations mark disrupting changes in *The Death of the Heart*.[20] Portia is described as sensitive towards these symbolic hints. "So, she shrank [...] from the shut-in room, the turned-in heart" (Bowen [1938] 1965, 73). "A shut door" (317) becomes the emblematic sign of exclusion or disconnection in this novel, mostly used with reference to the house at 2 Windsor Terrace, but also to less stylish places such as Eddie's or Major Brutt's room (342, 351). What goes on behind closed doors out of the reach of others is part of the various "betrayals". Similarly, representations of leave-taking occur so frequently with Portia that there is practically no character from whom she does not (have to) separate; additionally, Portia's father in the narrative past and Major Brutt on the brink of the near future irreversibly leave what they trusted to be a warm, sympathetic and familiar place. "Tough luck, but there you are", runs the personalised narrator's comment on such a "thoroughly decent fellow" (310).

Among the narrative devices, which in Bowen's novel implicitly transmit uncertainties and dissolution, a stylistic peculiarity of the text stands out: the use of double negation, at times repeated in consecutive sentences. It communicates a marked indeterminacy and complicatedness, a state which the author ascribed to the general mood at the end of the interwar years (cf. n. 20). Often the omniscient narrator uses double negation to depict the young protagonists. Portia observes and anxiously considers every word or action, sensing a truly plotted universe. "She could not believe there was not a plan of the whole set-up in every head but her own" (72), so that "nothing was not weighed down by significance" (73). In a similarly negating manner Eddie's vagueness and frivolity towards Portia are expressed: "she was the only person to whom he need not pretend that she had not ceased existing when, for him, she had ceased to exist" (231). Reiterated negation also veils Eddie's knowledge of his own lack of substance when he is confronted with Portia's passionate claim on him: "'the whole of me isn't there for anybody. In that full sense you want me I don't exist'" (259). Finally, double negation is again used by the narrator as a reflective comment on strained sorrowful individualism: "In fact, there is no consoler, no confidant that half the instinct does not want to reject" (326).

Uncertainty proves complementary to the general dissimulation ruling at 2 Windsor Terrace: "Crossing that springy door mat, the outside person suffered a sea change. In fact, something edited life in the Quaynes' house" (208). The unusual expression of life being "edited", that is "emended" or "revised" instead of spontaneous or unpolished, distinguishes the milieu at Windsor Terrace from the house at Seale-on-Sea. The "edited" condition raises questions, which overstrains Portia. By whom or what is life "edited", and to what purpose? Segregation? Fear of the other or the yet unknown? An exemplary conversation with a visiting couple reveals by dialogue and omniscient narration some views on the stratification of society, on dictatorship, responsibility and authority (310-14). The three collocutors are joined by Major Brutt, on whose behalf Anna is looking for "connections", but who remains humbly quiet, already aware that it is impossible for him to make them there. Emphatically, the meal and the discussion about social changes and the destruction of traditions (311) are interrupted by ruthless Eddie's phone call to his friend Anna. Ridiculing the innocent, constantly worried about appearances and social standing she is filled by indignation and permanent annoyance, as only omniscience can unveil. Anna and Thomas, dissimulators and double-dealers, have lost the faculty for empathy, regard and sincerity. The narrative discloses that theirs is a state of emotional and mental impoverishment, which leads to coldness. The ruling class raises doubts about whether values will be reassessed when so much is in the process of disintegrating and getting lost.

In Forster's, Orwell's and Bowen's novels discussed above, the orphan condition is not characterised by material poverty and the orphan's impossibility to find a place in a social community after the nuclear family is gone. The modernist writers' orphan figures, unconnected individuals, are robbed of a spiritual home and the binding commitments of others. Family as a closely-knit network becomes more problematic than enjoyable, where the orphan's accustomed domestic circle has ceased to exist. Consequently, the orphans' painful loneliness results from a bereavement produced by the lack of shared memories, values and ties; even with relatives the changed environment becomes "unfamiliar". Materialism, emptied traditionalism and ethical depletion produce the orphan's isolation and possible despair, which are in turn indicative of the lack of a community of shared values. Apart from individual identity, also social and national identity, with society and nation perceived as forming a kind of larger "family", is threatened by decline. Borrowing from a popularised phrase by Simone de Beauvoir one might say that in modernist fiction the parentless child is *made* an orphan in a sense that differs from the essentialist.[21] Orphanhood thus evolves into a condition fully effected by the socio-cultural ambiance in which the protagonist lives unconnected (cf. Puschmann-Nalenz, "Some Things" in this volume, 131, 155). In the sparse narrativisations between 1905 and '45 the orphan condition implies distress about a spiritual richness that is irreversibly lost or, in Rickie Elliot's case, not yet achieved. Orphanhood means deprivation of values, and the orphan thereby mirrors the society in which s/he has to live. For decades, development and maturing or "malleability" had marked the fictional orphan (Floyd 2014, 23). These features are superseded now by compromise, resignation and final succumbing, eventually obliteration. The orphan's physical death as a motif can thus substitute marriage, which frequently sealed—or crowned—his/her fate in earlier fictions. In the early-20th-century novel, marriage, formerly a symbol of the orphan's social integration or "accommodation", is replaced by his/her disappearance. The literary orphan's faculty for self-reinvention is being incapacitated, and as an iconic image s/he fades away.

On the metanarrative level, the orphan's near-vanishing for several decades from 20th-century fiction is heralded by the disappearance of an orphaned character before the end in several novels under consideration.[22] In the attempt to culturally contextualise this phenomenon the study of the thirties offers specific historical explanations, which show the difference from the Edwardian decade. J. Gindin, calling the 1930s "a dispiriting decade", states that its fiction is "dependent on metaphor that combines or does not distinguish between private and public experience. Often, individual and sexual experience is intrinsically related to the social and historical" (qtd from Darwood 2012, 112). Hence, the betrayal motif is stressed in *The Death of the Heart*, where it also signifies the fear of a socio-cultural and, according to Darwood, a historical danger (134-35). Whereas the frequency of the pathetic orphan figure in Victorian fiction had underlined the importance of lineage and family, the conspicuous later extinction of the orphan trope parallels the "sense of an ending" with regard to traditions and literary practices that had lasted for generations. Another critic characterises the modernist novelists as writing "of their time and social prospects with all the mixed emotions of those consciously addressing the last of their line" (DiBattista 2007, 219). The orphan as legacy and memento of virtues loses its function, until the sign itself has vanished.

Evelyn Waugh's retrospectively told *Brideshead Revisited* (1945) presents a linear account of England in the two decades between 1923 and '43. Charles Ryder, the middle-aged first-person narrator, who looks back on his life, reports that he lost his mother during the First World War. She was killed, he untruthfully tells his friend, on her way to Serbia, where she wanted to work for the Red Cross (Waugh [1945] 2003, 41). As a young man he believed that she followed a religious impulse, while she was travelling in an ambulance and died of exhaustion in Bosnia in the winter (83). His father, unwilling or incapable of offering him guidance (26), is depicted by Charles as a broken, absent-minded man, "rather odd in the head ever since" (41) and very distant. Rarely does the novel, which starts with Charles's first year in Oxford in the summer of 1923 and his romantic friendship with Sebastian Flyte, the Marquess of Marchmain's younger son, address the protagonist's orphaned condition. The narrative thus reflects the demand for control or suppression of emotions, which determines the education and behaviour of the social class into which Ryder is born. Accounting for the liberating effect which the comfortable and rather dissolute life of an affluent freshman at Oxford has upon him, the protagonist summarises his childhood very briefly after his first visit with his new friend to the sumptuous country house at Brideshead: "I had lived a lonely childhood and a boyhood strained by war and overshadowed by bereavement" (45). Toughened by "the hard bachelordom of English adolescence, the premature dignity and authority of the school system" (45), his disposition has become sad or even depressed. However, for a boy from his class the absence of parents does not mean social exclusion or destitution, since relatives—in Ryder's case first an aunt and then his cousin Jasper—partly assume the role of guardian or tutor with success. Materially he is well provided for, but lavish. Thus he can for some time happily enjoy his extravagant friendship with Sebastian and then the connection with the Marchmains until 1926, the year of the General Strike.

Apart from the sparse remarks about what Charles considers his barely noteworthy early years, literal orphans are only intertextually present in the narrative. When he accidentally meets Julia Flyte again about ten years later, in the mid-1930s, she ironically quotes the title of the movie *Orphans of the Storm* (1921), after she has spent the night with the first-person narrator during a storm at sea and they both fall in love (Waugh [1945] 2003, 249). In 1923, Sebastian's sister was not literally an orphan, but even then Charles had received enough information from his friend about the antagonising function of their family and home in his friend's generation. Thus the historical novel *Brideshead Revisited* continues a de-mythologising of the former domestic ideals. In their narratives, Forster, Orwell and Bowen initiated the dismantling of the family, while genre fiction, according to David Floyd's study, had already gruesomely depicted it in *fin-de-siècle* narratives. Waugh's retrospective conclusively assesses the discontinuity of the social imaginary as well as of cultural traditions, which supplied an "aesthetic education" in Brideshead, remembered by him as "Arcadia" (78). Ryder briefly participated in it through Sebastian. In the generation of parents, before 1914, traditions had apparently also still granted a dominant position to the aristocratic class-consciousness and lifestyle, especially if there were male heirs, "which at the time seemed to promise continuity to the line which, in the tragic event, ended abruptly with them [Lady Marchmain's three brothers were killed]" (134). The de-idealisation of the noble family—as well as Ryder's upper-middle-class family—inexorably proceeds: the tragedy of the First World War is followed by an unstoppable decline when Lord Marchmain leaves his wife and children for a dubious mistress, with whom he subsequently lives in Venice. Lady Marchmain, and with her their eldest, Lord Brideshead, are given to a relentlessly pious—if not bigoted—life as devout Catholics.[23] Their younger son Sebastian becomes an alcoholic, and their elder daughter, Julia, is unhappily married to a divorced Canadian businessman and politician. In *Brideshead Revisited* the characters' expressions of mourning for persons and sorrow about loss—especially loss that is linked to national identity—are only hinted at; to keep a stiff upper lip appears as a duty which also condenses in the literary narrative. On the other hand, the dissolution of relationships, of the accustomed life and above all the ambivalence towards the family are at the centre of the narrator's imagination. It becomes evident that fundamental changes of society are exemplarily present and that neither conventions nor nostalgic appreciation can stop the country's development. In the early forties the sea change finally turns a deserted Brideshead manor, which in Ryder's romantic imaginings is remembered as "a world of its own of peace and love and beauty" (306), into a military headquarters for the British Army. There, in the noble country house, Ryder, upon his return, eventually describes himself as once again orphaned in the narrative present: "I'm homeless, childless, middle-aged, loveless" (330). Despite the profanation of the manor's symbolic space, and regardless of the vanity it also indicated, Ryder is sure that the stately mansion with its chapel will not vanish: "and yet that [*vanitas*] is not the last word" (331).

The narratee is made to realise that the different displaced characters are "Orphans of the Storm" in more than one sense. Death, dislocation and loss of love have left all of the novel's characters in an isolated, destitute state. What could be perceived as a severe struggle for necessary social reforms in *The Longest Journey*, thereafter to be continued as Imperial crisis in *Burmese Days* and historical insecurity in *The Death of the Heart*, has culminated as upheaval and conspicuous change in *Brideshead Revisited*.[24] I maintain that the unparented individual and the orphanic condition lead a ghost-like existence as an almost completely absent presence in the mainstream novel between 1910 and the 1970s.

By fading out into an ultimate blank in literary texts the orphan figure—both as singular character and literary motif—fulfils a specific purpose in its multifunctional aptitude. The analysis of the motif in 18th-century novels has already stated that the "metaphorical level [to which the orphan is propelled] signifies an emptiness, a cipher-like quality, at the heart of the idea of 'orphan'. The orphan is thus a trope, always already abstracted from actual reality" (König 2014, 1). The disengagement from actual reality also becomes manifest in the near-disappearance of the fictional orphan in times following the two world wars.

For an in-depth assessment of the trope, the consideration of a particular analogy is illuminating. Such an analogy reveals itself between the use of the orphan motif and the island motif. Floyd very pointedly calls the island "the absolute orphanic space" (2014, 32).[25] Both the insular and the orphaned situation are empirically ascribed conditions persistently connected to certain states of mind, to society, nation and value systems, which explains their affinity to a use as existentialist metaphors. In the figurative sense "island" like "orphan" is common usage inside but also outside literature, as shown in "traffic island" or "orphan text". In literature either image is fraught with a number of connotations, which point to the metaphors' comparability. Similar notions of isolation, loneliness and insecurity, yet also of exceptionality, dissociation and difference are conjured up by the island and the orphan. The qualities that make the orphan as well as the island special are the disconnectedness from an entity and the tension between self-reliance and contingency.

In imaginative literature the insular and the orphaned condition are represented as an individual experience. "Island", the topographical signifier, becomes a powerful poetical image as in John Donne's "No man is an island". "Orphan"—literally the state of a young person bereaved of parents—may signify the expatriate, deserted or homeless. The orphan as signifier reaches beyond an individual's unparented state due to death. Like the trope of the island it overlaps with other concepts and transcends boundaries: the "orphan's" parents may have vanished never to return, abandoned their offspring, or vice versa, as with the migrant under age. "Parents" can assume a figurative meaning as ideological or cultural progenitors: the postcolonial or posthumanist "orphan" is a case in point. The fictional refugee's or soldier's loss of the fatherland, which represented paternal authority and protection, together with the loss of home shakes his national identity and may equally leave him/her in an orphaned state.[26]

These reflections lead to the question whether the doomed fictional orphan of the first half of the 20th century is a failed romantic figure, whose solitude and innocence may become tragic, but possibly also appear unsubstantial in the socio-cultural context of the time. The death of the orphan in the period of modernist representations indicated an extinction of the motif in highbrow literature and hinted at an already executed disruption of culture. With the vanishing of the signifier, a radical disconnection with previous ages and periods of literature was unmistakable. The long-time trope disappeared consecutively to the new orientation of the English novel in the early 20th century. A changed focus in semantics also supports this: at the centre of her study on the orphan in 18th-century fiction Eva König placed the "subject". As her introduction reveals, the term "subject" in the subtitle has to be understood in its double sense, thus emphasising the political dimension which novels focusing on an orphan figure also assumed. After about 1910, the "subject" as a psychological concept, which is transposed into the aesthetic dimension by narrativising, became an important issue in fiction. In *The Death of the Heart*, where interiority begins to be doubtfully blurred, this concept becomes ambiguous. Worse still, the inner life of a character is increasingly represented as empty (cf. Kitagawa). The hollowness of an individual, who is now imagined as lacking an "I", already reflects the complete abandonment of a unified self and inner "depth".

The supplementary thesis which I propose regards the absence of (war) orphans in the dialectics of fact and fiction during the interwar and post-1945 years. The inverse numerical relation of fictional and "real" orphans in the wake of two world wars doubtlessly requires further exploration. An American estimation claims that twenty million half-orphans lived in Europe at the end of World War II, in Germany 2.7 million war-orphans were counted, most of them children of killed or missing soldiers (Bulitta and Bulitta 2011). For 1918 the number of war orphans in Germany is given as 1,130,000 (Pieronti 2015, 19). Obviously, parts of social reality were ignored or silenced ("beschwiegen") by the neglect of the orphan in contemporaneous novelistic representation, where this figure leads no more than a spectral existence. An "absent narrative" as "counter-discourse", as I shall provisionally call the one about the orphan in post-war times, is, however, not an isolated case. Edward Said's essay "Permission to Narrate" (1984) states in pointed questions that narrativisation is to a high degree selective:

> What makes it possible for us as human beings to face the facts, to manufacture new ones, or to ignore some and focus on others? Answers to these questions must reside in a theory of perception, a theory of intellectual activity, and in an epistemological account of ideological structures as they pertain to specific problems as well as to concrete historical and geographical circumstances. (Said [1984] 2000, 266)

Said's deliberations refer to narrating in general and to the media representation of the 1982 war in Lebanon in particular. In the opening quotation of his article, the Lebanon war is called "the orphaned fight, scattered and banished from the center" (243). As I have tried to show, the text corpora of 20th-century fictions also have "to be discussed in terms of absences and gaps" (256). In the instance of the literary orphans being under-represented in "highbrow" British novels during the two decades following either world war, the obstacle to fictional portrayals is not an authorised national narrative, which would suppress their representation.[27] The obstacle, I believe, which imposed a silence lasting into the 1980s, could be recognised in the (too) short temporal distance from the events.

Several conclusive observations may yet illuminate the specific case of the orphan. Whereas the slaughtering of a generation of young men of Europe in the Great War was fictionally and above all poetically thematised during the interwar years, the existence of children orphaned by that war is missing from novelistic portrayals of the time. The dead soldiers are nearly always addressed as "sons", leaving orphaned parents behind, and not as "fathers" of a future generation. Similarly, in the earlier literary production of the post-World-War-II years fictional orphans lead a shadow existence; obviously novelistic works could not "accommodate" them. Only at first sight may it therefore appear surprising that in times of two world wars and their distressing aftermath the figure of the orphan had no place in literary narratives.[28] I propose that the trope became dysfunctional; its absence was often accompanied by scepticism about the family, after the domesticity had been a central concern of Victorian culture. The iconic image and literary hero/ine "orphan" was divested of its fascination and force of expression, while the literal orphan had become commonplace, demanding an enormous administrative and humanitarian effort mostly coped with by state and charity organisations. Regarding the First World War, the question arises whether a widespread silence equally surrounded the fate of war orphans in historiography. Asa Briggs' *Social History of England*, for instance, does not mention them at all in his listing and commentary of the losses and family break-ups subsequent to the Great War.[29] The orphaned children after the two world wars became an inconspicuous object and burden of the welfare state. In all likelihood, I want to state, the orphan had for post-war readers and writers lost the romantic touch; instead, one might recall the trauma of having sacrificed a part of the young generation.[30] Continuity itself seemed at stake and for many became a burning issue. In the handful of novelistic representations with an orphan figure s/he appears neither as rebel nor hero/ine, but faltering between adaptation and separateness. The orphans in the three narratives by Forster, Orwell and Bowen are unspectacular, lonely, even pathetic figures, who are unable to achieve respected participation in the wider community. In gendered representations, especially the orphaned men, who were physically marked and attached to the arts—Rickie Elliot and John Flory—are deemed failures by their social environment and die; their masculinity is judged as far from exemplary. The female orphans— Elizabeth Lackersteen and Portia Quayne—are accorded weakness as part of femininity; they are expected to submit and conform in order to survive. From the heterodiegetic narrators of the three novels the doomed orphans are granted neither pity nor empathy, but a certain degree of respect for their strife for authenticity. In contrast, Waugh's first-person narrator Charles Ryder, who thus is the master of his life's narrativisation, makes memory his theme, the past his very own possession, and narrating a method of self-assessment (see Waugh [1945] 2003, 215).

After the rare narratives with orphans from the thirties and forties, the novel of the 1950s and '60s testified to the absence of the orphan character.

Disconnected from the mainstream, its resurrection and relocation occurred as a displacement—in the Fantastic. There the restored orphan— enterprising, charismatic and adventurous in nature—metamorphosed into an otherworldly figure.

Notes

[1] Floyd's definition of "genre fiction" comprises novels that would usually be considered as canonical literary works, e.g. R.L. Stevenson's narratives. Since Floyd's concept is more important for the discussion of 19th-century fiction it is not debated here.

[2] For literature the term New Imperialism is especially connected with the name of Rudyard Kipling and the slogan of "the white man's burden" as the colonisers' reason for remaining in possession of overseas countries.

[3] Such a translatory shift of the character into the non-mimetic can again be observed after the middle of the 20th century, when fantasy literature celebrates the orphaned hero (cf. Sedlmayr in this volume).

[4] The following quotations are taken from "Mr. Bennett and Mrs. Brown" and "Modern Fiction". "Mr. Bennett and Mrs. Brown" was originally published as "Character in Fiction" in the July 1924 issue of *The Criterion*, a journal edited by T.S. Eliot; under the new title it came out in the Hogarth Press in October of the same year. "Modern Fiction" first appeared in Woolf's collection of essays *The Common Reader, First Series* (1925).

[5] Auerbach calls Joyce's *Portrait of the Artist as a Young Man* the exemplary text from modernist fiction with regard to the representation of the "self-orphaned" (=expatriate) protagonist. Its publication date 1916 certainly marks a historic turning point in Irish as in British and European history, apart from breaking new grounds in literature. Auerbach ignores, however, the rarity of orphan representations in modernist fiction.

[6] In an article published in 2014 I analyse the importance of the orphan figure for John Fowles's *The French Lieutenant's Woman* (1969) and Ian McEwan's *The Cement Garden* (1978), like Iris Murdoch's *A Word Child* (1975) with an orphaned protagonist early examples of a new turn in British Fiction.

[7] Pawel Wojtas (2010, 33) contests the novel's profile as a conventional *bildungsroman*. It certainly deviates from the usual templates and is marked as a "*bildungsroman* apart" by its outcome, its general gloominess and the "relentlessly deferred, indeterminate nature of the work" (49).

[8] The book's dedication by the author reads "Frateribus", "for (my) brothers" (at Cambridge). This underlines the novel's autobiographical elements.

[9] Much has been written on the homoerotic and "platonic" tinges Forster inscribed his novel with, but the explicit message of the text points to a higher appreciation of vital energy, of passion and the physical generation of life, which are curbed at

the narrated time by the middle-class regard for social convention and moral norms.

[10] Cf. Gopinath (2009). The "pukka sahib" ("great master") is, according to Flory, a mere pose among the British in colonial stations, often hypocritically propagated. With an ironic effect, Veraswami, the Burmese doctor, is shown as believing and eagerly defending this concept as successful and just (Orwell [1934] 1977, 36-39).

[11] Blackstock discusses at length women's role in connection with representations of imperialism in Kipling, Orwell and Forster's *Passage to India*.

[12] I hold it that not only Mrs Lackersteen, but all the female characters of this novel—apart from pointing at some of the socio-political issues of the decade following the end of World War I—provide a certain amount of social comedy in the general tragedy.

[13] "Connect" is a key-word not only in E.M. Forster's *Howards End*, but marks the exceptionality of the modern condition in T.S. Eliot's poem *The Waste Land* (1922).

[14] That several of the female orphans are sixteen when the story begins (for the novels by Dunham and Roberts, cf. the chapter "Some Things" in the present volume) points to the coming-of-age pattern, which connects the narratives also to the female *bildungsroman*.

[15] Darwood (2012, 123-24) indicates that the innocence appearing in Major Brutt or Portia has a subversive effect on the emotionally corrupted characters. The "undermining reproach" dialectically interlocks with Portia's unobtrusive adaptation, by which she displays a supportive attitude to her social environment. Generally, an alternatively subverting and supportive impact of the orphan on the dominant ideology of 18th-century society has already been claimed by König (2014, 4).

[16] Victoria Warren's argument (1999, 142) that Anna has to be regarded as the prime female protagonist in the same manner as Emma in Jane Austen's eponymous novel is unconvincing. Although based on a similar plot device and obvious resemblances in character constellations *The Death of the Heart* does not direct reader attention and sympathy primarily towards Anna, whereas Portia is far more central for Bowen's novel than Harriet in *Emma*. Jessica Gildersleeve (2014, 73-74) also regards Anna as the central figure because of her being traumatised by experiences in the narrative past, which left her cold and sealed.

[17] Cf. Kitagawa (2000, 484-86). The knowledgeable article contains an evaluative discussion of the major recent criticism of the novel. Its main thesis is that Bowen uses modernist concepts in a way which breaks with them.

[18] Regarding the non-presence of the orphan figure Harry Potter in the "normal" family surroundings, cf. Sedlmayr's chapter in the present volume, 189-92.

[19] Elizabeth, the orphan girl in *Burmese Days*, is equally absent from the novel's final chapter and only dealt with by the third-person narrator's report in a very blunt way. Her long-awaited "accommodation" is located at the very last turn of the plot, when she has already decided to leave the colony because she cannot belong.

[20] Bowen called *The Death of the Heart* a "pre-war" novel, "a novel which reflects the time, the pre-war time with its high tension, its increasing anxieties, and this great stress on individualism. People were so conscious of themselves, and of each other, and of their personal relationships because they thought that everything of that time might soon end" (qtd. from "Death of the Heart"). This opposes Warren's interpretation, according to which *The Death of the Heart* could not be termed a historical novel: "In basing her novel on the 'pattern' of Emma, Bowen underscores the continuity of experience." (148) I contend that the narrative comprises these contradictory characteristics.

[21] De Beauvoir's original phrase (in English translation) reads: "One is not born, but rather becomes, a woman".

[22] As a working hypothesis I distinguish between the narrative and the metanarrative level here, although postmodernist criticism does not use the distinction, because it spuriously "compartmentalises" interlinked areas presented in the texts. The synergetic effect is produced by their working inseparably together.

[23] The role of religion, represented by one of the few 20th-century Catholic authors who are English, has been variously discussed, e.g. by RoseMary Johnson (2012).

[24] So far *Brideshead Revisited* has been found reminiscent of Proust's *A la Recherche du Temps Perdu*. I believe that the literary work Waugh's memory narrative most obviously shares themes with is Thomas Mann's *Buddenbrooks* (1901), which in German bears the subtitle *Decline of a Family*.

[25] Floyd analyses texts where the insular situation causes an individual's orphanhood—such as the Robinsonade or SF novel.

[26] The dead soldiers as orphans, deserted and betrayed by their literal and/or metaphorical parent, are more than a figure of speech in Georgian poetry as in contemporary fictions (cf. Puschmann-Nalenz 2014, 197).

[27] The Irish national history contained "gaps" following the Civil War and the foundation of the Republic that have only lately been "filled" by historiographic fictional narratives (e.g. the movie *Philomena* or Sebastian Barry's novels).

[28] There are several examples in post-1980 fiction that include war experience, e.g. Graham Swift's *Last Orders*, where the topic of the war orphan emerges; I think it is justified to claim that the "orphan" narrative was for decades also in a "depressed condition" (Said [1984] 2000, 236).

[29] I quote the renowned social historian: "Asquith [PM of the UK from 1908 to 1916] himself lost a brilliant son killed in the Somme; almost one in five Oxford students were killed. Wives lost their husbands, sweethearts their fiancés, some women were never to marry" (Briggs 1987, 299). Where the historian addresses the fate of children and the attention they receive from the state after World War I it is in connection with children under fourteen at work in war time (305).

[30] More fictional consideration has meanwhile been given to the loss of brothers, respectively to the surviving sibling (e.g. Atwood, *The Blind Assassin*, or especially Graham Swift, *Out of this World*, *Wish You Were Here* and *Mothering Sunday*); in *Brideshead Revisited*, Lady Marchmain's three brothers are worshipped by her as poet-heroes who died in the Great War (Waugh [1945] 2003,

132-34). In literature those killed in action are often seen as deserted boys who died without having entrusted posterity with their legacy, which is instead bequeathed as a warning to the parent generation.

Works Cited

Beer, Gillian. 1989. "Discourses of the Island." In *Literature and Science as Modes of Expression*, edited by Frederick Amrine, 1-27. Dordrecht: Kluwer Academic.

Blackstock, Alan. 2005. "Beyond the Pale: Women, Cultural Contagion, and Narrative Hysteria in Kipling, Orwell, and Forster." *Ariel: A Review of International English Literature* 36 (1-2): 183-206. http://ariel.ucalgary.ca/ariel/index.php/ariel/article/view/370/366.

Bowen, Elizabeth. (1938) 1965. *The Death of the Heart*. Reprint, London: Jonathan Cape.

Briggs, Asa. 1987. *Social History of England*. Harmondsworth: Penguin.

Bulitta, Erich, and Hildegard Bulitta. 2011. *Kinder: Opfer der Kriege bis 1945*. Materialien zur Friedenserziehung. Volksbund Deutsche Kriegsgräber Fürsorge e.V., www.volksbund.de. www.100-jahre-erster-weltkrieg.eu/fileadmin/redaktion/Micro_Weltkrieg/Projekte/Handreichung_Kinder_Opfer_der_Kriege.pdf.

Crane, Ralph. 2011. "Reading the Club as Colonial Island in E.M. Forster's *A Passage to India* and George Orwell's *Burmese Days*." *Island Studies Journal* 6 (1): 17-28.

Darwood, Nicola. 2012. *A World of Lost Innocence: The Fiction of Elizabeth Bowen*. Newcastle-upon-Tyne: Cambridge Scholars.

"The Death of the Heart." lubimyczytac.pl. lubimyczytac.pl/ksiazka/232285/the-death-of-the-heart.

DiBattista, Maria. 2007. "Elizabeth Bowen and the Maternal Sublime." In *Troubled Legacies: Narrative and Inheritance*, edited by Allan Hepburn, 219-38. Toronto: University of Toronto Press.

Ellmann, Maud. 2011. *Elizabeth Bowen: The Shadow across the Page*. Edinburgh: Edinburgh University Press.

Floyd, David. 2014. *Street Urchins, Sociopaths and Degenerates: Orphans of Late-Victorian and Edwardian Fiction*. Cardiff: University of Wales Press.

Forster, E.M. (1907) 1962. *The Longest Journey*. London: Arnold.

—. (1910) 1921. *Howards End*. New York: Vintage.

Galsworthy, John. 1929. *A Modern Comedy*. London: Heinemann.

Gildersleeve, Jessica. 2014. *Elizabeth Bowen and the Writing of Trauma: The Ethics of Survival.* Amsterdam: Rodopi.

Gopinath, Praseeda. 2009. "An Orphaned Manliness: The Pukka Sahib and the End of Empire in *A Passage to India* and *Burmese Days.*" *Studies in the Novel* 41 (2): 201-23.

Hodgkinson, Will. 2004. "Cultural Quake: Manet and Post Impressionism." *The Telegraph*, June 14, 2004. www.telegraph.co.uk/culture/donotmigrate/3618913/Culture-quake-Manet-and-Post-Impressionism.html.

Johnson, RoseMary C. 2012. "Human Tragedy, Divine Comedy: The Painfulness of Conversion in Evelyn Waugh's *Brideshead Revisited.*" *Renascence Essays on Values in Literature* 64 (2): 161-75.

Kitagawa, Yoriko. 2000. "Anticipating the Postmodern Self: Elizabeth Bowen's *The Death of the Heart.*" *English Studies: A Journal of English Language and Literature* 81 (5): 484-96.

König. Eva. 2014. *The Orphan in Eighteenth-Century Fiction: The Vicissitudes of the Eighteenth-Century Subject.* Houndmills, Basingstoke: Palgrave Macmillan.

Maugham, William Somerset. (1915) 1966. *Of Human Bondage.* Reprint, London: Heinemann.

"Memsahib." *Merriam-Webster.com.* Merriam-Webster, http://www.merriam-webster.com/dictionary/memsahib.

Orwell, George. (1934) 1977. *Burmese Days.* Harmondsworth: Penguin.

Pieronti, Perluigi. 2015. *Kriegsopfer und Staat: Sozialpolitik für Invaliden, Witwen und Waisen des Ersten Weltkriegs in Deutschland und Italien (1914-1924).* Cologne: Böhlau. Google Books, https://books.google.de/books?id=uO1rDAAAQBAJ&pg=PA11&lpg=PA11&dq=zahl+der+kriegswaisen+1914-1918&source=bl&ots=Rn4MZav7cI&sig=doiSBtbeOPtgbLu6WSWUZfBemxo&hl=en&sa=X&ved=0ahUKEwjhi5TTv6fPAhUK7xQKHdLEAs4Q6AEISDAF#v=onepage&q=zahl der kriegswaisen 1914-1918&f=false.

Puschmann-Nalenz, Barbara. 2014. "The Figure of the Orphan in Contemporary Fiction." In *Narrating Loss: Representations of Mourning, Nostalgia and Melancholia in Contemporary Anglophone Fictions*, edited by Brigitte Johanna Glaser and Barbara Puschmann-Nalenz, 179-202. Trier: WVT.

Said, Edward. (1984) 2000. "Permission to Narrate." In *The Edward Said Reader*, edited by Moustafa Bayoumi and Andrew Rubin, 243-66. New York: Vintage.

Seshagiri, Urmila. 2001. "Misogyny and Anti-Imperialism in George Orwell's *Burmese Days*." In *The Road from George Orwell: His Achievement and Legacy*, edited by Alberto Lázaro, 105-19. Bern: Lang.

Warren, Victoria. 1999. "'Experience Means Nothing Till It Repeats Itself': Elizabeth Bowen's *The Death of the Heart* and Jane Austen's *Emma*." *Modern Language Studies* 29 (1): 131-54.

Waugh, Evelyn. (1945) 2003. *Brideshead Revisited: The Sacred and Profane Memories of Captain Charles Ryder*. London: Penguin.

Wojtas, Pawel. 2010. "E.M. Forster's Uneasy Bildungsroman: Exploring the Meanders of Existential Aporias in *The Longest Journey*." In *New Aspects of E.M. Forster*, edited by Krzysztof Fordonski, 31-51. Warsaw: University of Warsaw. https://www.academia.edu/358929/New_Aspects_of_E._M._Forster.

Woolf, Virginia. (1924) 1966. "Mr. Bennett and Mrs. Brown." In *Collected Essays* vol. 1, 319-37. London: Hogarth Press.

—. (1925) 1966. "Modern Fiction." *Collected Essays* vol. 2, 103-10. London: Hogarth Press.

CHAPTER THREE

"SOME THINGS REMAIN BROKEN FOREVER": ORPHANS AND ORPHANHOOD IN RECENT NARRATIVE REPRESENTATIONS

BARBARA PUSCHMANN-NALENZ

Introduction

In literary criticism of the past 40 years the rare depictions of the fictional orphan include very general as well as individual-psychological definitions. Nina Auerbach regards the orphan "as the primary metaphor for the dispossessed, detached self" (1975, 395) in the modern age. Kazuo Ishiguro, from whose work *When We Were Orphans* the heading of my chapter is taken, has probably received almost as much recognition for his use of the orphan motif as Dickens, who wrote his novels more than 150 years before. In an interview, Ishiguro gave an explanation of his intent to narrativise the orphan state. Usually, he argued, individuals are prepared and guided "as we come out of the illusionary world that adults have created for us as we grow up", yet it seems hard not to lose orientation, because "then you suddenly find yourself alone in this harsher world". And he adds about the purpose of his symbolic use of the motif: "I've taken characters who are literally orphans to exaggerate that point [= the separateness]" (Shaffer 2001, n. pag.). If we credit his own statements the orphan condition is, for the writer, primarily an individual-psychological and developmental stage; he wishes to communicate to his readers "the orphan within", that is, the state of a person's deeply felt loneliness and fundamental separateness at some time in life.

A divergent definition is offered by contemporary philosophers. The opening of Julia Kristeva's socio-cultural study *Strangers to Ourselves*, whose topicality makes the reader forget that it was first published 25 years ago, moves on to an investigation of the figure of the foreigner in the literary and intellectual history of Europe. She starts with a grave cultural interrogation, which soon leads to her definition of the stranger as orphan:

> Can the "foreigner", who was the "enemy" to primitive societies, disappear from modern societies? Let us recall a few moments in Western history when foreigners were conceived, welcomed, or rejected, but when the possibility of a society without foreigners could also have been imagined on the horizon of a religion or an ethics. As a still and perhaps ever utopic matter, the question is again before us today as we confront an economic and political integration on the scale of the planet: shall we be, intimately and subjectively, able to live with the others, to live *as others*, without ostracism but also without leveling? (Kristeva 1991, 1-2, emphasis in original)

The author, from her vantage point of psychoanalyst, subsequently urges "us", the addressees, to recognise the foreigner in ourselves (191-92) instead of denying him. The glory of individualism, celebrated since the 18th-century bourgeois revolution, she claims, is in the process of being subverted by the postmodern discovery of the individual's "incoherences and abysses, in short his 'strangeness'" (2).[1] In keeping with Kristeva, difference and otherness must be admitted as also lying in ourselves and causing a bereaved orphaned condition. Instead of a method of forgetting and levelling otherness its thematisation proves necessary, she claims. Following this demand, she offers a synthesis of the essentialist with the metaphorical or functional understanding of "orphanhood": Kristeva contends that the "foreigner" can be defined as "deprived of parents", but enjoying freedom—exile being identified as a "challenge to parental overbearance" of a young person. Consequently, she titles one of her sub-chapters "Orphans" (21).[2] The condition of orphanhood emerges when people surrounding the "foreigner" cannot know who his/her parents are and "murderously" ignore their existence (22), since the foreigner's ancestors are invisible and remain in obscurity. It is the exile him/herself who brought about this situation and has in turn become foreign to parents. This vanishing of the parents and/or close relatives—the loss of origins—, the author maintains, constitutes the condition of orphanhood in the subject—not necessarily a minor—, even if the voluntary exile is possibly experienced as a state of liberation. A community with strangers exists only by the strength of illusion, on which, she adds, perhaps all communities depend (23).

Kristeva's use of the term "orphan", we may conclude, is not purely metaphorical, since being bereft of parents proves crucial, whether by death, absence or unforced distancing through migration. Mourning as a response to the disappearance of parents, by contrast, is for the exile or emigrant a less obvious response than for those orphaned through death: beside melancholia Kristeva emphasises in the parentless "foreigner" also the various manifestations of intrepidity and ephemeral happiness that s/he experiences on account of his/her freedom—freedom from ties, strains and constraints. As the author's cultural theory suggests, melancholia as a state of paralysis is not necessarily characteristic of the orphaned "foreigner" or "stranger". The feasibility of defining him/her as "alien" (USA) is firstly derived from the concept of the cultural community and, after the turn to the 19th century, from that of the nation-state. If one follows Kristeva's statements, postcolonial fiction might be considered designated as the preferred place for representations of a "liberated", functionally orphaned protagonist.

The orphan emerges as one of those elemental metaphors which render conceptualisation difficult. In defining an elemental metaphor, Hans Blumenberg's essay *Shipwreck with Spectator: Paradigm of a Metaphor for Existence* (1979) interprets the use of the shipwreck image from ancient Greek and Roman philosophy through the literature of the Enlightenment and the 19th century (33-37). As Blumenberg shows, narrative representations of shipwreck and storms at sea picture the fundamental crises and life-threatening dangers an individual can be exposed to. This interpretation of the imagery also provides an illuminating approach to most of the orphan narratives under consideration here, some of them employing the voyage and the sea as plot elements. Several more depict the situation of a protagonist as precarious after a metaphorical "shipwreck" in his/her life. The "spectator" in Blumenberg's essay can be identified as the focaliser or an extra- or intradiegetic narrator who, from a point of safety, watches and reflects the catastrophic developments represented in the fictional text. As Blumenberg emphasises at the end of his work, a few special images are capable of expressing fundamental truths about human life and experience, which abstract conceptualisation and terminology cannot put into words with similar adequacy. He creates the term "nonconceptuality" ("Unbegrifflichkeit", 83) for the discursively inexpressible phenomena in human existence, which are communicable only by an elemental metaphor. When he maintains that "shipwreck with spectator", like "life—a journey", is one of them I would like to contend that "orphan" is another one.

In her monograph *The Orphan in Eighteenth-Century Fiction: The Vicissitudes of the Eighteenth-Century Subject* (2014), Eva König analyses a great number of novels and explores their socio-political background in Britain, as indicated by her use of the word "subject" in the triple sense of "subordinate", "self", and "citizen". In her introduction, she predicates her interpretations of 18th-century novels on the "productive analogy with Lacan's theory of subject formation" (König 2014, 7)—the psycho-analytical model of the child's individuation, whose stages are also to be found, if we follow König's propositions, in the development of the English novel in the long 18th century (cf. 8). Since during that age philosophical templates of identity were relevantly developed and especially engaged the man of the middle classes these ideas shaped what König calls the structures of "the political unconscious". She emphasises that "[t]he fictional orphan of this age plays a crucial role in this process" [that constituted the modern individual] (9), including gender formation. Analogously and on a metafictional level, the novel, a newly emerging "orphan genre", requires its place in the symbolic order of the literary universe. For Eva König this function of an analogy between orphan character and the novelistic genre remains of great importance throughout her book.

The diverse theoretical approaches—Ishiguro, Kristeva, Blumenberg and König—to the literary theme of the orphan briefly presented above provide several reference points for my analysis of the orphan motif in the narrative texts discussed below. The ensuing chapter's investigation of a range of fictional orphan figures is grounded on a sample of British and selected postcolonial novels that came out after 2000. In some instances of the argumentation the recourse to earlier works is useful to show the continuity or adverse connection with lately published works. It is my objective to explore in the gamut of orphan characters the multilayered forms and meanings the motif has assumed in the past years. For the purposes of this book and inspired by Kristeva's statements about the orphan and the foreigner, my opening sub-chapter focuses on the optimistic fictional orphan—the *persona* who has literally lost his parents and goes out of mourning. The analysis of the picaresque in orphaned characters will successively lead to a detailed section about "The Dead Mother", which is followed by considerations about surrogacy and substitution of parents in fiction. The mythical figure of the foundling in post-millennial novels and the significance of the notion of "home" in the narratives conclude my exploration of the literary orphan as cultural sign in the early years of the third millennium.

1. The Picaresque Orphan

1.1 "Go out of Mourning First"

In my contribution "The Figure of the Orphan" to the edited volume *Narrating Loss: Representations of Mourning, Nostalgia and Melancholia in Contemporary Anglophone Fictions* (2014), the bereavement by death or absence of the protagonist's parents was shown as basically symbolic of a state of lacking, rootlessness and frequently destabilisation. Despite the overwhelming weight given to mourning in contemporary culture this is not the only attitude which narrative fiction has inscribed the orphaned subject with, as especially 18th-century English novels and their protagonists reveal. European philosophy in the 17th century had reconceptualised man and the universe. As a result, the literary subject was conceived as bereft of a firm and consistent world picture and in search of a "place", spiritually as well as politically—for home, self, or meaning. The "orphan genre", as which the modern novel has been addressed, especially attended to these topics. Regardless of the orphaned subject's seriousness in the struggle with adversity, absurd and funny encounters abounded in fiction. They promoted a protagonist in whom the condition of orphanhood enlarged the possibilities to create him/her in the shape of a *picaro*. Tom Jones may be considered an obvious example of the picaresque orphan in the early stages of the English novel. The hero has to display his individuality and find a meaningful and satisfactory life, exposing English society and human frailty in the process, until he is eventually able to assess his biological parents and his happiness after having luckily escaped all vicissitudes.

Considering the historical origins of the fictional orphan figure in the 18th century, the question arises whether the novel in the age of postmodernism also creates roguish heroes, whose bereavement leads to a successful attempt at cheerfully striving for personal identity, and who then attain social recognition despite original destitution. In contrast to the *bildungsroman*, with which the picaresque novel shares several characteristics, the lopsided relation of merit and lucky circumstances in favour of the latter is crucial for the picaresque genre. Contingency decides whether those gifts and graces may be randomly bestowed on the orphaned hero/ine as a fundamentally bereft individual that render him/her fortunate. Providence and accident play a far greater role than the biological parents, about whose nature and status the picaresque orphan does not seem to care very much.

Among the frequent deviations from novelistic traditions in contemporary narratives the literary *topos* of the *picaro* presents a challenge. Obviously, the comic and satirical aspects, as in *Moll Flanders, Humphrey Clinker* or *A Sentimental Journey through Italy and France*, cannot seamlessly be transferred to recent developments in narrative representations. The picaresque novel has not disappeared, as critical essays about living authors from Timothy Mo to Peter Carey and Sarah Waters also show, but its protagonist is rarely an orphan now.[3] Contemporary fantasy literature, however, which is the object of the chapter by Gerold Sedlmayr in this book, illustrates striking and extreme variations of the orphaned hero. On the background of literary history the following question arises out of these preliminary reflections: where does the conflation of the orphan character with the *picaro* occur in very recent English fictions, and in how far do contemporary narratives about orphan characters obey the conventions of the picaresque genre?[4]

The *picaro* defies the mourner and mourning. Rarely has it been doubted that continuous mourning following loss by death or absence is considered adequate, yet in modernist narratives this attitude was already undermined. By subverting the coupling of loss/death and mourning they highlighted a taboo, which one of the most famous literary protagonists of the 20th century could easily break by irreverent reflections. Attending a funeral, Leopold Bloom's musings among the crowd of mourners contain an exhortation embedded in literary and popular associations which surround the topic of death:

> You must laugh sometimes so better do it that way. Gravediggers in *Hamlet*. Shows the profound knowledge of the human heart. Daren't joke about the dead for two years at least. *De mortuis nil nisi prius*. Go out of mourning first. Hard to imagine his funeral. Seems a sort of joke. Read your own obituary notice they say you live longer. […]
> Burying him. We come to bury Caesar. His ides of March or June. He doesn't know who is here nor care. […]
> Bury the dead. Say Robinson Crusoe was true to life. Well then. Friday buried him. Every Friday buries a Thursday if you come to look at it.
>
> > *O, poor Robinson Crusoe,*
> > *How could you possibly do so?*
> >   (Joyce 1971, 111, emphasis in original)

The implication that the eponymous hero of a canonised work of literature is dead and buried by the subsequent aversion from the so-called realistic novel comes in the stream-of-consciousness of Leopold—like his creator a "Friday" who buries a "Thursday"—after the advice to leave mourning behind. Nouri Gana has quoted this imperative in his book *Signifying Loss* (2011, 21).[5] The demand not to mourn the deceased—a preceding "Thursday"—any longer is also operative on the metafictional level as a challenge that was met by the publication of *Ulysses* in 1922. With regard to the postmodern turn, which in places threatened to bury modernism in "The Death of the Novel", the request will also gain further attention in the course of this chapter.

On the story level, deaths, bereavements and funerals, like representations of mourning, abound in contemporary fiction, which attests to present cultural faultlines. As far as the orphaned protagonists of English novels around the turn to the third millennium are concerned, mourning and melancholy undoubtedly characterise many of them. In the past 25 years separation and loss have become focal issues of British narrative fiction— loss of a loved person, of the familiar environment, one's self-image, national or personal identity, of an idea or great narrative.[6] Rarely do literary critics point at those writers who also produce works with a more optimistic outlook that disconnects loss from mourning: novelists such as David Mitchell (cf. Bayer 2014) and Tom McCarthy (cf. Vermeulen 2011) have been scrutinised with the result that they create central characters who successfully depart from generalised melancholia.

In contrast to the overwhelming majority of mournful narratives, renowned authors of deeply serious contemporary novels with a special emphasis on ethics occasionally untie the connection between loss and mourning through creating the orphan as a buoyant character or as one in whom the experience of hardships, luck, and zest for life are mixed. If the plots of these rare novelistic examples are examined, a traditional structural quality of the picaresque novel also emerges: its episodic design and "panoramic" view of society.

While the generic profile of the "*comic* epic in prose" (Henry Fielding) is not always fulfilled in the narratives discussed below, the confrontation with the unexpected, told from the perspective of the orphaned protagonist who defeats loss, trials and sea changes which he cannot influence, belongs to the picaresque genre. Among the novels that display these characteristics are *Black Dogs* by Ian McEwan (1992) as an early example of the non-melancholic orphan's history, contrasted with the recent *Lionel Asbo* (2011) by Martin Amis, and, as a representative of the popular novel, *Old Filth* by Jane Gardam (2004). The fact that the dynamic, mobile orphan figure is in the present sample male without exception does perhaps not surprise; the end of this chapter, however, will focus on "atypical", blessed female orphans. In examining the contrastive, non-melancholic figure, who has "go[ne] out of mourning" (Joyce), I wish to discuss the largely concealed potential inherent in the orphan character. The vacant position of the literary orphan's origins inspires the imagination—not least that of the fictional orphan himself.[7] A character whose history is a blank naturally allures the creative spirit of wilful, random novelistic exploitation. If the confidence and cheerfulness of orphan figures are isolated here for closer inspection, other aspects relevant for the general topic will be resumed in one of the following sub-chapters.

1.2 Narratives of Childhood or Youth and the Picaresque[8]

If picaresque elements can be traced in the (post)modern literary orphan, they lie in his/her early years. Even though mourning follows grievous loss, the childhood and youth of a protagonist without parents does not have to be restricted to melancholia, as the selected novels show in different narrative modes and perspectives. Jeremy, the orphaned first-person narrator of McEwan's *Black Dogs*, emerges as the author of his life narrative reaching from his childhood and the circumstances of his orphaned state to middle-aged adulthood. The boy Desmond, who appears in the first chapter of Martin Amis's *Lionel Asbo: State of England*, tells of his predicament in the family in a confessional letter, a form which is repeatedly used in the course of the novel. Typically, the picaresque orphan creates the past in his or her life narrative him/herself—sometimes allegedly reporting parts of it from other sources. The opening in the first-person epistolary mode of the mock-*bildungsroman Lionel Asbo*, however, is followed by a mostly third-person narrative about Desmond's and Lionel's divergent developments. In Jane Gardam's novel *Old Filth*, Sir Edward's life-story and judiciary career are throughout presented by an authorial but not omniscient narrator, who mostly adheres to the reflector figure's limited perspective. His by-name "(Old) Filth" was supposedly the hero's own invention and is an acronym of "Failed In London, Try Hongkong". Like "Asbo", which is not Lionel's civil last name, but an acronym of "Anti-Social Behaviour Order"[9] allegedly received by Lionel for the first time at the tender age of eighteen months, Sir Edward's nickname signalises sarcasm and humour. Very seriously, Jeremy, the narrator of *Black Dogs*, prefaces the rather gloomy historical novel about the agency of a "malign principle" (McEwan 1998, 19) by the story of his childhood. He subsequently presents the lives of his in-laws following a brief account of his own biography up to the point when he met them through his wife, from whom he had long been separated prior to a conciliatory gathering in the narrative present.

The fact that the representation of the protagonist's distant past takes up as little time and space in *Black Dogs* as in *Lionel Asbo* (Amis 2012, 10-13) is in tune with the construction of an orphaned hero who brusquely goes out of mourning. As these two novels word it, the protagonist "woke up" (Amis 2012, 10) from a paralysed melancholic state, or, as Jeremy remembers, when he surfaced from depression "I would come to life, then I would leave" (McEwan 1998, 18). An orphan such as Jeremy or Desmond seems to have become a sport of fate or a rambler, but not a mourner caught in the *stasis* of grief. Edward Feathers of *Old Filth* can in his old age apparently cope with his wife's death, but has suppressed every emotional response for more than 70 years. He remained unable to mourn after the traumatising brutal separation from his *ersatz* mother, a Malay girl, at the age of four, as the third-person heterodiegetic narrator discloses. Only when Edward has found again two of his "childhood companions-in-exile", who also share his secret from the remote past, can he feel sorrow.

In the opening sentence of the Preface to *Black Dogs*, Jeremy exhibits his immediate re-orientation after his bereavement: "Ever since I lost mine in a road accident when I was eight, I have had my eye on other people's parents" (9). Amis's orphan Desmond Pepperdine was twelve when he lost his mother Cilla; his dark-skinned father simply disappeared. At the beginning of the narrative, "(Desmond, Des, Desi), the author of this document, was fifteen and a half" (Amis 2012, 3) and has at the time embarked on a sexual affair with his maternal grandmother, mother also of his uncle and guardian Lionel and the reason why Des, who fears Lionel's revenge, writes a desperate letter to the agony aunt of a tabloid. The novel follows Desmond's development in the mode of a *bildungsroman* and puts the anti-father figure Lionel and their relationship centre stage, with protagonists and heterodiegetic narrator combining in their "involuntary" trend to expose the grotesque and the absurd.

The two novels by McEwan and Amis, fundamentally different in almost every other respect, leave no doubt that the orphan state is meant to provide the basic conditions for the evolution of the central characters, even though their explicit occupation with the past, with death and loss, remains brief. Jeremy becomes his own psychoanalyst when he describes his mindscape: "I never had any doubts about it, at some level you remain an orphan for life" (McEwan 1998, 10): the loss is never forgotten nor is it for him "buried" in the unconscious (as with Edward Feathers), but remains the driving force behind future actions and the protagonist's curiosity to find out more about the ways of other families and their parent-child relations. Desmond Pepperdine, in a parodic happy ending, finds bliss in the nuclear family he founds and a baby girl named after his mother, whereas Jeremy in his youth strives to belong wherever he finds an opportunity and eventually marries into a family. His friends, in contrast, are trying to solve their parental bonds in the struggle for freedom on their way to self-realisation. The unique feature of Jeremy's teenage life is the liberty he enjoys since he grows up without care or authority watching over him—a situation which implies the absence of outer as well as inner conflicts caused by parental expectations and gives rise to a protean identity of sorts. His peers even grudge him his plunge into a proletarian lifestyle, which he curiously undertakes for a change together with his elder sister, her husband and their little daughter. Desmond Pepperdine, who is submerged into criminal underclass life due to the "help" of his antisocial uncle, his senior by only a few years, tries to give himself an education and to leave this environment behind.

The orphaned heroes Jeremy and Desmond are portrayed in a struggle brought about by loss and lack, but this fight for survival in an emotional, cognitive and social sense is in an oblique way productive. Even though Jeremy describes himself as a grown-up with no persuasions or attachments he develops "a kind of moral capacity" (Doyle 2013, 131) even from his orphaned condition, namely an ability to respect dissent and accept a plurality of beliefs. On account of missing guidelines and inherited or imposed standards the orphan Jeremy becomes unusually open and tolerant; his emotional as well as intellectual state is characterised by fluidity. McEwan's first-person homodiegetic narrator does not conceive of his identity as indisputably relational, though as deficient in emotional ties. In his youth he shows an inclination to socially experiment and afterwards starts on a spatiotemporal itinerary that takes him across Europe and the past 50 years of European history. As an adult he develops a kind of disinterested, rational attitude, which makes it possible for him to reflect on different ideological positions without getting over-excited due to emotional bonds and familial inscription. Neither his mother-in-law's report of her religious conversion and mystic experience nor his scientific father-in-law's contempt for it, or the latter's—later abandoned— communist persuasions provoke hostility in Jeremy, nor do they cause a divide. The couple's children, by contrast, are totally estranged from their ideologically adamantly opposed parents. Jeremy's reflection "I am uncertain whether our civilisation at this turn of the millennium is cursed by too much or too little belief" (McEwan 1998, 20) exposes the assumption that a deficiency might turn out to be an asset; he is convinced that the same holds true with regard to his biography. On account of the young orphan's "childish unbelonging" state (17) the adult feels free to explore unknown intellectual, spiritual and empirical territory. This proves a gain out of loss, an opportunity seized by a protagonist who, on the cognitive level, appears as surprisingly "enlightened". Together with the lasting ties, which the protagonist has been lucky to eventually build with his in-laws June and Bernard Tremaine, his capacity for neutral tolerance enables him to become a humanist who acknowledges others' identities and has no trouble or fear in confronting them. Jeremy is uninhibited to philosophise about history and human nature, about good and evil, while those with deep ideological convictions and moral certainties draw dividing lines and engage in battles (172-73).

In contrast to the uncontrolled life of McEwan's young hero, a surfeit of inverted guidance and authority is bestowed on the orphan Desmond Pepperdine. The satirical portrayal of the successful criminal career of the boy's guardian—in a review referred to as a "Jackpot jailbird" ("Jackpot", n. pag.)—is seasoned with the scenic presentation of the fun awarded by talk about pornography or violence. It puts the reader in a doubtful mood. Finally, the novelistic treatment of the distortion of norms and the depiction of the celebrity cult following a great deal of money for Lionel amount to an overkill or hyperbole. Lucky circumstances like a lottery win and enormous public attention eventually result in a sort of mock-closure for the plot. After Lionel's departure Des, who worked as a reporter for the district's tabloid, afterwards read economics and obtained a degree, has the apartment to himself together with his girlfriend and dreams of a baby, his daughter Cilla. His career imitates that of the exemplary social climber against all odds, a pattern which leaves him as fabulously adapted to societal expectations as his uncle's conduct is anti-social. At 21, Des has already become a "tall, slender, well-spoken and delightfully assured young man, a graduate of Queen Anne's College, London" (Amis 2012, 150) with promising prospects.

The picaresque element in the concept of the self-made man has already been observed in American novels of the 19th and early 20th centuries. The balance between luck and merit in the picaresque hero's life story was revised when writers took into account the ongoing socio-economic changes by industrialisation and migration to the big cities. Desmond Pepperdine's is the satirical story of such a picaresque parvenu, Lionel Asbo's career that of the criminal as star. The farcical picture Amis displays, however, parodies or even perverts the condition-of-England novel as well as the *bildungsroman* or the novel of initiation. The reversed social norms Desmond is taught leave the orphaned youth perplexed: "As he continued on his journey, his journey from boy to man, Des found that the thoughts that stayed with him about his uncle were getting a little bit harder to file away" (61). Comic episodes and funny dialogues in *Lionel Asbo* usually result from a perversion of standards, like the advice Lionel gives Des to smash windows or steal a car in order to finally do something decent and sensible. The orphan, who may lay claim to the reader's sympathies, becomes a product of society's great expectations against the backdrop of his environment that antagonises these presumptions. The teen-aged Desmond Pepperdine has not changed his last name to his guardian Lionel's "Asbo" and would have no reason to do so. When Agony Aunt Daphne comes to interview Uncle Lionel in prison after he has won in the lottery with a stolen ticket she reports on the nephew as follows: "'A real pleasure to meet you,' says Des, and gives a graceful little bow. With his gorgeous smile and the light of true intelligence in his hazel eyes—what a radiant contrast to the pathetic gropings of his poor old uncle!" (151). Desmond's evolution comes closer to that of a middle-class model boy rather than a roguish character, while his uncle serves as a paradigm of criminal proles with firm principles and a code of honour.[10] The two-dimensional cartoon- and fairy-tale-style of *Lionel Asbo* mimics the picaresque tradition and propels the theme of "loss" onto a metafictional level, where in self-parodic manner it mocks the subtitle's claim to reflect the State of England in a novel. *Lionel Asbo* is not an anti-novel—it observes plot, characters, place and even the concept of linear time—but presents "the world turned upside down", following strategies we know from Jonathan Swift's satires, by establishing the picture of a "lawless" society that displays the carnivalesque disorder. On the meta-narrative level, however, this novel highlights "loss (of grand narrative)" as constitutive for contemporary artistic undertakings. The absence of "greatness" is emphasised by Martin Amis's declared endeavours to put more "anxiety" into this work. Tellingly, this includes "anxiety about the writing itself" (Lane 2012, n. pag.).

McEwan's and especially Amis's novel retains the episodic and adventurous structure of the picaresque genre and the positive outlook of a protagonist.[11] The view of society, on the other hand, is restricted due to the subjectivity of the narrator respectively the reflector figure. By contrast, Jane Gardam's well-made novel *Old Filth* offers a socially variegated picture of typified individual lives from the 20th century, which looks back on the era of the British Empire of the 19th century and its later demise.[12] Regarding the critical reception of Gardam's novel and its protagonist, honourable Sir Edward's nickname and especially his spontaneous or enforced errant displacements recommend him for an affiliation with the picaresque novel. The reviewer of *The Guardian* addresses the balance between the comic and the sad when he comments on *Old Filth* as "Eddie's odyssey [...] a sad mock epic version of the wanderings of the children of the British empire" (Davies 2004, n. pag.). Edward Feathers is a Raj orphan, a parentless exiled English child in times of the Empire.[13] His individual history presented by a third-person narrator and the intradiegetic characterisation by other figures unveil the discrepancies between his public person in the narrative present and his inner life disclosed in retrospect. When during his final journeys Sir Edward, aged and widowed, rests in the Inner Temple where senior and junior judges assemble for luncheon, his peers tax him as "'Rich as Croesus. But he's a great man.' 'Pretty easy life. Nothing ever seems to have happened to him. Nothing'" (Gardam [2004] 2013, 33). The ironic effect of this statement results from the contrast with the gradually revealed experience of Edward's personal drama. The narrator retrospectively also portrays what the protagonist could not remember: the distant past of his infancy.[14] The portrayal of the gloom resulting from bereavement that was missing from McEwan's and eliminated from Amis's depiction of an orphaned childhood receives great attention here. Gardam's narrative, the first part of her trilogy with the same protagonist, gives considerable room to a description of the childhood years of the recently deceased judge Sir Edward Feathers. After a distinguished professional career as a barrister in British Hong Kong prior to 1997—one of his scholarly articles is referred to as "Filth on Pollution" in the Inner Temple—he spent his retirement years with his now dead wife Betty in the scenic rural surroundings of Dorset. The dark secret—by himself called "filth" when he is 80 and dying—of his miserable time in a foster family in Wales remains concealed almost until the novel's end. After a reunion with two distant cousins who shared his fate as exiles Edward confesses to a priest that he intentionally caused the fatal accident of their sadistic foster mother when he was eight years old (245). To address the narrative as a tragicomedy with melodramatic elements, which is unfolded from a viewpoint "after Empire", renders it a historical novel of specifically British import.

Even though loss and sadness dominate some parts of Edward's life, the performative character of his biography, in which he acts the main part, marks him as a *picaro*. People enter his life and again leave the stage; they simply disappear from his view. Edward's mother died after his birth, his father, a widowed colonial district officer in Malaysia given to drink, could not relate to him and remained a stranger to the child who happily grew up among the indigenous people until the age of four, when the Baptist mission prepared him in a six-months course for his fate: "Because you will one day have to go to England. It is called Home" (28). To his hesitating parent the missionary briskly retorts, "it *is* the custom. […]. You went home yourself" (26, emphasis in original). The father's reaction discloses—beside the absurdity with which the word "home" is used—a shade of the cruelty of this childhood experience despite every good reason for the exile. Reasons of health, education, lifestyle and class are supplied for a small child's separation from a parent and his/her removal from the tropical colony. Edward becomes an orphan in every sense; upon his arrival in Wales his state of loss is complete, and while he has a name tag and an imposed—and pre-paid—course of life, the change is too early and confusing for him to consciously possess an identity. Following his itinerary—from Malaysia to Britain, thereafter from the Welsh foster family to prep school, to public school, to university, into the army, from post-war London back to the colonies, to England again and finally to the Far East—the narrative reveals the traumatising as well as the comically absurd stages in the life of the protagonist. When Edward is enlisted at the outbreak of World War II, because he could not get back to the East in time, fate puts him in a unit guarding Queen Mary, who has been evacuated from London. He becomes her favourite while the best of his school friends are killed serving in the RAF.

The mix of fortune and misfortune, misery and comedy continues to the end. "I cannot bear to think about the cruelty at the core of this foul world" (246) Edward Feathers utters after the three Raj orphans have made their confession. Impeccably traditional in appearance, he attends the Christmas service near Salisbury a little later and, praying, finds many things that turned out far better in his own life and for the other Raj orphans than he would have surmised. "How unaccountable it all is. How various and wonderful" (251) is his moral philosophy. When he decides to go to Malaysia ("Home") by himself for New Year's Day, chattering on the plane with a young lawyer who recognises him as the famous public figure, Sir Edward's wanderings have almost come to an end. The death of the protagonist on his arrival does not at all fit the conventions of the picaresque genre, nor does the third-person narrative about trauma and distress or global disaster like the two world wars and the austerity of the post-war years. And yet, the novel frequently embraces situational comedy—rarely social satire—in the life story of the orphaned character. Separation as one of the focal concerns of British narrative literature since the 20th century is epitomised in *Old Filth* with ambiguity: it means loss and a chance for progress. The orphaned protagonist, whose stiff upper lip has finally given way to sentiment, is revealed as responding with pain but also with amazement to the chaotic, indomitable life concealed under stifling order and control.

Evaluating the results of my above readings I would argue with regard to the three narratives that only *Lionel Asbo* fulfils the generic parameters of a picaresque novel, namely the dominance of roguish comedy, social satire and the invincible hero. The picaresque orphan is at present a rarity in literary English fiction despite the novelistic traditions of the 18th and 19th centuries. Possibly the young person "without parents—free of debt and duties" (Kristeva 1991, 21) is a taboo and simply too frivolous a character, considering the ethical turn in postmodern fiction where memory and the past have been pivotal. Some incompatibilities between the orphaned and the picaresque character add to the near-absence of the parentless *picaro*: the adventurous mind has not remained a general characteristic of the literary orphan. The reason for this circumstance lies in his/her frequently represented yearning for reliable bonds, a topic whose relevance became undeniable due to the tenets of modern psychology. As a consequence, we can conclude that contingency and dialectic contradictoriness are the hallmarks of the orphan character in recent mainstream narrative fiction. Elements of the picaresque novel with a frequent change of scenery and personnel, a protagonist whose biography shows the mixture of fortune and misfortune and leaves him to his own surprise independent from personal merit or influence, recur in all three of the above narratives. Indulgence and a pleasure in the comforts of life typical of the picaresque hero are added to the episodic structure. Therefore, the three texts show that the tradition of the picaresque narrative has not totally disappeared from the novelistic treatment of loss and separation around the millennium. Hartner, who addresses *Old Filth* as a postmodern *bildungsroman*, generally argues that genre concepts are basically still the same. This view has remained, however, highly controversial in the age of postmodernism. I would agree for the novel of character development that "most of the templates have neither been lost nor significantly altered or replaced" (Hartner 2013, 175). Though the picaresque orphan has become rare in English fiction he still illuminates the literary feasibility of disconnecting the link between loss and mourning.[15]

According to published research (cf. Ardila 2015, Doyle 2013, McCulloch 2007), the incidence of the picaresque orphan figure in contemporary American and Irish mainstream narrative literature appears higher than in Britain. This character type is, however, common in children's and juvenile fiction by British authors; in the genre of the romance with an appropriation of the *Cinderella* plot the social rise of the female orphan protagonist also claims a firm place. To point out the commensurability of loss and the picaresque in an American popular novel I briefly quote an orphan story by John Irving, well-known author of *The World According to Garp* (1978). In the opening chapters of *The Cider House Rules*, published in 1985, an authorial narrator shows how the orphan Homer Wells fails to be adopted after a series of abortive stays in different families for whom he had been thought suitable. He comes to permanently live in the orphanage in Maine that was meant to be only his temporary home. Mocking the protagonist as well as those around him— nurses, the local doctor, various adoptive families—the orphan condition itself also becomes the object of comedy, as does the history of the literary orphan, epitomised in Irving's novel by references to Charles Dickens' protagonists. When at the age of twelve Homer enjoys the prospect of being finally adopted by a sportsman and his wife, who is also an athlete, Dr Larch, physician and mediator for the adoption, is certain about the boy's hyperbolically described intellectual capacities: "He didn't fear for Homer's mind. A boy who has read *Great Expectations* and *David Copperfield* by himself, twice each—and had each word of both books read aloud to him, also twice—is more mentally prepared than most" (Irving 1985, chap. 1). Regardless of cultural coaching, the doctor's attempt to place Homer in this family of sportsmen again proves an incongruous combination, since the literary—or literate—orphan, even though he does credit to his first name, is of no interest to most people. In this case (fictional) life cannot successfully imitate art.

2. The Dead Mother and the Symbolic Order

In her study, Eva König initially states that in 18th-century fiction "lacking a *father* is a serious problem for eighteenth-century heroines, one often presented as an extreme form of orphanhood" (2014, 6, emphasis added). This observation results from the increasingly powerful patriarchal order, which reduced women's identity regarding name, property and agency. The author continues: "While fatherless children suffer abjection, motherless children can still thrive in eighteenth-century novels" (6). Her statement reveals another contrast with recent fictions, where the absence of the mother and the vanishing even of her memory are frequently striking dismal features.[16] König's comment, stating that not misogyny but neglect runs through 18th-century fictional representations of mothers, points at the near-irrelevance of the mother's disappearance. Even though König emphasises the positive presence of the mother, she adds: "Nevertheless, absent and dead mothers still often get short shrift from writers" (6). That, despite different accentuation in contemporary fiction, this remark still proves occasionally true will be demonstrated below. More often, however, recent novels attract attention to the missing mother of both male and female protagonists. The theories of Lacan and of feminist Luce Irigaray on the Symbolic provide the basis for my exploration of the novelistic development which causes the absence of the mother to take centre stage, whereby the overpowering presence of the father is unveiled. Such a dialectic process in contemporary fiction was enhanced or even stimulated by psychology and gender studies. In 1990 Margaret Whitford remarked: "Perhaps we have reached a period in history when this question of domination by fathers can no longer be avoided" (Whitford 1991b, 36).[17] The novel as genre participates and once more actively engages in the registration of cultural faultlines. That the fictional formation of a changing order is often conceived as a subversion of dominant social patterns complies with poststructuralist and feminist propensities.

Regarding British writer Graham Swift, reviewers have commented on the "remote fathers, the dead and deserting mothers" (Robson 2011, n. pag.) as a tiresomely recurring theme in his novels. The frequency of the motif in fiction is the more conspicuous since in Western European countries the death of the mother in childbed or soon after has become rare, whereas for Jane Austen, Mary Shelley or Charles Dickens it was part of their social experience. The assumption seems therefore well-founded that contemporary fiction's frequent "orphaning" of characters by death or absence of the mother does not reflect a historical reality. The addressing of "maternal deadness" and the protagonist's motherless-ness in novels, I contend with reference to Luce Irigaray, is more of a cultural than psychological significance today and illustrates that "this is not an account primarily of individuals, but of a whole cultural system" (Whitford 1991a, 76).[18] In 1987 Irigaray gave a concise description of the current system in her work *Sexes and Genealogies* (*Sexes et parentés*): "Patriarchy is defined by Irigaray as 'an exclusive respect for the genealogy of sons and fathers, and the competition between brothers'" (202, qtd from Whitford 1991b, 23). This structure—and the beginnings of a change in the past 25 years—becomes evident in the traditional family organisation, of which Whitford states with reference to Hegel's analysis of Sophocles' tragedies that "[o]ur current morality is still dependent upon these very ancient events". She continues, summarising: "When Patriarchy is established, the daughter is separated from the mother and, more generally, from her family. She is transplanted into the genealogy of her husband, must live in his house, must bear his name, and so must her children etc." (Whitford 1991b, 199).

Considering recent medical records on the premature death of women, compared to the early 19th century, I wish to argue that the mother's narrativised disappearance does not primarily serve to display the character development of a protagonist, but operates on the symbolic level as an acute manifestation of the absence/presence trope. The dominance of patriarchy expresses itself in the omnipresent "law of the father, of all fathers, fathers of families, fathers of nations, religious fathers, professor-fathers, doctor-fathers, lover-fathers, etc.", Whitford epitomises Irigaray (36). Irigaray's quoted explanation relies on psychoanalytical research: "Moral or immoral, they always intervene to censor, to repress, the desire of/for the mother" (36). According to Irigaray, the question of how and where Woman figures in Western culture remained unanswered at least until the 1980s. "What of that woman outside her social and material role as reproducer of children, as nurse, as reproducer of labour power?" (35) A repeated thematising of the mother's irreversible corporeal absence felt by the protagonist in a work of fiction also emphasises the writer's initial act to make her disappear by having her die. More generally, frequently creating this situation highlights the empty space in the symbolic order which dominates the Western socio-cultural system. In the heading of chapter 3 of *The Irigaray Reader* woman is addressed by Whitford as "the Silent Substratum of the Social Order'" (47). This may cause surprise and once more draws attention to Whitford's statement that in the prevailing paradoxical condition "[t]he maternal function underpins the social order and the order of desire, but it is always kept in the dimension of need" (35-36). This comment describes a deficiency, since woman's identity, according to Irigaray, is left in "exile". Moreover, the author observes that the maternal genealogy (especially mother-daughter) is persistently missing from representations in a patriarchal culture: it is the paternal line that "counts".

The recurrent motif of the mother's death in narratives symbolically hints at the failure or anxiety in reproducing the social order. Irigaray's following proposition was voiced in an interview translated by David Macey: "The substratum is the woman who reproduces the social order, who is made this order's infrastructure: the whole of our western culture is based upon the murder of the mother" (qtd from Whitford 1991b, 47). Implicitly this statement emphasises how important it is for the ruling socio-cultural paradigm to have the mother eliminated ("murdered") from the Symbolic Order. Julia Kristeva's theoretical reflections on the foreigner without parents, who experiences as "murderous" (Kristeva 1991, 22) the environment where they are ignored and therefore non-existent, echo Irigaray's pointed utterance about the importance of the "murder" of the mother for the social order.

2.1 Without a Trace

The way in which Margaret Whitford approaches Irigaray's theoretical conclusions can elucidate some of the objectives of the subsequent literary analyses:

> So I shall be discussing here, first, the major and most significant absence in the symbolic representations of a maternal line or genealogy; and second, the relationship between the systemic elements, of which this absence is a structuring factor. In the first section I want to look at the relationship which the symbolic has bypassed, the mother-daughter relationship, and argue that for Irigaray it is essential to bring that relationship into the symbolic (through interpretation of symbolic— philosophical or cultural—material). (Whitford 1991a, 76)

In perceiving the pertinence especially of the last sentence for the purposes of this chapter I add my thesis to the quote: in novels, which are part of the Symbolic as cultural material, this endeavour of "gapping" narrative representations with regard to the mother transpires as a focal point of substantial weight. The "'blank spaces of masculine representation'" (Howie 2008, 106) such as the missing mother present a challenge to the interpretation of literary works, which this section is trying to meet. It does not come as a surprise that in our culture female-authored fictions often equally hold these empty spaces, since women writers have been subjected to the same "laws" noted above. These representational blanks and the way they are being dealt with have inspired my analysis of novels by Graham Swift, Helen Dunmore and Jane Gardam. Also, and with particular awareness, postcolonial writers Margaret Atwood, Caryl Phillips and J.M. Coetzee are considered, together with one example by Toni Morrison, who after *Beloved* has continued to write about the North American colonial era. Their narratives are the objects of my exploration of the orphan character and the dead mother.

In terse words *Old Filth* portrays the death of Mrs Feathers, the Scottish wife of the District Officer in the Colonial Service, from puerperal fever following Edward's birth shortly after the end of the Great War. "Nobody had expected Mrs Feathers to die" (Gardam [2004] 2013, 19)—she was expected to be always there, yet she did not survive. The Welsh Baptist missionary who takes the new-born son back to his father assumes a role as administrator of a Christian's fate in the province; the native wet-nurse who had been provided remains desperate about the events, while the widower wordlessly turns to work and whisky and orders his servant to place the child in the villagers' hut: "Alistair Feathers never came near [his baby son]" (24). Edward has never known his mother and apparently does not learn anything about her. A young Malaysian girl, Ada, daughter of the wet-nurse, becomes his surrogate mother in terms of attachment. It shows in this narrative that in the consciousness of characters and narrator "there is only *the place of the mother*, or the *maternal function*", as Whitford paraphrases Luce Irigaray (1991a, 80, emphasis in original). Instead of the mother as an individualised woman baby Edward is assigned three females with different maternal functions, in tune with a society based on the division of labour. Tellingly, only the indigenous tribal people seem to have a memory of Mrs Feathers at all and a regard for the child's maternal origin: "Because of the memory of the child's kind mother, the Long House respected him and accepted him, an ivory child in their warm dust dun, and he was passed about, rocked to sleep, talked to and sung to and understood only Malay" (Gardam [2004] 2013, 24). Ada, embedded in her native environment, represents "home" in Eddie's life, yet he is separated from her when he is four years old and later unable to remember her. The enforced early departure leaves him in despair and bewilderment; he never mentions Ada again and thereupon develops a stammer throughout his youth. After the death of the mother following (and caused by) the birth of a son and, in congruence with this, the violent death of the foster mother in England, suppression and the Imperial law of the father reign supreme. At first they are represented by Alistair Feathers, the District Officer, who incorporates British administration in Malaya, later by "Sir", the headmaster of the English prep school. The third-person narrator treats these men at best with light irony which extends to Old Filth when he is Sir Edward and an admired representative of the law of the father(land). Flashbacks and flash-forwards ignore the existence—or the lack—of a mother.

In *House of Orphans* by Helen Dunmore, a writer popular in Britain for her historical novels, the dead mother and the memory of her are almost totally obliterated by the narration. The setting is Finland in the early years of the 20th century, with families in upheaval because the search for a better life forces people to emigrate. The nation is in a state of political unrest due to Russian usurping imperialism.[19] The main focaliser, Eeva, is a fifteen-year-old inhabitant of the orphanage for girls when the narrative opens. "Her mother had died when Eeva couldn't remember, and her aunt lived with them until she married. Eeva was seven then, and could manage the cooking. Her father worked in the shipbuilding yard" (Dunmore 2007, 29). Henceforth she regards herself as her father's talisman. "'Because of Mum dying when I was born'" (30) she imagines herself in her place, but when her father dies she is taken to the orphanage. There, at the bid of the doctor who is in charge of the institution, she assumes maternal functions for a sick child who like many children would otherwise die because "[t]hey have no mothers", as he states (6). Eeva has lost both parents, but it is only her father whom she remembers and who continues to shape her life by his presence in the girl's mind as her teacher and master of her childhood universe. Through her father's political involvement as a Communist and because of the familiarity with his ideas she develops into an unusually autonomous girl. At the age of thirteen, the threshold of her coming-of-age phase, she is by force taken from Helsinki to the orphanage in the sparsely populated countryside, with the intention of "changing her from what she was into an orphan, ready for service" (26). "An orphan" is not merely a parentless young person; the contemporaneous concept of "orphanhood" implies permanent immaturity, submission to the *weltanschauung* of an institution, later of a master or a mistress; it means exclusion from social processes, conformity, indeed de-personalisation. The girls in the orphanage are being drilled for domestic service and regarded as unable to read or to make mental or emotional progress, since they are perceived as bereaved of ancestry, moral guidance as well as material possessions and therefore incapacitated to develop identity, autonomy or intellect. The protagonist resists this transformation: "They'd taken her away and tried to make her into an orphan, but it hadn't worked. She was still Eeva. Inside her, where the jewel of her father's anger burned, she was Eevi" (35). To live in the hustle of the city again and join friends in the fight for Finland's liberty from Russian rule remains Eeva's prime objective when, at sixteen, she is placed in the same widowed doctor's household. Even though she can lead a relatively comfortable life there she does not settle, while he is torn between memories of his dead wife, who had terrorised their only daughter as a child, and the attraction towards the young girl. Eeva flees—eventually with Dr Eklund's consent—to Helsinki.

In microstructural portrayals Dunmore's and Gardam's novels reflect a society that is not only mentally and socially, but also biologically unable to reproduce social order and continuity from a problematic heredity: Edward Feathers and his wife Bess, like him a Raj orphan, remain childless; Anna-Liisa, the headmistress of Dunmore's Finnish orphanage, is—like the Baptist missionary in Malaya—not a mother and does not consider herself in the place of a mother (14); Doctor Eklund's motherless daughter is married, but has no child and eventually mentions pregnancy as a mere dream (318). Mothers whom he treats as a physician regularly almost die giving birth. Gardam's and Dunmore's narratives provide representations of a system that is coming to an end. In 1904 the house of orphans in Finland harbours the remains of a political, socio-cultural and economic malaise which the rule of the Tsar, the privileged position of Swedish Fins and the failed attempts at a civil revolution for autonomy brought about (cf. 128; 132; Oppermann 2015, 178-179); Edward Feathers, high-ranking member of the colonial administration of justice, represents "the last of the last" after Hong-Kong finally also became independent. The barrenness of a colonial situation is thus also figuratively expressed in each of the novels. Where the mothers of the young protagonists are dead without having left a trace of the living person the orphans themselves do not parent a child. Moreover, it is of importance that the diegetic strategies of these stories do not highlight the gap left by the dead mother as a blank in the symbolic order: in these popular novels the narrative fails to signal the empty space, while the mother's functions are to a certain degree ostensibly replaced. By contrast, the dominance of male characters, their ideas and dealings, appear overwhelmingly formative in the life of the male orphan Edward Feathers, who as an exiled child hushed up his Malay carer, later killed the Raj orphans' foster mother and then becomes a prime representative of the law. Patriarchal overbearance combined with an absence of the mother is equally present for the orphaned girl Eeva, whose engagement for male friends and political freedom is replete with traps and dramatic irony. In representations more unreflected and less complex than in other novels from this sample Gardam's and Dunmore's texts exhibit the elements of the incomplete symbolic order as if for a teaching lesson.

2.2 Blank Space

If in the above examples the representation of the mother's death/absence and the orphan's mourning are diegetically suppressed the reverse is true of Margaret Atwood's *The Blind Assassin* (2000), Graham Swift's *Wish You Were Here* (2011) or Toni Morrison's *A Mercy* (2008). In each of these novels the substance and symbolic meaning of motherless-ness receive an enormous impact, which raises the reader's awareness regarding a symbolisation of an absence in the imaginary prevailing in society. In *The Blind Assassin* the loss of the mother by death and of the father by absence, depression and finally suicide characterise a dysfunctional family. All of these events are explicitly presented in Iris's autobiographical narrative together with the emotional reactions of the two sisters—the narrator and her younger sibling. The interwoven and obscured identities of Laura and Iris Chase show how it is impossible for the orphaned sisters to cut their one remaining tie. It seems to be broken off when Laura commits suicide, but is insolubly revived through the writing and publication of the first "novel" embedded in the novel, which bears Laura's name but has been authored by Iris.

Margaret Whitford's exposition on Irigaray's psychoanalytic findings states "that [women] tend to relationships in which identity is merged and in which the boundaries between self and other are not clear. However she [Irigaray] presents this psychoanalytic diagnosis as a symptom or result of women's position in the symbolic order" (1991a, 80; cf. Whitford 1991b, 160-61). Therefore, she contends, portrayals of women and especially of mothers are also not individuated. In *The Blind Assassin* such a "confusion of identity" (Whitford 1991a, 81) can be considered as the foundation on which the first of the embedded novels rests: Iris, its true author and the first-person narrator of the framing autobiography, poses as Laura. On the story level, the frame tale depicts the impossibility to sever the bond between the sisters and their dead mother conceived as a living person, respectively the tie between Iris and Laura, as the following examples show. On her tenth birthday, the elder girl feels embarrassed because the birthday cake might hurt Mother's feelings, since they celebrate without her (Atwood 2001, 173). At the same time Iris cannot clearly remember their mother "or what she'd really looked like: now she looked only like her photographs" (173). Instead of a clearly revoked image in Iris's mind, only the photograph, a "secondary" visual representation of the icon "Mother" remains and shapes her strained memories. Iris reports how Laura regresses upon the loss of the mother and spends much time inside her mother's fur coat, buttoning it up completely—to merge with or "inhabit" her. Recognising that this is not a rational act, Iris calls it "conjuring Mother back" (167). Several weeks later, Iris rescues her younger sister from the river in which she had thrown herself on purpose, "'So God would let Mother be alive again'" (183), as she says. Exchanging her life for her mother's, which, the child believes, had been literally taken by the unborn baby her mother had lost, might revive her.[20] Tellingly, Iris's duty to guard her sister in the place of a parent cannot be fulfilled, since a woman is unable to shield another woman (see also below). It becomes impossible for her to protect Laura[21]—or herself— from the conspiracy of the Griffens: Richard, to whom Iris had been contracted or surrendered to save her father's reputation and his enterprise, and Winifred Griffen, Iris's sister-in-law. The evil that the Griffens commit turns the orphaned girls into victims of the ruling power which establishes itself due to financial and thereby socio-political superiority coupled with male oppression. Iris concludes that except for the faked authorship Laura—like her mother—will vanish into a void: "A few years more and it would be almost as if she'd never existed" (620). Laura can—

again similarly to her mother—only be remembered by her officially distributed photograph (622) as a renowned writer. While in the narrator these pictures raise doubts about their likeness with the original it is the destruction of another photo by which Iris had actually eliminated Laura's presence (631-32) as her *doppelgänger*: her sister's likeness has literally been cut out from the visual representation of a happy moment with Alex Thomas, their shared lover. That Iris's own existence has ever been precarious imposes itself on the aged narrator and the reader alike.

The maternal line in Atwood's novel does not cease to exist, however. Iris is the mother of a daughter whose name is Aimée, and Aimée was not fathered by Richard Griffen, Iris's Bluebeard-like spouse and destroyer of Laura. After Richard Griffen's death Aimée is taken from her mother by Winifred to destroy Iris as well; the law (law of the father, literally) is on Winifred's side. Winifred, acting out what her brother had planned, also determines the hegemonic narrative about his and the Chases' fate (624-25), whereas all Iris can do is to present an encoded "counter narrative": the first embedded novel *The Blind Assassin* and its frame tale. By writing it she implicitly claims the interpretational sovereignty over her sister's memory, yet she aims at yielding it again, because by the public Laura is wrongly perceived as a celebrated artist and author of the nested narrative *The Blind Assassin*. The narrator's struggle for identity and authenticity continues until she is close to death.

Iris Chase, however, is an exceptional orphan in one respect: she has given birth to a child. It is Sabrina, Iris's missing granddaughter, on whom the narrator's hope rests and whom she addresses with the revelation of an ancestry which altogether annihilates the paternal line: Sabrina's grandfather, she writes, is Alex Thomas, the rebel and lover Iris and Laura shared, himself an orphan whose father was unknown. "'You're free to reinvent yourself'" (627), Iris tells Sabrina. It is the continuation of the maternal line that assures Iris's being: "*Grandmother*, you will say, and through that one word I will no longer be disowned" (636, emphasis in original). Because "disowned" she was as a child and a mother as well as through the publication of the book of which she is the true author. Atwood's novel ardently exposes the problems of a woman's "presence"—the mother's, Laura's, Iris's own—by "conjuring" her up through thematising her absence as a stupefying blank and probing ways of representation. The narrator-writer addresses a woman's eradication as symbolically shown in the mutilated picnic picture. The instances of "absenting" her also point at the rule of the traditional symbolic order and its gaps or deficiencies.

(Self)annihilation is conspicuous as a theme with variations in Atwood's *Blind Assassin*. I wish to argue that the narrative communicates a discernible unstableness regarding the symbolic representation of the mother in the orphaned girls' memory, while the visual mark—the mother's photographic picture—is also too ambiguous to resist destruction. When gaps and absences take centre stage in the narrative the paradoxical effect will be that eventually a void "materialises". This achievement can be regarded as a representational bravery and this writer's act of resistance, since neither Dunmore nor Gardam allowed the empty space to become manifest. It may seem bold to continue this exploration by tracing the topic of orphanhood and the dead mother also in Atwood's dystopian novel *Oryx and Crake* (2003). Yet the author's inclination towards a representation of anti-utopian fantasies has been shown before, e.g. in *The Handmaid's Tale* and the innermost tale of *The Blind Assassin*, a work of speculative fiction allegedly composed by the sisters' lover. Dystopian Romance reappears in Atwood's 2015 novel *The Heart Goes Last*.

Snowman, the reflector figure of the third-person narrative of *Oryx and Crake*, embodies an orphan in a very radical sense: he is apparently the last survivor of the species *homo sapiens sapiens* on a destroyed and overheated planet. A book of revelation like *The Blind Assassin*, the novel uncovers the narrative past in retrospect, following the recollections of the focaliser Snowman. As a child he was deserted by his mother, who quarrelled with his father about the ethics of science. When he is still Jim, "he dreams again, it's his mother. No, he never dreams about his mother, only about her absence" (Atwood 2003, 277). Since as a person she is gone, Jimmy tries to retrieve her former presence by putting on her dressing gown, confusing his own self with her absent one, for which he hates her. Later, his friend Crake becomes aware of the problem her dispatch causes for Jim as a young man: his mother had disagreed with the experiments undertaken by super (or mad) scientists such as her husband or Crake. She joined the organised opposition, was sentenced for "treasonable crimes against society" (286) and eliminated.[22] The fact that true crimes against humanity have been committed by Crake in disseminating a lethal virus together with a new "bliss pill" for which only the three friends Jim, Crake and the girl Oryx have been administered the effective antidote, leads to Snowman's Robinson-like lonely survival. Out of revengeful jealousy, Oryx was killed by Crake, whom Jim killed thereupon. Jim-Snowman has by Oryx been obliged to assume responsibility as a pseudo-father for the Crakers—post-human creatures designed by their now dead eponym. Eventually Snowman takes them from the Paradice Dome, a sealed virus-free place where their god-like

creator had them raised, to an Edenic seashore landscape. There the
natural surroundings of Mother Earth and the living creatures seem to
reach a pre-lapsarian state, Snowman being the only one conscious of the
manipulated, denatured and polluted condition this whole world, which
mainly consists of simulacra, is in. For the Crakers, ultimate designer
babies or humanoid products of gene manipulation, the symbolic order is a
tabula rasa, even though they are able to talk, or rather to produce
intelligible sounds.[23] When the Crakers ask Snowman "'What is this place
called?'" he answers "'It is called *home*'" (354, emphasis in original).

The nature of the artificial post-humans, who possess shrunken brains
but no subconscious, poses yet another difficulty to Snowman. Their
psychological peculiarity propels the principles of this narrated world onto
a philosophical and psychoanalytical level: any symbolic representation
had been identified by the Crakers' creator as the beginning of all human
misery. Consequently, every artistic activity or cultural pursuit was by
Crake suspected of leading step by step to evils such as war or slavery
(361), and an introduction of such ambitions had therefore been forbidden.
When the Crakers, who also call the human—formerly Jim—"Snowman",
spontaneously fabricate an effigy of him to effect his presence while he is
temporarily absent, the initial step towards symbolisation has been taken,
and they are making fatal "progress" (cf. Mohr 2007, 21). Evolution of the
symbolic order, it becomes evident, cannot be prevented in the post-
humans—these beings already speak. The inevitability is accounted for by
Dunja Mohr's explanations of the role of language (18-20).[24] The
scarecrow-like semblance is destroyed after his return, and Snowman feels
"as if he himself has been torn apart and scattered" (Atwood 2003, 363).
The representation and the represented—like the signifier and its
referent—barely escape confusion. At the end, however, Snowman detects
three more human survivors on the shore, who are not aware of him.
Whether he will continue with destruction or save the ideals of a peaceful
human community remains an open question. It follows from the novel's
closure that the satirical aspects are meant to dominate this generically
hybrid narrative, where the dystopian and the feminist are woven together
with numerous intertextual elements.

Graham Swift's *Wish You Were Here* (2011) makes of Vera Luxton's
death the beginning of the end for the social microstructure of the novel.
The earlier *Waterland* and *Wish You Were Here* display parallels regarding
the novels' character constellations, a similarity which even extends to the
name of one of the male protagonists: the brothers are Dick and Tom in
the 1983 novel, Jack and Tom in 2011.[25] The analogies include
orphanhood: Dick and Tom Crick as well as Jack and Tom Luxton lost

their mother as children or teenagers; their fathers commit suicide in exactly the same manner.

Vera Luxton's death emerges as the crucial event in the narrative past, after which her sons, her husband, and the farm, which his paternal ancestors had owned and worked for centuries, decline. The family disintegrates like the place where they live and similar to the macrostructure of a globalised world "off its hinges" (Swift 2011, 300). Despite Vera's functional importance for the family, which cannot be overrated, she remains pale as an individual in Jack Luxton's, the main reflector figure's, memories. In one scene on Remembrance Day, often recollected by her elder son, she obligingly performed a social ritual with the Distinct Conduct Medal that had posthumously been awarded to one of her husband's uncles killed in the Great War. Vera, "like some diligent curator, placed the medal itself before [Jack's father]" (12), thus displaying a token of masculinity and patriotism. Her identity is concealed and disappears behind the traditions of the paternal line—also the line of the law of the father—, which has for decades been the source of national and family pride. This ritual is habitually accompanied by her with "a man's story coming from a woman's lips" (12), which Vera repeatedly tells about the DCM (10-11).[26] To the "plain—proud, illustrious—facts" (12) of the master narrative she authentically adds one moving detail of her own, namely that the two brothers would have divided and shared the medal had they survived; with her invention Vera intends to celebrate brotherly solidarity. The void in the representation regarding the person of the mother in the face of the powerful "law of the father", which means battles abroad and at home, poses a threat apt to undermine the ruling symbolic order. That the personal is political and that anxieties affect traditions as well as national concerns becomes first apparent in the question which precedes the narrative text. It portends the mythical and imaginary vision of the country: "Are these things done on Albion's shore?" (n. pag.), a quotation from William Blake's poem "A Little Boy Lost"—the orphan theme. The orphaned character, in whom the destabilisation of the existing order—including the symbolic—becomes manifest, is the protagonist of *Wish You Were Here*, who doubtfully oscillates between respect for and rejection of the law of the father and patrimony.

Woman, the mother, the secret guarantor of the social order and its substratum, as Luce Irigaray had defined her, has been silenced and dismissed in these novelistic representations—by having her die. But whereas in *Old Filth* and *House of Orphans* her existence has simply been annulled, her representation minimised, and the social world of the narrative closed ranks upon her, so to speak, Atwood's and Swift's novels in retrospect mark the empty space and draw attention to the vacuity of the mother's image. In the orphan's mindscape, the dead mother remains without personalised individuality, yet is identified as the emblem of a secure and supposedly lasting order. The explicit and surprisingly identical phrasing of the mother's death in *The Blind Assassin* and *Wish You Were Here* supports the significance: "*This event changed everything*" (Atwood 2001, 107, emphasis in original) and "it was anyway an event that changed everything, like a line in history" (Swift 2011, 20). It is a contingency whose significance extends beyond the psychological impact on a fictional child remembered by the adult narrator/focaliser. Atwood's and Swift's representations parade the blank that threatens the symbolic order with disintegration—an anxiety disregarded by Gardam and Dunmore, which Swift and Atwood articulate and which the minds of their protagonists reflect.

2.3 "Not a Grain Left"

Several important aspects of the condition of orphanhood can be investigated in works of postcolonial fiction, broadly defined. Novels set in colonial North America, South Africa or in Britain exemplify that the representations of an orphaned state and the death or absence of the mother explore cultural faultlines of particular topicality in recent decades. Therefore the present and the subsequent sections include narratives for which criticism has not specifically addressed the orphaned situation of the characters, even though the works have received scholarly attention.

"He tore a black strip from the lining of his mother's coat and pinned it around his arm. But he did not miss her, he found, except insofar as he had missed her all his life" (Coetzee [1983] 1998, 34). The negativing statement is a quotation from an enigmatic narrative, which was awarded the Booker Prize in 1983 and is reappreciated here because of the protagonist's solitariness, re-emerging in 2002 in another isolated young man in Coetzee's more recent novel *Youth*. The mother has been dead all his life to Michael, the disconcerting protagonist of J.M. Coetzee's *Life and Times of Michael K.*, who spends his time near his mother during her illness and carries her in a cart from Cape Town to the Stellenbosch hospital where she dies. The education he received first at the state school Huis Norenius, later in the camps from which he escapes, consisted of discipline, submission and manual work (cf. López 2011, 119); the tenor of these institutions corresponded to the one portrayed in other fictional orphanages (cf. Dunmore; cf. also the discussion of Roberts' *The Looking Glass* below).

At the beginning, only a third-person narrator can give information about the person and situation of Anna K. Her son Michael is a functional orphan with his mother still alive and even present—to him she was never there. Her life as a domestic servant, like that of her son, is a hardly perceived non-existence in the African underclass of South Africa during the time of apartheid.[27] Inarticulate and handicapped since childhood to the degree of muteness and considered dim by those who address him, he emerges as an odd focaliser, mostly distanced by third-person narration, at times complemented by the perspective of a white doctor.[28] The orphaned boy's odyssey leads him from the city into the country to become a cultivator after having been a carer, and at the end back to the place where they had lived in Cape Town. The state of homelessness and the condition of orphanhood—even though he is a grown man—fuse in his unrelational identity. "All these years, and still I carry the look of an orphan" who subsists on alms, he observes (Coetzee [1983] 1998, 181). Being a gardener and remaining silent he continues to live without want or need; his existence contradicts and subverts the templates of modernity and the value-system of the South-African apartheid regime as well (López 2011, 119-23).[29] As a pre-modern vegetable being, K. only wishes to reach "deep into the earth" for a spoonful of water on which "one can live" (Coetzee [1983] 1998, 184).[30]

In her sub-chapter "The double meaning of the word nature" (Whitford 1991b, 200-01) Luce Irigaray[31] elaborates how the connection frequently made between nature and woman/mother and "the fertility of the earth" (200) has become problematic.[32] The—according to Irigaray—ambiguous meaning of the word *nature* results from the working of the patriarchal order as dominating and exploitative. Its ambiguousness "corresponds to the beginnings of *non-respect for nature*" (200, emphasis in original) because of "the obligation for women, to give birth to children *within their husband's* [sic] *genealogy* (200, emphasis added). Therefore, Irigaray contends, a masculine and a feminine concept of nature exist, pejorative or assertive, accordingly. Anna's death and her son Michael's flight from servitude in the disciplinary system created by "the law of the father"—the ostensibly paternalistic apartheid regime—obliquely strengthen his awareness and love of nature and the earth, into which he almost wishes to crawl. The image of "a cord of tenderness" (66) is interpreted by a critic as an "umbilical cord", through which Michael feels himself connected to the fertile ground where his plants grow (Attridge 2004, 52). With reference again to Irigaray and clearly supported by the orphaned protagonist's wish

to depart without offspring, the previously defended argument is
strengthened that orphanhood may also prohibit future generations: the
literary orphans do not procreate. With Michael K. the orphan state
signifies a condition which does not even generate a presence in any
common imaginary—whether male or female, black or white. Nor does a
black man in that time and place occupy a space in the symbolic order or
is noticed as missing in it. Witnessing his mother's death and her
cremation, Michael K. realises his own vanishing: "There will be not a
grain left bearing my marks, just as my mother has now, after her season
in the earth, been washed clean, blown about, and drawn up into the leaves
of grass" (Coetzee [1983] 1998, 124). Only the bond with Nature proves
elemental.

Michael K. forms a contingent contrast to the reflector figure of Coetzee's
Youth (2002), a novel which addresses the hybridity of autobiographical
fiction, published twenty years after *Life and Times of Michael K.*.[33] The
reflector figure in *Youth*, a young white man, leaves his home, with defiant
intertextuality "proving something: that each man is an island; that you
don't need parents" (Coetzee 2003, 3) and escapes from his literature
studies and his paid job in South Africa to London to become a poet (40).
By abandoning a place, he also wishes to draw a line in his personal
history: "Will his mother not understand that when he departed Cape
Town he cut all bonds with the past?" (98). He appears as a voluntary
orphan, Kristeva's "stranger"-migrant, who struggles for identity and
fulfilment in an anonymous, indifferent or antagonistic environment. John
is alienated from the past, the oppressiveness of parents, and frustrated by
his fatherland. The despair which he had experienced there yields to a
gradual but infallible disillusionment in the European metropolitan city
and England's rural areas, where he is prepared to fight for his success but
only has to toil for survival and feels more and more estranged when
approaching a slow, gradual and entropic end: "At eighteen he might have
been a poet. Now he is not a poet, nor a writer, nor an artist. He is a
computer programmer, a twenty-four-year-old computer programmer in a
world in which there are no thirty-year-old computer programmers" (168).

His disappointment becomes more profound than the disappearance of
the longing for ideals and personal recognition would explain: "How can
anyone in England understand what brings people from the far corners of
the earth to die on a wet, miserable island which they detest and to which
they have no ties?" (148), he can only ask himself, since nobody is there to
whom he could communicate his frustration and defeat. Lack of
relationality and friendship ruins the life of John, who epitomises
Ishiguro's general definition quoted at the beginning of this chapter about

the disconcerted young person at a loss in the world. More specifically, he is a "postcolonial orphan," estranged and separated from the territory and the community of the former colonists. Upon the publication of *Youth* the reviewer in *TLS*, who obviously expected a coming-of-age novel in the pattern of a *bildungsroman*, complained about missed literary opportunities: "There are no picaresque adventures, no comic interludes, not even much in the way of illustrative *faux pas*" (Porter, qtd. from Attridge 2004, 157, emphasis in original). John is not only a mourner; he would, according to Freud's distinction, have to be classified as a melancholic.

After his prospects regarding professional work—which he considers a vocation—and love have failed, he knows that there is no return to the place he came from (Coetzee 2003, 140). Realising that at best he may have "a toehold in the British computer industry, in British society, in Britain itself" (168) since he is still young, he also faces that other possibility of complete failure, namely physical or psychological annihilation, towards which his colleague, another immigrant, is already steering:

> He and Ganapathy are two sides of the same coin. Ganapathy starving not because he is cut off from Mother India but because he doesn't eat properly, because despite his M.Sc. in computer science he doesn't know about vitamins and minerals and amino acids; and he [John] locked into an attenuating endgame, playing himself, with each move, further into a corner and into defeat. (168-69)

Lack of practical knowledge about everyday matters and neglect of the self seem to enclose them both in a stale, trite life.[34] Since they do not participate in any social, national or cultural community, either that of their place of origin or of the European country into which they immigrated, a state of life-threatening depression prevails, which renders them indifferent to pragmatic issues. They have arrived at a point where they are without ties or imagination, and the vision that they will cease to exist and vanish from any relation, context or affiliation becomes familiar to the protagonist. The closure of the novel does not open a perspective towards the youth's "double sense" of being a post-colonial person with a culturally hybrid identity (Naipaul, qtd. from Folks 2003, 76n1), but only offers a devastating balance which leaves an alternative between giving in (to socio-economic pressures), respectively giving up (aspirations and purposes), or slow physical self-destruction.

The narrator of *Youth* underlines the protagonist's coldness especially towards his mother as a reason for his flight from the Cape region—manifestation of a voluntary, definite separation which extends to the mother-country, like Ganapathy's "Mother India". The portrayals of Coetzee's male protagonists in the two novels and the "disappearance" of the mother that is not missed by either Michael or John receive an additional illumination against the theoretical background of Lacan's and Irigaray's explanations. *Life and Times of Michael K.* reveals that there is not just *one* symbolic order, as there is not simply *the* imaginary—unified and authoritative. Masculinity does in Coetzee's 1983 narrative not safeguard the black man against the absence from either the imaginary or the symbolic. Instead of *the* order one would have to speak here of the Western order of European derivation, whose traditionally hegemonic status several of the novels discussed in this chapter exhibit.[35]

John, the aspiring poet and scholar, felt already dislocated when and where he was ambivalently "at home" during the late nineteen-forties and -fifties. The reason was his awareness of South African realities, for instance when he faced a black workman. This added to his mood of "unbelonging", which he generally experienced as a young person and striving artist,[36] yet specifically as a descendant of the colonisers and therefore from childhood suffering from "contamination in the colonial legacy" (Head 1997, 7):[37]

> Deeper than pity, deeper than honourable dealings, deeper even than goodwill, lies an awareness on both sides that people like Paul [John's friend] and himself, with their pianos and violins, are here on this earth, the earth of South Africa, on the shakiest of pretexts. (Coetzee 2003, 17)

The focaliser senses there and then that in the eyes of South Africans of Dutch or British descent as well as black people he must appear a simpleton with his humanist or romanticising social notions, since he feels a gloomy future approaching for themselves and perhaps the country. Like Maureen Smales in Gordimer's novel *July's People*, John, whose ancestors had also arrived to unapologetically claim the land (cf. López 2011, 230), is orphaned in the aftermath of colonisation. Maureen, desperate and alone, tries to escape by air to save her life, while John flees from what he can neither consider his ancestors' rightful property nor his cultural and emotional "home". He flees to retain his self. European "cities of art"—Paris, London, Vienna (Coetzee 2003, 41)—seemed to promise him a full, inspiring and dynamic life with none of the despondency of the stalled situation that oppressed him in Cape Town in the late fifties; yet in England his yearning remains unfulfilled in the following decade. His orphaned condition, which cannot be tempered by the fleeting affairs he has with women, becomes manifest in a passage where he briefly meets his temporary girlfriend's English land-lady and tries to decode her facial expression:

> It is not a good time to be a South African in England. With great show of self-righteousness, South Africa has declared itself a republic and promptly been *expelled* from the British Commonwealth. The message contained in that *expulsion* has been unmistakable. The British have had enough of the Boers and of Boer-led South Africa, a colony that has always been more trouble than it has been worth. They would be content if South Africa would *quietly vanish* over the horizon. They certainly do not want *forlorn* South African whites cluttering their doorstep like *orphans in search of parents*. (86-87, emphasis added)

The communality of the microcosm as well as the macrocosm has disintegrated; John's own situation reflects that of the greater "family". A state of dislocation and exclusion, in which he finds himself in England, shatters his hopes and, moreover, makes him doubt whether he "is worth the trouble" other people might go to in appreciating and possibly befriending him.[38] As one of this special class of postcolonial orphans he cannot shed the past and the nationality he has left behind, nor can he enter another society with its own history, self-image and orientation, which he primarily notices in terms of it being a capitalist, competitive economy. To "quietly vanish over the horizon" expresses the way he also envisages his individual fate like that of his neighbour from India, whom nameless stretcher-bearers may soon bring out "with a sheet over his face" (169) that is veiling his identity. The protagonists of Coetzee's two novels intimate the notion to the reader that decolonisation only leaves orphans behind. Gordimer's July, the reader may speculate by means of extrapolation, forebodes a changing role and position for black people in South Africa.

2.4 "There Is No Protection"

(Post)colonial functional orphans such as John, who exemplify cultural orphanhood and dislocation, share major traits and situations with the literally orphaned protagonists by authors Margaret Atwood and Graham Swift. The following narratives about the orphan condition and the dead mother are set in diverse ages and parts of the world. They offer representations of the silenced and marginalised individuals whom the symbolic order has remained largely unaware of.

Breakup and social decline are conveyed by the life of the mother Monica Wilson née Johnson, the major figure in *The Lost Child* (2015) by

Caryl Phillips. The novel's title may refer to each of the protagonists in the main plot and the frame tale. It alludes to Monica, the prodigal daughter, who gets lost as an Oxford student and is estranged from her apparently well-meaning, educated father on account of her black lover/husband, by whom she is soon to be a mother. Furthermore, "the lost child" points at Monica's younger son Tommy, who disappears at the age of twelve and is found after a week, probably murdered by his mother's new boyfriend—a gloomy event and a riddle which remains largely unsolved. Finally, it applies to Ben, Tommy's elder brother, who is one of the focalisers and narrators. Ben literally becomes an orphan at fourteen after his mother's suicide following his brother's mysterious disappearance and death.

In fact, nobody can accept liability for the family's collapse of status, relatedness and belonging, even though scapegoating would make of Monica the real culprit of the disaster. In the eyes of the civil society of the sixties and its fictional representatives she is an upper-middle-class, educated but stubborn and inconsiderate young woman, who may be held responsible for her own life and that of her children. However, the narrative leaves little doubt that she has been rejected, abandoned, excluded or used by each of the male characters and that alienation prevails in Monica's experience. While after her divorce she does not seek reconciliation with her bourgeois parents her father realises her and her children's dislocation when she moves from Britain's South back to the North: "He saw them huddled together on the platform like evacuees, and all that was missing was their name tags" (Phillips 2015, 54). They are already "lost" even before the situation deteriorates. When Ben asks his mother "'Doesn't your mam and dad want us to stay with them?'" Monica evasively answers: "'No, love, we were *only visiting*. We just popped in to say hello, and now we're off to our own flat'" (196, emphasis added). Self-reliance, for the young woman, turns out to be synonymous with isolation. As they are growing, her small sons recognise that theirs is a dysfunctional family, which adds shame to precariousness and marginalisation to such a degree that Tommy, who is mobbed and victimised by his peers, at one moment wishes he were an orphan. Existentially, he already is one. Worries and concerns are largely caused by their mother who proves unable to hold a job, properly care for them, or get along with their teachers, father or grandparents—in one word who "cannot keep things under control". The omniscient narrator comments on Ben's response when the boy receives the news of his mother's death: "He had been sure that things couldn't get any worse than they already were" (201). Monica's own increasingly confused focalising exhibits her imaginary flight from an environment that appears invariably bleak and unwelcoming. In the face of the steady decline, her imaginings eventually become hallucinatory. In her dreams she again moves towards the prosperous South and higher education, while deterioration rules her everyday reality. Alternating backgrounds in Leeds and London show the desolation of council estates for children or their single mothers. The three lonely and forlorn characters move in a kind of "desert" or "blank"; they are in a state of abandonment, whether in the city or the countryside, alone or in busy surroundings.

The moors represent a place of crime and gloominess where Ben withdraws to mourn his younger brother: "I could feel the moors closing in on me, and for the first time in ages I began to feel close to my brother" (189). Separation and isolation can only be suspended in death, as this first-person narrator seems to impart, whereas accusations or assignments of guilt express above all the widespread helplessness in the light of a breakdown of family and social structures. Failed communication marks the one-parent family as well as Ben's foster homes (128, 176), the holiday camp or the contact with social institutions; examples are numerous, and Ben's summarising report on the depressing situation may suffice to illustrate desperate muteness: "And so we sat together for nearly an hour, me itching to get up and leave and Mam with that vacant look on her face, and neither of us able to talk about what had happened to my brother" (178). The characters of the main narrative—none of them depicted as evil, but as constricting, cut-off and difficult to approach or sympathise with—offer resistance to stimulation or empathy, including the reader's. The void in which they move encapsulates each of them, with the youngest and most vulnerable child as the easiest victim of alienation and unrelatedness. The novel is marked by unexplained riddles and obscurities with regard to plot, themes and characters, but even more by the absentism of mothers (cf. Woodward 2015, n. pag.) either through death, obliteration, drugs or mental disturbance. Questions remain unanswered, truths are withheld on both the diegetic and the extradiegetic level: "I stared out of the window at the stars and wondered again about our Tommy. Where was he?" (Phillips 2015, 176).

It seems natural that the setting of the Yorkshire moors triggers the association with another fictional lost child: Heathcliff.[39] An alternative spin-off of his life-story as Mr Earnshaw's illegitimate son by a black woman forms the framing tale to the main narrative about Monica, Ben and Tom. This in turn encloses, as the innermost story, a depiction of the last days of Heathcliff's authorial creator: a portrayal of Emily Brontë's imaginary wretched death is inserted into the multiperspectival representation of the lost children from the mid-to-late 20th century, which is framed by the Heathcliff story. With its nonlinear time structure, the novel produces a matrix of intertextual references among the three narratives, while changes in perspective enable an illumination of the same occurrence, e.g. the failed visit of Monica at her son's foster home on Christmas Day, from contrasting angles. The different stories are interconnected by the *topoi* of the lost child and the socially undesirable madwoman—in the docks of slave-trading Liverpool, on the margins of the big cities in the 1960s, or at her life's end in the parsonage on the West Ridings of Yorkshire. By Phillips's narrator, a young male person is given a slim chance of integration into the civil society of his time, as retrospectively seen from the early 21st century and the biographical author's situation.[40] Heathcliff, the dark motherless boy, is eventually taken from the Liverpool slums to his father's house. Ben Wilson, only survivor of the one-parent family in the main narrative, can enter Oxford University.

Obviously, a mimetic reading or classification of *The Lost Child* as working-class novel is thwarted by its postmodern features, not least among them the evasion of the narrative to tie up the loose ends. It equally avoids the depiction of cruelties and deviations, even though some reviewers felt reminded of the Moors murders (Miller 2015, n. pag.), and although Phillips himself had lived near their site (cf. Wade 2015, n. pag.). It is the condition of lostness which proves central to this novel and around which its different stories are constructed. The text opens with the first-person narrative of a nameless dying woman—later revealed as Heathcliff's mother—, herself a former slave, but also the mistress of a well-to-do English gentleman. The embedded main narrative about the Wilsons ends with the death of another uprooted mother, Monica. She is conceived as a woman who desperately tries to redress her "invisibility" or her barely perceived non-existence, and she tries the more so the less likely she is to succeed. In the end she is defeated. Both women leave orphaned male children behind when they disappear in death. Mr Earnshaw finally acknowledges his illegitimate son, and so does an aged and widowed Mr Johnson with his grandson Ben, whom he gravely tries to meet at the university. From the point of view of the "lost and found" children, neither of these reunions appears in a happy light, because the heavy burden of a miserable forlorn past counteracts a renewed tie to their buried origins and a quasi-paternal support. It is, however, through individuals—invariably male—or male-dominated institutions occupying a firm place in the symbolic order that the lost children can have the opportunity to prosper: only the white middle-class family patriarch respectively the modern educational system are able to provide it.

Toni Morrison displays the trope of orphans and the dead mother in a different geographical and historical context. The concepts of "orphanhood" and "home" are dramatically linked in *A Mercy*, from which the heading of this part of my book chapter is quoted (Morrison 2008, 162, 166). Set in Virginia and Maryland in 1682 and 1690, with slavery becoming the economic pillar of the American colonies, the novel is addressed by critics as a narrativisation of the origins of the nation or, alternatively, as a "postnational novel" (Karavanta 2012, 723). Karavanta's analysis, founded in Cultural Studies theory (esp. E. Said), emphasises Morrison's repeatedly displayed interest in the "before" of the nation, but also draws a line from the perceived pre-national disparity and forlornness to the "hybrid and marginal communities" (739) of our time that also, the critic says, claim and deserve representation. Post-national portrayals of the United States would include migration, impoverishment and dislocation of the "unbelonging" on the fringes of society, whom Karavanta calls "the Orphans of Modernity" (2012, 730).[41] The use of the word "orphan" in the metaphorical sense receives a special meaning in connection with African American fiction, as Morrison's novels exemplarily show.[42]

The characters in *A Mercy* are without exception "colonial orphans", left without parents either by death or expulsion.[43] The white girl Rebecca is an immigrant from London, Lina a Native American whose community died from diseases imported by Europeans. "She sorted and stored what she dared to recall and eliminated the rest" (Morrison 2008, 50) the narrator summarises her self-reinvention when she lives in the white woman's service. "One comes from Eden, one from a necropolis; it's too pat to convince" is the critical comment of the reviewer Hilary Mantel on the descriptions of Lina's and Rebecca's respective origins. She regards the novel as a weaker replica of *Beloved* (Mantel 2008, n. pag.). The third girl, of mixed ethnicity, is named Sorrow and has been mentally damaged by her suffering in a shipwreck, yet eventually gives birth to a daughter and re-christens herself "Complete". Florens, the main focaliser and first-person narrator, an African slave, is separated from her mother and brother at the age of eight when at her mother's solicitation she is handed over to the travelling farmer and tradesman Jacob Vaark, who, as a premature Northerner, is not distinctly in favour of slavery. Because of this early separation Florens perceives herself as non-existent, and consequently rejection repeats itself in her life.[44]

The four orphaned young women in Vaark's household totally depend on men, whether English-born husband and master, Portuguese slave owner, or freed African American artisan. All the new-born children die, the last among them being Jacob's and Rebecca's five-year-old daughter.

When Jacob succumbs to smallpox and Rebecca, during her illness, is cared for by Lina, the servant clearly realises the forsakenness and unbelonging existence of the exiled: "As long as Sir was alive it was easy to veil the truth: that they were not a family—not even a like-minded group. They were orphans, each and all" (Morrison 2008, 59). Two of the prevailing features of orphanhood are paradigmatically displayed by the characters, as Vega-González states in a generalising way: "*A Mercy* is ultimately a novel about survival and self-invention, features which are inextricably linked to the idea of orphanhood" (2011, 130). Florens represents the Africans in the American and Caribbean colonies. Hence, "Florens is a symbol of the African Diaspora insofar as her painful status as orphan mirrors the condition of collective displacement" (Wardi 2011, 24), which includes, beside lack of family and "death" of the mother, also "the lack of place" (36). The annihilation not only of origins but of identity, which Vega-González refers to, produced orphanhood in the sense of deracination and depersonalisation that is explored in novels such as *A Mercy*.

The female protagonists' experience commands that a woman can only be saved by men (cf. Morrison 2008, 133). Since the remaining hope for the unattached women after the death of the man called "Sir", Jacob Vaark, seems to be a man faraway the African blacksmith is called back, who might know how to cure Rebecca. He is also Florens's lover, and the slave girl is sent on her errand with a letter to fetch him and seeks shelter from a thunderstorm in the house of a white settler. Her rootlessness becomes evident when Florens is asked by his English widow who she is and where she comes from, who her father is and where he lives: "I say I do not know him and my mother is dead. Her face softens and she nods saying, orphan, step in" (107). Only her white mistress's accompanying letter documents Florens's existence and her identity: "*She is owned by me and can be knowne by a burne mark in the palm of her left hand*" (112, emphasis in original). Florens affirms her state and tries to assert her existence in spite of the de-personalisation: "I am a thing apart. With the letter I belong and am lawful" (115). Even enslavement grants a rudimentary security, in contrast to being an outcast of humanity—"the Black Man's minion" (111, 113)—, such as the white witch-hunters are seeking at Widow Ealing's house. The performance of their corporeal inspection of Florens and the fussing about the letter provides a scene not totally devoid of comic grotesqueness. It turns, however, into a personal tragedy for the sixteen-year-old girl (111-13), whose bare life is saved. Marked now as an outlaw or mythical changeling Florens continues to fulfil her errand.

The post-national novel, Karavanta maintains about *A Mercy*, completes the national narratives by presenting "discourses that remained in [the national's] margins and were silenced or represented as the national order's undesirable alterities" (740), which she also calls "negative communities". If they are "silenced" by discourse as non-existent in the imagined community there remains an empty space in the symbolic order that may explicitly be marked as such—by narrativising the blank—or implicitly left to threaten this order by subversion. That only a change in the Symbolic can cause a restructuring of the Imaginary belongs among the ideas Luce Irigaray developed. Whitford summarises that the female imaginary is hampered because of "the structuration of the imaginary by the dominant symbolic order" (Whitford 1991a, 89). Stimulating an awareness of the gap in the symbolic by representing the disappearance of the mother does have an impact on the imaginary, for "it is the symbolic which structures the imaginary" (91). Hence a writer's urge to ostentatiously uncover the empty space in cultural material such as the novel.

To present a "decentering narrative" (Karavanta 2012, 739) is, similarly to Morrison's novel, also avowedly part of the intentions Caryl Phillips pursues in *The Lost Child*; Monica Johnson's way leads from the centre to a heterotopian place and, socially as well as psychologically, to the borders of her human community. By considering Morrison's and Phillips's representational efforts about lostness, the analogy between the orphans of colonisation and those of social alienation or exclusion becomes visible. This can hardly be denied, as the reviewer of *NYT Book Review* bluntly (though, I believe, in a simplifying way) states about *The Lost Child*:

> By layering Monica's story with those of Heathcliff and Brontë, Phillips poetically suggests that women (and often enough their helpless children) are society's unwanted outcasts, victims of a patriarchal system that oppresses them as wantonly and unthinkingly as a colonial power oppresses its territories. (Allen 2015, n. pag.)

Phillips aims at an interlaced narrative to exhibit "the confusions that people have around British identity and British belonging", phenomena that are linked to "this very powerful mythology we have about ourselves [in Britain] that doesn't square with reality". The reader's consciousness is raised regarding the representational "gaps" in fiction. S/he can perceive the different realities and "the pressures incumbent upon somebody living a life in Britain, whether it's in 1957 or 2015 or 1817" (Wade 2015, n. pag.).

By narrative representations the blank in the symbolic order, where Woman and the maternal lineage are often missing, can be either concealed or uncovered. A number of works of contemporary fiction make it apparent by thematising "orphanhood" in connection with the "death of the mother". In the novels discussed in this part of the chapter the more general validity of the following statement, which the critic claims for Morrison's *A Mercy*, becomes evident: "Lacan's dictum that women cannot enter the Symbolic Order is borne out in this society where the law is made by men, for men" (Stave 2011, 144). The literary examples have revealed the significance of "cultural orphanhood" (Folks 2003, 68), whose exhibition is not restricted to postcolonial fiction, though most prominent there. "Orphanhood has been employed by many writers and critics as a metaphor for the postcolonial condition" (76).[45]

Kazuo Ishiguro, who immigrated to Britain from Japan as a very young child, apparently wants to focus in his novels on the psychological situation of the young person at the moment of transition or initiation into adulthood. Indeed, several of the narratives under consideration here could also bear the tag "growing-up novel", but in all of them "orphan" has an extended functional in addition to the literal meaning.[46] If we look at the literary contemporary, the cultural signification of the orphan condition has increased in importance during the past thirty years.

3. "In the Place of a Parent"

3.1 The Problems of Substitution

The disappearance of parents as a caesura in a protagonist's life has become a hallmark of contemporary narrative fiction. In this section of my chapter I wish to address the narrativisation of survival strategies and developmental opportunities, by which the absence of parents is accommodated or compensated for. Although the *parens patriae* concept ("parent of the fatherland") in its literal sense seems to have a reference only to former times with the sovereign as governing power and parent of all subjects it is still valid as a legal doctrine: the state can act as parent of a minor. This concept has, for example, emerged in McEwan's *The Children Act* (2014). The novel shows how in the place of natural parents, even though they are alive and present, the intervention of the state (through a court) in their place becomes necessary and legal, if the welfare of a child requires it.

It is, however, neither the legal nor the biological meaning of the terms "substitute parent" or "surrogate mother" which the present examples of recent fictions about orphans address. I wish to look at the representations of emotional substitution and social guidance for the parentless children that several of the novels in hand perform. It is moreover a topic that with the publicly realised importance of institutional care is receiving increased critical attention from psychological and sociological studies.

As regards narrative literature, much ink has been spilled on the topic of stepmothers in the interpretation of fairy tales, yet very little attention was given to a possible replacement of parents in contemporary fiction. Margaret Atwood in *The Blind Assassin* exposes aspects of failed relationships concerning "substitute parentage". After their mother's death Laura and Iris Chase are cared for by the housekeeper Reenie, whom they later, as adults, have literally to accept as a family member, since Reenie's daughter Myra is very likely their father's child and thus Laura's and Iris's half-sister. Even though Reenie, after their mother's death, becomes more a carer than an employee, she distinguishes herself vividly in the aged narrator's memory from Iris's dead mother. Barriers established by class and upbringing prove insurmountable, sc that the woman who looks after the girls during their childhood cannot assume the assignment of emotionally filling the place of their dead mother or giving them an education, nor can this task be accomplished by their father's new mistress. For eighteen-year-old Iris, the educational function is claimed by Winifred Griffen, her unloved husband's snobbish sister, whom one critic even calls an incarnation of the wicked stepmother of the fairy tale (Peled 2010, 58). The motherless girls thus find themselves successively caught between extremes of social class and yet remain emotionally impoverished. They are locked in a desolate situation without hardly any prospect of relief, since their mutual protection also proves futile. There is no help after the loss of parents, who were supposed to be the guardians of their welfare.

Black Dogs, on the other hand, shows a more fortunate if late "substitution" for dead parents in Jeremy's in-laws. Intellectual aspects and challenges prevail in his relation to them, which begins when he is an adult. Consequently, his relaxed attitude in discussions and his ability to bridge discrepancies render their relationship untroubled. McEwan's novel makes the reader amenable for the ambiguity inherent in loss and promotes a flexible identity with a detached yet conciliatory attitude regarding affective ties.

Jane Gardam's *Old Filth* presents a wide spectrum of "surrogate parenthood" for her protagonist, from the warmth of the indigenous girl who mothers the little boy in the tribal milieu of the Malayan long house before he is brutally separated from her, to the cruel foster mother in

Wales and the failing or fleeting connections with distant relatives or a friend's family during Edward's stay in prep and boarding school. In Helen Dunmore's *House of Orphans* the institution has become the determinant in the orphaned girl's life, until the local doctor takes her into his house. His patronising though sincere attempt to provide her with a good and secure existence while she works for him is eventually rejected by Eeva in favour of a return to the urban and politicised environment in which she had lived with her vividly remembered dead father. Dr Eklund, however, has assumed one important quality of a "substitute parent" for her: he is the last resort to whom she turns for help when her friend Lauri is in prison. Eklund's amorous designs remain unfulfilled; Eeva determinedly puts him in the position of a father and asks for a selfless gesture before leaving him behind and sending him back to his medical assignments. In Irving's briefly mentioned *The Cider House Rules*, the physician in charge of the orphanage also acts as a kind of substitute father for the boy Homer. In these novels, the doctor is the one and only person whose professional competence classifies him to watch over the health and prospect of a child entrusted to the institution.

Substitution or surrogacy in the sense of near-simulacra of a family reveals itself in the narratives as dysfunctional. At best, a substitute for dead parents is represented as a temporary helper providing shelter, financial means, or advice, in rare cases also affection and understanding for a limited time. At worst, a person with sadistic tendencies such as Edward Feathers's Welsh foster mother or someone with severe problems as in Ben Wilson's foster families only increases the difficulties in the lives of the fosterlings.[47] Different shades in-between enhance the conclusion that the substitution of missing parents in narrative representations is not an effective means to alleviate the condition of orphanhood. A substitute rather serves to reveal the complexity of the lack and, moreover, the ambivalence which characterises the state of the orphan. In the words of Ruth Cain, especially the disappeared mother "is a sticky immanence which does not allow any replacement" (2013, 421). In contrast to the fictional portrayals of nannies or black mammies, which, for example, William Faulkner presents in his fiction or Evelyn Waugh briefly delineates in *Brideshead Revisited*, novels in English after 2000 offer a sceptical approach to the motif of substitute mothers. The authorial "killing" of the mother in fictions proves to be an irreversible necessity to make the blanks in the imaginary as well as the symbolic visible.

3.2 The Orphan's Inverted Model Parent

Lionel Asbo, in truly Swiftean satirical manner, confronts the orphaned protagonist and the reader with a parent-replacement that eclipses Pip's benefactor in *Great Expectations*. Having sex with his seductive grandmother used to console Desmond Pepperdine when he was still mourning his mother three years after her death (Amis 2012, 4-5) in the narrative past. Ever since Desmond's father, a Trinidadian and Pentecostalist, had disappeared, his British uncle was appointed his legal guardian. Des introduces him in the letter to the agony aunt about the incest with his granny:

> *Apart from the legal question which is worrying me sick, theres another huge problem. Her son, Lionel is my uncle, and he's like a father to me when he's not in prison. See hes an extremely violent criminal and if he find's out I'm giving his Mum one, hell fucking kill me. Literally!* (5, emphasis in original)[48]

That Lionel has been "*like a father to* [Des]" is confirmed by third parties even later when Asbo is a rich prisoner and Desmond a promising, well-adapted young man. Interviewed after Asbo's release by a reporter for the daily paper the woman who talks to both uncle and nephew corroborates the boy's statement: "'More than once Des has claimed (in court) that Lionel was 'like a father' to him after he was orphaned at the age of 12. But there is nothing paternal about his greeting. 'Ah, here comes the soap-dodger,' says Lionel (for Des is of mixed race)" (150, parentheses in original).

Lionel Asbo, described as a "clueless foray into popular culture and working-class life, conducted with Amis's trademark gaudy, repetitive insistence" (Tait 2012, n. pag.), stages the proletarian and racist hero Lionel as a surrogate father to Desmond. Parenting, teaching and learning for life are enacted in a way unapproved by middle- or upper-class standards. Asbo's and his environment's authoritarian and exemplary methods are, however, revealed as efficient in so far as Desmond becomes a conservatively successful, law-abiding and happy citizen and family man! He follows the principle to always do the opposite of what his inverted education teaches him. The double negation of "normal" standards thus leads to affirmation. Asbo, however, remains true to his own self and his code of conduct, by which he makes the paternalistic mainstream society with their values and efforts look foolish. He has become famous and well-to-do when he lectures Des about the needs of his mates: "*These birds want a bloke with a bit of the devil in him, not ...*

*Not the good son. The grieving father. The caring partner—with his
empathy. Not the sad cunt who gives a fuck about West Ham* [Football
Club in East London]" (Amis 2012, 229). The absurdity of the provocative
confrontation of underclass stances and slang with middle-class notions—
including those of highbrow literature and its readers—renders this
sermon, like Lionel's advice to do something sensible, a softened mock
Modest Proposal.

The underworld of Lionel Asbo is a counterworld which adheres to
"mimicry in reverse" rather than to revolt; the lawless society obeys very
strict rules. There are law and punishment and a code of honour among
thieves. In the produced contrast with the established society carnivalesque
elements reign supreme. The *topos* of "the world upside down" mirrors the
hilarious and farcical in the standards of contemporary society. Not only
the celebrity cult, but education as well as child and youth protection
become the targets of satire in this novel. The world of Lionel Asbo
imparts to those outside that causality is nonsense, legal procedure absurd,
and goodwill folly. This is done in a narrative text which finally seems to
communicate confirmation and assent of the civil society after having
instigated anxieties. The exposure of hyperbole and a fun-loving style of
life are sideswipes at the bearing of mainstream society one decade after
the turn of the third millennium.

3.3 Mother Church and the Orphan

Among the representations of substitutes for disappeared parents an
outstanding parenting institution, whose importance was even greater in
the past, occasionally emerges in contemporary fiction: the Church. The
upbringing and guidance of orphaned children was traditionally a clerical
assignment, in modern times often transferred by subsidiary agreement
from the secular governmental authorities. In the two novels to be
explored here the clerical "parenting" is critically viewed.

The first literary example which shows a cleric as the guardian of an
orphan is an intertextual and metafictional historiographic novel about
medieval London by Peter Ackroyd, *The Clerkenwell Tales* (2003) (see
section 4 of this chapter). The second one is a feminist narrative, *The
Looking Glass* (2000) by Michèle Roberts, set in early-20th-century
Normandy. In either of the two novels, separated by a great distance
regarding the narrated time and disparate concerns of the authors, Mother
Church takes care of orphans in a dreary or joyless, possibly even
threatening, way. Roberts creates an orphaned girl, Geneviève, Ackroyd a
boy named Hamo, growing into a young man. Roberts's narrative

explorations parallel French feminist theories. *The Looking Glass*—like her *Daughters of the House* (1992)—could also be analysed under the heading "The Dead Mother" (cf. Cain 2013, 408-10; Gymnich 2013, 101, 109). As Roberts stated about her work in an interview in 2003, "a maternal body that is absent, dead or lost" can be regarded as a stamp of her novels (qtd from Martínez-Alfaro 2014, 132). The character and trope of the orphan is linked to the narrative about the "dead mother". I wish to focus here on the question how Roberts imagines a substitution of parents in an era at the end of which Europe was facing the outbreak of the First World War, before women had the right to vote and single mothers hardly ever found a way to take care of their children.

As in Dunmore's *House of Orphans*, the parentless state alone is not sufficient to produce the creature who is not born an Orphan, but made one—an emblematic figure. In addition to her loss of parents, the protagonist Geneviève in *The Looking Glass*, according to her own account, is shaped into an orphan by the treatment she receives in the orphanage: "Walk close to the walls, eyes lowered. Don't answer back. Silence at meals and in the dormitory. […] If we failed at self-control then the cane was there to teach us better" (Roberts 2000, 7). The female orphan is a humble, featureless young person prepared to meekly serve her superiors as an adult (7-11). Regardless of whether an institution run by the state or by a religious order is in charge, the female orphans are shaped in the image of de-personalised, passive beings.

Roberts is another woman writer who gives priority to traditionally marginalised female voices in the narrative. *The Looking Glass* connects alternating female focalisers who reflect events and other characters. The main first-person narrator Geneviève Delange, as the nuns had christened the parentless infant delivered at their door (9), recalls her time in the orphanage near Etretat in retrospect, starting her narrative at the moment when she leaves it to wait on a widowed woman who runs a café in the small town of Blessetot.[49] Geneviève's fantasies about the unknown woman who gave birth to her (7-9) exhibit her idealising nostalgia. Her employer Madame Patin soon represents the desired mother for the orphaned girl, who fervently attaches herself and will soon be deeply disappointed, as the girl's euphoria already leads the reader to expect:

> I was floating like a cloud in the sky. I loved Madame Patin. I had never loved anyone before. This was what it must be like to have a mother, I thought, this loving her and being allowed to be near her; normal and real; the most ordinary thing in the world. Love was so precious, yet it was so strong. It lifted me up and made me want to do great things. It made me capable of enduring anything. (33-34)

In the orphanage, daydreams were condemned as dangerous and recognised as subversive just like storytelling (cf. Gymnich 2013, 105). Significantly, the Church, which has traditionally played the role of maintaining patriarchal power structures (106), is here exclusively represented by women, namely the nuns at the orphanage with Sister Pauline as the only one who has a name, though not an individuality. Mme Patin represents the antagonist to the nun: when Geneviève has entered her service, she discourages the girl to kneel and say her prayers during the day: "'For heaven's sake, child, we haven't got time for that'" (Roberts 2003, 20). Madame Patin is the first to demonstrate that there exists something like an alternate way of life. Geneviève's response shows her lack of familiarity with a plurality of habits: "Nonetheless I was shocked at how an outsider was encouraging me to drop the orphanage ways. That was what made me feel I had really left" (20).

However, the most obtrusive mark left by the shaping in the orphanage on Geneviève is her recurring feeling of guilt about her sinful desires. It adds to the punishment through a violation which immediately follows her sexual awareness of her body in the looking glass and her open flirt with Frédéric Montjean, now Madame's husband and father of their child (94-95). Jealousy causes Geneviève to doubly hate him because of his harassment and his marriage. Though in danger of losing home and surrogate mother again, but also unable to bind Frédéric Montjean to herself and oust her friend she nevertheless continues to adore her, adding arrogance and pride to envy and hate. The baptismal ceremony of the couple's new-born child in the presence of the priest, neighbours and family members finally reduces the girl to what she was before:

> My status as a villager, as one of them, had slipped away like a shawl falling off. I was the outsider, their looks said, the orphan, the bastard, the odd girl who prowled the beach and the cliffs for hours and had no friends, and perhaps I had brought the family bad luck. (93)

The image of the shawl makes the temporary and fleeting nature of Geneviève's belonging visible. Other passages point at clothes as cultural symbols of status and therefore the way in which the orphan is to be perceived by her social environment: she continues to wear the shabby and worn clothes given to her at the orphanage a long time after she has left it.

Her desperate flight from unlawful sex in the Montjeans' house and the subsequent ostracism when the baby dies is followed by the nuns' rejection at the orphanage. The orphan's new job is to take care of the household chores elsewhere as well as of a little motherless girl, Marie-Louise, who lives with her grandmother and her uncle Gérard (101). The duplication of the orphan motif offers narrative alternatives concerning the life and education of an orphaned girl, but also leads to a confusion of female identities. Since the servant Geneviève and the English governess as well as the little girl herself are in love with Gérard, a writer and collector of pornographic photographs, all three females are punished by repeated loss (238). Geneviève tersely—not without satisfaction—states "I was the only woman left" (214). After Madame Colbert's death her corpse haunts Geneviève and incorporates the dead mother, "determined to exact vengeance" and kill her (224). The dead becomes the Other in a protean shape, merging with the mythical mermaid and Geneviève's own temporarily "buried" image: "She was the wicked girl who did not deserve a mother's love, who deserved to die, and so the ghost was coming for her and would get her and would not let her go" (223).[50]

The author uses Geneviève's voice to expose the mother-daughter relationship as pivotal and the mother's literal as well as symbolic death/disappearance as life-threatening. To heal the same wound in another orphan would become self-healing for the protagonist. Day-dreaming, Geneviève imagines herself in the role of the forgiven sinner and selfless female saviour:

> They [Gérard and his mistress] would be happy together and live happily ever after. Madame Isabelle would forgive me for having slept with Gérard. She would love Marie-Louise like a daughter. I would restore the child to the mother. I would restore the mother to the child. The child would not die. The mother would not die. The damage would be mended and the breakage healed. The mother would be reunited with the daughter (247).

This verbal panegyric symbolically establishes a counterweight to rational thinking such as an enlightened, cognitive—presumably masculine—discourse would present it. While the dreamlike mode characterises Roberts's novel in many places (cf. Gymnich 2013, 103), the hymn of the mother-daughter relationship also corroborates the emphasis Irigaray put on the female lineage. *The Looking Glass* makes the impossibility of a substitute palpable by showing that a restitution of the vital relationship can only take place in the imaginary.[51] The sexual offences the narrator Geneviève has committed will be forgiven by the miracle she will work in restoring the mother to the child, which appears like an atonement of the Fall, which—according to Irigaray—is the matricide.

Moreover, in *The Looking Glass* the rivalry of women in general appears either as destructive or comical (255-57, 266-67) and is variously exemplified. Gérard, the only man in the novel's female community and a poet, dies the death of a war hero, as a telegram imparts (268). With neither of the two contrasting female characters that, on the story level, might have acted as mother substitutes to Geneviève, Sister Pauline and Madame Patin, a cognitive as well as emotional transference proves successful. The nun as replacement in the convent-orphanage fails because of her vowed denial of offspring, the second woman is in a socio-psychological conflict "taken away" by a man. Consequently, the symbolic order can only maintain the blank. The Orphan—in the radical sense of Roberts's portrayal—is deprived of any kind of lineage; the impossibility of recovering the lost object leaves only the alternative between death as self-destruction or the life in the company of the similarly deficient.

The attraction of the spot where Geneviève almost ended her own life out of despair is the sea, the symbol of femininity (cf. Gymnich 2013, 102), which she feels could be her home (108). To walk along its edge together with the other orphans, "all my fears of telling my story dissolving, insubstantial as sea-froth", becomes her final daydream (Roberts 2000, 277). Narrating, of whose importance Geneviève has painfully become aware, is able to overcome her fixation on the "Orphan" chiffre as a de-individualised image, which related the de-personalised girls at the orphanage to the uniform picture of the nuns or to that of the soldiers, one of whom the artist Gérard has become in the end. Of his fate Geneviève is still ignorant "in this early summer of 1914" (277).

4. The Foundling—a Mythical Creature

As Eva König states on the opening page of her book (1), the archaic literary orphan—Moses, Romulus, Remus—was a foundling of unknown yet legendary origin, predestined to acquire heroic significance. The mysteriousness of his ancestry paved the way to monumental fame (cf. Gymnich in this volume, 19). I contend that the enigma of veiled origins can still surface in contemporary fictions and envelop the protagonist with a certain charismatic aura. However, "Longing for Origins in Postmodern Times" became characteristic of literary orphan figures towards the end of the 20th century.[52] Actually, the topic mirrors current legislation, which respects this wish and grants every individual the right to know and trace his/her biological father and mother. In fiction, the quest for lost parents has turned out to be essential for the identity, happiness and self-image of the orphaned protagonists.[53] Contrary to a young exile's impulse to rid him-/herself of ancestral oppression and prove that "you don't need parents" (Coetzee 2003, 3; cf. also 32), the experience that every man *is* an island proves alarming to most orphans in the literary sample of this chapter. The construction of identity or individual life planning seems impossible to the orphan characters in the "foundling" novels, because they remain without concrete information about parents probably forever unknown. Kristeva's statements about the "foreigner" point to the conflictual novelty of an existence in surroundings where the social environment is ignorant of the stranger's ancestry (cf. 1991, 2-3). When the protagonist himself possesses no memory of his/her biological parents—a situation re-emerging and emphasised in fiction after 2000—a restless journey in search of them begins and may lead to a finish rather than to a rewarding closure which satisfies curiosity. The gaping hole in such a figure's biography robs his/her existence of legitimateness, and it entails a blank space in the self. Orphan characters of 19th-century fiction did not seem to care about the details of who their parents were, what they looked like, whether they had an education, property, friends or special qualities, nor about what they thought, felt, did or suffered. In the early-20th-century novels discussed in the chapter "The Gap" of the present volume, the orphaned characters were able to save their own early history and the childhood memory about their parents before they had died or gone absent. The destiny and image of the orphan without memory or past in contemporary novelistic portrayals will also be the subject of the following exploration.

4.1 The Flouted Orphan

The foundling reappears in different shape and role in 21st-century fictions. Hamo Fulberd, the orphan boy in Ackroyd's pseudo-medieval alternative narrative to Chaucer's *Canterbury Tales*, is a minor character. The novel *The Clerkenwell Tales* remains a minor work, a kind of vigorous frolic or *étude* with numerous movements in the wake of *London: The Biography* by the same author, for whom the city is a living person. The plot—in the double sense of the word—revolves around a visionary nun and a conspiracy by the name of "Dominus", which consists of clerics, aldermen and nobles. They establish a secret link with a group of religious fundamentalists, "the predestined men", through one of its clandestine members, the Austin Friar William Exmewe, who is also the head of Dominus. The conspiratorial meetings lead to murders and terrorist attacks mainly on churches with the aim of removing King Richard II from the throne, to be succeeded by Henry Bolingbroke as King Henry IV (Ackroyd 2004, 74). Accordingly, the narrated time of religious and political upheavals is 1399, the year before Chaucer's death, and as the true protagonist the medieval city herself emerges in her multi-faceted liveliness.

Beside the significance of religion this work is marked by generic hybridity with the tributaries of Gothic, mystery, crime and historical novel including elements of occultism. Violent death seems one of the most natural motifs in this blend, and violent death often seems to have an affinity to the fictional orphan. I would like to argue that the orphan's (justified) fear of being killed, which recurs here as in most of the novels in hand (Atwood, *The Blind Assassin*; Amis; Coetzee, *Michael K.*; Morrison; Phillips, and Roberts) validates the multiple manifestations of the orphan's social precariousness to the point of total exclusion. To physically liquidate the orphan—a lost child in most of the above-mentioned narratives—presents itself to members of society as a sensible way to eliminate someone who holds no legitimate position in it. Legitimacy results above all from parental origins and their transparency, as protection follows from a parent's presence.

Hamo's first appearance in *The Clerkenwell Tales* shows the typical stigmata of the orphan as which he is later revealed: he walks through London with bowed head closely behind Exmewe and Richard Marrow, the carpenter, who both ignore him (Ackroyd 2004, 14). Like Roberts's Geneviève Delange allegedly of unlawful and sinful origin, he has no memory and no individual past, since he was left at the gate of St. Bartholomew Cloister, taken in by the friars and then apprenticed as an illuminator in their scriptorium (16). Known as silent and simple he does not consider himself belonging to a community, even though he lives in the priory. "From infancy, he had been a natural exile. […] He was familiar with loneliness" (17), so that he draws comfort only from familiar objects and the company of stones. Surprisingly, he has begun to follow Exmewe around, trying to stay concealed, but with the obvious desire to attach himself, unnoticed. "The connection between the two was impossible to fathom except that, in some obscure fashion, Hamo Fulberd had found a father" (17). Hamo acquires endangering knowledge about the conspirators and their objective from listening to the conversations Exmewe has with various sympathisers (107). The friar suspects the boy of conspiring with the mad nun, to whom the orphan, a mysterious child of darkness, appears as a holy hermit (108).

Hamo is hardly ever given a voice or assigned focal sense perception in the narrative; he has no agency except in his work with the manuscripts. A third-person heterodiegetic narrator, intertextually focusing on various characters borrowed from Chaucer, makes them surface in their "tales", in scenes and dialogues. The orphan is easily manipulated by his authoritative and powerful "father", who uses him to commit arson in a church, so that the boy will be persecuted as a heretic and wanted felon. Indifference towards the orphan's fate seems a natural attitude for the leaders: "If Hamo were to die, well, what cannot be mended must be ended. Need knows no law" (109). The boy is sacrificed by the friar like the symbolic sculpture of the Lamb of God, a wax statue of which nothing remains because it stands on the altar in the church and is immediately destroyed by the fire. The series of burning churches causes turmoil, subverts religious and political order and promotes anarchy (126); the orphan becomes one of the instruments used to create the desired social unrest. As a precaution he is killed by the monk's own hands after Hamo has carried out his order. While Hamo awaits his end in fatalistic apprehension he remains a marginal figure whose life or death is of no consequence either in the mindscape of the agents or on the diegetic level of the story.

My interpretation of this figure is deduced from the contention that the fictional orphan functions as a cultural signifier filled with variable meanings. Caused by his environment's craving for power and disregard for the individual, the foundling, cut off from his past and (therefore) with no right to a future, serves in *The Clerkenwell Tales* as the sign of a life as impermanent as the waxen candle, "signifying nothing" in a world bared of humanistic illusions. I consider this portrayal of an orphan's fate part of the novelistic contribution to the present discourse on "the disappearance of the ideals of humanism" (Földváry 2014, 218), to which dystopian novels also contribute. "The Author's Tale" from a new era (Ackroyd 2004, 207-13) concludes *The Clerkenwell Tales* with a meta-narrative chapter and shows how recent developments of urban renewal have made efforts to obliterate the late medieval city. Laying the blame of power-craving inhumanity on the doorstep of the medieval Londoners the contemporaries of a post-Enlightenment age may recognise some of the features of their times in the mirror of the text.

4.2 The Happy Orphan

William Shakespeare is the godfather of Jeanette Winterson's novel *The Gap of Time* (2015), a hypertext and "updated" narrative version of *The Winter's Tale*, whose plot she summarises on the first pages.[54] "New Bohemia. America […] used to be a French colony. Sugar plantations, big colonial homes" reads the description of the initial setting (Winterson 2015, "Watery Star"). Later in the novel it is explicitly defined as contemporary New Orleans ("I Would Not Prize Them"). A middle-aged

African-American man takes a baby left in the nearby hospital's baby-hatch home and decides to raise her as his daughter—Perdita, the lost one. In a few paragraphs the reader learns by temporal prolepsis the story of her detection after eighteen years, while the subsequent full-length account of her getting lost and growing up imitate step-by-step the plot of Shakespeare's play, through a diegetic transposition set in contemporary London and the US. Each of Shakespeare's characters is replaced by a 21st-century equivalent: the jealous and suspicious father, the innocent friend, the hurt wife and several allies or servants who faithfully obey either of them. Following Shakespearean tragic complications, the end is equally a happy one; in the 21st century the miracles take place on a psychological level, first when the baby saves her foster father from an abysmal depression, later, when after eighteen years the former friends who were in enmity are reconciled and the estranged wife, Perdita's mother Mimi, a famous singer, returns to husband and lost child. Four supposed orphans, including Perdita, who are foundlings with lost parents, join in a girl group, calling themselves "The Separations" ("The Day of Celebration").

The orphan protagonist characterises several of Winterson's novels (cf. Onega 2012, 201). The narrative of *Lighthousekeeping* (2004) navigates around the existential metaphor *Shipwreck with Spectator* (Blumenberg):[55] the ancient lighthousekeeper Pew has survived calamities at sea. The girl Silver miraculously also lives, whereas her mother falls to death from the cliffs when Silver is ten.[56] Since nobody can put the orphan to use, she is taken in by the old blind lighthousekeeper at Cape Wrath in Scotland, later to be orphaned a second time like the two girls in Roberts's novel. Despite the blows of fate, the child Silver, when interrogated by the local teacher, can count her blessings: "'If I hadn't been an orphan, I would never have known Pew'". Miss Pinch's questioning reply unveils her disregard for both the blind old man, whose job will soon become superfluous by technological progress, and the orphaned girl: "'What possible difference could that have made?'" Silver's blunt answer "'[t]he difference that love makes'" (Winterson 2004, 106) reveals the author's focal point: the higher significance of emotional attachment over blood-relationship. The parallel between the character constellations Silver-Pew here and Perdita-Shep in *The Gap of Time* ten years later is as obvious as the confident expanse of emotion and redemption in the novels' intertextual fantasy.[57] Considering *Lighthousekeeping*, Julia Kristeva's statements about the stranger-orphan find a confirmation in the portrayal of the protagonist's life. Old Pew's love and storytelling, reciprocated by the child, save Silver, who is regarded by other people as an intruder and illegal stranger: "Because the police discovered that as I had no mother or father, I didn't officially exist. I asked them to telephone Miss Pinch, but she claimed never to have heard of such a person as myself" (145; cf. 138). Silver recognises that, although others deny her existence, life itself is the ultimate gift. She must listen to other tales as well as tell her own story to save her life—thereby recalling another ancient and famous intertext.[58] "The book is thus a meditation about mourning and melancholia, but also about the redemptive powers of storytelling", Anne-Julia Zwierlein states about *Lighthousekeeping* (Zwierlein 2014, 171). Silver clings to storytelling like Pew did to his plank and his tales in the shipwreck, a disaster which he relates to the "spectator" Silver. Blumenberg points out the analogy with the shipwreck and the significance of the storytelling: "The change of the spectator's spatial distance towards a stranger's distress at sea into the temporal distance of the memory of one's own" (1979, 54, my translation) takes place at the lighthouse. To spin a yarn is the major occupation there besides "watching". Silver's "defiant resolution to hold on to happiness" (Winterson 2004, 171) following Pew's departure by boat into the unknown Hereafter results from her awareness of meaningfulness. Her reorientation foreshadows Perdita's, another orphaned protagonist's, innocent working in *The Gap of Time*.

For those around her, the foundling Perdita becomes a token of unexpected grace, healing a deep wound She herself has been saved and signifies the proverbial second chance for individuals in the novel whose life seemed to be heading towards a desperate end. In *The Gap of Time*, Perdita's love of others is not the only source of the spreading of emotional warmth. Most of the characters experience tenderness and affection towards another person for the first time. A similar human kindness like the one that saved Perdita as a lost infant enables others to overcome ethnic and psychological barriers as well as geographical boundaries. In a world dominated by toughness, capitalist economy and the service industries, it is love which makes reconciliation and atonement for guilt as well as new or renewed affective bonds possible. Symbolically, harmony is also signified by music, which as a theme runs through the whole narrative. The more fluid identity and a flexibility with regard to "belonging", which Perdita and her peers represent, open the optimistic view into a future with better prospects than the previous generation in *The Gap of Time* gave rise to fear.

If the foundlings Hamo, Silver and Perdita are rooted in a wondrously mythical world, the foundling in Graham Swift's recent novel *Mothering Sunday* (2016) is involuntarily involved in the wake of the original catastrophe of the 20th century: the Great War. She received a lovely

name in the orphanage where she was found and raised as Jane Fairchild.
At 22 she enters the household of the well-to-do Niven family in rural
England as a maid.[59] The Nivens have lost two sons in World War I, just
like their neighbours, the Sheringhams. It is 30 March 1924, Mothering
Sunday and a glorious springtime day, when Jane receives a phone call
from 24-year-old Paul Sheringham asking her to visit him while his
parents are away and Jane has her day off like other domestic servants to
see their mothers on this particular day. "All over the country, maids and
cooks and nannies had been 'freed' for the day, but was any of them—was
even Paul Sheringham—as untethered as she?", Jane the orphan ponders
(Swift 2016, pos. 855). She has been Paul's lover for some time and is
even called a friend by him. On her way back home after an unforgettable
encounter she joyfully cycles along country roads, ignorant of Paul's
simultaneous suicidal drive towards the posh restaurant, where he is
awaited by his fiancée, a fortnight before his wedding with a member of
his social class. Jane Fairchild believes she benefits from a freedom no one
else can feel. The experience of this day is told in personalised third-
person narrative with limited perspective:

> Could she have done what she'd done today if she'd had a mother to go to?
> Could she have had the life she didn't yet know she was going to have [she
> later becomes a well-known novelist]? Could her mother have known,
> making her dreadful choice [to abandon the new-born girl], how she had
> blessed her?
> [...]
> Girl? She was twenty-two. The air up her skirt and a Dutch cap up her
> fanny (Pos. 870).

That her euphoria is not totally ephemeral proves later in her life. As an
old woman—without a past or origins, without "natural" obligations or
credentials—she serenely thinks she was ideally predestined for the
profession of fiction writer, which she repeatedly states in interviews:

> "I was an orphan," she would divulge for the umpteenth time. "I never
> knew my father or mother. Or even my real name. If I ever had one. That
> has always seemed to me the perfect basis for becoming a writer—
> particularly a writer of fiction. To have no credentials at all. To be given a
> clean sheet, or rather, to *be* a clean sheet yourself. A nobody." (Pos. 898,
> emphasis in original)

Though at first devastated by her young lover's fatal accident and later by
her husband's early death she presents herself at eighty or ninety a very
cheerful interviewee. Linking her biography closely to her profession,

since, as she claims, "she had come into the world with an innate licence to invent" (pos. 912), she regards herself the born fiction writer. This character approaches the 18th-century picaresque orphan more closely than the mournful figures in numerous contemporary narratives.

The hours spent with her lover on Mothering Sunday, March 30th, 1924 leave the focaliser Jane happy, until she learns upon her return to her master's house that now "all five [sons]" of the neighbouring families are dead. There are hints that Paul deliberately caused the accident—he steered his car into an old English oak on the roadside—, because he silently felt that he was under a heavy social and familial pressure. The burden of expectations, which rested upon him as the only surviving son of an upper-class family after the Great War, had crushed his hopes as an individual. This probability is hushed up by the relatives like the circumstances of his death.

Jane Fairchild, without history or relationships, provides the contrastive foil to the Nivens and the Sheringhams, including Paul. They have suffered a terrible loss by the death of their children or brothers. She remains one of the few figural representations for whom loss of parents, especially of the mother, is not a formative experience in life, nor does she miss such an attachment. Enthusiastic about her sexual experience with Paul Sheringham and even more elated by his appreciative respect for women in domestic service she regards her personal freedom as an asset which others, including the man who had made love to her, were not endowed with. To have addressed the analogy between the "untethered" orphan's freedom to enjoy and that of the novelist to invent remains the innovative element of the story material in Swift's recent novel. In 1975 Auerbach pointed at the unencumbered freedom of the artist achieved by James Joyce's 'orphaning' of his hero Stephen Dedalus (cf. the chapter Puschmann-Nalenz, "The Gap" in the present volume, 83), even though this appeared still debatable in the text of *A Portrait of the Artist*.

The ambiguity of the loss of origins with its propensity to the picaresque, which was discussed above, has been brought up by more audacious writers as a subject of contemporary fiction; yet Graham Swift, as a conservative, does not evade this aspect in his story of an orphan girl. In works of socio-psychological theory, the detachment from ancestry was already proclaimed in the 1980s as a chance opposing grief about loss (cf. 113, 125 of the present chapter). In narrative literature, this disentanglement became a topic raised on the intradiegetic as well as the metafictional level once the threshold to modernism had been crossed. The figural narrator in *Ulysses*, quoted above, stated that, as with a natural law, "Every Friday buries a Thursday, if you come to look at it" (Joyce 1971, 111). This hints at a required—perhaps indispensable—generational relief and the intrinsic departure for a new day. Like several of the fictional characters depicted above, the Early Modern English novel, variously referred to as an orphan genre without the parenthood of tradition (cf. König 2014, 8; Auerbach 1975), experienced a second orphaning by the loss of the grand narrative during its later development.

5. Home and Orphan

In conclusion, I wish to briefly address the frequency with which the idea of "home" is linked to orphanhood in the fictions under consideration here.[60] The orphaned protagonist, lacking parents, is also characterised by not possessing a home and finds only a temporary abode either in an institution or in other people's homes. The cultural orphan, in danger of losing or having already lost his/her cultural inscription with the original surroundings, occupies an important place not only in the postcolonial but also in the posthumanist imagination.

In the novels *Old Filth* and *Oryx and Crake* the identical sentence "It is called home" defines diverse, unknown spaces as the pseudo-familiar. "Home" has to be England to little Edward in Malay; to the posthuman Crakers, who were raised in a completely artificial world under a bell jar, a delusively unpolluted stretch of land and sea is designated as their "home" by their pseudo-father Snowman. The strangeness which, from the viewpoint of the colonial child, or, respectively, the posthuman creatures, is inherent to the spaces they never set eyes on, contradicts the traditional concept of "home". The result is an immediate disparity of signifier, signified and interlocutor. "Home" here signifies something totally alien to the addressee. Thereby the arbitrariness of language as a means of communication on the one hand and a semantic breach of convention on the other are revealed. The addressed posthuman beings are unable to name and recognise the place called "home" by their tutor as linked to memory, emotional ties and belonging. The power of signifying and authentication, to which the phrase "It *is called* home" draws attention, lies one-sidedly with the speaker: Auntie May, the Baptist missionary, and Snowman, the supposedly last of the human race. They fully use the authority connected with this signifying power.[61] For Auntie May as for Alistair Feathers in *Old Filth* England is convincingly "home", and the delusive landscape into which Snowman has led his wardens recalls "home" for him. "Home", for either designator, is some place belonging to the past and forever internalised by memory as "home within", whereas for the fictional addressees it is a mere word separated from an unknown referent. In contrast to the Crakers, who were created as capable of speaking yet presumably without access to the symbolic, Edward Feathers possesses a notion of "home", which differs from his father's or the Baptist woman's. "For he was Home" are the final words of the narrative about old Sir Edward (Gardam [2004] 2013, 258); for him "home" is the East (257), where he was born, the place he longed for and where he arrives to die. "Home" is revealed as a construct.

For the female protagonists of *House of Orphans* and *The Looking Glass* the emblematic image of "home" cannot be transferred to an institution, the orphanage: they are aware of what they connote with "home". Eeva never stops remembering "home" with her father in Helsinki. Even though without a concrete experience, Geneviève longs for "home" when she builds the illusion that she has found it at Madame Patin's, the place where she falls in love with her employer. Toni Morrison attaches a political dimension to the idea of "home" (Wardi 2011, 23 and *passim*), since almost none of the characters is or feels "at home" either on the farm or later in the big house. Jacob Vaark may be considered the *pater familias* of the household, to which slaves, servants, workmen and family members belong.[62] Only the white couple of direct European descent can tackle the task of building a house and making themselves "at home". Vaark's three consecutively erected houses are spaces that can barely connote "home", because no memory or person is attached to them, and the first two are meant to be only transitory abodes. Jacob's houses, like the Portuguese planter's estate, work as social signifiers. As such they are conceived by Vaark himself (Morrison 2008, 88-89), who dies in the last unfinished one, "a profane monument to himself" (44) in his servants' eyes. "It was still the grandest house in the whole region and why not spend eternity there?" (143).[63]

Lastly, *The Lost Child* represents the mutability of "home" among these fictions. Especially from Ben Wilson's point of view, hardly any of the places where he stays connotes "home" in the sense that it is more than a roof over his head, neither the flats where they live nor the foster homes where he is sent. He does not belong to the literally "homeless", because social welfare—the law of the father—can provide housing for the boys' mother, who left home never to return; yet the problem where home is remains—is it anywhere? In the framing story about Heathcliff's fate the narrative concern with the idea of "home" is emphasised at the end. Each of the frame story's concluding chapters finishes on the word "home" (Phillips 2015, 252, 260), even though the man (Mr Earnshaw) means by it something unknown to the child. For the man who is his father "home" is the big house on the Yorkshire heath. Again, a father has the power to designate and promise "home" to his motherless son. Only paternal care could secure, procure or deny "home" for a child, as we can see in the narratives by Phillips as well as Morrison, Roberts, Gardam or Dunmore. In each of these novels "home" remains, however, either utopian or a postponed promise. As a study based on psychoanalytic theory contends about Atwood's *The Blind Assassin*, where the father fails in keeping up "home", the notion of "home" is linked to the disappeared maternal line and, like the person of the mother, is represented by a blank:

> *The Blind Assassin* employs a vast array of images of gaps, absences, zeros, and nothings. But perhaps the most gaping hole of all, situated at its center, is the family home, Avilion, once filled with people and things but now boarded up and empty. The place is haunted by maternal memories. Even before the death of their own mother, the sisters have been (in a sense) "brought up" by their dead grandmother. (Parkin-Gounelas 2004, 690-91; parentheses in original)

The place called home is conceived of as furnished with connotations which reach deep into a person's memories and affections, comprising sense perceptions, emotions and ties to human beings, animals, objects and ideas. To annihilate them all may create a posthuman world: *Oryx and Crake* presents a narrative which even more sweepingly exhibits "zeros" that include the precarious position of the new-world patriarch. A Robinson without his "kingdom" and little chance to return to a humanised earth, Snowman is determined to consider the moment at which he has arrived as "Zero Hour" (Atwood 2003, 374), from where one must start anew.

In postmillennial fiction, the concept of "home" and the trope of "orphan" have entered a trying, often burdensome association. The empty space of an absent parent extends into the blank wherein the imaginary "home" is located and where the symbolic portends the closely linked void of "the dead mother". The orphans' situation of a permanent loss produces repeated crises and usually interferes with new experience, except for those figures that dare take the leap to a still largely undefined communality.

Notes

[1] Kristeva refers to and quotes Camus' novel *L'Étranger* (1942) as the literary example for her theoretical explanations (1991, 5, 25-29). A fictional model for the hero with self-imposed exile in English literature is, also according to Auerbach, Stephen Dedalus in Joyce's *A Portrait of the Artist as a Young Man* (1916).

[2] In the first half of the 19th century institutions in London which raised and educated parentless children were officially called "orphan asylums", meaning an abode for the unprotected abandoned children.

[3] For the history of the picaresque in Western literature up to the turn of the second millennium see Ardila (2015). Novels such as *Lucky Jim* or *The Tin Drum* notably exhibit the occurrence of a picaresque (anti-)hero in the second half of the 20th century. Studies in the American novel name John Dos Passos, Saul Bellow, Thomas Pynchon and Jonathan Safran Foer as writers some of whose works re-create the *picaro* and continue the corresponding literary tradition. Jamie McCulloch (2007) compares Martin Amis's *Money: A Suicide Note* and *The Information* to American examples of the postmodern picaresque.

[4] Máire Doyle elucidates the appropriation of the literary orphan, who is called a rare figure in Irish fiction, with novels by John McGahern. She explains that the protagonist of *The Pornographer* "demonstrates not only characteristics of the literary orphan but also of the picaro", who is by unforeseen circumstances forced "to confront society unaided by family" (2013, 130). Doyle's article is primarily based on Nina Auerbach's theoretical reflections.

[5] I leave the obvious association of Bloom's interior monologue aside here, namely that Robinson, the white Anglo-Saxon Protestant explorer, has died and is buried by his coloured subjugated former servant.

[6] Juliana Schiesari (1992, 1) maintains that loss has become the prime thematic concern in European theoretical discourse at least since 1990.

[7] See Margaret Atwood, *The Blind Assassin*, where—in contrast to Iris and Laura Chase—the male orphan Alex Thomas with origins unknown to the narrated world is capable of inventing his own history and remaining master of it (cf. Puschmann-Nalenz 2014, 193-94). This character type increases the intradiegetic unreliability of narrating.

[8] A complementary analysis of the picaresque element in the orphan figure is provided in Gymnich's section about the late-Victorian "adventurous orphan".

[9] This acronym is common usage. A dictionary defines it as "an official order that a person must stop behaving in a way that annoys or harms other people".

[10] The intertextual reminiscence of Dickens's orphaned boys and depicted poverty has been observed in Amis's work by critics (e.g. Barnes, n. pag; cf. also Peters 2016, 90-92).

[11] Desmond has by some readers been called the only male figure in his recent work with whom the reader can sympathise.

[12] The trope of the Raj orphan illuminates imperialism from an angle different from Rudyard Kipling's novels *The Jungle Books* and *Kim* (cf. Gymnich's part on "the adventurous orphan" in this volume, 60-69).

[13] The term "Raj orphans" also confirms the equation of literal orphan and exile. In Kazuo Ishiguro's 2000 novel *When We Were Orphans*, Christopher Banks and his friend are marked as "pseudo-orphans", whose melancholia is also adequately described by the quote heading this chapter.

[14] Hartner (2013, 172-74) discusses *Old Filth* as an education novel and focuses on the theoretical framework appertaining to the narrative hybridisation of the postmodern novel and the traditional *bildungsroman*.

[15] For instances of the confident, serene female orphan see section 4.2. In postcolonial fiction such a figure seems to occupy a more important rank (cf. Tönnies 2016, 113, 122-23).

[16] Ian McEwan's novel *The Cement Garden* (1978) is an early example of contemporary narratives about the death of the mother. For an interpretation cf. Puschmann-Nalenz (2014, 182-85).

[17] Whitford quotes from the English translation of Irigaray's *Sexes et Parentés* (1987). She summarises the ancient origins of the matricide motif and the fight for patriarchal order (Whitford 1991b, 36-38).

[18] Irigaray developed her philosophical theories starting from her position as psychoanalyst. Despite her scholarly foundation in psychoanalysis she is critical towards Freud as well as Jacques Lacan, partly because she regards them as firmly rooted in the patriarchal system.

[19] See Eva Oppermann for the historical background of the novel. Her comprehensive article, informed by the theories of Michel Foucault and Gaston Bachelard, focuses on the semantic importance of spaces which the novel's protagonist inhabits.

[20] That the child is dangerous for the mother is repeatedly expressed in Graham Swift's novels as well: e.g. mothers have died giving birth (*Out of this World*), or the unborn child damaged the mother's mental health (*Waterland*).

[21] As a young girl, Laura is abused by Iris's husband Richard, who, together with his sister, fools his wife. This varies the topic of the ruined orphan girl in the Victorian novel (cf. Gymnich in this volume 33).

[22] Banerjee deals with this deserting mother figure as exceptional, because she opposes the ruling system. Her absence from husband and son is an act of self-assertion. Dunja Mohr argues that Atwood creates a feminist "post-human utopia" (2007, 17) disguised as dystopia. This is justified considering that the mother is a strong character with traits that she alone represents. Perhaps Snowman's conclusive tentative reflections on pacifism equally support the evaluation as utopia.

[23] Kinga Földváry investigates the motif of the posthuman child as one of the "forms of the nonhuman 'Other'" (2014, 209) in European Anglophone fictions. The Crakers would, if one follows her argumentation, echo "the innocent *tabula rasa* of Romanticism" (210, emphasis in original) instead of incorporating the dark materials of dehumanised virtual technology, a function which, in Atwood's

dystopian vision, is assigned to the villains among the extinct species *homo sapiens sapiens*. It would be interesting to further explore the question whether the Canadian author discloses a basically different outlook compared to writers whose works "envision a future that terrifies the aging societies of Europe, which fear their own demise at the hands of their own children, creatures they are increasingly reluctant to acknowledge as their own" (Földvary 2014, 211; cf. 212).

[24] In the new world of *Oryx and Crake* the symbolic and language do not appear simultaneously and are not interdependent. Instead, one succeeds the other in reverse order: the symbolic emerges after the verbal. The production of the visual symbol comes unrehearsed from the Crakers. Lacan's statement that he is "prepared at any time to say that the symbol reaches beyond spoken language" (2006, 58, my translation) has been resolved into a succession of actions surrounding the Crakers in the novel.

[25] In both novels the younger sons, Tom Crick or Tom Luxton respectively, are the smart ones. The elder brother, Dick Crick, the mentally retarded fruit of incest between father and daughter Atkinson (Swift 1999 229-30), parallels Jack Luxton, the sensitive blockhead and main focaliser of *Wish You Were Here*. Jack is, like Dick, sometimes ridiculed by other characters.

[26] The third-person narrator gives an account of the circumstances which led to the awarding of the medal from the perspective of the commanding officer in the battle of the Somme, who refers to "the day's unspeakabilities" and shows awareness of the de-personalising effect of war on the soldiers (10). Cf. also Puschmann-Nalenz (2015, 11).

[27] Slightly earlier, in 1981, Nadine Gordimer published *July's People*, which imagines the war-like state South Africa would be in under the regime of the eighties before the end of Apartheid. It shows the white woman Maureen Smales, a literal orphan, born Maureen Hetherington into the liberal upper class of the former colonisers, as another kind of "postcolonial orphan". Maureen, who has to flee with husband and children from her home in Johannesburg, is bereaved of a world that does not exist anymore and a past left behind in the often-conjured "back there". From the family's hiding in their black servant's village she runs towards a mysterious helicopter to escape alone.

[28] Attwell states that when Coetzee was looking for resources for this protagonist he found them in Kafka, in Dostoevsky's Holy Fool and Melville's Bartleby (2015, 121-22).

[29] López (2011) presents an analysis of the novel, mainly based on Michel Foucault's *Discipline and Punish* and Max Weber's *The Protestant Ethic and the Spirit of Capitalism*. The novel, López claims, can be considered a cultural representation of South Africa in the early eighties.

[30] In the part of the world where the beginnings of hominisation are placed this protagonist, after his mother's death, is permanently concerned with the earth, its fertility, organic growth and his immersion in it. An instinct makes him feel that he belongs to this earth; the notion that the reverse might also be true remains alien to him. It becomes an issue touched by the narrator's reflections in *Youth* (see below) and Coetzee's later work.

[31] The chapter is an English translation by David Macey from *Sexes et parentés*.

[32] In her introduction to the section "Ethics and Subjectivity", Whitford (1991b, 161) explains Irigaray's reference to Hegel and the connection he makes between woman and family as follows: "While men can be spirit (universal), the family represents 'nature'." Hence, woman is associated with nature.

[33] Both novels by Coetzee comprise historical references and concrete details, but especially *Life & Times*, like *Waiting for the Barbarians*, has also been interpreted as an allegory (cf. recently Griem 2013; also Attridge 2004, 32 and Attridge's references). Coetzee himself wrote in his notebook during the composition of *Life & Times*: "What I need is a liberation from verisimilitude!" (qtd. from Attwell 2015, 116). This remark is in accordance with the novels' allegorical features.

[34] Enclosed spaces and especially rooms as signifiers of oppressiveness and isolation are frequently represented in *Youth* (cf. López 2011, 227-29).

[35] Apart from the "family's" (also the Imperial "family's") disintegration *July's People* by Nadine Gordimer demonstrates how the ruling imaginary order can be shattered subsequent to the socio-political: Maureen loses faith in her "emasculated" husband, whom she sees in a state without power or counsel (significantly, after their flight, he loses first his car and then his gun). She vaguely realises that the black man has entered the symbolic order—a development which disconcerts her to the point of confusion, not least of identity. She escapes.

[36] The intertextual connection of the narrative with Joyce's *Portrait of the Artist as a Young Man* is uncovered by López (2011, 239-40).

[37] In his seminal introduction on "the writer's place" Head (1997) explains and discusses the author's ambivalences towards "place".

[38] Evidently, the personal is for the central character closely connected to the political. Commenting on the writer's subjective dilemma, Pieter Vermeulen elucidates "Coetzee's ambiguous political position in South Africa" and the author's awareness of "his own inescapable complicity" with the privileged whites (2010, 273). Cf. López (2011, 220).

[39] Cf. Gymnich in this volume (54-62) for the analysis of the character in Brontë's novel. *Wuthering Heights* was famously published under a male pseudonym and thus remained an "orphan work" until 1850, when Charlotte Brontë revealed her dead sister as its author.

[40] Caryl Phillips immigrated to Britain from the Caribbean as a baby. He grew up in Leeds and read English Literature in Oxford, where he is a fellow now.

[41] From a viewpoint of political philosophy, Susan Strehle (2013), in her reading of the novel, considers American society as resting on binary oppositions of different kinds—racial, religious, material, national or gender-related—, a pattern which, Strehle claims, is reflected in *A Mercy*.

[42] Vega-González explains the role of orphanhood in postcolonial African American fiction, especially the frequency of the motif in Morrison's work, together with the significance of the mother-daughter relationship (2011, 119-20). Her close reading of *A Mercy* contains the descriptions of each of the female characters' unbelonging and self-invention. She calls Florens "the quintessential

orphan" (126), who experiences a "rebirth" (128) through eventual detachment and the writing of her story.
[43] Shirley Ann Stave (2011) uses the psychoanalytic approach of Jacques Lacan to discuss identity and relationality of the protagonists in *A Mercy*.
[44] For an interpretation of *A Mercy* based on psychoanalysis and trauma theories cf. Wyatt (2012), who also relies on the repetition of a traumatic experience: when Florens beholds Malaik, the little orphaned boy whom the desired blacksmith is taking care of (Morrison 2008, 136-37), a scene unfolds that in Florens reactivates the removal from her mother, who intended to keep her baby brother.
[45] Folks quotes Homi Bhabha as well as Naipaul and Ishiguro as references.
[46] "Banks's eventual acceptance of his orphaned state signals the possibility of an escape from the symbolic parent/nation authority and the possibility of a far more fluid and syncretic understanding of the self as the basis of future relationships. Orphanhood becomes a trope for a post-national identity", writes Tim Christensen (2007/2008, 202) about *When We Were Orphans*.
[47] The polarisation of the functional surrogates of a parent in good and evil resembles the "helper" or, respectively, the witch-like stepmother in fairy tales.
[48] Passages in the first person with Des as letter-writer are in the novel always printed in italics, as are the instructions a lecturing Lionel gives his nephew.
[49] Regardless of disparities, the heroines in *The Looking Glass*, *House of Orphans* and *A Mercy* are each portrayed at the age of sixteen when the plot unfolds and they begin a new stage in their life and enter "the world". The marks of rites of passage, connected with the awakening of sexual desire in or for the girls and symbolised by the *topos* of the journey, are evident. The ambivalences inherent in this transitional state are enhanced by the lack of support or companionship because of the "dead mother". Geneviève and Eeva are about to enter service (soon to leave it again), Florens accomplishes her errand to save her mistress's life and begins her life-narrative.
[50] For Roberts's thematisation of ghosts and the maternal undead cf. Cain (2013, 413-14, 423, 432), who offers an interpretation of *Daughters of the House* and *Impossible Saints* (1997) based on psychoanalysis and trauma theory.
[51] Ruth Cain, in her analysis of Roberts's novel (2013, 408), points out that the 20th century produced a number of critical studies on the "blanks" in the representations of mothers. According to Cain, the frequent occurrence of the motherless figure testifies "to the persistent denigration of maternity within the symbolic systems we have available" (408).
[52] The quotation is the title of an article on Kazuo Ishiguro published in 2007 by Christian Schmitt-Kilb.
[53] In Jon MacGregor's *So Many Ways to Begin* (2006) the search for the hero's biological mother becomes an obsession and a leitmotif, in Roberts's *The Looking Glass* it appears veiled in the protagonist's odyssey to find a surrogate.
[54] Shakespeare's last-but-one play has recently stimulated "contemporised" remakes in different genres. Stage director Roberto Ciulli transposed the plot and the characters into a Mafiosi society with the Sicily setting in his stage adaptation

of 2015/16. It was performed for the German Shakespeare Association in November 2015.

[55] Beside Winterson, also—though less pointedly—Atwood's *Oryx and Crake*, Morrison's *A Mercy* or the framing narrative about Heathcliff in *The Lost Child* present the sea (voyage) as a symbol of utter, dangerous change.

[56] See Anne-Julia Zwierlein's article (2014, esp. 170-71) on the importance of the Death of the Mother for *Lighthousekeeping*.

[57] The foster-father as loving carer of the orphaned girl has also a forerunner in the Victorian novel (cf. Gymnich in the present volume, 37-42, 53, 56).

[58] The majority of female protagonists in the novels in hand turn out to be the daughters or sisters of Scheherazade in saving their lives by telling stories.

[59] Swift's heroine shares her fate as foundling and servant with the protagonist of William Trevor's last novel *Love and Summer* (2009). The girl Ellie becomes the wife of a widowed Irish farmer and devotes her life to his fortune. Like the central female figures in Trevor's preceding novels she is and remains an almost saintly innocent.

[60] For this connection in modernist narratives, cf. the statement about E.M. Forster's canonised novel *Howards End* in the chapter "The Gap" in the present volume (89). For Victorian fictional orphans and the idea of "home" cf. Gymnich in this volume (60-61).

[61] In fact, the father (figure) decides in both narratives what and where "home" is: Alistair Feathers has the last word about sending his son to England, and Snowman, who acts as surrogate father to the Crakers, takes them to the shore.

[62] The interpretation of Vaark's name as VA-ark points at the settler's monumental charge.

[63] It is worth noticing that Sorrow, the shipwrecked orphan, is called Complete after her daughter's birth, while Jacob Vaark cannot complete the building which was to demonstrate his material success and prosperity.

Works Cited

Ackroyd, Peter. (2003) 2004. *The Clerkenwell Tales*. London: Vintage.

Allen, Jeffery Renard. 2015. "'The Lost Child' by Caryl Phillips." *The New York Times Sunday Book Review*, May 08, 2015. http://www.nytimes.com/2015/05/10/books/review/the-lost-child-by-caryl-phillips.html?_r=0.

Amis, Martin. 2012. *Lionel Asbo. State of England*. London: Jonathan Cape.

Ardila, J.A. Garrido. 2015. *The Picaresque Novel in Western Literature*. Cambridge: Cambridge University Press.

ASBO http://dictionary.cambridge.org/de/worterbuch/englisch/asbohttp://.

Attridge, Derek. 2004. *J.M. Coetzee and the Ethics of Reading: Literature in the Event*. Chicago: University of Chicago Press.

Attwell, David. 2015. *J.M. Coetzee and the Life of Writing: Face-to-Face with Time*. New York: Viking.

Atwood, Margaret. (2000) 2001. *The Blind Assassin*. London: Virago.

—. 2003. *Oryx and Crake*. London: Bloomsbury.

—. 2015. *The Heart Goes Last*. London: Bloomsbury.

Auerbach, Nina. 1975. "Incarnations of the Orphan." *English Literary History* 42 (3): 395-419.

Austen, Jane. 1969. *Northanger Abbey* and *Persuasion* (in one volume). London: Dent.

Banerjee, Suparna. 2013. "Towards 'Feminist Mothering': Oppositional Maternal Practice in Margaret Atwood's *Oryx and Crake*." *Journal of International Women's Studies* 14 (1): 236-47.

Barnes, Jonathan. n.d. "Martin Amis's Asbo." http://www.the-tls.co.uk/tls/public/article1064536.ece.

Bayer, Gerd. 2014. "Loss and the Nation in David Mitchell's *Black Swan Green*." In *Narrating Loss: Representations of Mourning, Nostalgia and Melancholis in Contemporary Anglophone Fictions*, edited by Brigitte Johanna Glaser and Barbara Puschmann-Nalenz, 15-26. Trier: WVT.

Blumenberg, Hans. 1979. *Schiffbruch mit Zuschauer. Paradigma einer Daseinsmetapher* [*Shipwreck with Spectator: Paradigm of a Metaphor for Existence*. Translated by Steven Rendall. Cambridge, MA: MIT Press, 1996]. Frankfurt: Suhrkamp.

Cain, Ruth. 2013. "The Buried Madonna: Matricide, Maternal Power and the Novels of Michèle Roberts." *Women's Studies: An Interdisciplinary Journal* 42 (4): 408-38.

Christensen, Tim. 2007/2008. "Kazuo Ishiguro and Orphanhood." *Anachronist* 13: 202. http://connection.ebscohost.com/c/literary-criticism/34999589/kazuo-ishiguro-orphanhood.

Coetzee, J.M. (1983) 1998. *Life and Times of Michael K.* London: Vintage.

—. (2002) 2003. *Youth*. London: Vintage.

Davies, Stevie. 2004. "Pearls Beyond Price: Review of *Old Filth* by Jane Gardam." *The Guardian*, November 20, 2004. http://www.theguardian.com/books/2004/nov/20/featuresreviews.guardianreview13.

Doyle, Máire. 2013. "Exploring the Alternatives: The Orphan and the Family in John McGahern's Fiction." In *New Voices, Inherited Lines: Literary and Cultural Representations of the Irish Family*, edited by Yvonne O'Keeffe and Claudia Reese, 125-46. Bern: Lang.

Dunmore, Helen. (2006) 2007. *House of Orphans*. London: Penguin. Kindle.

Földváry, Kinga. 2014. "In Search of a Lost Future: The Posthuman Child." *European Journal of English Studies (EJES)* 18 (2): 207-20.

Folks, Jeffrey J. 2003. "Richard Marius and Cultural Orphanhood." *Southern Quarterly: A Journal of the Arts in the South* 41 (4): 68-77.

Gana, Nouri. 2011. *Signifying Loss: Towards a Poetics of Narrative Mourning*. Lewisburg, PA: Bucknell University Press.

Gardam, Jane. (2004) 2013. *Old Filth*. Hachette Digital ebook. Kindle.

Gordimer, Nadine. (1981) 1982. *July's People*. New York and London: Penguin.

Griem, Julika. 2013. "Postkoloniale Grabungen? J.M. Coetzee's 'Kunst am Bau'." In *Die Räume der Literatur: Exemplarische Zugänge zu Kafkas Erzählung "Der Bau"*, edited by Dorit Müller and Julia Weber, 195-213. Berlin: De Gruyter.

Gymnich, Marion. 2013. "Privileging Female Voices and Breaking Taboos: Michèle Roberts's *The Looking Glass*." *Anglistik: International Journal of English Studies* 24 (1): 101-10.

Hartner, Marcus. 2013. "Hybrid Genres and Cultural Change: A Cognitive Approach." In *The Cultural Dynamics of Generic Change in Contemporary Fiction: Theoretical Frameworks, Genres and Model Interpretations*, edited by Michael Basseler, Ansgar Nünning and Christine Schwanecke, 163-82. Trier: WVT.

Head, Dominic. 1997. *J.M. Coetzee*. Cambridge: Cambridge University Press.

Howie, Gillian. 2008. "Feminist Generations: The Maternal Order and Mythic Time." In *Luce Irigaray: Teaching*, edited by Luce Irigaray with Mary Green, 103-11. London: Continuum.

Irigaray, Luce. 1991. "Interview with *P.L.*" In *The Irigaray Reader*, edited by Margaret Whitford, 47-52. Oxford: Basil Blackwell.

Irving, John. (1985) n.d. *The Cider House Rules*. Harper Collins Imprint. Kindle.

"Jackpot Jailbird: Low-lifes [sic] in London." *The Economist*, June 30, 2012. http://www.economist.com/node/21557737.

Joyce, James. (1922) 1971. *Ulysses*. Harmondsworth: Penguin.

Karavanta, Mina. 2012. "Toni Morrison's *A Mercy* and the Counterwriting of Negative Communities: A Postnational Novel." *Modern Fiction Studies* 58 (4): 723-46.

König, Eva. 2014. *The Orphan in Eighteenth-Century Fiction: The Vicissitudes of the Eighteenth-Century Subject*. Basingstoke: Palgrave Macmillan.

Kristeva, Julia. 1991. *Strangers to Ourselves*. Translated by Leon S. Roudiez. New York: Harvester Wheatsheaf [French original 1988].

Lacan, Jacques. 2006. *Namen-des-Vaters*. Translated by Hans-Dieter Gondek. Wien: Turia+Kant [French original 2005].

Lane, Johanna. 2012. "Needed: Anxiety." (Review of Lionel Asbo). *Publisher's Weekly*, July 2, 2012.
http://search.ebscohost.com/login.asp?profile...

López, Maria J. 2011. *Acts of Visitation: The Narrative of J.M. Coetzee*. Amsterdam: Rodopi.

Malkmus, Bernhard. 2009. "The Birth of the Modern Picaro out of the Spirit of Self-Reliance: Herman Melville's *The Confidence Man*." *Amerikastudien / American Studies* 54 (4): 603-20.

Mantel, Hilary. 2008. "How Sorrow Became Complete. Review: *A Mercy* by Toni Morrison." *The Guardian*, November 08, 2008.
http://www.theguardian.com/books/2008/nov/08/a-mercy-toni-morrison.

Martínez-Alfaro, María Jesús. 2014. "Dark Histories of the Soul: Loss and Haunting in Michèle Roberts's *Daughters of the House*." In *Narrating Loss: Representations of Mourning, Nostalgia and Melancholia in Contemporary Anglophone Fictions*, edited by Brigitte Johanna Glaser and Barbara Puschmann-Nalenz, 123-38. Trier: WVT.

McCulloch, Jamie. 2007. "Creating the Rogue Hero: Literary Devices in the Picaresque Novels of Martin Amis, Richard Russo, Michael Chabon, Jonathan Safran Foer, and Steve Tesich." *The International Fiction Review* 34 (1+2): 13-26.

McEwan, Ian. (1992) 1998. *Black Dogs*. London: Vintage.

Miller, Lucasta. 2015. "*The Lost Child* by Caryl Phillips, review." *The Guardian*, April 18 , 2015.
http://www.theguardian.com/books/2015/apr/18/the-lost-child-caryl-phillips-review-wuthering-heights-emily-bronte.

Mohr, Dunja M. 2007. "Transgressive Utopian Dystopias: The Postmodern Reappearance of Utopia in the Disguise of Dystopia." *Zeitschrift für Anglistik und Amerikanistik (ZAA)* 55 (1): 5-24.

Morrison, Toni. 2008. *A Mercy*. New York: Knopf.

Onega, Susana. 2012. "Portraits of the Artist in the Novels of Jeanette Winterson." In *Portraits of the Artist as a Young Thing in British, Irish and Canadian Fiction after 1945*, edited by Anette Pankratz and Barbara Puschmann-Nalenz, 187-205. Trier: WVT.

Oppermann, Eva. 2015. "Houses to Buy and Dreams to Buy: Heterotopian Places in Helen Dunmore's *House of Orphans.*" *Anglistik: International Journal of English Studies* 26 (2): 175-84.

Parkin-Gounelas, Ruth. 2004. "'What Isn't There' in Margaret Atwood's *The Blind Assassin:* The Psychoanalysis of Duplicity." *Modern Fiction Studies* 50 (3): 681-700.

Peled, Nancy. 2010. "Motherless Daughters: The Absent Mothers in Margaret Atwood." In *Textual Mothers/Maternal Texts: Motherhood in Contemporary Women's Literatures*, edited by Elizabeth Podnieks and Andrea O'Reilly, 47-61. Waterloo, ON: Wilfrid Laurier University Press.

Peters, Susanne. 2016. "A Proletarian Comedy of Manners: Martin Amis's *Lionel Asbo.*" *Anglistik: An International Journal for English Studies* 27 (1): 85-98.

Phillips, Caryl. 2015. *The Lost Child*. New York: Farrar, Straus and Giroux.

Puschmann-Nalenz, Barbara. 2014. "The Figure of the Orphan in Contemporary Fiction." In *Narrating Loss: Representations of Mourning, Nostalgia and Melancholia in Contemporary Anglophone Fictions*, edited by Brigitte Johanna Glaser and Barbara Puschmann-Nalenz, 179-202. Trier: WVT.

—. 2015. "Space and the Globalization of Violence in Graham Swift's Works." *PhiN Philologie im Netz* 72: 1-23. http://phin.de.

Roberts, Michèle. 2000. *The Looking Glass*. London: Little, Brown & Co.

Robson, Leo. 2011. "*Wish You Were Here* by Graham Swift: review." *The Telegraph*, June 20, 2011. http://www.telegraph.co.uk/culture/books/bookreviews/8579300/Wish-You-Were-Here-by-Graham-Swift-review.html.

Schiesari, Juliana. 1992. *The Gendering of Melancholia: Feminism, Psychoanalysis, and the Symbolics of Loss in Renaissance Literature*. Ithaca, NY: Cornell University Press.

Shaffer, Brian W. 2001. "An Interview with Kazuo Ishiguro." *Contemporary Literature* 42 (1): 1-14. http://web.b.ebscohost.com/ehost/delivery?sid=723fe4ed-fe96-41a8.

Stave, Shirley Ann. 2011. "Across Distances without Recognition: Misrecognition in Toni Morrison's *A Mercy.*" In *Toni Morrison's 'A Mercy': Critical Approaches*, edited by Shirley A. Stave and Justin Talley, 137-50. Newcastle-upon-Tyne: Cambridge Scholars.

Strehle, Susan. 2013. "'I Am a Thing Apart': Toni Morrison, *A Mercy*, and American Exceptionalism." *Critique: Studies in Contemporary Fiction* 54 (2): 109-23.

Swift, Graham. 1999. *Waterland* and *Last Orders*. London: Picador.

—. 2011. *Wish You Were Here*. London: Picador.

—. 2016. *Mothering Sunday: A Romance*. London: Simon & Schuster (a Scribner e-book). Kindle.

Tait, Theo. 2012. "*Lionel Asbo* by Martin Amis." *The Guardian* June 08, 2012. http://www.theguardian.com/ books/2012/jun/08/lionel-asbo-martin-amis-review.

Tönnies, Merle. 2016. "The Use of Comic Effects in Memoirs of British Asian Adolescence: 21st-Century Writers Looking Back at the 1970s and 1980s." *Anglistik: An International Journal for English Studies* 27 (1): 113-24.

Trevor, William. 2009. *Love and Summer*. London: Penguin. Kindle.

Vega-González, Susana. 2011. "Orphanhood in Toni Morrison's *A Mercy*." In *Toni Morrison's 'A Mercy': Critical Approaches*, edited by Shirley A. Stave and Justin Talley, 119-35. Newcastle-upon-Tyne: Cambridge Scholars.

Vermeulen, Pieter. 2011. "The Novel after Melancholia: On Tom McCarthy's *Remainder* and David Mitchell's *Ghostwritten*." In *The Literature of Melancholia, Early Modern to Postmodern*, edited by Martin Middeke and Christina Wald, 254-67. London: Palgrave Macmillan.

—. 2010. "Being True to Fact: Coetzee's Prose of the World." In *J.M. Coetzee and Ethics*, edited by Anton Leist and Peter Singer, 269-89. New York: Columbia University Press.

Wade, Francesca. 2015. "Caryl Phillips: 'If they don't look at my picture they think I'm a woman'." *The Telegraph*, March 16, 2015. http://www.telegraph.co.uk/culture/books/authorinterviews/11470135/Caryl-Phillips-If-they-dont-look-at-my-picture-they-think-Im-a-woman.html.

Wardi, Anissa. 2011. "The Politics of 'Home' in *A Mercy*." In *Toni Morrison's 'A Mercy': Critical Approaches*, edited by Shirley A. Stave and Justin Talley, 23-39. Newcastle-upon-Tyne: Cambridge Scholars.

Whitford, Margaret. 1991a. *Luce Irigaray: Philosophy in the Feminine*. London: Routledge.

—, ed. 1991b. *The Irigaray Reader*. Oxford: Basil Blackwell.

—. 1991c "Introduction to Section I." *The Irigaray Reader*. Oxford: Basil Blackwell, 1991b: 23-29.

Winterson, Jeanette. 2004. *Lighthousekeeping*. London: Fourth Estate.
—. 2015. *The Gap of Time: The Winter's Tale Retold*. Hogarth Shakespeare. Kindle.
Woodward, Gerard. 2015. "*The Lost Child* by Caryl Phillips, book review." *The Independent*, March 26, 2015. http://www.independent.co.uk/arts-entertainment/books/reviews/the-lost-child-by-caryl-phillips-book-review-wuthering-heights-.
Wyatt, Jean. 2012. "Failed Messages, Maternal Loss, and Narrative Form in Toni Morrison's *A Mercy*." *Modern Fiction Studies* 58 (1): 128-51.
Zwierlein, Anne-Julia. 2014. "Lost at Sea: Mourning, Melancholia and Maritime Mindscapes in Early 21st-Century British and Irish Fiction." In *Narrating Loss: Representations of Mourning, Nostalgia and Melancholia in Contemporary Anglophone Fictions*, edited by Brigitte Johanna Glaser and Barbara Puschmann-Nalenz, 161-77. Trier: WVT.

CHAPTER FOUR

ORPHANS, MYTH, AND CONTEMPORARY FANTASY LITERATURE: *HARRY POTTER, HIS DARK MATERIALS, A SONG OF ICE AND FIRE*

GEROLD SEDLMAYR

Laura Peters, in her work on the orphan figure in Victorian literature, has fruitfully availed herself of Jacques Derrida's conception of the *pharmakon*; or, more correctly, of Derrida's reading of Plato's use of this very concept (cf. Peters 2000, 22-23, 26-27). In this chapter, I would like to follow Peters' example and take Derrida's essay "Plato's Pharmacy" as a point of departure for my own reading of the orphan figure, albeit with a slightly different angle. In fact, I would like to explore the specific function of the orphan figure with a view to its status in texts that are designated as belonging to the genre of "fantasy". What I am especially interested in is the particular connection between the orphan, myth, and fantasy. As for the link between the two latter terms, I proceed on Brian Attebery's assumption that "fantasy, as a literary form, is a way of reconnecting to traditional myths and the worlds they generate" (2014, 9). With regard to the first two terms, I follow Derrida's suggestion that, at least within the framework of the Western metaphysical tradition (which the term "Platonism" probably represents like no other), there is a close relationship between the orphan and *mythos*, the classical Greek word for "story": "The orphan is always, in the text of Plato—and elsewhere—the model of the persecuted creature. We had begun by stressing the affinity between writing and *mythos* created by their common opposition to *logos*. Orphanhood is perhaps another side of their kinship. *Logos* has a father; the father of a myth is almost impossible to find" (Derrida, 1981, 183n69). Before turning to some of the most iconic fantasy texts of our time in order to situate them within this thematic complex, it is necessary to briefly discuss the Platonic texts on which Derrida focuses, as well as define the term "fantasy".

Plato's Monsters: Writing—Myth—Fantasy

Derrida derives the notion of a family scene which structures the opposition *logos*/*mythos* from a discussion of two myths to which Socrates alludes in Plato's *Phaedrus*. One is the story of how the god Theuth (Thoth) comes to the god-king Thamus of Egypt, who in turn embodies Ammon, the chief of gods, and offers several of his inventions as gifts for the good of the Egyptians, among them the invention of writing. Describing its use, he claims it is a remedy, a *pharmakon*: "'This invention, O king,' said Theuth, 'will make the Egyptians wiser and will improve their memories; for it is an elixir [*pharmakon*] of memory and wisdom that I have discovered.'" (Plato, 274e). However, Thamus immediately rejects Theuth's invention, claiming that instead of supporting their memories and making them wiser, writing "will produce forgetfulness in the minds of those who learn to use it, because they will not practice their memory. Their trust in writing, produced by external characters which are no part of themselves, will discourage the use of their own memory within them" (275a). Writing is indeed a *pharmakon*, but for Thamus the term rather implies one of this highly ambiguous term's other meanings, not "remedy", but "poison". While *logos*—living speech—guarantees the presence of meaning and of truth (*aletheia*), written language is deadening. According to Thamos, the "external characters" of writing, i.e., the written words and the letters of which they consist, have a "strange quality": "you might think they spoke as if they had intelligence, but if you question them, wishing to know about their sayings, they always say only one and the same thing" (275d). With spoken language, Socrates holds, the creator/progenitor, when producing speech, is necessarily present, which in turn guarantees the presence of meaning—if need be, he can immediately react and clarify. Written language, in contrast, lacks the presence of such a "father figure" and hence assumes the status of a helpless and disoriented orphan (Derrida 1981, 82-83): "every word when once it is written, is bandied about, alike among those who understand and those who have no interest in it, and it knows not to whom to speak or not to speak; when ill-treated or unjustly reviled it always needs its father to help it; for it has no power to protect or help itself" (275d-e). Divested of its paternal origin, the written word is deprived not merely of the presence of meaning, but also of its "social status": without distinction (in Bourdieu's sense), it addresses itself to and seeks assistance from those who understand as well as those who do not.

The other myth that Socrates discusses with Phaedrus (in the chronology of the dialogue, this discussion actually comes first) concerns the fate of the Athenian princess Oreithyia, who rejects the advances of Boreas, the god of the cold north wind. Boreas, in tune with his icy character, angrily kidnaps her while, together with her playmate Pharmacea, she is dancing at the banks of the river Ilissus. He abducts her to some far-off place, wraps her up in a cloud and rapes her. When Socrates and Phaedrus, during a walk outside of the city gates of Athens, come to the very spot at the river where Oreithyia was allegedly carried away by Boreas, Phaedrus asks Socrates whether he believes this tale to be true and hence raises a more general question about the nature of mythic tales and the fantastic creatures inhabiting them. Socrates claims that one could approach such tales in a rationalistic way and attempt to unearth the "real" kernel behind them. One could assume, for instance, that Oreithyia was thrown off the edge of the cliff by a gust of wind and killed; subsequently, this "normal" incident has become clad in the cloak of an invented story, hence rendering its factual truth invisible. However, as Socrates adds, such a probabilistic approach could only ever yield very limited success, because people would be hard put to find explanations for all mythic tales and the huge variety of fantastic creatures they feature. According to him, finding out about their nature can only be of any interest as long as a certain precondition is fulfilled. It makes no sense to inquire into the "reality" of fantastic creatures *before* another inquiry has been completed, namely the inquiry into the nature of one's self: "I am not yet able, as the Delphic inscription has it, to know myself; so it seems to me ridiculous, when I do not yet know that, to investigate irrelevant things" (Plato, 229e-230a). Importantly, this "knowing oneself" implies knowing "one's own monsters": "I investigate […] myself, to know whether I am a monster more complicated and more furious than Typhon or a gentler and simpler creature, to whom a divine and quiet lot is given by nature" (230a). Hence, Socrates—for philosophical reasons—dismisses mythic or fantastic creatures like "the Centaurs, […] the Chimaera, […] Gorgons and Pegas" (229d). For him, they are so extraneous to the proper purpose of human existence that he is not even inclined to decide between a rational explanation for their appearance in mythic tales, which would degrade them to mere figments of the imagination, or their potential reality. This, in turn, forces Socrates' listener Phaedrus and Plato's readers to decide for themselves whether they follow Socrates and totally dismiss the issue concerning the nature of mythic tales and creatures, or try to investigate it nonetheless.

From the later discussion of the myth of Theuth and Thamos, the trajectory of Plato's argument appears to be straightforward: both mythic tales and the art of writing are an impediment to the attainment of true knowledge. Strangely enough, though, in order to find out about the "propriety and impropriety in writing" (274b), Socrates has recourse to a myth, namely the myth of Theuth and Thamos, the truth of which can never be ultimately established (Derrida 1981, 79-80). My argument in the following is that fantasy tales like J.K. Rowling's *Harry Potter* or Philip Pullman's *His Dark Materials* take up Socrates' questions about the "truth value" of mythic storytelling, not least in order to renegotiate and put into perspective the legacy of Western metaphysics. The question is not whether this is done intentionally—at least in *His Dark Materials*, it is. Rather, this sort of investment is taken to be characteristic of fantasy literature in general. To borrow Attebery's words: "Fantasy is an arena—I believe the primary arena—in which competing claims about myth can be contested and different relationships with myth tried out" (2014, 9).

While Nina Auerbach has claimed that "the orphan can be thought of as a metaphor for the novel itself" (1975, 395), this is arguably even more true of fantastic and fantasy tales. Fantasy again and again takes up elements from old mythic tales, often via a detour through other texts that have in turn incorporated myth in one way or another; what John Clute refers to as "taproot texts" (1997b, 921-22). Fantasy thus is both connected to and disconnected from older "originals". For Auerbach, the novel is the "faintly disreputable and possibly bastardized offspring of uncertain parentage" (1975, 395); with regard to the fantasy novel, the qualifiers "faintly" and "possibly" can safely be discarded. Often discredited as relatively worthless products of popular culture, fantasy texts have long been pushed to the margins of scholarly attention. At first glance, this may be due to the proliferation of "genre fantasy" (Attebery 1992, 9-11), much of which indeed is commercially oriented formula fantasy that unimaginatively avails itself of the motifs, storylines, and characters of the genre classics, without adding any innovative twist for their part; ironically, as John Grant holds, genre fantasy therefore "is not at heart fantasy at all, but a comforting revisitation of cosy venues, creating an effect that is almost anti-fantasy" (1997, 396). The scholarly rejection of fantasy, though, may also have more fundamental reasons. Lucie Armitt, who conceives of fantasy not as a genre but rather a mode of writing, proposes in *Fantasy Fiction: An Introduction*:

> "Fantasy" is a word commonly disparaged by literary and nonliterary voices alike. Summed up in the dismissive phrase "castles in the air," fantasy takes on a kind of vertical trajectory that must be flattened,

smoothed out, replaced with a more acceptable "horizontal" outlook. [...]
What *is* fantasy writing? Utopia, allegory, fable, myth, science fiction, the
ghost story, space opera, travelogue, the Gothic, cyberpunk, magic realism;
the list is not exhaustive, but it covers most of the modes of fiction
discussed in this book as "fantasy." Where fantasising is "airy-fairy," then
realism is "grounded" [...]. It is, from this point, an easy slippage to glide
from "realistic" to (literary) realism. Literary realism is certainly the type
of fictional writing adopted most readily by the canon, seen as most fitting
for serious or weighty subject matter. (Armitt 2005, 1)

In short, Armitt believes that the tendency to consider "realistic" fiction as
superior has led to the concomitant depreciation of fantastic literature,
simply because the former is given credit for being able to describe the
world "as it is".[1] In order to counter this conception, Attebery, just like
Armitt (cf. 2005, 2), stresses that "[t]hough they are contrasting modes,
mimesis [i.e., 'realism'] and fantasy are not opposites. They can and do
coexist within any given work; there are no purely mimetic or fantastic
works of fiction" (Attebery 1992, 3). Nonetheless, the simple fact that this
binary, as well as the implicit hierarchical relation between its poles, often
seems to be accepted as a given, is proof of the lingering influence of
"Plato-style" rationalism.

When I use "fantasy" in the following, I do not so much refer to
"fantastic literature" as it developed from the 18th century, particularly in
the shape of the gothic novel, but rather to the kind of narratives by and
written in the wake of George MacDonald, J.R.R. Tolkien, C.S. Lewis and
others. Avoiding terms like "high fantasy" or "sword and sorcery", I rather
adhere to Attebery's influential conception of fantasy in terms of a "fuzzy
set": "Genres may be approached as 'fuzzy sets,' meaning that they are
defined not by boundaries but by a center" (1992, 12). While, at the
boundaries, "[f]antasy edges into science fiction; science fiction impinges
on mainstream fiction; [and] mainstream fiction overlaps with fantasy"
(13), the most likely candidate for the position at the centre is J.R.R.
Tolkien's *The Lord of the Rings*: "Tolkien's form of fantasy, for readers in
English, is our mental template, and will be until someone else achieves
equal recognition with an alternative conception" (14). Attebery published
these words in 1992. It may well be that, in the meantime, *Harry Potter*
has usurped the towering status of *The Lord of the Rings*. At the same
time, if this were the case, it is questionable whether Rowling's series has
also replaced the generic template offered by Tolkien's trilogy. Attebery
delineates this template by way of three constitutive aspects (content,
structure, reader response), all of which are also true for *Harry Potter*:
"The essential content is the impossible, or [...] 'some violation of what

the author clearly believes to be natural law'[.] [...] Second, the characteristic structure of fantasy is comic. It begins with a problem and ends with resolution'" (14-15). The third aspect pertains to the effect fantasy produces in the reader, which Attebery—by way of Tolkien's term "eucatastrophe", Russian formalism and Brecht—variously describes as "wonder", "estrangement", "defamiliarization", and "alienation" (16). In *The Encyclopedia of Fantasy*, a standard work of reference for scholars of the field, John Clute defines fantasy very similarly, particularly regarding the first aspect: "A fantasy text is a self-coherent narrative. When set in this world, it tells a story which is impossible in the world as we perceive it [...]; when set in an otherworld, that otherworld will be impossible, though stories set there may be possible in its terms" (1997a, 338). Without having to elaborate on the implications of Clute's phrasing, it is striking how the emphasis put on impossibility again seems to echo Socrates' reservations against myth, which returns us to Auerbach's above-quoted claim that the novel is the "faintly disreputable and possibly bastardized offspring of uncertain parentage" (1975, 395).

In addition to the other reasons, the fact that fantasy texts shamelessly—and maybe sometimes unwittingly—exploit older texts has probably contributed to separating them with even more intensity from what are considered to be their incomparably worthier and therefore canonised "parental" texts. This complicated and apparently haphazard family relationship especially to mythic tales, however, also harbours an advantage that should not be underestimated. To quote Attebery at some length:

> Like dream or myth, [fantasy] uses symbols to tell the truths that the conscious mind cannot grasp or fears to face. Yet unlike myth, fantasy speaks with no cultural authority. It pretends to be a mere game, a simple amusement for children or a pastime for an idle hour. Like a jester in a Shakespeare play, it is free to speak forbidden truths because no one pays it any mind. And, like the Elizabethan theater, the genre of fantasy has become a space for cultural negotiation, to borrow Stephen Greenblatt's term, in part because of its seeming inconsequentiality. Whereas Marlowe and Shakespeare dramatized contesting models of gender, knowledge, and authority, fantasy pits different myths and responses to myth against one another. Those responses include different levels of belief, from literal through figurative and secondary to complete rejection. They also include different kinds of engagement—moral, social, liturgical, psychological—and different kinds of obligation. Fantasy can be used to weigh the claims of myth against those of its Modern rivals, history and science. (Attebery 2014, 21-22)

Attebery's argument that "fantasy speaks with no cultural authority" is reminiscent of Socrates' contention that *mythos*, like writing in general, lacks the paternal presence of the *logos*. Just like Thamus, the embodiment of the Father, denies the use value of Theuth's invention, literary studies scholars, as well as the whole community of those who have amassed cultural capital, have long tended to deny that fantasy carries much inherent originality. Fantasy texts, of course, do have "parents"—the above-mentioned "taproot texts"—but in most cases, their legacy has become obscured to the point of unrecognizability.[2] For Attebery, though, this lack of the paternal presence—fantasy's uncertain orphan status—is exactly what provides it with its potential to question and re-negotiate the authority of "father discourses". Of course, this does not imply any guarantee whatsoever that the potential will be fulfilled. It is for this reason that the orphan character in fantasy fiction attains such prominence: as the embodiment of the genre itself, he or she represents fantasy's potential to renegotiate the power and influence of myth. Ultimately, this happens not so much in order to finally erase myth, like Socrates suggests, but to bring it into position against those discourses that, throughout the course of modernity, have come to dominate and displace it. History and science are just two of the possible candidates.

Harry Potter

The Real and the Fantastic

When the reader encounters Harry Potter for the first time, the scene taps into a long tradition of foundling characters in myth, legend, and literature (cf. Gymnich in this volume, 19; Puschmann-Nalenz, "Some Things", in this volume, 158-66). Similar to the biblical Moses, Fielding's Tom Jones, Wilde's Jack Worthing, or Michael Ende's Jim Button, he is discovered as a helpless baby by his future substitute family and raised by them. However, unlike many of these foundling predecessors but very much like other orphan characters, his fate with those who raise him is not enviable. Like Cinderella—Ximena Gallardo C. and C. Jason Smith, for instance, have called Harry "Cinderfella" (cf. 2003)—or Jane Eyre, he is seriously neglected by his kin, the Dursleys. Harry's new residence, number four, Privet Drive, is situated in the non-magical part of the world, the sphere of the "Muggles": as the narrator stresses right at the beginning, the Dursleys "were perfectly normal" and "the last people you'd expect to be involved in anything strange or mysterious" (*PS*, 7).[3] Recognisably, the Dursleys' is *our* world, a thoroughly secularised world of suburban middle-class complacency: they are a nuclear family with a father occupying a leading professional position in a company, a housekeeping mother, and a spoilt single child.

According to Farah Mendlesohn's distinction of different rhetorical strategies employed in fantasy fiction, the first chapter clearly is akin to what she calls an intrusion fantasy: the fantastic in the shape of "strange and mysterious things" (*PS*, 7) intrudes into the primary world and disturbs its "normality".[4] Mr Dursley, on his way to work, witnesses "a cat reading a map", but explains it away as "a trick of the light" (*PS*, 8); there is an uncommon number of cloak-wearing people in the streets ("weirdos"), whose appearance he also tries to rationalise. Only when he incidentally overhears the name "Harry Potter" is he temporarily thrown off the track. After all, his family's relation to the strange, "unDursleyish", Potters is their big "secret, and their greatest fear was that somebody would discover it" (*PS*, 7). Hence, from the perspective of the Dursleys, the arrival in Privet Drive of Dumbledore, McGonagall, Hagrid, and of course baby Harry is indeed unsettling: as in other intrusion fantasies, "the world is ruptured by the intrusion, which disrupts normality and has to be negotiated with or defeated, sent back whence it came, or controlled" (Mendlesohn 2008, 115). Obviously, the Dursleys opt for control. However, since the reader's sympathies, from the beginning, are narratively steered away from them (by way of satire), the reader is never even close to sharing their point of view and opinions. As a consequence, Rowling subverts the usual functioning of the intrusion fantasy. While commonly in such fantasies, "the fantastic is the bringer of chaos" (Mendlesohn 2008, xxi), the abhorred, unfamiliar and rejected Other (which, for the Dursleys, it is), the reader does not encounter it as such: rather, it is constructed as a desirable alternative reality, the "preferable Other", if you will.

This reversal of perspectives is again suggested at the beginning of the second chapter, "The Vanishing Glass". By way of ellipsis, the narrative fast-forwards nearly a decade so as to introduce us to the then ten-year-old Harry. Interestingly (and in tune with the narrative device of ellipsis), Privet Drive is described as a place that gives the impression of being frozen in time. As the narrator mentions, "Privet Drive had hardly changed at all" (*PS*, 19) in the years between Harry's arrival in 1981 and the narrative present in 1991. The notion of a place outside of time seems to evoke a motif commonly found in fairy tales, as for example with the enchanted castle in Sleeping Beauty. However, in this case, it is not magic that is responsible for the timelessness in which house and family are caught; on the contrary, the impression of stasis is entirely a characteristic of a thoroughly mundane world whose inhabitants are not at all interested in the dynamics of newness, in the challenge posed by what is not explainable within the parameters of the already familiar. In fact, "[o]nly the photographs on the mantelpiece really showed how much time had passed" (*PS*, 18), but tellingly, the photographs exclusively document the "development" undergone by Dudley, Harry's bullying cousin. In contrast, "[t]he [living-]room held no sign at all that another boy lived in the house, too" (18). Harry, "the boy who lived" (18), by leaving no sign, paradoxically signifies as an absence in the Dursleys' home and lives: "The Dursleys often spoke about Harry like this", i.e. disrespectfully and in the third person, "as though he wasn't there—or rather, as though he was something very nasty that couldn't understand them, like a slug" (22). It is as if he were invisible, at least invisible as a fellow human being.

With respect to the position occupied by the Dursleys, Harry's "invisibility" is obviously linked to his strangeness, a strangeness that is interpreted as being a legacy of his parents. As Aunt Petunia avers: "I knew you'd be just the same, just as strange, just as—as—*abnormal*" (44). The difference between Harry's surrogate and his real parents, then, is one between two modes of being-in-the-world. In the world of the Dursleys, Harry can hardly *be*, which becomes evident from the diegetic fact of him being "invisible" in the Dursleys' household as well as the extradiegetic fact that the narrator gives us hardly any glimpse of the everyday reality of Harry's growing up with them in the first decade of his life: there is hardly any place for Harry in a "realistic" narrative. This double absence is indicative of his orphan status (cf. Puschmann-Nalenz, "Gap", in this volume, 96).

Two years later, during Aunt Marge's visit, Uncle Vernon again explicitly berates Harry for his "*abnormality*" (*PA*, 20). Aunt Marge, who—very much like the propagators of a racist "pure blood" ideology in the magical world—reveals herself to be a late-19th- and early-20th-century-style believer in the necessity to fight a threatening biologically and culturally induced degeneracy ("Bad blood will out" [26]), even suggests that she would have put Harry in an "orphanage if [he]'d been dumped on *my* doorstep" (23). The reason for the Dursleys' harsh rejection of Harry is never really explained, yet one need not look far for the answer: they reject him as abnormal because he represents everything they cannot explain. He literally is a "foreign body" that irritates the perfection of their middle-class milieu. Obviously, as the reader learns later, Aunt Petunia especially knows very well about her late sister's wondrous capacities, but this knowledge makes it even worse, because Harry, by his very presence, constantly reminds her of her own inability to access this other world, the world of magic. After all, when she was as old as Harry is at the beginning of *Philosopher's Stone*, Petunia even wrote a letter to Dumbledore and asked whether she could also attend Hogwarts with her sister, but was denied (*DH*, 537) and painfully felt excluded. Accordingly, from the point of view of the Dursleys, and particularly in the case of Petunia, the fantastic comes to occupy a space and assume a function common to that in other intrusion stories. As Rosemary Jackson writes: "Far from fulfilling desire, these [fantastic] spaces perpetuate desire by insisting upon *absence*, lack, the non-seen, the unseeable" (1981, 45). This, then, is the first function of Harry's orphanhood: it stands for the fantastic itself. In a thoroughly secularised and rationalised post-Enlightenment world, Harry is a singularity that needs to be contained. By the Dursleys' suppression of information pertaining to his parents, they effectively cut him as well as themselves off from a tradition and worldview that have been denied to them and hence deemed "false". Two years later, when "none of the Dursleys", on their nephew's 13th birthday, "gave any sign that they had noticed Harry enter the room" (*PA* 18), this is of course not because he is really invisible, but because they choose to ignore him, to un-see him. While "[t]hat which is not seen", according to Jackson's analysis of the critical potential of fantasy fiction, "can only have a subversive function in relation to an epistemological and metaphysical system which makes 'I see' synonymous with 'I understand'" (1981, 45), the case is slightly different with the Dursleys. Actually, they do see—young Petunia clearly sees her sister Lily soar in the air after launching herself from the swing (*DH*, 532), Vernon distinctly recognises the cat reading a map—but they are unable to understand; and precisely because they cannot understand, they choose to un-see, to render invisible that which is beyond explanation. They seek to deprive Harry of meaning and of life, thereby prefiguring Voldemort's relationship to him.

All of the aforementioned tropes—time and timelessness, the power to signify, invisibility, as well as the binary life/death—structure Harry's existence as an orphan, just as they determine the structure of the story as a whole. At the end of the septology, Harry will once and for all decide against the possibility of omnipotent power and a perverse form of immortality by rejecting the Deathly Hallows. Significantly, of the three artefacts, he will only keep the Cloak of Invisibility (*DH*, 599), that powerful magical item which his ancestor, Ignotus Peverell, had allegedly received from Death in order to hide from him (*DH*, 572) and which Harry, at first unknowingly, had inherited from his father. Harry, however, does not hide from death, but, by willingly sacrificing himself, proves his humanity and so can eventually free himself from his orphan status by founding a family and hence enable the future. In the following, we will have to look at these processes in more detail in order to shed light on their connections and implications.

The Orphan's Call for Signification

Harry of course does not remain in his abject situation with the Dursleys for long. Significantly, the first sign announcing the change of his fate is a letter that unexpectedly arrives by post and is addressed to him: "No one, ever, in his whole life, had written to him. Who would? He had no friends, no other relatives—he didn't belong to the library so he'd never even got rude notes asking for books back" (*PS*, 30). Harry, though, does not have a chance to read it, because Uncle Vernon immediately strips him of it. Vernon's action, shocking though it is, is only logical. After all, throughout Harry's life with them, the Dursleys have tried to turn him into a cipher devoid of meaning, a "nothing" without history. Now, this history is on the point of catching up with Harry. When he shouts, "I WANT MY LETTER!" (*PS* 31), he in fact calls for signification and hence the insertion into a historical trajectory. The boy "who didn't belong to the library" demands to be linked to a signifying system and a history of which he has been deprived, an archive in which to trace his origins and construct a future. Tellingly, this human urge for meaning cannot be blocked by the Dursleys: every day, new letters keep arriving, and on top of that, an exponentially growing number. Not even their flight to a forlorn little place out on a tiny island in the sea can prevent the inescapable. On his 11th birthday, Hagrid, the "Keeper of Keys and Grounds at Hogwarts" (*PS*, 40), personally arrives to deliver the letter and tell Harry about that other world to which he belongs, precisely and straightforwardly because his parents belonged to it as well: "*our* world, I mean. *Your* world. *My* world. *Yer parents' world*" (*PS*, 41). The letter of acceptance, which invites him to become a pupil at Hogwarts School of Witchcraft and Wizardry, literally re-inscribes him with a meaning that the Dursleys had attempted to erase.

Strictly speaking, it is not entirely correct to say that Harry's mode of being in the world is analogous to a "blank page" before the arrival of the letters. When, more than ten years earlier and under an "inky sky" (*PS*, 18), baby Harry is brought to number four, Privet Drive, by the very same Hagrid, Dumbledore places a letter into the child's hands in which he explains the situation to the boy's future foster family. It is this older letter that identifies the boy as an orphan in the first place and so, by transferring the responsibility of bringing the boy up to the Dursleys, indirectly triggers Harry's period of suffering. Apart from this, however, and much more importantly, there is Harry's scar, which figures as an ostensible, clearly decipherable and non-erasable mark of his identity, at least within the signifying system of the magical world. The scar is a sign, a Socratic "external character", which, more than anything, represents Harry's orphan status in all its ambiguity. On the one hand, it will always and unfailingly remind him as well as everyone else of the non-presence of his parents; it is a sign of loss, of lost meaningfulness and unfulfilled desire. On the other hand, it re-presents his parents' unconditional love for him and hence the non-erasable bond that exists between the three of them; in this sense, it is a sign of complete fulfilment, a sign of the absolute, of love in the full Platonic sense. As Dumbledore explains: "[Voldemort] didn't realise that love as powerful as your mother's for you leaves its own mark. Not a scar, no visible sign … to have been loved so deeply, even though the person you loved us is gone, will give us some protection for ever" (*PS*, 216). Semiotically speaking, what ultimately counts is not the signifier, the materiality of the scar, but rather the signified which magically connects to its abstract referent, the highest Platonic *eidos*: love and its power of protection.

Hagrid, who is astonished at the degree of Harry's ignorance regarding his background ("But yeh must know about yer mum and dad" [*PS*, 41]), gets to the heart of the problem when he says: "It's an outrage! A scandal! Harry Potter not knowin' his own story when every kid in our world knows his name! [...] Never wondered how you got that mark on yer forehead?" (*PS*, 44, 45). The scandal consists in the fact that Harry plays a leading role in a story (*mythos*), namely the story of his life, of which he is not conscious. His status as an orphan is symbolic of this aporetic position of being "inside" and "outside" at the very same time: Harry, to pick up on the topic raised before, is invisible to himself. While the gap can never be wholly bridged—Harry will "have that scar for ever" (*PS*, 17), as Dumbledore observes—he can at least connect to his story by attempting to achieve control over the role he is supposed to play in it. This, however, is not that easy, precisely because he is the "Chosen One": it seems as if his whole story has already been written by a power beyond himself, namely fate, the employment of which in turn conforms to the established generic conventions of fantasy writing.

Considering Harry's ambiguous status as an orphan, it is indeed fitting that Voldemort is not only Harry's antagonist, but also his uncanny *double*. As James Michael Curtis notes: "In terms of its treatment of the orphan figure, one of the most interesting features of the Harry Potter series is the juxtaposition of Harry and his archenemy, the evil Lord

Voldemort. Despite standing at nearly polar opposites of the moral spectrum, the two characters are, in fact, extremely similar" (2016, 101-02). Like Harry, Voldemort/Tom Riddle was raised an orphan and also is a so-called half-blood. While his father, the rich and handsome upper-middle-class Tom Riddle Sr., was a Muggle, his plain-looking mother Merope hailed from one of the oldest, though impoverished, wizarding families, the Gaunts, who could trace their ancestry back to Salazar Slytherin. However, in contrast to Harry's parents, Voldemort's had never been truly in love: freed from the tyranny exerted by her father and brother due to their temporary imprisonment in Azkaban (*HBP*, 200), Merope magically made Riddle fall in love with her, probably by way of a love philtre, i.e. a *pharmakon*.[5] After she had ceased to apply the potion, because, according to Dumbledore, she "could not bear to continue enslaving him by magical means" anymore, he immediately left his pregnant wife and "never troubled to discover what became of his son" (203). When Dumbledore meets the young Tom Riddle for the first time, he is in a Muggle orphanage somewhere in the London of the 1930s. Merope, who had come to the orphanage in a highly destitute state, gave birth to him there and died shortly afterwards (249). More than with Harry or any of the other orphans or half-orphans in the series, Tom's situation in the orphanage is reminiscent of those in Charles Dickens' novels: "The orphans […] were all wearing the same kind of greyish tunic. They looked reasonably well-cared-for, but there was no denying that this was a grim place in which to grow up" (*HBP*, 251). Yet in contrast to *Oliver Twist*'s Mr Bumble, the matron, Mrs Cole, seems to be a rather friendly woman; and in contrast to Oliver Twist himself, who retains his goodness in spite of all adverse circumstances, Tom becomes a "bully" (250) and a thief (cf. 255-56), who scares and mistreats the other kids by secretly using magic, which he instinctively begins to master. "Tom Riddle", as Sarah Fiona Winters remarks, "is a nightmarish version of the neglected orphan" (2011, 219). Significantly, like Harry, Tom is totally unaware not only of his magical ancestry but the existence of the magical world as such. As an orphan, he is not simply cut off from his parents, but from everything they stand for—his father's affluence and his mother's belonging to the world of magic. When Dumbledore tells him that he is offered a place in Hogwarts, Tom, never having heard of the school, is even afraid that he is about to be committed to an asylum for the insane (*HBP*, 253). More importantly, like Harry, Tom has been marked, yet not by a scar, but by his very name. Actually, apart from his looks (which derive from his father) and his magical abilities (which derive from his mother), Tom's only inheritance is his name. As her last wish, Merope told Mrs Cole that

the boy "was to be named Tom, for his father, and Marvolo, for *her* father
[…] and she said the boy's name was to be Riddle" (249). As Tom's
reaction reveals when being confronted with his name, he is not happy
about it at all. As he believes himself to be special, he despises his first
name as too ordinary: "There are a lot of Toms" (257). The only thing that
reconciles him with it is the fact that it is his father's, but only as long as
he wrongly believes that his magical abilities derive from his paternal side:
"My mother can't have been magic, or she wouldn't have died" (257). He
does not understand that the will to survive can be shattered. For him,
survival is everything: throughout the series, his major impulse is to outdo
and attain power over death.

It is at this point that the dissimilarities between Harry-the-orphan and
Tom-the-orphan become apparent. "[T]he series", Curtis notes, "gives us
two very different paths for the orphan child" (2016, 102). While Harry,
from the beginning, seeks to connect to others and find a meaningful place
within a larger community—within an established and dynamic social
signifying system—Tom's urge is rather to further dis-connect himself and
thereby potentiate his orphan status. As Dumbledore comments: "Even
then", as a boy in the orphanage, "he wished to be different, separate,
notorious" (*HBP*, 259). Ultimately, he seeks to stand *outside* the system,
but only in order to control it: he does not want to be organically
connected to the world and derive meaning from it, but instead intends to
form it, to impose meaning on it. Still, in contrast to the legions of pop-
cultural baddies who seem to lack any motive for their evilness,
Voldemort's hunger for power is not something that has been part of his
character from the beginning; it is not an essentialist trait. The reader
learns that during his years in Hogwarts, young Tom still tried to find a
connection to a paternal legacy, to a larger system of meaning and parental
protection: "Riddle was obsessed with his parentage […] [but] searched in
vain for some trace of Tom Riddle Senior" (339) in the archives of the
wizarding world. When he finds out that his father is a Muggle and that his
magical talent derives from his mother's side, this comes as a severe blow
to a traditional understanding of ancestry that solely works along
paternal/patriarchal lines, the more so because he considers his dead
mother as weak. The subsequent decision he takes at the age of 16 is
momentous. After setting out from the orphanage during the summer
holidays (which is telling in itself), he finds and kills his father and
grandparents, "thus obliterating the last of the unworthy Riddle line and
revenging himself upon the father who never wanted him" (343-44). In
addition, he slyly manages to throw suspicion on his mother's brother, his
uncle Morfin, who ends up in Azkaban, where he eventually dies, and with

him the old line of the Gaunt family. Very efficiently and cold-bloodedly, Tom hence annihilates his whole family, thereby turning himself into a "true" orphan, someone irrevocably severed from his family and its history. Notably, after having found out about his father being a Muggle, he also changes his name (339): he erases what he considers to be the shameful, stigmatising mark of his original identity and replaces it with another one, which Dumbledore aptly terms "the mask of 'Lord Voldemort'" (259). Ironically, though, the old name is as inerasable as Harry's scar: the mask he dons is not wholly "new", not indicative of Tom's self-creation from scratch, but it is a rearranged version of the "original" chain of signifiers—which, in fact, is not so original either, as Tom's disdainful commentary about the commonness of his first name reveals. To put it differently, his "new" name is literally a "Riddle", but a riddle that is still solvable within the given semiotic parameters. As Tom in the shape of his embodied memory—the version of Tom Riddle that has sprung from his diary—demonstrates to Harry by *writing letters and words into the air*, "TOM MARVOLO RIDDLE" anagrammatically metamorphoses into "I AM LORD VOLDEMORT" (*CS*, 231). His new name is not *radically* (Lat. *radix*, the root) different from his old; it is merely the result of a (magical) sleight of hand.

Repetition-in-Difference: Voldemort and Harry

It is thus possible to interpret Tom's/Voldemort's actions in terms of a desire to *write himself anew*, to re-inscribe himself with a new identity. His "desire of writing" is indeed a "desire for orphanhood and patricidal subversion. [...] The status of this orphan, whose welfare cannot be assured by any attendance or assistance, coincides with that of a *graphein* which, being nobody's son at the instant it reaches inscription, scarcely remains a son at all and no longer *recognizes* its origins, whether legally or morally" (Derrida 1981, 82). Yet Voldemort is not prepared to leave it at that. To disavow his legal and moral origins is not enough, because the notion of disavowal is meaningful only *within* the parameters of the old order. Disavowal thus further cements his orphan status, which in fact is the root cause of all his distress. By way of the patricide, he indeed brings his existence as an orphan to a head, but, so he obviously intends, only to ultimately get rid of it and the stigma it carries. The only way to do so is to become the origin and centre of an entirely new system. To put it differently, he is not content to be an orphaned *graphein*, but intends to become the origin of "living *logos*" (Derrida 1981, 82) himself. The means to do so, his *pharmakon*, is the ritual that is set at the end of the central

book of the septology, *The Goblet of Fire*: the ritual through which
Voldemort brings about his own rebirth and hence becomes his own father
and mother.

Tellingly, the ritual takes place in the graveyard in which Voldemort's
father is buried. Harry is tied to the headstone on which Voldemort's
father's name is engraved, with the legend *"TOM RIDDLE"* (*GoF*, 554)
clearly standing out on the page for the reader to see. Whereas in Socrates'
tale, Thamus, the god/father, is in the position of the originator of *logos*,
discrediting writing as a fatherless orphan, the scenario is reversed in this
scenario: the father is put into the position of the dead written word. At the
beginning of the scene, Voldemort appears as a deformed, snake-like, but
"almost helpless" baby-child (556) that is being brought to life in a
perverted, black-magic version of a birth ritual, at the conclusion of which
he appears as a full-grown man: "Lord Voldemort had risen again" (558).
At the beginning of the ritual, the baby is lowered by Wormtail into a large
cauldron, into whose liquid content three further ingredients are then
thrown: one of Voldemort's father's bones, Wormtail's right hand, and a
drop of Harry's blood. It may not be too far-fetched to read this as a
perverted version of a fertility ritual, which, according to James Frazer and
other "myth and ritual" theorists, can be considered as one of the central
mythic paradigms. Fertility rituals re-enact the cycle of life and death and
hence assure the continuation of life's power to assert itself, particularly
with regard to the existence and survival of the community. They are
based on the assumption that there is a "magical connection between the
drama of the dying and reviving god on the one hand, and the seasonal
cycle on the other. The king is dead; long live the king" (Coupe 1997, 25).
In contrast to such traditional fertility rites, Voldemort's rite is neither
performed with a view to the well-being of the community as a whole nor
is it staged as the *representation* of a mythic story. There is no god-figure
whose mythic fate Voldemort and Wormtail *imitate* by way of what Frazer
identifies as the "Law of Similarity", one of the two principles of
"Sympathetic Magic" (Frazer 1994, 26). Rather, he intends this ritual to be
wholly original, an act of self-foundation, a performance through which he
ultimately brings himself forth. By becoming his own father, he severs the
connection to his actual father. As he explains to Harry, his first
motivation is to posthumously revenge himself on Tom Riddle Senior for
leaving his mother and him, thereby rendering him an orphan:

> "You stand, Harry Potter, upon the remains of my late father," he
> hissed softly. "A Muggle and a fool … very like your dear mother. But
> they both had their uses, did they not? Your mother died to defend you as a

child ... and I killed my father, and see how useful he has proved himself, in death ..." [...]
"You see that house upon the hillside, Potter? My father lived there. My mother, a witch who lived here in this village, fell in love with him. But he abandoned her when she told him what she was ... he didn't like magic, my father ...
"He left her and returned to his Muggle parents before I was even born, Potter, and she died giving birth to me, leaving me to be raised in a Muggle orphanage ... but I vowed to find him ... and I revenged myself upon him, that fool who gave me his name ... *Tom Riddle* ..." (*GoF*, 560-61)

Yet Voldemort's revenge, which consists in the ritualistic severing of his ties to the father, has larger implications. Instead of dramatizing the *cyclical* nature of natural processes, which is the whole point of fertility rites, he intends to eliminate death once and for all, but not for everyone— like Jesus, for instance—but only *for himself*: "You know my goal—to conquer death" (566). In this sense, Voldemort truly is an anti-Christ figure.

In *A General Theory of Magic*, the anthropologist Marcel Mauss holds that "[m]agic is the art of preparing and mixing concoctions, fermentations, dishes" (1972, 66). It is in this respect that Mauss refers to the cauldron and the actions performed around and with it as "cuisine, pharmacy, chemistry" (66). Following up on this, the perverted resurrection ritual is indeed meant to assume the function of a remedy, a *pharmakon*, by which Voldemort intends to heal himself from his orphaned status by founding himself anew. Indeed, he has even begun to establish a new signifying system by stigmatising his followers with the Dark Mark, a device that allows them to summon each other, make themselves *present* at all times and be conjured from anywhere (*GoF*, 560). However, as with Plato's *pharmakon*, this one has a highly ambiguous nature, subverting Voldemort's intentions from the outset. The reason for this is to be sought in the fact that all ritual is a form of language and hence needs to be understandable (and repeatable) within a larger meaning system. The narrator does not mention where Voldemort derives the ritual from, whether the "recipe" has come down to him in some way or whether he has devised it himself. What is mentioned, however, is that particular sacrificial ingredients are needed, namely his father's bone, Wormtail's hand, and Harry's blood, as well as specific incantations that Wormtail mutters when throwing the items in: "*'Bone of the father, unknowingly given, you will renew your son'*" (*GoF*, 556) etc. As Mauss claims, not only is it commonly the case with magical rituals in all cultures that "[t]he peculiar and weird nature of non-verbal ritual is paralleled by the enigmatic muttering of spoken rites" (1972, 72), it is also generally true that "all ritual is a kind of language; it therefore translates ideas" (75). One of the "ideas" that is being "translated" is precisely the idea of the utter impossibility of an absolute self-foundation. For one, he simply cannot do without the connection to his father, which becomes evident both in the fact that his father's bone is a necessary component of the resurrection rite and the above-discussed paradoxical anagrammatic nature of his "new" name. And neither can he do without upholding the legacy of his mother, since it is through her that he can do magic in the first place. In addition, he is inescapably tied to Harry, who is not only the living sign of his failure but also his double, both Other and (displaced) Self. After all, as it turns out, Harry himself is the seventh Horcrux, one of the containers of Voldemort's split soul. As such, he is the living proof that Voldemort's power can never be *absolute*. In fact, then, what Ronnie Carmeli has fittingly referred to as "Voldemort's splitting tendency" (2009, 28) is always already subverting Tom Riddle's desire for closure, for overcoming his orphan status by fathering himself.

Their specific relation is also the reason why Harry, in the duel that he is forced to fight with Voldemort, can successfully (and unwittingly) oppose the evil wizard's death spell, the *Avada Kedavra* (*GoF*, 575), by way of his non-violent disarming spell, *Expelliarmus*, which effectually turns into a powerful counter spell, "Priori Incantatem", as the chapter's title indicates.[6] And it can become such precisely because their wands, but more so they themselves, have a share in each other's being: Harry has incorporated a part of Voldemort's soul as a consequence of his mother Lily's sacrificial act, and Voldemort has been resurrected with the help of Harry's blood. They are a *repetition* of each other, but a *repetition-in-difference*. It is precisely through their connection—"*Don't break the connection*" (576), he tells himself—that Harry can oppose Voldemort's death-bringing power. Not only does a "golden, dome-shaped web [...] of light" erect itself as a protective egg-like shell around them (preventing the Death Eaters from assisting their master), the atmosphere is moreover charged by the "unearthly and beautiful sound" of the "phoenix song" (576): the song of the mythical bird that traditionally represents the cycle of life and death, as well as the power of resurrection. Apart from the (acoustic) presence of the phoenix, the scenario in itself references classical creation myths, for instance the one connected to Socrates' Thamus, who is the god Ammon-Ra in Egyptian mythology: "The world came out of an egg. More precisely, the living creator of the life of the world came out of an egg: the sun, then, was at first carried in an eggshell. Which explains a number of Ammon-Ra's characteristics: he is also a bird, a falcon [...]. But in his capacity as origin of everything, Ammon-Ra is also the origin of the egg" (Derrida 1981, 92). And by way of possible allusions like this one, it again becomes clear that Voldemort's intention to inhabit the position of the Father-without-father, of the absolute origin, is doomed to fail from the beginning. While he craves to "conquer death", he stands for nothing *but* death. The difference between the two types of orphans is hence revealed in the course of this duel: while Voldemort, as has been argued, seeks to *potentiate* his orphan status in order to free himself from it,[7] Harry is able to come to terms with and overcome it by actively connecting not only to his past—his parents—but also the present, namely his friends and the community at large. Unlike Voldemort, Harry does not aspire to be the Lord over Life and Death, to take God's place, but is strong and perseveres precisely because he accepts his place within a larger order of things, within a context that gives him security and provides him with meaning in the first place—which is signified by the egg-like "dome shaped web" around him.

Harry Potter as Literary Myth: Casting Off the Orphan Status

On a meta-level, Harry's integration within a larger order of things indicates *how* Rowling's fantasy, like so many other fantasies, takes a stand both against the traditional Platonic rejection of myth and the specifically modern "myth of mythlessness" (Coupe 1997, 13) that has come to dominate Western thinking since the Enlightenment. It goes without saying that Rowling's *mythos* does not have the status of the old, sacred mythical stories: it lacks "cultural authority" (Attebery 2014, 21). Self-evidently, it is not the kind of handed-down, anonymous myth that exerts religious binding power for an entire community. For this reason, it is surely tempting to denounce it, as well as fantasy in general, for its haphazard, "postmodernist" appropriation of bits and pieces of older mythic stories, which now, in their isolated, secularised and thoroughly commodified condition, are far from being able to constitute any overarching, organically connected field of meaning anymore. Viewed from this perspective, fantasy is arbitrary pastiche and hence cannot but result, to borrow Fredric Jameson's words, "in anything but 'heaps of fragments' and in a practice of the randomly heterogeneous and fragmentary and the aleatory" (1991, 25). The "golden, dome-shaped web" created by fantasy would be nothing but a hoax, an illusion, a sleight-of-hand, comparable to Voldemort's donning of the mask that is his new name. In a way, then, this sort of criticism resembles Socrates'/Plato's criticism not only of myth, but also of the written word. However, if this is so, if the criticisms work analogously, it is advisable to take note of the fact that whereas the *pharmakon* of writing, for Socrates, is poisonous, he nonetheless can never wholly cancel out the possibility of conceiving it as remedy. As mentioned above: is it not the case that he uses myth in order to be able to make his point in the first place? Irrevocably, then, *pharmakon* means both, poison and remedy. When transferring the issue to contemporary fantasy, this in turn leaves us with the chance to recover it as viable (to raise it from the dead, so to speak). But how? In order to answer, it is worthwhile to quote at some length from a passage in which Derrida summarises Plato's argumentation in *Phaedrus*:

> As a living thing, *logos* issues from a father. There is thus for Plato no such thing as a written thing. There is only a *logos* more or less alive, more or less distant from itself. Writing is not an independent order of signification; it is weakened speech, something not completely dead: a living-dead, a reprieved corpse, a deferred life, a semblance of breath. The phantom, the phantasm, the simulacrum (*eidolon*, 276*a*) of living discourse is not inanimate; it is not insignificant; it simply signifies little, and always the same thing. The signifier of little, this discourse that doesn't amount to much, is like all ghosts: errant. It rolls (*kulindeitai*) this way and that like someone who has lost his way […], like someone who has lost his rights, an outlaw, a pervert, a bad seed, a vagrant, an adventurer, a bum. Wandering in the streets, he doesn't even know who he is, what his identity—if he has one—might be, what his name is, what his father's name is. (Derrida 1981, 144)

Does this not recapitulate all of the above-sketched charges against fantasy? That it is an illusory "phantasm" that cannot properly re-establish a living connection to its (still?) meaningful "parent discourses"? Fantasy, according to this view, is a *ghostly* entity, the simulacrum par excellence. However, as even the title of the chapter under consideration, "Priori Incantatem", indicates, "curses" can be reversed: the orphan Harry unwittingly manages to summon the ghosts of the dead, most importantly his parents, to defend himself against the deathliness of Voldemort. In their *presence*, he can escape from death. When it comes to his parents, it is interesting to note that his father's ghost arrives first, but not because he takes pride of place; this is what the patriarchally structured tradition represented by Plato would "naturally" posit. On the contrary, James' short speech indicates that he is there primarily to herald the coming of Harry's mother, who subsequently arrives and promises Harry to "give [him] time" (*GoF*, 579). Significantly, Harry uses this given time to grasp Cedric's corpse in order to "[t]ake [it] back to [his] parents", pursuant to Cedric's injunction. The ghost parents of an orphaned son assist in returning the remains of a dead (but spiritually present) boy to the latter's now "orphaned" parents: the closing of a circle, the integration of life and death.

After having considered Harry's connection to the ghosts of friends and family in the duel scene, it can be claimed that *Harry Potter* is positively mythopoeic in the sense that it tends "to create or re-create certain narratives which human beings take to be crucial to their understanding of the world" (Coupe 1997, 4). Of course, this is not to say that fantasies like *Harry Potter* are automatically or inherently apt to say anything "essential", to do more than intertextually *play* with mythic elements: fantasy "pretends to be a mere game" (Attebery 2014, 21). However, deconstructively speaking, play—i.e. the play of *différance*—is "the condition for the presence of essence" (Derrida 1981, 155), and hence is itself "foundational" for being (while not being itself). In this context, and although "play" is not synonymous with "game" (156), it is interesting to note that the retrieval of the philosopher's stone in the first instalment of *Harry Potter* is *preceded* by the necessity of mastering a chess game, which is simply impossible to accomplish on one's own. If one takes further note of the fact that the philosopher's stone, in alchemical lore, was not only connected to the notion of a "primary matter", but also to the orphan, the role of this figure attains even more complexity. In *Psychology and Alchemy*, for instance, C.G. Jung mentions in passing that "Hermes Trismegistus is said to have called the stone 'orphan'" (1968, 319). The Jungian scholar Rose-Emily Rothenberg elaborates: "The term orphan was used by the alchemists as the name of a unique stone, a gem similar to our modern solitaire that was found in the Emperor's crown. The alchemists equated the orphan stone with the lapis philosophorum, the Philosopher's Stone. The stone represents the totality, or the 'one'; it corresponds to the psychological idea of the Self" (1983, 182). What is decisive for the present argument is that while "the *prima materia* [...] represents the unknown substance that carries the projection of the autonomous psychic content", "[i]t is of course impossible [for the alchemists] to specify such a substance, because the projection emanates from the individual and is consequently different in each case" (Jung 1968, 317). Unsurprisingly, then, the nature of the philosopher's stone is always ambiguous: "it is both worthless and precious, a set of opposites familiar to the orphan" (Rothenberg 1983, 182). In terms of Jungian archetypal psychology, this implies that the orphan, who often finds him- or herself in the "innocent child position", "elicits the compensatory witch-bully archetype on the other side" (187), which in literary myths, for instance in fairy tales, is often represented by the evil stepmother. However, the ambiguity of the orphan also allows for the possibility of reversal: "The orphan may begin

to behave exactly like the witch or the bully, and assume his/her
characteristics and behavior patterns. Living out either of these roles—the
victim or the oppressor—suggests that he is possessed by the negative side
of the parent-child archetype" (187; cf. also Vanderbeke in the present
volume, 244 and 276-277). Quite obviously, if applied to *Harry Potter*, it
is clear that Voldemort has taken on the role of the oppressor—for
Jungians surely a sign of an unresolved personality development. If we
choose to read Voldemort as an *aspect* of Harry's personality, which is
eliminated in Harry's self-sacrificial act at the end of the septology, it
becomes clear why he leaves the philosopher's stone behind: his
maturation is completed; he has finally cast off the debilitating
implications of his status as an orphan and is hence free to found his own
family. All in all, then, to complete this short foray into Jungian theory,
"Harry Potter as an orphan appeals to our collective unconscious—and
displays Rowling's brilliance for preserving a time-tested aspect of mythic
storytelling" (Weiss 2013, 30).

   In a highly illuminating article on "Harry Potter and the Quest for the
Domestic", Ximena Gallardo C. and C. Jason Smith convincingly suggest
that Harry, as his adventures draw to a close in the last novel, "is not so
much pursuing *things* as engaging with *competing* narratives" (2009, 100).
To be more precise, these narratives are, on the one hand, the tale of "The
Three Brothers", which Gallardo C. and Smith characterise as a "'closed'
masculine narrative", and, on the other, "the unfolding 'open' feminine
narrative of Voldemort's Horcruxes" (100). In the end, Harry will decide
against the promise of absolute power—the power over death that the
possession of the Deathly Hallows would give him—and instead opt for
destroying the Horcruxes, which involves sacrificing himself. In contrast
to Harry, Voldemort fails precisely because he is unable to understand the
implications of the legend of "The Three Brothers" (*DH*, 330-332).[8] One
very mundane, but telling, reason for this is that he was socialised in a
context in which the tale did not exist and hence could not carry any
meaning, as Harry realises: "Voldemort had been raised in a Muggle
orphanage. Nobody could have told him *The Tales of Beedle the Bard*
when he was a child, any more than Harry had heard them" (*DH*, 350).
However, this is obviously not reason enough, precisely because, after all,
Harry, who was also raised in complete isolation from the wizarding
culture and its mythic and legendary tales, turns out to be the only one
who interprets the tale correctly.

   For a long time, Dumbledore, Harry's most important surrogate father
figure, has also *misinterpreted* the tale. Like Voldemort, he sought to
attain the power promised by the possession of the Deathly Hallows. And

like Voldemort, his reason to do so was a direct consequence of his very own status as an orphan. When he was 17,[9] he tragically lost his parents and his sister Ariana (cf. *DH*, 454-57). Most problematically, Dumbledore had his own share in the death of Ariana, precisely because he neglected her for the sake of the power fantasies he cultivated with his friend Grindelwald, which involved supporting the racist project for Wizard supremacy. While Grindelwald and he both strove for power and hence searched for the Hallows, Dumbledore's own quest for them was ultimately motivated by his intention to find the Resurrection Stone and bring his family back from the dead. However, just like Voldemort, he did not understand the gist of the tale. While Voldemort, as well as Grindelwald before him, is chiefly interested in the Elder Wand, the "unbeatable wand", Dumbledore mainly sought after the Resurrection Stone: "it meant the return of my parents, and the lifting of all responsibility from my shoulders" (*DH*, 574). None of them focussed on the Invisibility Cloak, least of all Voldemort: "[Voldemort] would not think that he needed the Cloak, and, as for the stone, whom would he want to bring back from the dead? He fears the dead. He does not love" (577). Of course, Harry is not free from temptation. During the time in which he, Hermione and Ron are in hiding, Harry feels the strong pull exerted by the idea of absolute power, which carries the threat of dividing him from his friends: "Harry's belief in and longing for the Hallows consumed him so much that he felt quite isolated from the other two and their obsession with the Horcruxes" (353). Yet ultimately, he realises that he must give up on possessing the Hallows. He learns how to read the legend of the "Three Brothers", and he tellingly learns it by following his mother's example, who willingly gave her own life in order to save his. Now it is his turn to do the same for those he loves and thereby assume *parental authority*. As Dumbledore comments: "You are the true master of Death, because the true master does not seek to run away from death" (577). Harry's decision to cancel his quest for the Deathly Hallows is taken after he has buried Dobby at Shell Cottage, a sort of safe house, the name of which again indicates protection, like the dome webbed of light in the duel scene in *Goblet of Fire*. According to the logic of the narrative, Harry's choice "*not to act*" (406) is one of his most momentous decisions. In the words of Gallardo C. and Smith:

> as a consequence of understanding the meaning of 'The Tale of the Three Brothers' and choosing instead to enter the "open" tale of the Horcruxes, Harry becomes the master of both narratives—he has actively destroyed the Horcruxes and through *inaction* become the master of the Hallows—

and thereby of the masculine/feminine duality the narratives represent. (101)

In the context of the present line of inquiry, it needs to be added that Harry can only master these narratives because he consciously inserts them into the "narrative" of his family. Learning "the lesson of the mother" (Gallardo C. and Smith 2009, 101) means understanding how his own narrative, his "life story", ties in with the life narratives of his parents. Just like Harry, in *Prisoner of Azkaban*, realised that the person on the other side of the lake is *not* his father but his future self, a self that has learned to conjure the protective "Patronus" spell (*PA*, 282, 300), he now realises that he has to step into his parents' shoes and continue the narrative that they had begun. And the same goes for other narratives, in particular those of his various surrogate parents. As Lisa Damour for instance notes: "Armed with insight into Dumbledore and Snape's early lives, Harry suddenly, and completely grows up" (2009, 7). It is not surprising, therefore, that on his way to Voldemort at the beginning of the Battle of Hogwarts, Harry is again guarded by the ghosts of his parents and two of his substitute fathers (Sirius and Lupin; *DH*, 560-61), and neither is it surprising to learn that these ghosts "vanish" (*DH*, 563) as soon as he drops the Resurrection Stone, casts off the Invisibility Cloak and confronts Voldemort, who—unsuccessfully—kills him: Harry has finally emancipated himself from his orphan status.

In summary, Voldemort's plan has many flaws, but arguably his major mistake is that he does not see how his story is inevitably entwined with the stories of others, most importantly Harry's. This entanglement with the fate of others is symbolically represented by the drop of Harry's blood that Voldemort, in order to resurrect himself, has incorporated: "He took into his body a tiny part of the enchantment your mother laid upon you when she died for you" (*DH*, 568). Precisely because Lily's motherly protection is harboured *in* Voldemort, Voldemort is unable to kill Harry—he merely kills the part in Harry that is the splinter of his own soul. What Voldemort, the parricide, intends to function as a remedy for his orphaned status, a means to anchor the force of life within him, namely Harry's drop of blood, has thus unwittingly turned out to be a destructive *pharmakon*. In Laura Peters' words: "The orphan […] can be read as text; a supplement in which is embodied difference within a notion of sameness. The orphan as supplement functions then in the same way that Derrida conceives of the *pharmakon* (scapegoat) which 'acts as both remedy and poison'; self-introduced 'into the body of the discourse with all its ambivalence'" (Peters 2000, 26). Voldemort's attempt to *write himself* as a wholly original story, a story without precedent and without roots elsewhere, is doomed from the beginning: he does not see that no story can exist on its own, that all stories are crossed, influenced, overwritten by other stories. Most unexpected for him, perhaps, is the fact that someone he had considered to belong to his closest allies, in the end, is revealed to have been one of his most committed opponents: Severus Snape. Though not an orphan, Snape, who, like Voldemort and Harry is a half-blood (*HBP*, 593-94), grew up in unhappy and poor (*DH*, 534) conditions, with parents who did not care for each other and a Muggle father who did not show any tolerance for his wizarding wife and son (535; *OP*, 521). Voldemort has never even guessed the extent of Snape's love for Lily and hence could not estimate the impact Snape's story would have on his own (*DH*, 593). The same goes for many of the other characters that resist him, many of whom have an orphan background: the half-giant Hagrid is an orphan, whose giant mother left when he "was abou' three" and whose father died just "after [he] started school" (*GoF*, 372; cf. *OP*, 384, 497); Neville Longbottom is a quasi-orphan, whose parents have been in a mental asylum since they were magically tortured by Bellatrix Lestrange, Barty Crouch Jr. and other Death-Eaters and who was then raised by his grandmother (*GoF*, 516-517); Luna Lovegood is a half-orphan, whose mother died when she was nine (*OP*, 760). Ultimately, all of their stories become interwoven and viably support each other. Voldemort is defeated precisely because he has never been interested in the stories of others and fails to acknowledge how his story is connected to theirs: he remains an orphan. In contrast, Harry is on the winning side because he is willing to abstain from creating a master narrative for himself: of the three powerful artefacts, the Deathly Hallows, he only keeps the Invisibility Cloak and therefore symbolically chooses to remain inconspicuous, one among many, but one who is linked to those others in a meaningful way.

His Dark Materials

Lyra's In-between-ness

At first glance, the case of Lyra and Will, the protagonists of Philip Pullman's *His Dark Materials*, is quite different from that of Harry Potter in that they are what Maria Nikolajeva refers to as "functional orphans", that is, children "whose parents are alive but do not [or, in Will's case, cannot] care about them" (2002, 172). At the beginning of the story, we learn that the 12-year-old Lyra, on whom I will concentrate, has grown up in Oxford's Jordan College, with the college's scholars as "all she had for a family" (*HDM*, 21).[10] Significantly, she does not really miss having a

"proper" family, since she has never had one and thus is unfamiliar with
the concept: "[The scholars] might even have felt like a family if she knew
what a family was, though if she did, she'd have been more likely to feel
that about the College servants. The Scholars had more important things to
do than attend to the affections of a half-wild, half-civilized girl, left
among them by chance" (21-22). As this passage reveals, Lyra's is
essentially an in-between position with respect to several aspects: "class"
(between servants and scholars), "education" (measured on a scale
between the problematic binaries "wildness" and "civilisation"), as well as
her "locatedness" within a familial structure. Indeed, from a traditional
point of view according to which one's position in the family serves as a
microcosmic indication of one's position in society and the world at large,
the aporetic fact that, in the scholars and servants of Jordan College, she
has and has not found a family at the same time, necessarily implies the
non-decidability of her class and educational positions.

In addition, Lyra's ambiguous status is also expressed in spatial terms.
Regarding space, however, attention is not so much drawn to her "in-
betweenness" but to her occupying "marginal" positions, although both
notions are of course connected. While "Oxford", in terms of the
connotations this name evokes, serves as the epitome of learning, culture
and civilisation, Lyra is not fully level with this image, and literally so.
Instead of using her energies to deepen what she is taught in the
haphazardly conducted lessons with the scholars (cf. 62)—she does not
have any regular schooling –, she rather spends her time with her friend
Roger, the kitchen boy, exploring the roofs above and vaults underneath
Jordan College or engaging in battles with the children from the other
colleges or the town; battles fought *outside* the college walls. Nonetheless,
Lyra's in-between-ness and marginality do not constitute a shortcoming,
but rather an advantage; they grant her freedom to grow up relatively
untouched by the constrictions otherwise imposed by class, educational
and gender norms, as well as childhood ideology. In contrast to the gender
restrictions one associates with the late-Victorian atmosphere pertaining to
Lyra's Oxford, for example, it strikes the reader as conspicuous for a girl
that she smokes cigarettes, immediately "recogniz[es] the cue for a fight"
(51), and is the uncontested boss in her gang, who "consider[s] it a
deplorable lapse on the part of her subjects not to tell her everything and at
once" (54). In short, Lyra feels extremely comfortable in Oxford.

While this is true, Oxford can certainly be characterised as a failed
home. It lacks well-defined parental identification figures and is not
conducive to a "morally" and intellectually beneficent education, at least
regarding the ideological standards of classic children's literature, whose

plot typically has the "adult normative effect of revealing to children, after the journey, what a great home they left" (Wilson and Short 2012, 131). At the same time, Oxford is not exactly the sort of failed home Wilson and Short claim to be a defining feature and "the starting point" of what they call the "postmodern metaplot" often employed in recent children's literature. Apart from the fact that it is doubtful whether the common labelling of *His Dark Materials* as "children's" or "young adult fiction" is correct—it is as much and as little literature for children as Blake's *Songs of Innocence*—Lyra's home is only a failure from a traditional "adult normative" perspective, but not from hers. While "[t]he theme of a failed home is synonymous with a failed parent" (Wilson and Short 2012, 135), Lyra does not conceive of it as such, precisely because she believes her parents to be dead; she is not aware that her parents are failed parents.

In contrast to Harry Potter, then, who spends his first ten years at number four, Privet Drive, as an outsider in a painful stasis, she, although being an outsider as well, longs for permanence and wants her life to remain as it is. This of course is illusory, and the "trigger" that gets the plot going and hence is indicative of the fact that ultimately growing up cannot be prevented is telling with a view to our argument on the status of orphanhood: "This was her world. She wanted it to stay the same for ever and ever, but it was changing around her, for someone out there was stealing children" (*HDM* 57). While she herself, without knowing, had been abandoned by her parents when still a baby, a group of child kidnappers, the so-called Gobblers, have begun to snatch children away from their parents in order to submit them to cruel experiments conducted in a research facility in the thinly inhabited regions far in the icy north. Unsurprisingly, many of these children are torn from homes that do not match the still potent Victorian middle-class ideal, but, like Billy Costa, hail from travelling communities, or, like Tony Makarios, come from socially disadvantaged backgrounds (39-41). Thereby, as Laura Peters has illuminatingly suggested, Pullman's depiction of the Gobblers and their practices critically echoes Victorian emigration schemes, through which orphans were denied a position at what was considered to be the centre of the civilised world by forcefully deporting them to "marginal" regions. These schemes were particularly aimed at orphan children living on the street ("street arabs"), since their very existence signified a potential threat to the stability of a social order ideologically based on an idealised image of the bourgeois core family (cf. Peters 2011, 99-102; cf. also Gymnich in this volume, 16, 60). This possible historical reference to imperial practices gives an idea of how strongly Pullman's trilogy engages with questions concerning the authority and truth claims of hegemonic master narratives.

Accordingly, and analogous to the foregoing discussion of *Harry Potter*, it will be asked in which way Pullman makes use of the orphan figure in order to negotiate the status and legacy of the Father/Logos, not least with a view to the relation between *logos* and *mythos*. In order to prepare the ground, I will again make reference to the legacy of Western metaphysics as shaped by Plato. More precisely, without having been explicitly identified as such by Pullman, Plato's *Timaeus* will be treated as one of the intertexts relevant for an understanding of *His Dark Materials*; this is justified by the fact that the trilogy, in spite and because of its nature as a fictive text, may be characterised as offering a critical investigation of the Western metaphysical legacy.

Creator Fathers and Sinful Mothers: Lyra's "Platonic" Parents

In Plato's dialogue *Timaeus*, the eponymous dialogue partner offers a cosmological—and, if you like, mythic—account of the creation of the universe and the world. He begins his creation story by proposing a fundamental distinction, namely between "that which is Existent always and has no becoming" (27d-28a) and "that which is Becoming always and never is Existent" (28a). Very clearly, for Timaeus, precedence is to be given to the first, since only that which is "ever uniformly existent" and hence remains the same is "apprehensible by thought", "whereas the other is an object of opinion with the aid of unreasoning sensation, since it becomes and perishes and is never really existent" (28a). In other words, nothing that is physically present and therefore accessible via the senses ("unreasoning sensation") can belong to the order of (essential) Being, but only to that of Becoming. Accordingly, precisely because the cosmos "is visible and tangible and possessed of a body" (28b), it cannot have existed forever, hence must have a beginning, and so is part of the order of Becoming. This in turn implies that the cosmos itself must have been created; it must have a "Cause", a "Maker and Father" (28c). The origin of all becoming therefore is not only anthropomorphised in Timaeus' creation story, but also inserted within a familial scene in that the creator, the demiurge, is posited as a Father—as in so many other creation myths. According to Timaeus, the question remains, though, which of the two "Models" the paternal "Architect" (28c) had in mind when creating the world, that of Eternal Being or that of Becoming. While the Cosmos has undoubtedly been made and hence is inevitably caught in the process of becoming, Timaeus argues, the inherent perfection of the Maker has nonetheless brought about the best of all possible worlds, the "fairest of all that has come into existence", which implies that it was created according to the model posed by Eternal Being: "it has been constructed after the pattern of that which is apprehensible by reason and thought and is self-identical" (29a). In line with Plato's theory of forms, true knowledge is always tied to the recognition of the unchanging essences that underlie the ever-changing physical world.

In the first part of the trilogy, *Northern Lights* (or, in the US-American edition, *The Golden Compass*), Mrs Coulter and Lord Asriel—the parents that Lyra at first does not recognise as her parents; whose true nature she does not see through—both seem to represent a "Platonic" world view: Mrs Coulter because she spearheads the Church's war against carnal desire; Lord Asriel because of his demiurgical desire to connect the worlds, a desire for whose fulfilment he does not even shy away from sacrificing Lyra's friend Roger. In Marisa Coulter's case, the classical dichotomisation of Form (Being / Substance / Idea / Reason / Mind etc.) and Matter (Becoming / Accident / Image / Unreason / Body etc.), with Form hierarchically dominating Matter, appears in the shape it has assumed in the Christian tradition from the early Middle Ages. According to Elizabeth Grosz, in Christianity, "[t]he matter/form distinction is refigured in terms of the distinction between substance and accident and between a God-given soul and a mortal, lustful, sinful carnality" (1994, 5). After all, the whole point of the cruel experiments conducted by order of Mrs Coulter at Bolvangar serve one aim only: to prevent children from maturing sexually and so from falling into original sin. In Lyra's world, which is a world parallel to ours, all conscious beings have a visible dæmon, which is an entity that has an animal shape, is able to talk, has a character of its own, and normally is of the opposite sex. Most significantly, the dæmon represents something like the person's "soul". During childhood, the dæmon is able to constantly change its shape; only after the child has reached puberty, turned into an adolescent, gradually acquired a steady notion of who he or she is, and hence matured, does the dæmon assume a fixed form. Apart from the dæmon's consolidation, maturation is also indicated by the concentration of "Dust" around the newly grown-up being, enigmatic particles that cannot be seen by the (human) naked eye. To reveal the mysterious nature of Dust is the driving motive of all of those who not only seek to understand the world, but also to control it. For Mrs Coulter, who is a representative of the most conservative sections of the institutionalised Church in Lyra's world, maturation always also implies the awakening of sexual desire, which in turn epitomises humans' "inborn" potential for sinfulness, their inherent tendency to let themselves be tempted by evil. As Mrs Coulter explains to Lyra:

> Dust is something bad, something wrong, something evil and wicked. Grown-ups and their dæmons are infected with Dust so deeply that it's too late for them. [...] You see, your dæmon's a wonderful friend and companion when you're young, but at the age we call puberty, the age you're coming to very soon, darling, dæmons bring all sort of troublesome thoughts and feelings, and that's what lets Dust in. A quick little operation before that, and you're never troubled again. (*HDM*, 234-35)

According to this worldview, each individual's move from a state of "innocence" to a state of "experience" inherently and necessarily *repeats* Adam and Eve's fall into original sin, whose story is centrally featured also in the version of the biblical Genesis that exists in Lyra's world (*HDM*, 304-05). Perversely, then, Mrs Coulter's scientific experiments, by which dæmons are brutally severed from their humans, are motivated by the ideologically grounded urge to sever and hence save humans from what is considered to be the disastrous legacy of their "first parents", Adam and Eve. In other words, Mrs Coulter endeavours to turn humans into orphans in a radical sense by preventing them from taking their ur-parents' place. It is only logical therefore that Mrs Coulter willingly dissociated from her child soon after Lyra's birth and allowed her to grow up in the belief that her parents had died in an accident. After all, Lyra is the "product" of Mrs Coulter's adulterous affair with Lord Asriel; she is the visible sign of her own "weakness of the flesh", her own sinfulness. For these reasons, and unsurprisingly, it comes as a shock to Mrs Coulter to learn that her daughter, according to the witches' ancient prophecy, is supposed to be the New Eve: "Eve! Mother of all! Eve, again! Mother Eve!" (*HDM*, 580). Far from annulling the curse that, according to Christian doctrine, has subjected humankind to a life of hardship inevitably ended by death, Mrs Coulter, by way of her own offspring, seems to even have promoted and advanced it. At least ostensibly, the consequences are clear: "I shall have to destroy her [...] to prevent another Fall" (580). In hindsight, however, the reader will recognise that this is a lie, partly at least. While she indeed wants to prevent Lyra from falling, she does not intend to destroy, but to save, her.

In the beginning, Lyra's relationship with her father, Lord Asriel, is different from that to her mother. In the time before she knows about their true affiliation, Lyra admires both and even wishes that "[Asriel] and Mrs Coulter would fall in love, and [...] get married and adopt Lyra" (76). However, in a further ironic twist, after having realised that Mrs Coulter is the leader of the Gobblers and learned who her parents really are, she distances herself from her mother and instead venerates her father even more. She is proud when she hears how Asriel in the past had selflessly helped and supported the gyptians several times (117) and even begins dreaming of "her great imprisoned father" (154), whom she intends to set free. In consequence, "whereas Lord Asriel was now 'father', Mrs Coulter was never 'mother'" (192). This 'imbalance' in Lyra's perception of her parents is soon righted when Lyra, in her first conversation with Lord Asriel about his paternal role, accuses him of not caring about her and not being interested in what she has done for him: "You en't human, Lord Asriel. You en't my *father*. My *father* wouldn't treat me like that. Fathers are supposed to love their daughters, en't they? You don't love me, and I don't love you, and that's a fact" (302). In the dramatic finale of *Northern Lights*, the situation becomes much worse, in ways unexpected by Lyra, since Asriel, in order to build a bridge into the worlds seen through the Aurora, cruelly sacrifices Roger. In this moment, the man, who had figured as a liberating rebel against the constricting authority of the Church, avails himself of the Church's cruel method of intercision and hence potentially becomes what he had seemingly opposed before. However, the inversion of his character is not as neat as might be supposed. After all, his own scientific discoveries have made possible the "intercision" process in the first place (226).

Be that as it may, although Lyra primarily blames herself for having unwittingly betrayed Roger, it is implied that she equally accuses Asriel of having betrayed her. After all, while she had risked her own life in order to save Roger's when he was in the hands of the Gobblers, Asriel has annulled her endeavours by sacrificing the kitchen boy for the sake of his very own aims. Hence, Asriel appears to come up to Lyra's accusation that he "en't human" in more senses than one: he appears to be *inhuman* not only because he willingly kills a child, but also because, by building a bridge into another world, he assumes the role of a Romantic overreacher; someone who craves to rival God and take His place. Instead of "merely" endeavouring to save human beings from the "sinful" influence of Dust, like Mrs Coulter, Lord Asriel intends to do a lot more, namely to get to the root cause of it all and eliminate it: "Somewhere out there is the origin of all the Dust, all the death, the sin, the misery, the destructiveness in the world. Human beings can't see anything without wanting to destroy it, Lyra. *That's* original sin. And I'm going to destroy it. Death is going to die" (309). In a way, then, Lord Asriel, at this point, is similar to Lord Voldemort in *Harry Potter*. Not only does he intend to destroy death; in addition, by doing so, he plans on annulling the currently valid master discourse and, all by himself, set up a new one. The most obvious intertextual reference at this point, surely, is to Milton's Satan; after all, even the title of the trilogy is taken from *Paradise Lost* (cf. Milton 2004, 51: Book 2, l. 916). After the creation of the bridge, he stylises himself as the new bringer of the light, a new, but literally enlightened, Lucifer: "This will mean the end of the Church, Marisa, the end of the Magisterium, the end of all those centuries of darkness! Look at that light up there" (322).

By the end of *Northern Lights*, then, the family constellation has become severely complicated. While Lyra has lost her status as a true orphan because it turns out that her parents are alive and kicking, she has ultimately and painfully come to reject them *as* parents. In denying them parent status, she willingly returns herself into the situation of an orphan. At the same time, Mrs Coulter and Lord Asriel wage their very own wars against parental figures of a supposedly much higher existential nature: Mrs Coulter intends to cut off humans from the legacy that ties them to their mythical ur-parents, Adam and Eve; Lord Asriel begins a war against "the Authority", i.e. that entity that arrogates to himself the privilege of being the creator of the cosmos, the origin of Truth, and hence the Father of all. To accomplish their goals, Mrs Coulter and Lord Asriel proceed ruthlessly, not least at the expense of Lyra. After having created the bridge, their self-love and their mutual attraction seem to overpower their love for Lyra, as they both try to shift the responsibility for her to the other (323). Suggested by her dæmon Pantalaimon, that is, by a process of inner recognition, Lyra ultimately comes to the conclusion that "if *they* all think Dust is bad, it must be good" (325). This epiphany in itself marks an act of emancipation: Pantalaimon and Lyra realise that they have only believed that "Dust must be bad [...] because [Mrs Coulter and Lord Asriel] were grown-up and they said so" (325). From this point on, however, the parental *logos*—"they said so"—will be radically questioned. In its place, Lyra, with Will's help, will see to it that *mythos*—the art of telling meaningful and true stories—will come into its own again.

Mythos—Logos—Khōra: Lyra in Plato's Cave

For heuristic reasons, let me return to Plato's *Timaeus*. While Timaeus' cosmology is meant to be a truthful account of the creation of the cosmos and the world—one which, significantly, is meant to demonstrate the absolute priority of the *logos*—he himself concedes that it cannot help being a story, though a highly plausible one: "we should be content if we can furnish accounts that are inferior to none in likelihood, remembering that both I who speak and you who judge are but human creatures, so that it becomes us to accept the likely account of these matters and forbear to search beyond it" (29d-e). In addition, in order to be able to properly understand the status of Timaeus' long speech, his "likely account", it is necessary to also take into account the preceding shorter contribution by Critias, who equally recounts "a tale which, though passing strange, is yet wholly true" (20d). Actually, what we are presented by Critias is a story within a story within a story. At its centre is another history of origins that was once, Critias alleges, told by an old Egyptian priest to Solon, who in turn related it to Critias' grandfather, an incident at which the then ten-year-old Critias was present and which he is able to fully remember: "Marvellous, indeed, is the way in which the lessons of one's childhood 'grip the mind,' as the saying is. For myself, I know not whether I could recall to mind all that I heard yesterday; but as to the account I heard such a great time ago, I should be immensely surprised if a single detail of it has escaped me" (26b). Accordingly, only children are capable of remembering properly, whereas grown-ups either must take recourse to auxiliary means or forget. No wonder, then, that the Egyptian priest charges the Greeks, represented by Solon, with being forgetful: while they believe that only one catastrophic deluge had afflicted the world, the Egyptians know that there were many. And they know, not because they remember, but because they have mastered the art of recording these events in writing and building up a historical archive (23a-23c). Analogously, certain story elements—for instance that Lyra finds invaluable support and guidance with the *gyptians* (boatpeople whose name not only recalls the loaded term "gypsies" but also refers to "Egyptians") or that, in her Oxford, there is a River *Isis* and a *Jordan* College—are subtle clues that remind us that western culture and thinking have their roots not exclusively in classical, *logos*-fixated, Greece and Rome, for whose legacies Oxford University may well stand, but also in older Near-Eastern and North African cultures, like those of Mesopotamia and Egypt. In this sense, it is also interesting to note that the gyptians' Ma Costa had nursed baby Lyra after her "Platonic" mother had abandoned her (*HDM*, 112).

All in all, then, the cosmology at the heart of Plato's *Timaeus* is embedded within, and complemented by, a frame whose intricate employment of mythic elements allows us to read it against the grain and hence expose the precarious nature of the truth claims regarding the Platonic *logos*—counter to the text's ideological trajectory. In order to do so and ultimately utilise this deconstructive reading for the analysis of *His Dark Materials*, it is necessary to mention one last relevant aspect. In Timaeus' creation story, the binary relationship between Being and Becoming, which is analogous to the binary *logos* and *mythos*, is complicated by the introduction of a *third* "Form that is baffling and obscure", *khōra*, which is "the receptacle, and as it were the nurse, of all Becoming" (49a). Without being anything in itself, *khōra* "is" that which is necessary in order to allow an Idea to become manifest in/as a sensually perceptible object in the material world. It "is" the unformed "Place" (52a) in which the four elements find a first expression and by way of which the demiurge can then shape the cosmos. What is relevant with a view to our argument is that Timaeus continues to employ the image of a family constellation in order to clarify the complicated trinity of Being (source), *khōra* (recipient), and Becoming:

> For the present, then, we must conceive of three kinds,—the Becoming, that "Wherein" it becomes, and the source "Wherefrom" the Becoming is copied and produced. Moreover, it is proper to liken the Recipient to the Mother, the Source to the Father, and what is engendered between these two to the Offspring; and also to perceive that, if the stamped copy is to assume diverse appearances of all sorts, that substance wherein it is set and stamped could not possibly be suited to its purpose unless it were itself devoid of all those forms which it is about to receive from any quarter. (50c-d)

By way of gendering the creation process, the female principle, the Mother, is limited to serve as a passive surface of inscription; a "substance" which, while being able to "receive within itself all the kinds [of forms,] should [in itself] be void of all forms" (50e). In contrast, the male principle, the Father, stands for "the self-identical Form, ungenerated and indestructible, neither receiving into itself any other from any quarter nor itself passing anywhither into another, invisible and in all ways imperceptible by sense, it being the object which it is the province of Reason to contemplate" (52a). As I will show in the following, Pullman, in a radical way, attempts to pull down this Platonic family scene, along with all its implications. In this, the figure of the orphan is of central importance; it is vital for Pullman's criticism of the legacy of western metaphysics.

At the beginning of *The Amber Spyglass*, the third and last instalment of *His Dark Materials*, the reader finds Lyra in a cave somewhere in the Himalayas. She has been kidnapped by Mrs Coulter, who, by way of a drug, has put her in a state of permanent sleep. The situation is important for at least two reasons. While the reader, as well as Will, still believes Mrs Coulter to be evil, it turns out later that, by that time, she has already changed sides: she has fled to this remote place in order to protect Lyra from those who try to harm her. In addition, the location itself provides a clear nod to Plato's allegory of the cave. The sleeping and forcefully drugged Lyra is in the position of those men whom Socrates describes as being fettered in the same spot of a cave from their childhood (*Republic*, 514a). Like them, she sees shadows. However, while Socrates' imagined prisoners are fated to see nothing but untrue phantoms so that, accordingly, they "deem reality to be nothing else than the shadows of [...] artificial objects" (515c), the shadows Lyra perceives are decidedly real and true. In her dream state—and only in her dream state—is she able to communicate with a very specific shadow, namely Roger's ghost in the Land of the Dead. It is only because she perceives him and the other shadows that she is able to see through the nature of things and realises what to do. In that, Pullman renegotiates Timaeus' suggestion that the existentially antecedent space or ground that "is" *khōra* is comparable to the space we perceive in dreams: "when we regard this [i.e., *khōra*] we dimly dream and affirm that it is somehow necessary that all that exists should exist *in* some spot and occupying some *place*" (*Timaeus*, 52b). Problematically, then, *khōra* can never be understood in a conscious, "waking", state: "we are unable also on waking up to distinguish clearly the unsleeping and truly subsisting substance, owing to our dreamy condition" (52b). Accordingly, in order to grasp this Third Form at least in an approximative manner, we are required to employ "a kind of bastard reasoning" (52b). Who else but the dreaming "bastard" girl Lyra could accomplish such a feat?

Indeed, it must be agreed with Millicent Lenz that Pullman ties in with "a long tradition in literature" that clings to the "idea that one must be in an awakened state to be truly alive" (2005, 3). Since Pullman, if anything, is a Blakean, it is perhaps not too far-fetched to refer to yet another intertext, namely William Blake's epic *Jerusalem: The Emanation of the Giant Albion*, a literary myth, at the beginning of which Jesus calls out to the sleeping Albion, the representative of humankind: "Awake! awake O sleeper of the land of shadows, wake! expand!" (plate 4, line 6, p. 146). The point for Blake, as well as for Pullman, however, is that the called-for "wakefulness" must not be equated with pure Reason in the Platonic sense, and that truth therefore must not be sought in an invisible and eternally fixed metaphysical space *beyond* the mutable and sensually perceivable material realm. At the same time, an exclusive confidence in physical reality will not do either, at least not if it is reduced to the kind of "demonstrative truth" (*Jerusalem*, plate 28, line 11, p. 174) associated with "Bacon & Newton & Locke" (plate 70, line 15, p. 224). Actually, for Blake, both approaches to truth are connected to the sleep of humankind in that they are ideological systems that serve to oppress life, that is, the creative potential within each and every human being. In Blake's own mythic creation story, *The Book of Urizen*, Urizen, one of the so-called Eternals, after his Fall, egoistically sets himself up as the sole Creator God and forms the phenomenal world by devising instruments that allow it to be ordered according to unchanging physical laws. Not only does he form "a line & a plummet", "a dividing rule", or "scales to weigh", but also "golden compasses" with which "to explore the Abyss" (*Book of Urizen*, plate 20, ll. 33-40, pp. 80-81). In the constricting atmosphere of the ensuing world, which is regulated both by way of Urizen's materialistic "iron laws" (pl. 23, l. 26, p. 81) yet also by what is termed "The Net of Religion" (pl. 25. l. 22, p. 82), human beings forget how to connect to and understand themselves as creative entities within an infinite, dynamic multi-dimensional universe. Instead, as a consequence of the hegemonic Urizenic systems of Science and Religion, their five senses shrink (pl. 25, l. 29, p. 82) so that humans are henceforth only able to experience the world as a finite, strictly measured three-dimensional space in which they feel powerless and so accept their oppression. The point, though, is that these oppressive systems are ultimately self-made, that our "manacles" are "mind-forg'd" ("London", l. 8, p. 27), that Urizen is an *aspect* of the human state. As Blake puts it in *The Marriage of Heaven and Hell*: "If the doors of perception were cleansed every thing would appear as it is: infinite. / For man has closed himself up, till he sees all things thro' narrow chinks of his cavern" (plate 14, p. 39). Mrs Coulter's cavern, I propose, stands for all of these aspects at the same time: for what Immanuel Kant calls the "*self-incurred minority* [*Unmündigkeit*]" (Kant 1996, 17) of humankind, the restricting and oppressive aspects both of the Western metaphysical tradition ("Platonism") as well as of modern materialism ("Newtonianism"), and the disabling and demeaning possessiveness associated with an authoritative kind of parenthood. While Mrs Coulter, not least on account of her being a *femme fatale*, has come to take a position similar to Blake's Rahab, who symbolises a deeply hypocritical "Religion of Chastity, forming a Commerce to sell Loves / With Moral Law" (*Jerusalem*, pl. 69, l. 34-35, p. 223), Lord Asriel is closer to the mad Urizenic scientist, whose steam-punky Fortress in the Sky, featuring "[h]ammers the size of houses" and "gigantic slicing machines and rollers" (*HDM* 769), is reminiscent of Albion's "cruel Works / Of many Wheels" (*Jerusalem*, pl. 15, l. 17-18, p. 159). Being unable to identify with either of these positions, Lyra assumes a third one.

In her dream in the cave, Lyra is able to leave her place in the material word and reach into the World of the Dead, which she perceives as a "*great plain*" (*HDM*, 603). On the one hand, this is not so strange as it appears. After all, the trilogy rests on the conceit of a multiverse. Cleverly availing himself of quantum physics, and particularly of one of its sub-branches, namely the so-called many-worlds theory, Pullman finds a way to question the taken-for-granted-ness of Newtonian physics while at the same time holding on to a materialist worldview. As I have argued elsewhere:

> while certain facts seem to have the status of an undisputable law in our world, there might be another frame of reference (the quantum frame) in which these laws lose their authority. *His Dark Materials* discusses the implications of switching from one system of thought to another with respect to laws of different "natures": scientific (physical), religious (metaphysical), moral etc. This is not to suggest that *His Dark Materials* favours scientific over religious thinking, or quantum speculations over morality. It implies instead that the validity of any one truth depends on a particular perspective, so that shifting it might easily entail a corresponding shifting of truths. (Sedlmayr 2017, 470)

Accordingly, no place in Pullman's cosmos is unambiguous. Lyra's above-discussed status of marginality in Oxford, which is emphasised by the spatial semantics implied in her spending much of her time above and below ground level, as well as outside of the college walls, becomes even more pronounced when taking into consideration that there are other Oxfords besides hers, particularly the Oxford from which Will comes and which is the one in "our" world. Significantly, these Oxfords are similar to and different from each other at the same time. For instance, while in Will's Oxford, she once notes that on "a particular worn stone at the corner of Catte Street—there were the initials SP that Simon Parslow had scratched, the very same ones! She'd seen him do it! Someone in this world with the same initials must have stood here idly and done exactly the same" (*HDM*, 390). The crucial insight derived from this observation is that such uncanny doubles might ultimately be true for herself as well: "There might be a Simon Parslow in this world. Perhaps there was a Lyra"—and if there was, this other Lyra would likewise be same and other with regards to her. Of course, the differences between Lyra's and Will's worlds are as striking as the similarities, amongst others because Lyra's has the feel of the early 20th century (or even earlier) rather than its last decade, with no cars or planes but instead carts, zeppelins, and gyrocopters, to say nothing of humans featuring external dæmons. The point is that the cosmos as Pullman depicts it is not limited, but full of possibilities: one in which each action by a conscious being can potentially bring forth a new world which in turn offers new options (cf. e.g. *HDM*, 541; Sedlmayr 2017, 471).

Lyra's "Originality" and the Truth of Storytelling

Nonetheless, within the endless variety of worlds in the multiverse, the world of the dead has a singular status, because in it, *"time had been stilled* [...]. *This was the end of all places and the last of all worlds"* (*HDM*, 603). As the reader learns, the Authority, who had once set himself up as the Father-God with absolute powers (766), had created it as the ultimate destination for all conscious beings: after their death, everyone will end up in this dreary world, no matter which promises of Heaven had been made to them before (623). Graham Holderness, who avails himself of Mircea Eliade's differentiation between "sacred" and "profane" spaces, characterises Pullman's world of the dead as profane:[11] "'sacred' space is rich, complex, open; 'profane' space is closed, one-dimensional, homogenous" (Holderness 2007, 276). Moreover, as a "non-place" in Marc Augé's sense, it "is a dead end, leading only back into itself. You could be anywhere; you are nowhere". Yet, it has to be added, while Marc Augé typifies transit zones like airports as non-places, which may be true for the suburb of the world of the dead, the world itself is literally a dead end; it is the opposite of a transit zone. There is no way out, not even the way the dead have entered. As the boatman who takes them over the underworld's river claims: "I have taken millions, and none came back" (*HDM* 824). It is in the world of the dead that the trilogy's use of the trope of orphanhood finds its climax. And this is due to two reasons.

1) In order to be allowed access to the world of the dead, Lyra and the others have to leave their dæmons behind—no matter whether they are externally visible, like Pantalaimon, or whether they are "hidden within", as with Will and the Gallivespians. What is probably Lyra's most courageous deed, in fact, is simultaneously the great betrayal that the prophecies have foretold. In splitting herself from herself, she betrays Pan and therefore her human nature. However, in this case, both the notion of "betrayal" and that of "splitting" are highly ambiguous.

According to Christian myth, Adam and Eve betray God in that they violate His law and give in to temptation. Their punishment is their expulsion from paradise and their fall into an earthly existence structured by hardship and mortality, and burdened by the weight of original sin. In other words, their punishment consists in the fact that they are split up: what dominates them henceforth is their mortal nature, while their divine and eternal aspect—their "true" being—becomes hidden. As discussed above, Lyra's mother subscribes to the truth of this narrative and hence, paradoxically, attempts to relieve humans of the burden of original sin by severing them from their dæmons, which causes them even more pain and turns them into pseudo-human zombies (*HDM*, 363). Within the semantic system of Pullman's own narrative, Mrs Coulter's mission and deeds, however, are of course not condoned. Quite the contrary, her cruel destruction of the kidnapped children is clearly condemned. After all, the practices at Bolvangar are, for instance, reminiscent of the eugenic experiments conducted by the Nazis: severing dæmons from their humans is indeed an unacceptable betrayal of human life. In this respect, it is also illuminating to again take into account William Blake's mythic system, which serves as a major intertextual reference point for Pullman. In Blake's so-called prophecies, the self-betrayal of human nature—which results in "fallenness" or "generation"—is *always* accompanied by a destructive splitting up of formerly harmoniously unified elements. What is split off in such a process, amongst others, is what Blake calls the Spectre, which represents "self-centered Selfhood" (Damon 1988, 381), a negating power, and finds expression in Pullman's "Spectres of Indifference" (*HDM*, 438) that haunt Cittàgazze.

Lyra's act, however, is of a different kind: unlike her mother, she does not violate another human being, but *herself*: "Lyra was doing the cruellest thing she had ever done, hating herself, hating the deed, suffering for Pan and with Pan and because of Pan" (*HDM* 825). Hers is a freely willed and voluntary deed. As such, it is neither aimed at supporting the notion of an inherently sinful world—as is Father Gomez's self-flagellation (655)—nor is it self-centred. On the contrary, her division from Pan is an act that literally renders her self-less. As such, it is also an unprecedented deed: "Pan, no one's done this before" (825). This implies that hers is a truly foundational act, an act without any "parental" models. Hence, it qualifies as *original*, without, however, being able to claim absoluteness. On the one hand, since it is self-less, it cannot even make a claim to *be* anything substantial. On the other hand, hers is not a solitary action: it is not a *unique* foundational act, since Will and the Gallivespians equally leave behind their dæmons.

2) Courageous though Lyra's deed is, it cannot make a change in itself. Its significance stems from the fact that it serves as the condition of possibility for her and her friends' greatest accomplishment, namely the opening up of the world of the dead. Crucially, the freeing of the dead is brought about by a rather simple act, namely by Lyra recounting *true* stories "about the world she knew" (*HDM* 849). Amongst others, she tells the ghosts "the story of how she and Roger had climbed over Jordan College roof and found the rook with the broken leg" or "about the great battle between the Oxford townies and the clay-burners" (849). The value of these stories lies in their details: the lively description of colours, different smells and sounds, even the consistency of the mud in the

claybeds. By presenting such particulars in a meaningful way, Lyra is able to re-build and *make present*—to *re-present*—her own world *within* the world of the dead, and thereby manages to infuse the ghosts with life, to rekindle life by triggering long forgotten memories: "As she spoke, playing on all their senses, the ghosts crowded closer, feeding on her words, remembering the time when they had flesh and skin and nerves and senses, and willing her never to stop" (850). It is important to notice that these stories are no fictive grand narratives, like the pompous yarn about her father and mother being the "Duke and Duchess of Abingdon" which she told before, a narrative that includes many of the time-proven stock elements of sensational adventure stories and hence unsurprisingly features an orphaned protagonist: "*parents dead; family treasure; shipwreck; escape ...*" (832). While her tall tale is successful with the miserable humans in the holding area of the suburb, she cannot fool the harpy No-Name, the chief guardian of the land of the dead, who sees through her and accuses her of being a liar: "*Lyra* and *liar* were one and the same thing" (833). It is only when she begins to tell true stories about her life in Oxford that she manages to impress even the harpies; stories of a time when she still believed herself to be a real orphan. The representation of her previous orphanhood, then, is doubled and *repeated* on a metalevel by her status as narrator of her own life story. Lyra, by recounting her life as a child and making the Oxford of her childhood present, becomes a "parentless" *creator* of worlds. This amounts to a critical subversion of Timaeus'/Plato's cosmology: instead of holding on to the distinction between Being and Becoming, between abstract *eidos* and material *simulacrum*, Pullman insists on the materiality of life and truth: Lyra becomes a demiurge that makes use of bodily rendered words which, in their very materiality, are truly life-giving; they give substance to the shadows. While before, "the ghosts passed through their bodies, warming themselves on the way" (*HDM*, 836), Lyra's words are now enough to accomplish the same feat. Even the harpies listen, because, as No-Name admits, "[Lyra] spoke the truth. Because it was nourishing. Because it was feeding us" (*HDM*, 852). It is very important to stress that, within the logic of Pullman's narrative, these are no metaphors. Just as Lyra's words make the ghosts remember their bodily selves—life as expressed and communicated via the senses— they satisfy the harpies not only "spiritually" or "mentally", but also physically. As Judith Butler claims, "[s]poken words are, strangely, bodily offerings" (2004, 172). If this is so, Lyra's offering is of a specific kind: it is confessional speech, since she does not try to hide anything, but freely grants the ghosts and the harpies insight into the truth of her life. While her confession tellingly does not imply any notion of guilt, it is part of a larger sacrificial act that is motivated by love. Like in the traditional metaphysical creation stories, her act of giving life is hence inherently characterised as an act of love; yet in contrast to the old metaphysical creation stories, it is not meta-physical, but decidedly physical. Judith Butler's conceptualisation of "bodily confessions" perfectly fits Lyra's case:

> If transference is a form of love or, minimally, an enactment of a certain relation to love, then we might say further that it is a love that takes place in language. This is not to say that language substitutes for the body, since that is not quite true. The spoken word is a bodily act at the same time that it forms a certain synecdoche of the body. (173)

For this reason, there is no capital-lettered Truth beyond the material. Dust, which is the locus of consciousness and hence the origin of human creativity and truth, is both spiritual and material at the same time. It is variously described as atoms, particles, or pixels on Mary's computer screen (another 'Cave'!).

In addition, while Lyra's storytelling in the World of the Dead is akin to foundational acts in mythical creation stories, it is significant that Lyra, in stark contrast to other creators, has not *intended* her action to be of the world-building kind. It may be claimed that Lyra, feeling "sick with apprehension" (*HDM*, 849) but giving in to the ghosts' entreaty to reconnect them to the living world, *exposes* herself. Crucially, "[w]ithout this moment of exposure, a moment in which one displays something more than one intends, there is no transference" (Butler 2004, 173). In fact, then, there's no calculus of power motivating Lyra's deed, no intention of creating forms of life bound and subjected to her will. She is simply telling her story—*a* story, not *the* story—in order to feed the ghosts, to help them recall and re-feel their previous lives. In *His Dark Materials*, *mythos*—the power of story—hence triumphs over *logos*. And it does so by activating the topos of orphanhood. As Derrida writes: "the mythic saying resembles a discourse without a legitimate father. Orphan or bastard, it is distinguished from the philosophical *logos*, which, as is said in the *Phaedrus*, must have a father to answer for it and about it" (1995, 124). Lyra's story does not answer to any father, nor any mother, simply because these stories are stories about a time in which she did not know she still had any parents.

The Rejection of the Paternal *Logos*

In this connection, it is only logical that Lyra and Will are instrumental in destroying the Authority. However, they do not intentionally kill the "ancient of days" (*HDM*, 926), the embodiment of the old concept of the commanding, "hidden" creator god, the representative of the *logos*. Rather, without knowing who he is and what they are doing, they free him from the crystal litter in order to reach out to and "comfort him; because he was so old, and he was terrified, crying like a baby" (925). The fact that "his form began to loosen and dissolve" (926) as soon as he is touched by the wind stresses that his power has been sustained for so long only by artificial means: that he has suffered a miserable existence not dissimilar from that of the ghosts in the World of the Dead. What is decisive, though, is that Lyra and Will do not represent a new version of the Authority. Lyra's foundational stories—the stories she tells in the World of the Dead—do not have the untouchable status of the Word of God. They do not represent a new paternal law. On the contrary, they remain what they are: simply episodes of a (relatively) common life. In contrast to the Word of the Father, it is not necessary to codify or even repeat them. Not any fixed meaning is important, but what Lyra is doing by telling them. In fact, as the pact Tialys successfully suggests to the harpies reveals, every true story told by any individual is as important and valuable as hers: "Every one of these ghosts has a story; every single one that comes down in the future will have true things to tell you about the world" (852). In this sense, all of these stories are truly foundational and original in their own right; a master discourse is not required.

Precisely because the rejection of the absoluteness of the paternal *logos* is so crucial in *His Dark Materials*, it is equally crucial to understand that, after all, Lyra is *not* a genuine orphan. Just like it is true that all individuals have their own stories, it is also true that no story can exist and make sense all on its own. Each story relies on other stories, though never in an absolute sense. This is what both Mrs Coulter and Lord Asriel have come to realise by the end. Like in Blake's "The Little Girl Found", in which Lyca's selfish parents are ultimately confronted with the parental models offered by the lion and the lioness, Lyra's own parents equally rediscover their true calling as parents. In an act of unselfish love for Lyra, and in fact for all beings in the living worlds, they sacrifice themselves in order to kill the Authority's tyrannical regent, the demonic angel Metatron. Similar to Lyra's sacrifice before, theirs is also unique because they will be the only dead who will not end up in the World of the Dead and hence will not get the chance to pass through it and fuse with the cosmos. Although they know that they "won't survive like the ghosts" if they succeed in dragging Metatron into the abyss, they accept their fate "to give Lyra time to find her dæmon, and then time to live and grow up" (*HDM*, 921). Their voluntary death marks the point at which Lyra eventually turns into a true orphan—and in a very radical sense. Unlike Will, whose Dust particles, after his death, will have the chance to reunite with those of his parents, Lyra is being barred from such an option. What counts, though, is that their deeds have enabled life, creativity and truth to continue, yet not in any authoritative paternal sense, but in a decidedly open manner. Pullman's universe is not about fixity, but dynamism; it is not about sameness, but diversity. As the angel Xaphania explains regarding the nature of Dust and hence the nature of the cosmos: "Dust is not a constant. There's not a fixed quantity that has always been the same. Conscious beings make Dust—they renew it all the time, by thinking and feeling and reflecting, by gaining wisdom and passing it on" (994). This notion of "passing it on" is the central point: as the episode in the World of the Dead makes clear, everyone is in possession of something to pass on; and this something is a story, the true story of his or her life. We have a sense of self only because we have formed it by way of a narration, a *mythos*. And this *mythos*, in turn, will never be isolated, but depends on the stories of others. In Pullman's world, hence, existential orphanhood is nearly impossible, since you can only be a true orphan if there is nothing that has been passed on to you. No wonder, then, that Lyra, at the beginning of the tale, is presented to us as a functional orphan only. And no wonder, too, that Pullman's *His Dark Materials* is not a philosophical tract, but a fantasy tale, a *mythos* in its own right.

The Conditionality of Destiny

In order to reach a conclusion to this part, it is worthwhile to briefly return to Plato's *Timaeus*. As the above summary of Plato's *Timaeus* will hopefully have shown, *Timaeus* leaves the reader "caught in a [complex] scene of reading" (Derrida, "*Khōra*", 98) Even though not in terms of narrative construction, the question of "reading" also lies at the heart of *His Dark Materials*. Just like Lyra learns and unlearns to read the intricate symbolism of the Alethiometre—literally, an instrument to measure truth—we, as readers, are equally challenged to decipher the many meanings contained but not exhausted in Pullman's trilogy. Amongst others, the impossibility of exhaustion lies in the fact that Pullman's text "partakes in" and "feeds on" a large number of (parental) intertexts, from Plato via the Bible to Milton's *Paradise Lost* and Blake's prophecies, to name just some of the most conspicuous, whose meanings in turn are equally inexhaustible. Indeed, on account of the trilogy being a *fantasy*, it is easy to charge Pullman with presenting us with nothing but an invented myth: "myth derives from play [and] [h]ence it will not be taken seriously" (Derrida 1995, 112). However, as Timaeus' own creation myth reveals, which, as he admits, is itself nothing but an *eikōs muthos*, a "probable tale", "when one cannot lay claim to a firm and stable *logos*, when one must make do with the probable, then myth is the done thing [*de rigueur*]; it is rigor" (Derrida 1995, 112). The same holds true for Pullman's fiction, with the exception that it is not even geared to "lay claim to a firm and stable *logos*".

In his critique of the trilogy, David Gooderham claims that Pullman's all-too explicit use of (anti-)ecclesiastical terminology and the many negative allusions to institutionalised Christianity ultimately thwart his innovative employment of mythic language. In this, Gooderham avers, Pullman's anti-doctrinalism slyly justifies and consolidates a new doctrinal belief system, one that might be labelled "secular humanism": "This is the Grand Narrative to end all grand narratives, the High Fantasy to end all fantasies, the Eschaton to end all kingdoms of heaven! After this"—i.e., the destruction of the Authority and Metatron—"there are just plain human dimensions, human tasks and human stories" (Gooderham 2003, 164). However, while Gooderham surely has a point, he tends to overlook the productive ambiguity inherent in Pullman's literary myth, which finds its most potent expression in the conceit offered by the World of the Dead. By the creation of an opening in/exit from "*the end of all places and the last of all worlds*" (*HDM*, 603), the World of the Dead comes to signify both the end and the beginning of life. In this way, it comes to resemble what Timaeus calls *khōra*: "it is laid down by nature as a molding-stuff for everything, being moved and marked by the entering figures, and because of them it appears different at different times" (50c). This difference is not a difference in outward appearance, but stems from the fact that the World of the Dead, due to Tialys' pact with the harpies, becomes an echo chamber for a never-ending number of stories, none of which will ever be the same. Importantly, utterly at variance with Plato's metaphysical model, it is *not* the case that "the figures that enter and depart are copies of those that are always existent" (50c). In Pullman's cosmos, there is no fixed *logos*, just as there are no eternal abstract original ideas, and neither is there a towering divine Father or Author Figure. Hence, the paradoxical prophecy by the witches that it is Lyra's destiny to "put an end to destiny" (*HDM*, 549) is part of Pullman's own intricate "reading scene". While stories have the potential to be true, their truth can only emanate from a particular situation, a here and now that dynamically connects to a specific past and a possible future. According to *His Dark Materials*, there simply can be no overarching story that serves as reference point for all other stories, which means that no story is *destined* to carry only one meaning, to deserve only one interpretation. As with the interpretation of Plato's *khōra*, while "[e]verything happens as *if* the yet-to-come history of the interpretations [...] were written or even prescribed in advance" (Derrida 1995, 99), this conditionality—"*as if*"—implies that the belief in the one Truth is a wishful projection. Just like *khōra* "'is' nothing other than the sum or the process of what has just been inscribed 'on' her" (99), any text—even that of my own life story—will be/mean nothing but the sum of its interpretations. It is in this sense that every interpretation indeed becomes part of a larger destiny. It is also in this sense that the World of the Dead, the once profane non-space, is "reconsecrated" by Lyra's and all ghosts' stories in order to serve as a space of possibility, and as such functions as symbolic of the space offered by Pullman's literary myth. In Graham Holderness' words:

> The space of Philip Pullman's fiction is analogous to Mircea Eliade's "sacred space". To enter it is to cross a threshold from the ordinary to the enchanted. The place the reader then finds him or herself in is an aperture, a horizon, a place filled with "images of an opening". Pullman's primary fictional method is to invent ways of effecting a "break in plane", so "communication between the cosmic planes" becomes possible. In particular, he opens that space between the world of the living and the Land of the Dead. Pullman also defines human "being" as nomadic, never quite at home, restless and hungry for elsewhere. (2007, 288)

Existentially, then, all human beings are homeless. Their state of "never being quite at home", though, is not a shortcoming, but offers a chance to progress, develop, live. It is important to remember that neither the notion of home nor that of parents is rejected by Pullman. However, Lyra's parents only become "true" parents from the moment in which they realise that parenthood, in order to enable life, must not be limiting. For Pullman, it simply will not do for parents to avail themselves of Urizenic "iron laws". In this connection, the fact that Lyra and Will must separate in the end is perhaps equally part of Pullman's conception of an enabling "existential orphanhood". While a classical happy ending would imply a narrative closure that would render the trilogy's "message" void, Lyra and Will are not totally separated, after all. They will meet each year at the same time and each sit on that same bench in the Botanic Garden (another version of Paradise), each in their own Oxford. In this way, "we *would* be close, if you sat here and I sat just *here* in my world" (*HDM*, 1007).

Coda: *A Song of Ice and Fire*

George R.R. Martin's *A Song of Ice and Fire*—which, since its adaptation as a TV series, *Game of Thrones*, surely must be counted the most popular fantasy of the present time (apart from *Harry Potter*, perhaps)—brims over with orphans and half-orphans, particularly among the protagonists. After the beheading of Eddard and the later murder of Catelyn during the Red Wedding, the (remaining) Stark children become orphans—or half-orphans, depending on the motherly status of Catelyn after her resurrection as Lady Stoneheart. Apart from them, Daenerys Targaryen, commonly called Dany, is surely the most prominent orphan. Since she is a true orphan from the very beginning of the series, I will concentrate on her in the following. At the time of writing, only the first five instalments have been published (up to *Dance with Dragons*), so my interpretation has a provisional character.

When the reader encounters Dany for the first time as a then-13-year-old girl, she is on the verge of getting married to Khal Drogo, a powerful leader of the Dothraki, nomadic warrior tribes living in the grasslands of Essos. The marriage has been arranged by her brother Viserys, who is eight years her senior, and the businessman Illyrio. Dany's and Viserys' assessments of the situation could not differ more radically from each other. Full of self-confidence and focused only on himself, Viserys proclaims: "When they write the history of my reign, sweet sister, they will say that it began tonight" (*GoT*, 29).[12] In contrast, Daenerys, standing at the window and looking down on Pentos, secretly yearns to enter a time *beyond* history: "Dany could hear […] the shouts of ragged children playing games beyond the walls of the estate. For a moment she wished she could be out there with them, barefoot and breathless and dressed in tatters, with no past and no future and no feast to attend at Khal Drogo's manse" (29). As her daydream reveals, by divesting herself of her class status as well as her dynastic legacy, Dany would concurrently step out of a linear, teleologically oriented conception of time. Consequently, the scene spells out not merely Dany's subordinate role, her object status, but also her ambivalent position as orphan.

On the one hand, she is an orphan in the narrow, literal, sense: "She had been born on Dragonstone nine moons after their flight, while a raging summer storm threatened to rip the island fastness apart. […] Her mother had died birthing her, and for that her brother Viserys had never forgiven her" (30). Accordingly, while she must have been procreated shortly before the murder of her father (her birth takes place "nine moons after their flight"), her mother died in childbed. Dany's entry to life was thus flanked by her parents' deaths. On the other hand, Dany is also an orphan in a wider, more general, sense: she is a refugee, an expatriate on the continent of Essos, who has been separated from her father-/motherland, Westeros. Ever since her flight from Dragonstone the siblings have been on the run and led a nomadic life: "They had wandered since then, from Braavos to Myr, from Myr to Tyrosh, and on to Qohor and Volantis and Lys, never staying long in one place" (31). In the final analysis, Dany's entire story revolves around the question how to resume the severed connection to her father-/motherland. Her natural parents being irretrievably lost, Dany does not even yearn for them. Yet what she considers to be her home—her mother-/fatherland—is still there, is physically real: a retrieval of what was lost appears to be possible. The problem, however, is that she knows Westeros as well or as little as she knows her parents. Since she has lived in exile since her birth, the image she has of this lost and never experienced homeland is a glorified, nostalgic, and hence ultimately unreal and fictive, one: "Somewhere beyond the sunset, across the narrow sea, lay a land of green hills and flowered plains and great rushing rivers, where towers of dark stone rose amidst magnificent blue-grey mountains, and armored knights rode to battle beneath the banners of their lords" (*GoT*, 29-30). It is a land of which Viserys claims that it is his by right of the royal blood of the Targaryens flowing in his veins, and most of the knowledge Dany has both of this land and of her family has come down to her via Viserys' stories. She herself cannot recall anything.

> [Viserys:] "Ours by blood right, taken from us by treachery, but ours still, ours forever. You do not steal from the dragon, oh, no. The dragon remembers."
> And perhaps the dragon did remember, but Dany could not. She had never seen this land her brother said was theirs, this realm beyond the narrow sea. (*GoT*, 30)

Particularly in her current situation, shortly before she is sold by her brother like a slave, Dany is unable to feel the connection to her homeland. She is feeling lost.

Although Dany, as noted above, momentarily yearns for a life *beyond* history, her wish does not imply entering "mythic time". Rather, in her daydream, she longs to bypass the fate tied to her dynastic legacy: to put it bluntly, she does not want to be a passive plaything in the game of thrones, but would sooner exchange her high birth for that of a poor street urchin. Hence, in this very moment, if Dany could decide upon the nature of her own story, she would choose herself to be what Northrop Frye calls "the hero of the *low mimetic* mode", a hero who is "superior neither to other men nor to his environment" (2000, 34). To have her story shaped by this mode would move her farthest from the three modes that, according to Frye's chronological system, have preceded it: the mythic, the romantic, as well as the high mimetic mode. Of course, in hindsight, Dany's wish is void: rather than being a common heroine, she will, in the different phases of her development, nearly always have a power of action much greater than the average human. While Dany, as "mother of dragons", may almost qualify as a divine, mythic heroine, she probably best fits the category of a heroine from the mode of romance, "whose actions are marvellous but who is [herself] identified as a human being" (Frye 2000, 33). As claimant to the Iron Throne and ruler over the great slaver cities in the East, Dany is undoubtedly "superior in *degree* to other men [and women] and to [her] environment" (33). And yet, keeping in mind Frye's proposition that "while one mode constitutes the underlying tonality of a work of fiction, any or all of the other four may be simultaneously present" (50) as well, I suggest that the low mimetic mode, which Frye deems to be characteristic for "realistic fiction" (34), and even the ironic mode are equally and productively employed in *A Song of Ice and Fire*. Arguably, much of the series' attraction lies in the narrative's ostentatious "realistic" style, achieved not least via multiperspectivity.

Hence, considering Dany's initial situation in the light of her further journey, I will conclude my reflections on the connection between orphan, myth and fantasy by tracing some lines of tradition that connect Martin's cycle to the orphan novel and hence, mainly, to literature categorised by Frye as having been written in the low mimetic and ironic modes. According to Auerbach (1975: 396), the orphan figure in the 18th-century novel is primarily a *pícaro*, a rogue, who, since s/he does not have any past by way of which s/he could socially stabilise his or her position, is required to create a future out of him- or herself. In a genre sustained by the rising middle class, the orphan epitomises the newly-to-be-defined place of this very class in a deistic universe; a universe in which it becomes increasingly difficult to have recourse to God as a father figure just like that. On the one hand, then, orphans represent the modern individual, whose status was constituted through the empty spaces left behind by the disintegration of the premodern metaphysical order of things: spaces, however, which could not be wholly satisfactorily filled by the new, increasingly market-oriented structure of the world. On the other hand, it is particularly the orphaned heroes of this new genre, the novel, that could constructively make use of these empty spaces by their cleverness, but also by their moral impartiality. "[The 18th-century orphan] stands supreme and a little monstrous, the great artificer, the self-made man" (Auerbach 1975, 403). Timaeus' demiurge has returned, disposed of his metaphysical nature, but still endowed with a divine nature: someone who has assumed the power to *make himself* and therefore shape the world. As Barbara Puschmann-Nalenz shows in the present volume, while the "picaresque orphan is at present a rarity in literary English fiction despite the novelistic traditions of the 18th and 19th centuries" (cf. her chapter "Some Things", 124), traces of the picaresque do remain, particularly perhaps in the fantasy novel (as well as serialised comics; cf. Vanderbeke in the present volume, 267). Although Dany is certainly no *picaro* in the narrow sense—if only because she lacks that character type's unburdened and easy-going nature—she still may be described as "self-made", not least because of her being a *woman* in a man's world. While her lineage and her magical power over dragons are certainly helpful, her attraction as a character mainly stems from her desire to shape the world according to her own will. Hardly anything remains in Dany of the 19th-century tradition of the orphan as pathetic figure, whose helplessness and disadvantaged state mostly pertained to women and child characters (cf. Gymnich in the present volume, 25ff.). Rather, Dany easily slips into the role of the (formerly male) adventurer, complete with all the imperial undertones characteristic of the respective texts.

In a particular way, the story of Dany therefore reveals and repeats what Auerbach calls the "amphibious nature of the eighteenth-century orphan novel" (1975: 403). While her somewhat headstrong dragons seem to provide a fitting image for this, she herself is indeed monstrous as well. Karin Gresham, who reads Dany against Bakhtin's concept of the carnivalesque, persuasively claims that her body can be understood as a grotesque body that not only breaks down the boundary lines between male and female (in that, when taking Khal Drogo's place as the leader of the khalasar, her body becomes hardened and assumes "male" qualities [cf. Gresham 2005, 157]), but also carries in itself an animal-like, bestial nature: "Martin grants Dany [...] her greatest strength when she appears in these liminal states that embrace in combining imagery from the empowering aspects of the feminine, masculine and bestial" (151). Another aspect that Dany shares with the *picaro*, then, is the "capacity for perpetual rebirth" (Auerbach 1975. 398). Her ritualistic self-immolation at the end of *A Game of Thrones* enables not only the birth of her dragons, but also her own rebirth. At the end of *A Dance with Dragons*, the ritual is renewed and repeated by her undergoing another baptism of fire through Drogon, complemented by her flight with the black dragon (*DwD*, 764-66).

Particularly after her rebirth as mother of dragons, Dany is self-confident and self-determined. She is a doer, not only because she never loses sight of her goal to reclaim the Seven Kingdoms but more particularly because she decides to create a world without slavery. And yet, the pressure exerted by a world that is forming her, instead of the other way round, becomes steadily more severe, in the shape of prophecies, dreams, but especially because of the political responsibility she takes upon herself as a result of her military campaigns against Astapor, Yunkai and Meereen. After the capture of Meereen she has to admit to herself that victory and defeat are two sides of the same coin: "*All my victories turn to dross in my hands*, she thought. *Whatever I do, all I make is death and horror*" (*SoS*, 983). Ultimately, she therefore decides to bring her wanderings to an at least temporary close. She intends to remain in Meereen until the situation has stabilised and she has understood what it means to rule efficiently. Both to the slave traders and herself, though, she appears less as a saviour than a demonic bringer of pain and destruction, a state of affairs for which the girl Hazzea, who has been killed by Drogon, assumes a tragic symbolic character (see *DwD*, 50, 174-75).

All in all, then, it may be claimed that the orphan character, from the 18th century, has represented the condition of a gradually secularising world, in which old authorities are replaced by new ones so that the erosion of formerly binding grand narratives corrodes certainties about one's own origin as well as the origin of the community at large. In the 20th and 21st centuries, these tendencies become even more relevant and pronounced. As Barbara Puschmann-Nalenz argues:

> It is evident that the figure of the orphan as a trope of the loss of origins in contemporary fiction, closely connected to themes of history and belonging, signifies specific situations [...]; it can serve to highlight loss of orientation, breakup of relationality and disintegration of selfhood, as it can signify desertion and abandonment of (national) affinity and communal ties. (2014, 199)

In a paradoxical manner, fantasy, as a specific mode of world building, seems to both amplify and resist the topic trends associated with the orphan character. There seems to be some agreement that fantasy has a pronounced anti-secular tendency—just like fantastic literature as a whole. It is a genre that braces itself against the "disenchantment" of the world, against the dilution of the metaphysical substance of the cosmos, which, on the diegetic level, is often expressed by what John Clute calls "thinning".

Fantasy tales can be described, in part, as fables of recovery. What is being regained may be (a) the primal STORY that the surface tale struggles to rearticulate, (b) the primal TRUE NAME, or home, of the protagonist, (c) the health of the land [...] through a process of HEALING, or indeed (d) the actual location of the land itself [...]. But, although it is true most fantasy stories *finish*—and tend to end in a EUCATASTROPHE—it is also true that the happy endings of much fantasy derive from the notion that this is a *restoration*, that before the written story started there was a diminishment. (1997c, 942)

As has become evident in the above discussions, the search for and investigation of a possible "primal story" is highly relevant for *Harry Potter* and *His Dark Materials*, just as it is in *A Song of Ice and Fire*. In each case, this primal story is in some way connected to the protagonist's parents and their legacy, which in turn relates to the search for home and, for instance *ex negativo* in Voldemort's case, for a true name. Although it is not possible as yet to evaluate the notion of the "healing of the land" in the case of *A Song of Ice and Fire* (since, at the time of writing, only the first five volumes have been published, with two more to come), both *Harry Potter* and *His Dark Materials* definitely conclude with such a healing process. It is safe to say, though, that, in all three cases, the story revolves around the "painful THINNING of texture, a fading away of beingness" (Clute 1997a, 339). Even in the case of Pullman's anti-metaphysical narrative, there is a pervasive sense of what it means to *truly* be, pitted against the corroding influence of deadening, authoritarian forces. These stories spell out notions of true "beingness", which are invariably connected to some "higher" value system, i.e., a "texture" of values, a signifying system apt to embrace the protagonists and "locate" them in a "sacred space", a home, and hence restore them to an "un-orphaned" status.

Very often, such "thinning [. .] manifest[s] itself through a loss of MAGIC" (Clute 1997a, 339), which perhaps becomes most evident in *A Song of Ice and Fire*: no Gandalf-type wizards appear, no wand-wielders and spell-casters as in *Harry Potter*. In large sections, it appears to be a highly "modern", "down-to-earth" world, which is devoid of magic. Unsurprisingly, the lack or loss of magic pre-eminently pertains to those who inhabit the west of the known world: "Magic had died in the west when the Doom fell on Valyria and the Lands of the Long Summer, and neither spell-forged steel nor stormsingers nor dragons could hold it back, but Dany had always heard that the east was different" (*GoT*, 235). Not least because of this, many of the authorities in the south of Westeros do not believe in the sudden strengthening of the white walkers, the "Others", north of the Wall; not least because of this, many claim that the stories about the Targaryen girl with the three dragons are nothing but myths. The political intrigues, all of them motivated by very mundane reasons, and the brutal, spectacular and mostly pointless violence that characterises the "game of thrones" contribute to the representation of a disenchanted world given to a continuing disintegration in ever smaller units of meaning, held together only by the pursuit of power.

In a quite blatant way, the so-called Unsullied, Dany's eunuch army, represent the costs occasioned by a world which is primarily shaped by violence and the secular striving after wealth and power. Although it is possible that many of the Unsullied still have parents, they may qualify as "true" orphans. Already sold as slaves at a young age, they are systematically robbed of every form of emotion and their attachment capabilities. As Kraznys explains (*SoS*, 318), all Unsullied, in order to master the last initiation phase in order to become a warrior, have to kill a newborn baby that they need to snatch from its mother. For them perhaps even worse than this is the test at the end of an earlier phase, when they are obliged to strangle that dog to death which was given to them as a puppy on the day of their own castration. The murder of the dog and the baby by their own hands symbolises the effacement of even the last spark of familial feeling, the ultimate obliteration of compassion. To dispossess them of their names is another means to alienate them from their identity and humanity. What this means is demonstrated to the reader by way of the freed ten-year-old slave girl Missandei, whose three brothers have been trained as Unsullied. Although they are still alive, Missandei tellingly refers to their family relationship in the past tense: "Three of them were my brothers once, Your Grace" (*SoS*, 373). It is tempting to declare the Unsullied representatives of the lost postmodern subject, divested of all ethnic and familial bonds. As Dany exclaims in disappointment: "[The Unsullied are] eunuchs, not men. Shall I buy eight thousand brick eunuchs with dead eyes that never move[?]" (*SoS*, 326). These are zombie-like warriors, comparable to Mrs Coulter's army of "intercised" soldiers, whose identity, it seems, has irretrievably drifted apart, yet not in the liberating sense in which Pullman's ghosts become one with the cosmos.

The (preliminary) climax of Dany's forlornness and disorientation is reached in the last "Daenerys" chapter published so far (which, if not counting the "Epilogue", is also the last chapter in *Dance with Dragons*). In this chapter, Dany wanders through the immenseness of the Dothraki sea (which, in fact, is a prairie) and, once again, makes an effort to imagine a future without past: "*Keep walking. If I look back, I am lost*" (*DwD*, 1019). It is at this point perhaps that the difference between fantasy and other, more "realistically" oriented, varieties of contemporary fiction becomes plain. Much fantasy, including Martin's, is ultimately inclined towards essentialism. Arguably, fantasy does exactly what Dany here is afraid of. It looks back; somewhat nostalgically, it looks back to the metaphysically constituted wholeness of a premodern world, a world in which all things still were intrinsically and meaningfully connected with each other. Even in the moment of severest forlornness Dany feels her being integrated in a larger cosmic context, particularly when she again has a vision of the masked Quaithe, a spiritlike figure that seems to function as the mouthpiece of fate: "[Dany] saw. *Her mask is made of starlight.* 'Remember who you are, Daenerys,' the stars whispered in a woman's voice. 'The dragons know, do you?'" (*DwD*, 1026). To put it provocatively: precisely because fantasy commonly looks back, to pre-historic, quasi-medieval or quasi-Renaissance worlds, in which the divine and the fateful still were essentially connected with the human sphere, it undoubtedly has conservative leanings. As genre or mode, fantasy braces itself against the disintegrating tendencies of an orphaned world that seems to have dismissed notions of wholeness. Fantasy looks for our lost origins, which it imagines in the shape of magical creatures, fulfilling prophecies, and the perpetuation of monomythical hero stories. Dany's understanding of her queenship is medieval in that it implies that the body of the king/queen and the body of the land organically coincide. Not for nothing does she—who is no natural mother anymore, who has lost her child and so is an orphaned mother—become the mother of her (orphan) dragons and of her people, including her orphaned slaves. As queen, Dany seeks to end the overarching orphan condition once and for all. Yet by which right? Undoubtedly, this is a right based on old and overthrown conceptions of dynastic sanctity and nobility by blood.

Obviously, though, this argument would be too one-sided if it were meant to serve as a general indictment of fantasy literature. It is too one-sided not only because other fantasies—like the *Harry Potter* series and especially *His Dark Materials*—very strongly act against such outdated conceptions on the level of content—but also in a more general sense. With reference to the passage in Plato's *Phaedrus* which was briefly discussed at the beginning of this chapter—the passage in which Socrates concedes priority to speech over writing, because speech happens in the here and now, and hence can guarantee presence of meaning—Cathy Caruth argues:

> Writing, here, is *orphaned language,* communicating the distress and potentially dangerous loss of legitimacy, not only of writing itself, but also of all language affected by the possibility of rootlessness introduced into the linguistic family tree.

[…] [W]e may also hear a literary story in this philosophical speech, in which writing emerges *as a figure*, the figure of the orphan, a figure that transmits a rift, or an orphaning, a rupture within language, signified by writing. (Caruth 2011, 240)

Writing itself, hence, is subjected to orphanhood. In writing and especially literary writing, ambiguous semantic systems are conceived within which the readers are perpetually sent on journeys in search of origins, meaning and sense.

While *A Song of Ice and Fire*, on the diegetic level, hence seems to create a metaphysically holistic world, the series is clearly a postmodern product when considered from an extradiegetic perspective. Indeed, in the tradition of Tolkien's writings, Martin designs a very detailed, "deep", world, which is provided with a persuasive historical dimension not least through his many references to the past. However, the excessive way in which Martin engages in the historicisation of a purely fictive world reveals at the same time that the depth he creates is nothing but virtual, simulacral. To avail myself of Fredric Jameson's words, *A Song of Ice and Fire* figures as a further "symptom of the waning of our historicity, of our lived possibility of experiencing history in some active way" (Jameson 1991, 21). When Dany, in the last chapter, appears as a fallen queen whose "clothes were hardly more than rags" (*DwD*, 1019), then her initial wish to bypass history and join the company of the "ragged children […], barefoot and breathless and dressed in tatters" (*GoT*, 29), seems to have come true. In a way, Dany seems to have been degraded to a hero of the low mimetic, maybe even the ironic, mode. However, her preceding, quasi-ritualistic, reunification with Drogon, whose fire had burned her hair but not the rest of her body, thereby recalling and repeating her birth as mother of dragons, has already offered a clear indication of the fact that linear earthly history might transform into cyclical mythic time and hence start anew, as what Mircea Eliade refers to as "a living world—inhabited and used by creatures of flesh and blood, subject to the law of becoming, of old age and death" (1998, 184). On a metaliterary plane, it might analogically be argued that the rise in popularity of fantasy signifies a return to myth. In Frye's words:

[T]he mimetic tendency itself, the tendency to verisimilitude and accuracy of description, is one of two poles of literature. At the other pole is something that seems to be connected both with Aristotle's word *mythos* and with the usual meaning of myth. That is, it is a tendency to tell a story which is in origin a story about characters who can do anything, and gradually becomes attracted toward a tendency to tell a plausible or credible story. [...] Reading forward in history, therefore, we may think of our romantic, high mimetic and low mimetic modes as a series of *displaced* myths, *mythoi* or plot-formulas progressively moving over towards the opposite pole of verisimilitude, and then, with irony, beginning to move back. (2000, 51-52)

The important point is that while fantasy may well signify a "move back" to myths, this move will necessarily be characterised by the traces left by the other—preceding—modes, not least the ironic. Hence, in a paradoxical manner, specifically the orphan characters in fantasy open up spaces for active reading. It is possible to understand the orphan as an "emancipatory" sign, which—due to the "clipping" of its referential structures—is potentially well suited to open up new and dynamic options to refer both to "reality" and "myth". Just as Dany only knows Westeros from the stories her brother told her about it, we only know Westeros from what Martin's narrator has told *us* about it. These stories are not myths in the old sense, but—as the popularity of the three fantasies under discussion well proves— they have the potential to convey a sense of what the old myths must have meant, yet without claiming to be as exclusive and binding. After all, we *know* that this is fiction, and we also *know* that contemporary fantasy has cast off and even reacts against ur-fantasies like those by Tolkien and, even more so, C.S. Lewis, with all their sometimes overburdening ideological and symbolic baggage. At the same time, fantasy offers a space that allows the negotiation of the legacy of the Western *logos*.

Notes

[1] Undeniably, Armitt's argumentation is very general here, maybe too general to remain uncontested. Regarding her list, many of the texts that have been categorised as "magical realism", for instance, are certainly credited with having enough "weight" to be canonised. However, I am mainly interested in fantasy in the narrower sense.

[2] Certainly, it is possible to identify, for example, the ways in which Tolkien has incorporated Norse mythology in his writings. However, these influences are only evident to the experts, to those in the know—not merely because there are no explicit references to them in Tolkien's stories, but also because Norse mythology in general has lost its currency today.

[3] For all references to the *Harry Potter* novels, the following abbreviations will be used: PS = *Philosopher's Stone*; CS = *Chamber of Secrets*; PA = *Prisoner of Azkaban*; GoF = *Goblet of Fire*; OP = *Order of the Phoenix*; HBO = *Half-Blood Prince*; DH = *Deathly Hallows*.

[4] From the fifth chapter, though, "Diagon Alley", *Harry Potter* turns into a "portal-quest fantasy". It is for this reason that Mendlesohn categorises *Harry Potter* among "The Irregulars" (cf. 2008, 246-47).

[5] As Derrida notes, *pharmakon* can be translated "by 'remedy,' 'recipe,' 'poison,' 'drug,' 'philter,' etc." (1981, 77).

[6] Tellingly, the same sequence of spells will lead to Voldemort's ultimate demise in their last duel (*DH*, 595-96). The last duel is a *repetition* of this one, with the *difference* that Harry has fully matured by then, while Voldemort has not developed at all.

[7] His claim that the Death Eaters are his "*true* family" (*GoF*, 561) is obviously self-defeating. As Dumbledore mentions more than once, Voldemort does not care about friendship or family.

[8] In the tale, three brothers prevent their drowning in a dangerous river by magically spanning a bridge across it, thereby tricking Death. Death, hoping to trick them in return, offers a wish to each of them. The first brother wishes for a wand that cannot be defeated, the Elder Wand; however, after having boasted of his invincibility, he is murdered in his sleep and the wand stolen. The second wants to have "*the power to recall Others from Death*" (*DH*, 331), receives the Philosopher's Stone, and resurrects his deceased lover; however, since the girl is nothing but a cold, suffering shadow, he ultimately commits suicide. The youngest, who suspects Death's motives, "*asked for something that would enable him to go forth from that place without being followed by Death*" and is given the Cloak of Invisibility which allows him to live a peaceful life until old age, at the end of which he passes the Cloak on to his son.

[9] Since wizards in *Harry Potter* come of age at the age of 17, it is debatable whether Dumbledore qualifies as a "true" orphan. What is decisive for the present argument, however, is that Dumbledore's past actions ultimately derived from the experience of losing his family. Rita Skeeter, in her biography of Dumbledore, explicitly refers to him as an orphan (*DH*, 290).

[10] For all references to *His Dark Materials*, the abbreviation *HDM* will be used.

[11] In this context, Dirk Vanderbeke has made me aware of the important fact that Lyra's surname, Belacqua, refers to the sinner Belacqua in Dante's *Divine Comedy*. After having passed through the nine circles of Hell (*Inferno*), Dante, accompanied by Vergil, meets Belacqua on one of the terraces on the way up the Mountain of Purgatory. Belacqua, who made himself guilty by committing the deathly sin of sloth, is not yet allowed to further proceed upwards, towards Paradise, but instead has to wait for the exact same amount of time that he put off doing penance for his sins during his life (cf. Dante, *Purgatorio*, Canto IV, ll. 98-135). In stark contrast to Dante's Belacqua, Lyra is neither prepared to wait nor is she indolent. It would certainly be quite rewarding to consider the intertextual references to the *Divine Comedy* in more detail.

[12] In the following, I will use the following abbreviations: *GT* = *A Game of Thrones*; *SoS* = *A Storm of Swords*; *DwD* = *A Dance with Dragons*.

Works Cited

Armitt, Lucie. 2005. *Fantasy Fiction: An Introduction.* New York: Continuum.

Attebery, Brian. 2014. *Stories about Stories: Fantasy and the Remaking of Myth.* Oxford: Oxford University Press.

—. 1992. *Strategies of Fantasy.* Bloomington, IN: Indiana University Press.

Auerbach, Nina. 1975. "Incarnations of the Orphan." *English Literary History* 42 (3): 395-419.

Blake, William. 1988. *The Complete Poetry and Prose of William Blake*, edited by David V. Erdman. Newly Revised edn. New York: Anchor Books.

Butler, Judith. 2004. "Bodily Confessions." In Judith Butler, *Undoing Gender*, 161-73. New York: Routledge.

Caruth, Cathy. 2011. "Orphaned Language: Traumatic Crossings in Literature and Culture." In *A Companion to Comparative Literature*, edited by Ali Behdad and Dominic Thomas, 239-53. Chichester: Wiley-Blackwell.

Carmeli, Ronnie. 2009. "Four Models of Fatherhood: Paternal Contributions to Harry Potter's Psychological Development." In *Harry Potter's World Wide Influence*, edited by Diana Patterson, 11-33. Newcastle-upon-Tyne: Cambridge Scholars.

Clute, John. 1997a. "Fantasy." In *The Encyclopedia of Fantasy*, edited by John Clute and John Grant, 337-39. London: Orbit.

—. 1997b. "Taproot Texts." In *The Encyclopedia of Fantasy*, edited by John Clute and John Grant, 921-22. London: Orbit.

—. 1997c. "Thinning." In *The Encyclopedia of Fantasy*, edited by John Clute and John Grant, 942-43. London: Orbit.

Coupe, Laurence. 1997. *Myth.* The New Critical Idiom. London: Routledge.

Curtis, James Michael. 2016. *In Absentia Parentis: The Orphan Figure in Latter Twentieth Century Anglo-American Children's Fantasy.* Dissertation thesis. The University of Southern Mississippi. Aquila. http://aquila.usm.edu/dissertations/322/.

Damon, Foster S. 1988. *A Blake Dictionary: The Ideas and Symbols of William Blake.* Rev. edn. Hanover: University Press of New England.

Damour, Lisa. 2009. "Harry the Teenager: Muggle Themes in a Magical Adolescence." In *Reading Harry Potter Again: New Critical Essays*, edited by Giselle Liza Anatol, 1-10. Santa Barbara: ABC-CLIO.

Dante. 1997-1999. *Divine Comedy*. Princeton Dante Project.
    http://etcweb.princeton.edu/dante/index.html.
Derrida, Jacques. 1995. "*Khōra*." [French original 1993]. In Jacques
    Derrida. *On the Name*, edited by Thomas Dutoit, 87-127. Translated by
    Ian Mc Leod. Stanford: Stanford University Press.
—. 1981. "Plato's Pharmacy." In Jacques Derrida. *Dissemination* [French
    original 1972], 67-186. Translated by Barbara Johnson. London:
    Continuum.
Eliade, Mircea. 1998. "Myth and Reality." In *The Myth and Ritual Theory:
    An Anthology*, edited by Robert A. Segal, 180-89. Malden: Blackwell.
Frazer, James George. 1994. *The Golden Bough: A Study in Magic and
    Religion*. A New Abridgement from the Second and Third Editions.
    Intr. Robert Fraser. Oxford World's Classics. Oxford: Oxford University
    Press.
Frye, Northrop. (1957) 2000. *Anatomy of Criticism: Four Essays*.
    Princeton: Princeton University Press.
Gallardo C., Ximena, and C. Jason Smith. 2003. "Cinderfella: J.K.
    Rowling's Wily Web of Gender." In *Reading Harry Potter: Critical
    Essays*, edited by Giselle Liza Anatol, 191-203. Santa Barbara: ABC-
    CLIO.
—. 2009. "Happily Ever After: Harry Potter and the Quest for the
    Domestic." In *Reading Harry Potter Again: New Critical Essays*,
    edited by Giselle Liza Anatol, 91-107. Santa Barbara: ABC-CLIO.
Gooderham, David. 2003. "Fantasizing It As It Is: Religious Language in
    Philip Pullman's Trilogy *His Dark Materials*." *Children's Literature*
    31: 155-75.
Grant, John. 1997. "Genre Fantasy." In *The Encyclopedia of Fantasy*,
    edited by John Clute and John Grant, 396. London: Orbit.
Gresham, Karin. 2005. "Cursed Womb, Bulging Thighs and Bald Scalp:
    George R.R. Martin's Grotesque Queen." In *Mastering the Game of
    Thrones: Essays on George R.R. Martin's* A Song of Ice and Fire,
    edited by Jes Battis and Susan Johnston, 151-69. Jefferson: McFarland.
Grosz, Elizabeth. 1994. *Volatile Bodies: Towards a Corporeal Feminism*.
    Bloomington, IN: Indiana University Press.
Holderness, Graham. 2007. "'The Undiscovered Country': Philip Pullman
    and the 'Land of the Dead'." *Literature & Theology* 21 (3): 276-92.
Jackson, Rosemary. 1981. *Fantasy: The Literature of Subversion*. London:
    Routledge.
Jameson, Fredric. 1991. *Postmodernism, Or, The Cultural Logic of Late
    Capitalism*. Durham: Duke University Press.

Jung, C.G. 1968. *Psychology and Alchemy*. 2nd edn. Translated by R.F.C. Hull. London: Routledge.

Kant, Immanuel. 1996. "An Answer to the Question: What Is Enlightenment?" In Immanuel Kant. *Practical Philosophy*. Translated and edited by Mary J. Gregor. The Cambridge Edition of the Works of Immanuel Kant, 15-22. New York: Cambridge University Press.

Lenz, Millicent. 2005. "Introduction: Awakening to the Twenty-First Century: The Evolution of Human Consciousness in Pullman's *His Dark Materials*." In *His Dark Materials Illuminated: Critical Essays on Philip Pullman's Trilogy*, edited by Millicent Lenz with Carole Scott, 1-15. Detroit: Wayne State University Press.

Martin, George R.R. (1996) 2005. *A Game of Thrones: Book One of A Song of Ice and Fire*. New York: Bantam. [*GoT*]

—. (2000) 2011. *A Storm of Swords: Book Three of A Song of Ice and Fire*. New York: Bantam. [SoS]

—. (2011) 2012. *A Dance with Dragons: Book Five of A Song of Ice and Fire*. New York: Bantam. [DwD]

Mauss, Marcel. 1972. *A General Theory of Magic* [French original 1902/1950]. Translated by Robert Brain. London: Routledge.

Mendlesohn, Farah. 2008. *Rhetorics of Fantasy*. Middletown: Wesleyan University Press.

Milton, John. 2004. *Paradise Lost*. A Norton Critical Edition, edited by Gordon Teskey. 3rd rev. edn. New York: Norton.

Nikolajeva, Maria. 2002. *The Rhetoric of Character in Children's Literature*. Lanham: Scarecrow Press.

Peters, Laura. 2000. *Orphan Texts: Victorian Orphans, Culture and Empire*. Manchester: Manchester University Press.

—. 2011. "Revisiting the Colonial: Victorian Orphans and Postcolonial Perspectives." In *Critical Perspectives on Philip Pullman's His Dark Materials: Essays on the Novels, the Film and the Stage Productions*, edited by Steven Barfield and Katharine Cox, 93-110. Jefferson: McFarland.

Plato. 1966. *Phaedrus*. In: *Plato in Twelve Volumes*, vol. 1. Translated by Harold N. Fowler. Cambridge, MA: Harvard University Press; London: William Heinemann. Perseus Digital Library. data.perseus.org/texts/urn:cts:greekLit:tlg0059.tlg012.perseus-eng1.

—. 1935. *Republic*. In: *Plato in Twelve Volumes*, vol. 5-6. Translated by Paul Shorey. Cambridge, MA: Harvard University Press; London: William Heinemann, Reprint 1969-1970. Perseus Digital Library.

http://data.perseus.org/texts/urn:cts:greekLit:tlg0059.tlg030.perseus-eng1.

—. 1929. *Timaeus*. In: *Plato in Twelve Volumes*, vol. 9. Translated by Robert Gregg Bury. Cambridge, MA: Harvard University Press; London: William Heinemann, Reprint 1966. Perseus Digital Library. www.perseus.tufts.edu/hopper/text?doc=urn:cts:greekLit:tlg0059.tlg031.perseus-eng1.

Pullman, Philip. 2012. *His Dark Materials*. London: Scholastic. [*HDM*]

Puschmann-Nalenz, Barbara. 2014. "The Figure of the Orphan in Contemporary Fiction." In *Narrating Loss: Representations of Mourning, Nostalgia und Melancholia in Contemporary Anglophone Fictions*, edited by Brigitte Johanna Glaser and Barbara Puschmann-Nalenz, 179-202. Trier: WVT.

Rothenberg, Rose-Emily. 1983. "The Orphan Archetype." *Psychological Perspectives* 14 (2): 181-94.

Rowling, J.K. 1997. *Harry Potter and the Philosopher's Stone*. London: Bloomsbury. [*PS*]

—. 1998. *Harry Potter and the Chamber of Secrets*. London: Bloomsbury. [*CS*]

—. 1999. *Harry Potter and the Prisoner of Azkaban*. London: Bloomsbury. [*PA*]

—. 2000. *Harry Potter and the Goblet of Fire*. London: Bloomsbury. [*GoF*]

—. 2003. *Harry Potter and the Order of the Phoenix*. London: Bloomsbury. [*OP*]

—. 2005. *Harry Potter and the Half-Blood Prince*. London: Bloomsbury. [*HBP*]

—. 2007. *Harry Potter and the Deathly Hallows*. London: Bloomsbury. [*DH*]

Sedlmayr, Gerold. 2017. "Philip Pullman, *His Dark Materials* (1995-2000)." In *Handbook of the English Novel of the Twentieth and Twenty-First Centuries*. Handbooks of English and American Studies, vol. 5, edited by Christoph Reinfandt, 461-80. Berlin: De Gruyter.

Weiss, Meri. 2013. "The Role of Maternal Females in Harry Potter's Journey." In *Legilimens!: Perspectives in Harry Potter Studies*, edited by Christopher E. Bell, 19-31. Newcastle-upon-Tyne: Cambridge Scholars.

Wilson, Melissa B., and Kathy G. Short. 2012. "Goodbye Yellow Brick Road: Challenging the Mythology of Home in Children's Literature." *Children's Literature in Education* 43: 129-44.

Winters, Sarah Fiona. 2011. "Bubble-Wrapped Children and Safe Books for Boys: The Politics of Parenting in *Harry Potter*." *Children's Literature* 39: 213-33.

CHAPTER FIVE

THE ORPHAN IN COMICS AND GRAPHIC NOVELS[1]

DIRK VANDERBEKE

Introduction

In literature, childhood has traditionally been a time of perils and uncertainties. Unclear parentage or abandonment have been standard motifs in heroic tales since the earliest recorded myths—in the Gilgamesh epos, Enkidu has no parents as he is created from clay by the goddess Aruru, Moses is found by Pharaoh's daughter in the bulrushes of the Nile, Oedipus and Paris are abandoned by their respective parents in an attempt to prevent the unfavourable predictions of oracles. Moreover, as one of the Gorgons points out in Neil Gaiman's *The Sandman*, the gods "never seemed to care where they spurt their seed. Not keen on their responsibilities as fathers" (*The Kindly Ones* #61, 2), and so divine or semi-divine descent usually means that the hero has a tough start in life and grows up with at least one absentee parent. The pattern of the solitary hero, who has to fend for himself from early childhood onward, was adapted to literary works. As supernatural interference and godly impregnation have gone out of fashion, however, orphanhood at least partly replaced the story of the divine but absent parent. Thus, the life expectancy of the parents is severely reduced by the necessity to give the protagonists a fresh start in life unhindered by familial restrictions or domestic affiliations. Kimball suggests that "Orphans begin with a clean slate because they do not have parents to influence them either for good or for evil" (1999, 559); and Fingeroth argues that this openness and lack of restrictions offers a challenge as well as a potential:

> That's the side to which the orphan myth plays. The idea, so emphasized and mythologized in American popular culture, is: we are all alone. We

fight our own battles, make our own rules, defy those who would destroy
us. We are alone to succeed or fail, to triumph or succumb.
We make our own destinies. (2004, 70-71)

Blakemore, while less optimistic, argues that orphans are nevertheless "a
boon for authors—they come with lots of baggage, but few family ties"
(Blakemore 2014, n. pag.). Of course, the children do not grow up in
blissful or fearful solitude. The animal helpers that nursed various heroes
of antiquity—e.g. Paris or Romulus and Remus—are no longer suitable
figures in realist fiction, and therefore foster parents or institutions, for
better or for worse, fulfil parental duties, but also throw into sharp relief
the forces that act on the child and thus contribute to its future failures or
successes.

The new beginnings, however, not only affect the orphaned protagonist
of the story, they can also be seen as a useful narrative device, as orphans
are perfect guides for the reader, who is also introduced to unknown
territories and new social environments. Characters like Moll Flanders or
Oliver Twist allow us to accompany them when they take their first steps
into new social spaces, when they need to make sense of new experiences,
meet with supporting or threatening figures of authority, and enter happy
or precarious relationships. Empathy is then evoked not only by the pity
for the solitary child facing uncertainty and unpredictable changes, but
also by the joint encounter of dismal or promising circumstances and the
experience of co-learning the specific rules that govern the unfamiliar
fictional world.

As Puschmann-Nalenz points out, the interest in literary orphans is
usually focused on the 18th and 19th centuries (2014, 179), that is, a time
when a low life expectancy still rendered orphanhood a significant social
phenomenon. The chance to grow up with two living parents was diminished
by diseases and epidemics, war, famine, and not the least by the very fact
that, in particular in the 18th century, childbed mortality was still a factor
to be reckoned with (Loudon 1986, 13-14), leaving 1-2% of all children
motherless from the very start of their lives. But then not only the loss of
one or both parents left children orphaned; foundlings, abandoned children
or runaways have to be included in the number of orphans, too. Indeed,
orphanhood may not have been the worst fate, and in 1759, the social
reformer Jonas Hanley suggested that the death of parents was socially and
psychologically preferable to illegitimacy and/or abandonment (Nixon
2011, 6). Moreover, the traditional and archetypal image of the homeless
street urchin or guttersnipe as depicted in 19th-century realist literature
stands in stark contrast to its valued counterpart, the "well-maintained

eighteenth-century orphan situated in the centre of a domestic space and receiving attention from a replacement family" (6).

The orphan, then, is a contradictory phenomenon, either being doomed to suffer abandonment and solitude or rising to prosperity and success with or without the help of a foster family or supporting mentors. "Orphans are at once pitiable and noble. They are a manifestation of loneliness, but they also represent the possibility for humans to reinvent themselves" (Kimball 1999, 559). Thus, their domestic and social environments may in fact be more important than their status as orphans. Do they live in impoverished or prosperous circumstances? Have they been abandoned to lead a largely solitary existence, or are they integrated into a social community of similarly lost children or possibly a loving and protective foster family? In this respect, Moll Flanders is orphaned even though her mother lives and so may her father. Huckleberry Finn, who has a living father, may appear to be "more orphaned" than Tom Sawyer or Sid, who live with a caring aunt and do not seem to be traumatized in any way about the death of their parents.

All these aspects are also present in the comic, but while in 20th-century mainstream literature orphans occur less frequently, in comics and graphic novels, as in genre literature, they remain very prominent. As many genres, e.g. fantasy, romance, and some subgenres of detective fiction and science fiction, draw on narrative patterns that have a long pedigree—from mythology via Arthurian romances and fairy tales to the picaresque and gothic novels—orphaned heroes here still play a significant role, and so they do in comics and graphic novels, particularly in those that employ fantastic or non-realist elements.

The following survey of orphans in comics and graphic novels must, of course, remain incomplete, as the sheer mass of material cannot be considered in the scope of this chapter—or even in a book-length study. I have, nevertheless, tried to address the most important aspects and texts.

The Early Comics or Worlds without Parents: From the Youthful Anarchists to the Lovable Urchin

The beginnings of the comic as we know it are usually dated to the late 19th century. This was also the time when new medical achievements reduced childbed mortality, and improvements in hygiene slowly increased the chances for children to grow up with both of their parents. Over time, orphans became exceptions rather than familiar, if mostly pitiable, elements of society. But this did not diminish their presence in the comics, where the orphan is as ubiquitous as in the early novel. Nina

Auerbach suggests that "the orphan can be thought of as a metaphor for the novel itself: a faintly disreputable and possibly bastardized offspring of uncertain parentage, always threatening to lose focus and definition, but, with the resilience of the natural victim, always managing to survive; a particular product of the modern world" (1975, 395).

The same could ultimately be argued for the comic, which made its appearance when the novel had gained respectability, and now the new medium for the masses was looked upon with disdain as the improper and vulgar bastard of word and image (for a humorous rendition of this point cf. Rowson 2013, 237-43). However, if the format was beneath respectable appreciation, it was nevertheless very popular and may well have been a decisive factor in the marketing strategies and sales battles of the yellow press, which actually received its name from *The Yellow Kid*, a comic run simultaneously in Joseph Pulitzer's *New York World* and in William Randolph Hearst's *New York Journal* (Meyer 2012, n. pag.).

The 19th century also saw the rise of children and adolescents as protagonists, not only in children's literature but also in books for adults, and the constructions of childhood are often cast in dichotomies behind which we can easily recognize a Christian or Hobbesean view, based on the idea of original sin or warring nature, and the Rousseauian vision of natural purity—the innocent child versus the sinful child, the child as moral guide versus the child in need of guidance and chastisement, the cute or picturesque child versus the filthy rascal. In her introduction to *The Child in Literature*, Adrienne E. Gavin contrasts an older and more pessimistic perspective with a Romantic or modern vision of childhood (2012, 3); her assessment is informed by Susan Honeyman's distinction between a childhood that is "irrational, in the worst cases primitive, and in need of taming", or "intuitive, natural, and untainted by civilization" (Honeyman 2005, 80), as well as Chris Jenks's "Dionysian child", who is "impish and harbours a potential evil" (2005, 63), and the "Apollonian child", who is "angelic, innocent and untainted by the world" (64). The orphan, of course, allows for a particularly precise presentation of these alternatives, as here the child can be shown with minimal external influence either in its purity or depravity. In consequence, Jennifer Duggan sees orphans as "paradoxical figures to be both pitied and feared, signalling either the fulfilment of potential or its loss, and they often metamorphosed to reflect their inner moral state, good or bad" (2016, 51). In contrast to the strict division between the good child with an inherent morality and its counterpart, the evil imp, there is, however, also the lovable rascal, the dear dirty devil, the child whose lawlessness we can admire from the elevated perspective of the detached observer.

All these versions are, of course, also present in comics, and have been ever since their inception. As a consequence of the specific format of the early comics it is, however, not always easy or even possible to determine whether the children presented are, actually, orphans or rather belong to families which remain invisible. In novels and even most short stories, the most basic facts of the protagonist's life are usually presented, and thus in texts focusing on children their domestic circumstances are an important element in the characterization. Comics, however, were originally extremely reduced narratives with only a few images focusing on one specific situation; in consequence, the action is not embedded within a larger context and the domestic environment of the children remains undetermined unless it has a specific impact on the tale. Occasionally, a familial status of the child in question is presented after years of omission, but this clarification is not necessarily coherent with the previously published stories. The protagonists can be seen as "functional orphans" (Nikolajeva 2002, 172), i.e. children or juveniles whose parents are absent, possibly disinterested or incapable of parental care, and most often seem to be quite irrelevant to the youngsters who seem to fend for themselves and live by their own wits, means, and rules. It is a world in which children and adults seem to be natural opponents, fighting endless battles which usually follow the pattern of "crime and punishment".

Wilhelm Busch's famous series about Max and Moritz is a perfect example. The two boys are obviously part of a rural community, and we learn that they have an Uncle Fritz, as he is the victim of their fifth prank (Busch 1967, 23), but their parents are never mentioned—nor is the boys' specific relationship revealed: if they have an uncle in common they would have to be cousins or brothers. Even after the boys have been killed rather cruelly—being ground in a mill and then fed to some geese—the joy about their demise and the ensuing peace is unanimous, and grieving parents are not mentioned. The naturally mischievous children are orphaned in death, as they are not mourned and their end does not leave any gap in a bereaved family. This pattern can be found quite regularly in Busch's narratives about drastic pranks and even more drastic punishment, which can be meted out by any victim or witness of the misdeeds. If necessary, the recalcitrance of nature and various objects joins in the punishment—e.g. the naughty boys of Corinth harass Diogenes, but when they roll his barrel downhill, their shirts are caught on two nails and they are steamrolled and flattened out like dough (Busch 1962, 131-33). Again, death seems to be the appropriate reward for mischief—even if these graphically grotesque retributions obviously contribute to the humour and possibly pave the way for the later indestructibility of comic and cartoon figures, which can survive explosions, falls from immense heights and other calamities without serious harm.

Such unruly and uncontrollable boys have become stock figures of the comics and are still present today. Among them are Rudolph Dirk's Katzenjammer Kids, Hergé's Quick et Flupke, the British Dennis the Menace (who, in contrast to his fairly mild American namesake, is far more violent and basically a hooligan), Rodger the Dodger, or The Bash Street Kids. Most of these figures are not orphans, but their parents do not seem to be intimately related to the boys and, more rarely, girls and are of less importance than the best friends and other partners in crime. The stories mostly take place in a world beyond adult control, and parents are as likely to suffer from their kids' malice as anyone else. Again, every victim or witness may chastise the culprits once they have been caught.

The Katzenjammer Kids are a good example. The German immigrant urchins are obviously derivatives of Max and Moritz, "an exercise in raucous vulgarity" (Sabin 2001, 24), but they do not come to a cruel end after only a few pranks—indeed they made their first appearance in 1897 and are still syndicated today, which makes this the longest-running strip in comic history. Fritz and Hans are half-orphans, living with their mother, and the role of the father is taken by "The Captain". Quite regularly, he is the victim of the pranks and also the executioner of the almost inevitable spanking. The humour is anarchic, and the kids turn against every form of authority, including "The Inspector", a school representative. In their destructive rebellion against all rules, order and the world of adults, the kids appear as juvenile versions of the American Adam as described by R.W.B. Lewis, "an individual emancipated from history, happily bereft of ancestry, untouched and undefiled by the usual inheritances of family and race" (1955, 5). They are orphans by choice and behaviour, always ready to "avoid 'civilization'" (Fiedler 1966, 26) and to "light out for the Territory" (Twain 2004, 263), even if this territory should only be the backyard, whence the next assault on life as we know it can be launched.

Sabin suggests that with the rise of kids as consumers with their own pocket money, "comics became a private reading space for children, a place where they could negotiate adult power and authority, and where juvenile fantasies could be played out: a world of naughtiness, make believe violence and what primary school teachers used to call 'messy play'" (2001, 28).

The stories, then, serve two purposes: they fulfil the dreams of havoc and rebellion against parents, teachers, policemen and other figures of authority, but simultaneously also allow for a dollop of gloating when the young anarchists are inevitably found out and receive their usually painful

punishment. The bad boys are once more abandoned and orphaned, this
time not only by their own inconsiderate choice or the narrative
requirements of the format but also by their readers, who observe them
gleefully from the safe distance of domestic conformity.

The mischievous and occasionally nasty outlaws are, however, not the
only variant of children in the early comics; there are also more lovable
urchins with or without family ties, among them, most famously Mickey
Dugan, a.k.a. the Yellow Kid. Marked by a yellow nightshirt, a bald
head—probably shaved to rid him of lice—large ears and buckteeth, the
Yellow Kid was, according to his author Richard F. Outcault, "not an
individual but a type" (qtd. by Blackbeard 1995, 135). Once more, the
Yellow Kid may technically not be an orphan, but then he seems to live
permanently on the streets, and his parents are hardly, if ever, present on
the pages. A panel from May 3, 1896, "Moving Day in Hogan's Alley",
shows the move of a Dugan family, but as the Yellow Kid seems to be
delighted about their departure and obviously remains on the premises for
another four months he can hardly be a member of this family. It seems as
if Outcault had not yet decided upon the name of the kid (Blackbeard
1995, 39)—he would do so a few weeks later on June 21st, when the kid's
nightshirt bears the declaration "I am de Dugan Kid". Balzer and Wiesing
mention that in October 1896 he moved with his family not only from the
New York World to the *New York Journal* but also from Hogan's Alley to
McFadden's Row of Flats (2010, 21-22) but later they point out that he is
rather accompanied by his friends when he changes his haunts (23). And
indeed, that is also what is shown in the first full page panel for the *New
York Journal*: "In the first McFadden Flats (October 18, 1996), the Yellow
Kid and his gang, dogs, and loyal smoking goat move wholesale from
Hogan's Alley to their new neighborhood" (Blackbeard 1995, 66). Adults
may carry the furniture out of the old lodgings, but it is a huge group of
kids who are on the move. And when they arrive at their new destination,
this is what the story accompanying the comic tells: "Then there were
introductions, which did not, however, disclose the identity of the Yellow
Kid. 'Whose little one are you, dear?' asked Mrs. Murphy of the kid,
observing the omission. 'Say, I ain't nobody's child. I belongs t' de gang.
See?' answered the Kid" (Outcault, plate 40). Later, when the rest of the
gang is "distributed according to their family connections in the recently
vacated portions of the flats" (plate 40), there "was no room or portion of a
room assigned to the Yellow Kid, but he discovered a little closet in the
hall adjoining to the door of Tim's room" (plate 40).

Within this world of urchins, the Yellow Kid serves as a guide and
master of ceremonies. The panels usually display a spectacle or a scene of

havoc and disorder under one specific topic, e.g. "The Great Lawn Tennis Tournament in Hogan's Alley" (August 30, 1896), "Opening of the Hogan's Alley Athletic Club" (September 27, 1896) or "Receiving the Returns in McFadden's Row on Election Night" (November 1, 1896), with the Yellow Kid, frequently looking directly at the reader, in a central position with his nightshirt, in lieu of a speech balloon, offering some kind of comment on the chaotic activities that surround it. It is thus a transitional figure, creating a link between the audience and the story and at the same time marking the distance which necessitates some explanation, however ironic and absurd it may ultimately turn out to be.

(Richard F. Outcault, *Hogan's Alley*. August 30, 1896, *New York World*, from Outcault, plate 36, Kitchen Sink Press)

Mary Wood suggests that the Yellow Kid managed to address and attract several audiences simultaneously: "The character probably appealed broadly to the working class because of his dialect and ridiculing of the rich, but there is plenty of evidence that the middle class was the primary audience" (Wood 2014a). Such a broad appeal required an intricate employment of multiple and ambivalent messages which met each of the intended audiences on their own grounds. Social commentary went hand in hand with caricatures of the poor and an early kind of 'poverty porn', but also with parodies of high society life reminiscent of the satirical methods employed by John Gay in *The Beggar's Opera*. The obvious tenacity and creativity with which the kids survive and even enjoy themselves in the most unfavourable conditions evoke the American spirit of inventiveness, resilience and pride, but also create the image of a picturesque and idyllic niche in the urban jungle, the inhabitants of which do not seem to require any support and scorn the interference of social workers, policemen or educators. Accidents, injured children, starvation and death are present on the pages, but also quickly succeeded by, or even juxtaposed with, more entertaining motifs or hilarious scenes, merging tragedy and comedy within the overcrowded panels.

Like Charlie Chaplin's tramp, the "orphan" of Hogan's Alley or McFadden's Flats is a victim and a survivor, a fool and a trickster, a rebel and a rogue, but additionally he is also a child deserving our pity and compassion. He may always wear the same yellow nightshirt, but he is nevertheless a quick-change artist, a floating signifier, a free metaphor that can be endlessly reassigned to serve new contexts and messages. As an orphan, he is not restricted by family or kin; he is a free agent, an infant version of the rugged individual, proudly presenting his peers and his habitat to the various audiences.

The Yellow Kid quickly became iconic. Within the panels he is regularly the blandest and most recognizable figure—as Scott McCloud has pointed out, simplicity in design favours reader-identification (1994, 44). His yellow nightshirt bearing his utterances may well have been reminiscent of billboards (Harvey 1994, 6) or of the sandwich men who were part and parcel of the cityscape and advertisement in the late 19th century, but then the kid himself was "recognized throughout the city on billboards and sandwich boards" (Watson and Hill 2012, s.v. "Yellow Kid") as he himself became part of the battle between Pulitzer and Hearst. In January 1896, Hearst had lured Morrill Goddard and his whole editorial staff from Pulitzer's *New York World* to his own *New York Journal*, and in the fall of the same year he brought Outcault and "The Yellow Kid" to the *Journal*. There was a little problem, though, because Outcault had merely been able to copyright the name of the Yellow Kid, but not the figure itself, and so the *World* kept publishing *Hogan's Alley*, now drawn by George Luks. Thus, the Yellow Kid was press-ganged into the service of two warring masters, bought at a princely price by Hearst, but simultaneously held hostage by Pulitzer. The Kid turned into a profitable commodity, the orphan sold, and his promotional power was not restricted to the newspapers he served. Ostensibly an "anti-establishment celebrity" (Wood 2014b), he was simultaneously used not only as a "commercial selling point for yellow journals" (Wood 2014b), but also for "numerous unauthorized Yellow Kid products, including songbooks, buttons, chewing gum, chocolate figurines, cigars and ladies' fans" (Gordon 1998, 32).

Little Orphan Annie

Similar to Outcault, who claimed that the type of the Yellow Kid was a common sight in the slums of New York, Harold Gray, the author of *Little Orphan Annie*, suggested that he had met a model for his creation on the streets of Chicago.

> I talked to this little kid, and liked her right away. [...] She had common sense, knew how to take care of herself. Her name was Annie. At the time, some 40 strips were using boys as the main character; only three were using girls. I chose Annie for mine, and made her an orphan, so she'd have no family, no tangling alliances, but freedom to go where she pleased. (Qtd. from Heer 2008, 24)

But then there is, of course, also the poem "Little Orphant Annie" by James Whitcomb Riley, which was very successful and widely known and thus may well have been the source for the comic and the protagonist's name. In the poem, a little orphan girl tells the children of her foster family "witch tales" that culminate in the punishment for misbehaving children; those who do not say their prayers or ridicule their parents will be snatched away by goblins:

> You better mind yer parunts, an' yer teachurs fond an' dear,
> An' churish them 'at loves you, an' dry the orphant's tear,
> An' he'p the pore an' needy ones 'at clusters all about,
> Er the Gobble-uns 'll git you
>   Ef you
>   Don't
>   Watch
>   Out! (Riley 1994, 2)

In this poem, the orphan appears as a moral authority, looking at family life from the outside and passing harsh judgement on those who do not comply with middle-class standards of conduct. Moreover, she becomes an advocate for her own peers, and while the children cluster around to hear her stories, the orphans and the poor and needy ones "cluster about" the more affluent members of society and require our support—and those who refuse to aid them will suffer the children's version of being condemned to hell.

Within the world of the poem, however, charity and the support of the orphan do not come without a price, and little Annie is not simply adopted, and thus equal to the family's kids, but has to work for her living almost like Cinderella:

Little Orphant Annie's come to our house to stay,
An' wash the cups an' saucers up, an' brush the crumbs away,
An' shoo the chickens off the porch, an' dust the hearth, an' sweep,
An' make the fire, an' bake the bread, an' earn her board-an'-keep; (Riley
1994, 1)

This aspect is taken up in the very first Little Orphan Annie strip from
August 5, 1924. In the first panel Miss Asthma, the asphyxiating and
generally unpleasant matron of the orphanage, tells Annie: "You have
been sheltered, clothed and fed since you were a baby entirely by
charity—you should be very grateful" (Gray 2008, 36); in the following
three panels, however, we see her at work, scrubbing the floor and
washing dishes—and, of course, praying before going to bed, always
hoping that she will eventually be taken up by a nice family, even if this
may not necessarily mean that her chores are over: "And then maybe I
could have two dresses, and there wouldn't always be dishes to wash and
scrubbing and mending—but I wouldn't mind working hard every minute
if only they weren't always telling me I'm an orphan" (36).

Orphanhood carries a stigma Annie wants to escape. Within the
semantic system of the comic, she may be a free agent, unbound by family
ties, kinship, or normative behaviour,—after all, the reader knows that she
will always manage to escape all hardship and trials with the help of her
moral compass, strong will and the "no-nonsense determination of a little
girl in hard times" (Petersen 2011, 134)—but she feels very much tied
down by the classification as an "orphan", its implications and the social
practices which in the story remain an inescapable consequence of her
status.

Askeland suggests that "[t]he 'blank slate' of healthy orphaned infants
holds an especial power in American culture: an innocent victim
completely cut off from any potentially still-interested parent, available to
be rescued from appalling living conditions and to be given a chance at a
better life" (Askeland 2001, 489). In the case of Little Annie, these dismal
conditions resurface repeatedly. She will always live under the threat of
being returned to the orphanage in case of misbehaviour or simply because
of the arbitrary decision of a foster parent, and whenever this actually
happens, she will not be received with care and compassion but with the
sadistic matron's glee and a few 'I told you so's. She is thus permanently
kept in a precarious situation, and in spite of her self-determination, her
pluck and her willingness "to fight back with a sharp tongue and a good
left hook" (Heer 2008, 11), she will time and again be in need of a saviour.

Still in the first week of publication, on August 11, a visitor tells Annie the story of Cinderella, an indication that the comic adapts some of the values of the fairy tale to the social environment of America in the 1920s. According to Bruce Smith, "Her motto is short and sweet. 'Tell the truth, work hard, save your money, and keep your nose tidy.' As her creator Harold Gray, once remarked, 'That's good advice for any kid, and especially for an orphan'" (1974, 2).

Of course, there will be no prince to marry Little Annie—her age is frozen at 11 and thus she never reaches the age at which that would be of any interest—but then some elements of the fairy tale can be detected in the comic strip. There are at least two evil stepmothers present in the panels, Miss Asthma and the equally cold-hearted and hypocritical Mrs. Warbucks, her on-and-off foster mother who takes her up "only on trial" (Gray 2008, 38) and later repeatedly tries to return her to the orphanage. The role of the prince, then, is taken by Mr. Warbucks, the richest man in the world, who becomes Annie's beloved "Daddy". He is immediately enamoured of the kid and sides with her against the machinations of his wife; and he rejects the condescension with which his wife treats Annie. When she claims that she took Annie from the orphanage because she felt she "should do something for charity", he explodes: "Charity, eh—Charity!!! If I was as full of charity as you are I'd be the most successful mortgage-loan shark outside of Sing-Sing. Annie does not need charity—just give her an even break and she'll do the rest—Charity!!—Bah" (Gray 2008, 51).

He is, however, obliged to go on numerous business trips during which Annie may be returned to the orphanage by Mrs. Warbucks or otherwise lost, and thus we find a "cycle of separation and hardship, rescue and reunion that framed Annie's adventures and the quest motif that animated them throughout the strip's run" (Harvey 1994, 99).

Annie's origin remains a mystery, even though Miss Asthma seems to know the necessary details, and she tells a trustee of the orphanage that "we know more of her antecedents than in the case of most other orphans" and that "Annie herself may have these records when she is 21 if she desires, but not until then." Unfortunately, she closes the door before Annie can hear anything else, but the response to the news is striking, indicating the solitude and self-doubt of the orphan:

> Well, I'll be a sardine! What do you know about that? So I have a history with parents in it and everything—I'm glad I have something of my own, even a history—and parents—I never could be sure whether orphans even had any parents—I can't remember any—Wait till I'm twenty-one—I'll

have to hurry and grow up real soon—Isn't it funny to be someone but not know who? (Gray 2008, 38)

And when Mr. Warbucks asks her "Whose kid are you" she answers just like the Yellow Kid did: "I'm nobody's kid", adding, "I'm just an orphan Mrs. Warbucks took on trial" (Gray 2008, 51).

As usual, Annie is the most iconic character in the comic strip, but in her case the blandness of the image is carried to an extreme: she is known for her empty pupil-less eyes. In the very first strips she was still drawn with black dots and later with small circles for eyes, and she looks like a lively girl, but her image quickly became more simplistic while the eyes grew larger and produced a unique, but also haunting gaze.

(August 12, 1924 / May 24, 1927, from Gray, *Complete*, 38 and 338, © 2018 Dick Tracy. Tribune Content Agency, Llc; Used by Permission.)

These vacant eyes have become a fixed term in America—indeed, in 1971, Nancy E. Warner, Professor of Pathology at University of Southern California, coined the term "Orphan Annie-Eyes nuclei" for "tumor cells with empty nuclei or those showing just a thin rim of peripheral chromatin in sections of papillary thyroid carcinoma" (Bave 2013, 1).

Unquestionably, Harold Gray was politically reactionary, "for most of his life on the far right of the Republican party" (Heer 2014). The comic strip celebrates American entrepreneurship and the rise of the hard-working and industrious self-made man, who succeeds in the face of all obstacles—usually in the form of bureaucratic government interference, union leaders, hypocritical social workers or evil competitors. Annie and Daddy Warbucks share the essential virtues and, to some extent, also the background of basic solitude in an "indifferent America" (Schwartz 2010, 130). In his first meeting with Annie, Warbucks stresses the similarities—and it also becomes clear that his name is quite accurate:

> Ever since I can remember, Annie, I've been alone same as you—nobody ever helped me—I had to help myself—see? [...] I had a little machine shop—Then the war came along—I was too old to fight but I wanted to do my bit so I made munitions—Well I made a fortune too, and everyone hates me for it—Maybe I did wrong, Annie—but I did the best I knew. (Gray 2008, 53)

This solitude turns the benevolent capitalist into another kind of functional orphan: he is orphaned by the very society and government the alleged virtues of which he embodies and promotes. Heer suggests that the comic is "an allegory about how the poor (in the form of the heroine) are best aided by their own gumption as well as the occasional helping hand by the rich (in the form of Annie's adopted father "Daddy" Warbucks as well as other benign representatives of the .01%)" (Heer 2014).

This is only partly accurate. Of course, there are the "good" rich who will recognize American virtues wherever they may be found in the poor and also in the racially oppressed—Gray was "surprisingly progressive on racial matters" (Heer 2014), and African-Americans as well as Orientals play positive roles in the strip. Moreover, in times of desperate need, Annie is also sheltered and comforted by the poor, e.g. in *Little Orphan Annie in Cosmic City* by Mr. and Mrs. Futile, who are in peril of losing their home to the rich Phineas P. Pinchpenny, a danger that will, of course, be averted with the help of Annie. In this comic Annie also beats up a lazy and cheating paperboy who bullies her when she complains about his questionable work ethics. She then takes over his job with lots of goodwill and energy—which quickly earns her a rise in wages. Thus, she drives the point home:

> That just goes to show yuh—th' boss knows when yer cheatin' or when yer tryin'—I'll bet a lot o' birds, who never get ahead, would have lots of better luck if they'd quit squawkin' 'bout their tight boss and really get to work and <u>do</u> something to <u>earn</u> more dough." (Gray 1974, 133, emphasis in the original)

It seems as if Gray tried to forge an alliance between the deservedly rich and the undeservedly poor against the machinations of an allegedly ineffective and hypocritical welfare state and its lazy recipients, the conspiracies of the left, and the evil, i.e. greedy, selfish and ruthless capitalists.[2] Gray was quite direct in promoting his political agenda in *Little Orphan Annie*, which has been described as "the first nationally syndicated comic strip to be unabashedly, unrelievedly, 'political'" (Harvey 2013). This was already an issue and point for concern in the fairly early days of the comic strip:

> On September 9, 1935, *Time Magazine* reprinted an editorial by the publisher of the Huntington, West Virginia *Herald-Dispatch*, a self-identified progressive conservative, calling the strip a "vehicle for a studied, veiled, and alarmingly vindictive propaganda" promoting "rugged individualism." The publisher asserted, "The creator of the comic strip *Little Orphan Annie* has violated his sacred reader trust... In the latest instance, all political leaders, and it follows every public official, are at once indicted as 'crooks' and to accept such a sweeping indictment is to permit the creator of *Little Orphan Annie*... and Chicago's Tribune Syndicate, to attack and condemn all persons, all institutions, and all ideas save those they choose to label acceptable." (Santod 2015, 30; quotations from "Veiled Vindictive Annie", *Time*, 9 September 1935)

Gray's introduction of politics into the comic strip was, however, revaluated by Ben Schwartz as "a pivotal moment in moving 'the funnies' onto more mature ground" (2010, 130). Of course, it was Roosevelt's New Deal and the liberal welfare politics that most infuriated Gray, and when Roosevelt was nominated for the fourth time in 1944, he expressed his protest by letting Warbucks die the symbolic death of American entrepreneurial liberty—when Roosevelt died in 1945 Warbucks was resurrected, suggesting that: "Somehow I feel that the climate has changed since I went away --- we'll see" (qtd. from Harvey 2013, emphasis in the original). After having been abandoned by his country and his social environment, the "orphaned" capitalist may now return and once more reap the fruits of his hard and selfless labour.

In *Little Orphan Annie* then, orphanhood is presented not only in the eponymous heroine but also as a state of mind and as a social and political condition of the individual. As such it is a burden as much as a potential; on the one hand, it indicates a fundamental solitude as an inherent ingredient of the American way of life, a solitude that can only be overcome temporarily before the individual again has to fend for itself; but on the other hand, it also allows for self-reliance, non-conformism and individual action.

Lucy "The Orphan" or: The Anti-Annie

With her curly hair, a red dress, and the final twinkle in her eye, Lucy Johnson, the orphan, shares some features of Annie. Like her famed counterpart, she suffers and wishes for a foster home where she is no longer maltreated but finds love and acceptance, and with her pluck and determination, she is finally able to achieve her dream and to live happily ever after. However, there are some decisive differences: The story is not one of the endless serial comic strips, but only eight pages long. It did not appear in the newspapers but in EC's *Shock SuspenStories* #14 in April-May 1954 (script Al Feldstein, pencils and ink Jack Kamen), and its fame does not rest on its endearing heroine and her cheerful way to overcome all obstacles and difficulties but on its notoriety as one of the most scandalous publications in American comics' history.

EC was founded by Max Gaines and started out as *Educational Comics*, "specializing in decidedly uncommercial titles like *Picture Stories from the Bible, Picture Stories from American History*, and *Animal Fables*" (Wright 2001, 135). After Max Gaines's death in 1947 his son William took charge of the ailing company, and soon a reorientation took place. EC became *Entertaining Comics* and now turned to horror, science fiction, crime, and war as subjects of the frequently truly graphic tales. New titles were, for example, *Tales from the Crypt, Shock SuspenStories, Weird Science, Frontier Combat*, but also *MAD*. And while the comics were available for all ages and had a large audience among children, the stories did not always address topics usually considered suitable for younger readers but rather "mature themes like murder, lust, psychosis, and political intrigue" (Wright 2001, 136). The stories were, "tangible evidence of a youth culture slipping out of parental control" (149).

Orphans had appeared before on the pages of *Shock SuspenStories*. In the story "Halloween!" (#2, April-May 1952), the matron of an orphanage realizes that the manager has been stealing from the funds. When he tries to kill her to keep her quiet, the orphans intervene and later use his hollowed-out head instead of a pumpkin. The orphans here change from victims to agents who are quite capable of acting on their own behalf and manage to turn misery into happiness. This also applies to "The Orphan" and its heroine Lucy, a ten-year-old girl.

In the caption of the first panel of "The Orphan", the reader is told by Lucy that ultimately "everything worked out swell" (Feldstein and Kamen 1954, 1), but at present things look bleak. She is, however, not an orphan, not yet, but lives with her father and mother. In this story, the parents neglect and abuse the child, who is persistently referred to as "the brat".

The father is an alcoholic who beats his wife and daughter mercilessly; the mother never wanted the child in the first place and regards her daughter as a mistake, conceived when the father was too drunk to take precautions. Lucy's hopes rest in her Aunt Kate who would love to adopt her, but out of sheer malice the father rejects the suggestion, preferring to force the child on his wife. When Lucy finds out that her mother has taken a lover and wants to run away with him, there is momentarily new hope that they might take her along, but this again is thwarted when they secretly pack with the intention of leaving her behind. When the couple departs without Lucy, they are met by the drunken father who comes home earlier than expected. Lucy watches the scene from an upstairs window: there is a shot, the mother faints, the lover flees the scene of crime, and when the police arrive they find the mother with the gun in her hand and Lucy crying over her dead father. At the trial, the mother and her lover are charged with premeditated murder and sent to the electric chair. The last two panels show Lucy happy as she has finally been adopted by her loving aunt. Winking at the reader she now offers her own version of the fatal night:

(Feldstein and Kamen 8, © 2018 William M. Gaines, Agent, used with permission)

It is striking that in the 1954 Senate Subcommittee Hearings into Juvenile Delinquency, which followed the attacks on comics by Fredric Wertham and led to the establishment of the Comics Code Authority, the interrogation of Gaines was chiefly concerned with this comic (for the background and procedure of these hearings cf. Nyberg 2005). A few other stories and some rather graphic covers of magazines were briefly touched upon—regularly with the question whether Mr. Gaines considered them in "good taste" which he invariably confirmed—, and the distribution, sales, and advertisement strategies were also addressed, but "The Orphan" was the crucial comic discussed at some length. As the imagery in this story is comparatively realistic and without excessive graphic motifs like open or decaying bodies, dismemberment, or murder in action, all of which frequently appeared on the pages of *Entertaining Comics*, it was clearly not the artistic realization of the comic that came under attack, but rather its content.

The most important argument against "The Orphan" was that it subverted the common notion that "crime should not pay", and that "as a result of murder and perjury, [Lucy] emerges as triumphant" (Senator Hennings in Gaines, "Testimony", n. pag.). Gaines's claim that the last panel constituted an "O. Henry finish" which surprised and entertained the audience did not pull any weight, and instead the assumption that the ending "makes her a wonderful looking girl" (Herbert J. Hannoch in Gaines, "Testimony", n. pag.) seems to have carried the day. There are, however, numerous other stories in EC publications in which crime does pay and murder goes unpunished, which raises the question why this particular comic drew the attention and the fire at the Senate Hearings, and whether issues not addressed by the interrogators—but evoked by Gaines—may have contributed to the harsh critique.

"The Orphan" not only presents a "perfect murder", it also undermines the American celebration of the family with an image of misery and parental cruelty which might be acceptable in literary works like Stephen Crane's *Maggie: A Girl of the Streets*, but certainly not in a comic for young audiences. In an interview, Gaines claimed that some of his stories contained a relevant form of social critique (Gaines, n. pag., cf. also Wright 2001, 136), and Feldstein suggested that they carried a "plea to improve our social standards" (qtd. from Wright 2001, 137). In addition, Gaines argued that they had a moral basis and that the victims of the atrocious crimes usually deserved a *lex talionis* style retribution: "If somebody did something really bad, he usually 'got it.' And of course, the EC way was he got it the same way he gave it" (Gaines 1983, n. pag.). Lucy thus performs an act of justice, if not quite impartial justice, and the parents are punished in the same drastic ways a villain or witch is dealt with in traditional fairy tales.

It is, however, also possible to read this story as a cynical re-enactment or possibly even parody of the American foundational myth, of the violent severance of unacceptable ties with an authoritative institution that has lost its legitimacy by neglect and maltreatment. In this respect, Lucy, cruelly beaten by her father and coldly rejected by her mother, asserts her inherent and inalienable rights of life, liberty, and the pursuit of happiness—quite successfully, as it turns out, and she also makes it from a rather miserable home to prosperity and all the toys she wants. In the Senate Hearings,

Gaines suggested that the American children "are citizens, too, and entitled to select what to read or do" (Gaines, "Testimony", n. pag.), thus arguing that a ban of his comics would amount to a form of censorship incompatible with the American liberties. He then addressed precisely those problems that were also relevant in "The Orphan":

> There are many problems that reach our children today. They are tied up with insecurity. No pill can cure them. No law will legislate them out of being. The problems are economic and social and they are complex. Our people need understanding; they need to have affection, decent homes, decent food. (Gaines, "Testimony", n. pag.)

"The Orphan" thus "challenged the cult of domesticity" (Carver, n.p.), it staged a rebellion against "core American values" (Carver, n.p.) and the unfulfilled promises of suburban family life—which were also questioned in movies of the same time like *The Wild One* or *Rebel Without a Cause*. Lucy chooses orphanhood and a kind of "self-selected" affiliation over "natural" parents, and the solitary spinster over the married couple as foster parent. In addition, the comic is arguably a parody of *Little Orphan Annie* and its celebration of the American way of life, of hard work and self-determination. Like Annie, but with very different means and to very different ends, Lucy refuses to be a victim and achieves agency; and she finally lives her very own version of the American Dream—a version that was obviously unacceptable at the time of its creation.

The Orphan on the Doorstep

Little Orphan Annie celebrates the individual and the meeting of like minds—which happens not in a mature sexual relationship but between "Daddy" Warbucks and Annie. Marriage in this comic does not seem to be a particularly promising endeavour—and this is one of the persistent topics in American comics. In this respect, the comics employ patterns from 18th and 19th century literature, but while in the 18th-century novel marriage usually concludes the narrative, the seriality of the comic and the timelessness of the storyline indefinitely postpone the end of courtship and the beginning of married life—Donald and Daisy, Mickey and Minnie, or Popeye and Olive Oyl are examples of endlessly wooing couples. Those couples who are already married are more often than not unhappy—alternatively, they may also be the object of satire and ridicule (e.g. Li'l Abner and Daisy Mae or Blondie and Dagwood Bumstead) or victims who occasionally provide more orphans (e.g. various parents of orphaned superheroes).

But then married couples are also not necessarily the preferred foster parents—in this respect Annie and Superman are not the rule and Lucy Johnson is a fairly common case. Orphans or functional orphans frequently end up with same-sex single foster parents in all-male or all-female groups—again the Disney universe offers several examples, with Donald and his nephews or Daisy and her nieces (the children of ever-absent siblings).

In Frank O. King's *Gasoline Alley* (reprinted by Drawn and Quarterly and edited by Chris Ware as *Walt & Skeezix*), life seems at least for quite some time to be fairly segregated between men and women, even though most of the characters are married; in their daily lives men usually keep among themselves and chiefly discuss cars and home-brewed hooch while women appear either in the role of nagging wives or as erotic distractions. But then an orphan unexpectedly appears in a basket on Walt's doorstep on Valentine's day 1921 and is with no further ado adopted and named Skeezix by the bachelor—the name is cowboy slang for an orphaned calf. The baby subsequently bridges the division into male and female spheres; it is the women who inspect the newly found child and inform Walt that it is, actually, not a girl but a boy, and they 'borrow' him when Walt needs to work on a car. To help Walt with the kid, there is also the African-American nurse and housemaid Rachel, rendered as a stereotypical Mammy but also with more complexity than was usual at the time (Heer 2006, 10). And, of course, Skeezix also acts as a catalyst between Walt and his love interest Phyllis Blossom, and the inveterate bachelor is softened by his future wife's obvious interest in, and rapport with, his adopted son. Heer describes the gender politics in *Gasoline Alley* as a kind of complex misogyny (2010, 142), and indeed, in the years before he walks the aisle, Walt regularly rejoices in his independence whenever his peers face marital obligations or scorn, but one might also argue that his role as a single step-father allows Walt to take up an in-between position. The orphaned child serves as a link between male and female groups, and Walt partakes of both spheres and their discourses, discussing child welfare with the ladies and the usual car lore with his cronies.

The female interest in Skeezix reflects the intentions of the publisher and the creator who wanted to increase the comic's impact and, in particular, to attract a female audience. As it would have taken too much time to get Walt married and have him produce a child, the delivery to the doorstep—in consequence Walt calls Skeezix his stepchild—was chosen as a quick alternative, and it could serve easily as a demonstration for a juvenile audience that children are brought by the stork or some other mysterious entity. The child is discovered in the early morning after Walt has been woken up by the doorbell, and he claims that he has seen "a shadowy figure slink away in the darkness." He finds a note saying: "I have never seen you but I have seen your picture. I know you are kind hearted. Please care for and give the baby a good home" (King, February 14, 1921), and that is exactly what he does without any further inquiry into the child's past or search for the natural parents. The note in the basket may well be seen as a metafictional element and express the assumed perspective of the intended audience—after all, the readers have only seen Walt in pictures, they know that he is kind-hearted, and they seem to want him to adopt a child and expect him to provide a good home. And so he does. The sudden appearance of an abandoned child does not raise any eyebrows or questions among his friends and neighbours; the child was found on Walt's doorstep and so he will look after it—with support and advice from the women and full acceptance from the men.

Only several years later, in 1926, does the question of Skeezix's origins gain some relevance when his biological mother Helena Octave, an opera singer, appears, and once more in 1927 when the biological father, Colonel Henry Coda, files a suit to get custody of Skeezix. By then Walt has married Phyllis Blossom after a long phase of indecision: "Walt knows that he needs a wife to complete his happiness, yet he always yearns to return to the all-male island of happiness he has when he is alone with his son" (Heer 2010, 142). Leslie Fieldler suggests that the typical male in American literature tried to avoid "the confrontation of a man and a woman which leads to the fall, to sex, marriage, and responsibility" (Fiedler 1966, 26), but while Walt tries to evade Phyllis and the looming prospects of matrimony for a considerable time, he has already taken responsibility. If at the time when these events of *Gasoline Alley* were published small children usually belonged to the domain of the mother, the orphaned child raised by the single male called for a transgression of traditional gender roles and allowed Walt to develop a 'female' domestic side. It is precisely this aspect of his physically as well as psychologically well-rounded personality which will ultimately lead to his triumph when the trial over custody is settled by a verdict of the Supreme Court, which claims to be "in conformity with the trend of the authorities generally" (King 1927). This verdict, read out by Walt's attorney, celebrates the care and tenderness of the foster parent:

> The instinct of fatherhood was not aroused in Col. Coda until the child was past six years old, years in which Walt Wallet watched over in anxiety and travail, as well as in joy, the developing life, and felt the full force of the growing love of Skeezix for him. For the welfare of this child and in the interest of thousands of other children whose parents are those of adoption

and not of blood, we believe [...] the retention of Skeezix in the home of
Walt and Phyllis Wallet to be vitally important and that the claims of the
appellee be deemed inferior to those of the appellant. (King 1927)

In the story of the trial and generally in the early years of *Gasoline Alley*,
the orphan does not take centre stage but serves as an additional element
that contributes to the personality of the protagonist. As such, the child is
not always present but can drop from the narrative whenever the focus
turns to other topics or events. While in *Gasoline Alley*, however, this
happens only temporarily, it remains a permanent aspect in later comics
like *Popeye*, in which once more a baby boy, Swee'Pea, is found on the
doorstep and adopted by the protagonist, or in the world of Duckville. But
while Swee'Pea, the various Disney nephews and nieces, and also Little
Orphan Annie are condemned to eternal childhood, *Gasoline Alley*
introduced a new way of handling the life of its protagonists. Here, the
story of Walt & Skeezix is not frozen in the era of its first inception, but
the characters age in real time. Thus, we watch Skeezix grow up in an
expanding family as Walt and Phyllis also have biological children; he
goes to school and later to war, marries his childhood sweetheart, has
children and takes over his father's garage—which later passes into the
hands of his daughter Clovia when he in turn retires. The orphan is located
at the core of the American family; there is no trauma and no prejudice,
but an unexpected normality. The threats come not from an orphanage or
other forms of institutions but only temporarily from the biological
parents, who abandoned the kid but later try to regain it—the court,
however rules, as in Bertold Brecht's later *Caucasian Chalk Circle*, that it
is not the biological bonds that count but affection and care. Orphanhood
does not carry a stigma but offers a promising start into life, and the comic
celebrates an America in which the small town community is perfectly
able to solve problems through individual compassion and goodwill. It is
perfectly well summed up in a wordless strip in which people in cars, on
horseback or at campsites greet each other, waving amicably at passing
strangers (King, *Walt & Skeezix*, September 5, 1921).

As mentioned above, Popeye the sailor, created in 1929 by Elzie Segar
in his strip *Thimble Theatre*, finds his boy-kid similarly to Walt: Swee'Pea
is delivered in a box to his doorsteps. In contrast to Skeezix, however, the
impact the foundling had on the comic strip was far less momentous. First,
Swee'Pea does not really develop, even though he learned to speak, and in
1957—Segar had died in 1938 and new artists had continued the strip—he
suddenly made a jump from his usual baby's nightshirt to a boy's sailor
suit which he would wear until 1959 and occasionally afterwards
(Grandinetti 2004, 11-12). He nevertheless remains an unchanging child in

the care of an eternally middle-aged sailor, sharing some of his foster father's abilities, e.g. he sometimes also becomes incredibly strong after having eaten spinach. Moreover, as an adoptive father, Popeye, of course, has to protect Swee'Pea, but this does not include a major change in his personality or a new perspective in his life. Swee'Pea appears in some strips and stories, but he is not a permanent presence on the page or in the mind of the protagonist. Unlike Walt, Popeye never moves beyond the courtship phase in his relationship with Olive Oyl, with Bluto as a persistent competitor for her affections, and his independence as a bachelor is never really in peril: at the end of *Little Swee'Pea* (1936), in which the kid first appears on the screen, Popeye sings "There's no ifs and maybes, I'll never have babies ... I'm Popeye the Sailor Man" (qtd. from Grandinetti 2004, 164), and so far he has remained true to this pronouncement.

Comic figures occasionally have multiple origins and histories, and in long runs of strips, serialized stories and animated movies, different artists develop their own ideas about their characters' backgrounds. Swee'Pea is a good example. In the comic strip, he is found by Popeye and without any legal procedure continues to live with him ever after (he was actually officially adopted on November 21, 2004 at a ceremony officiated by Judge Greg Mathis and hosted by the *National Council For Adoption* in New York City). In a story that began in September 1937, his mother returns and tries to win custody over her abandoned son. "The resultant tug-of-love tale ran until December 5th and displayed genuine warmth and angst amidst the wealth of hilarious antics by both parties to convince the feisty 'infink' to pick his favourite parent" (Wiacek). In the story *King Swee'Pea*, written when Segar was terminally ill, it turns out that the abandoned child is, in fact, the crown prince of the country Demonia, whose father has been killed and who now needs protection from his evil uncle, who wants to win the throne. In his book *Superman on the Couch*, Fingeroth argues that: "To be an orphan means that our possibilities are endless. We are not from the small town, the confining neighborhood, the constricting ethnic roots that we have been told are ours. We could be the King of England, the scions of industrial wealth" (2004, 67). This is to some extent realized in Swee'Pea's new story of origin, but these origins are no longer pursued by later artists; moreover, in the animated movies we get a very different history. Here Swee'Pea seems to be under Olive Oyl's care—in *Li'l Swee'Pea* Popeye picks him up at her house, takes him to the zoo, and then returns him to her—and sometimes he is referred to as 'Cousin Swee'Pea'. "Evidently, the creators of the animated cartoons did not hesitate to rewrite Swee'Pea's family history whenever the plot demanded" (Grandinetti 2004, 165). The orphan becomes a kind of wild card which in the narration can fill any position and change with every new game.

The World of Disney

The motif of the foundling on the doorstep also resurfaced in the comics and short films of the Disney universe, where rather unruly and mischievous orphans first appeared in *Mickey's Orphans* (1931). In this animated Christmas short film, a hooded figure—akin to the "shadowy figure" that Walt claims to have noticed when Skeezix was deposited at his home—brings a basket with dozens, if not hundreds, of cute but uncontrollable anthropomorphic kittens to Mickey's and Minnie's house. They quickly create havoc which is later even amplified when Mickey, dressed as Santa, brings them some ill-considered Christmas presents: tools like saws and hammers, and quite well-functioning toy guns. Furniture, windows, tableware, lamps and vases quickly fall prey to the destructive infant forces, and even the hosts are the targets of some rather violent pranks. But as it is Christmas, there is no punishment: goodwill, understanding and forgiveness reign supreme as kids will be kids, and the movie ends with the presentation of a splendid Christmas tree, which the rowdy kittens reduce to a bare skeleton in seconds.

These orphans are akin to the youthful anarchists discussed above, e.g. Max and Moritz or the Katzenjammer Kids, but they are not there to stay. They constitute a temporary invasion, a visitation of chaos that may put the protagonists' nerves to a severe test, but which will also pass like the seasonal holiday that entails their presence. And in contrast to the early juvenile outlaws, they go unpunished and actually leave the scene victorious.

Similar orphans appear in the more usual form of anthropomorphic mice in *Orphans' Benefit* (1934), *Orphans' Picnic* (1936) and *Mickey's Circus* (1937). In each of these films the orphans are an immense group of indistinguishable, disrespectful and uncontrollable kids. No orphanage is mentioned, and the origin of the orphans remains obscure. The stories present a clash between one or two adults and the wild horde of orphans which quickly escalates into an all-out battle, but, again, in these short films and stories there is no punishment, and two different results are possible. While *Mickey's Orphans* ends in a kind of precarious Christmas harmony, later stories regularly culminate in the adult victim's complete defeat. In particular Donald Duck, who is hardly more rational or mature than his juvenile opponents, suffers badly and ultimately goes down in shame rather than glory.

The general idea of these short films was taken up again in the first introduction of Donald's nephews Huey, Dewey and Louie in a comic strip on October 17th, 1937. Similar to the previous Duckburg orphans, they were basically identical in their looks as well as in their characters— only distinguishable by the colours of their jackets and caps. In the strip, the nephews are announced by letter ("Dear Donald! I am sending your angel nephews, Louie, Huey and Dewey, to stay with you while their father is in the hospital. A giant firecracker exploded under his chair. The little darlings are so playful. I hope you enjoy them. Your cousin Della!") and delivered to Donald's door—and they quickly assault Donald with high voltage and water. Originally, their stay was only planned to be temporary, but they were simply never picked up again, and so they later were present in those stories in which they were needed and finally ended up living with their uncle on a permanent basis. More or less abandoned, they appear as functional orphans, and most readers probably never realize that they do, indeed, have parents. In an early critical assessment of the Duck universe, for example, the parents are never mentioned and on the family tree their names are marked as doubtful (Gans 1972, 10-11); moreover, Della's relation to Donald is uncertain as she is introduced as his cousin in 1937 but later appears as his twin sister.

Over the years and with the transition of the comics from the original creators, the writer Ted Osborne and the cartoonist Al Taliaferro, to Carl Barks, Donald's nephews underwent a complete transformation. Originally, they were mischievous and geared to bring out their uncle's worst tempers, but later, possibly under the beneficial influence of the Junior Woodchucks, they mutated to paragons of rationality and virtue in contrast to the lazy und frequently ignorant Donald. This shift is indicative of a new perspective and didactic agenda in the comic. While the gap between the adult generation and the orphaned children is maintained, the foster parent is no longer the source either of neglect and exploitation or guidance and support. Instead, the organized community, slightly satirically based on the Boy Scouts of America, seems to offer knowledge, trains the kids in useful outdoor skills, and endows them with self-confidence and a collective identity. In consequence, the children take over the role of the foster parent, offer advice, supply necessary information from the inexhaustible *Junior Woodchucks' Guidebook*, and balance Donald's choleric temper with rationality and logic.

As in *Gasoline Alley*, the various functional orphans in Disney comics allow for the presence of children without the need of previous courtship and marriage. In the case of Disney and his strict conservatism, the sudden appearance of children on the doorstep thus evades any indication of sexuality. Such functional orphans are an added ingredient to an already existing serialized narrative, and the success of the first stories determines whether they will become integral parts of the series or simply be dropped from the pages. In contrast to Walt and Skeezix's real time development of father-stepson bonding and later family life, their presence can be turned on and off without further explanation.

In all these comics, the integration of the orphans into their new environment is unproblematic. There is no trauma—Skeezix and Swee'Pea are too small to experience any loss of their home or unfamiliarity with their foster parent and new living conditions, and the Disney children smoothly move from a visit to a permanent presence in their respective foster parent's home. They are the orphans of the funnies or of publications for children, and the problems which arise cannot dampen the general merry mood for long. Of course, sadness and grief exist in these worlds, but they are soon overcome and give way again to more cheerful and optimistic attitudes which may boost the spirits of the readers in their daily chores or provide untarnished entertainment for the kids. Of course, the situation is quite different in the Disney feature films, which also abound in orphans but here they are often traumatized and grow up in precarious circumstances, e.g. Bambi, Cinderella, Mowgli, Peter Pan, Simba etc. However, these orphans are not in the scope of this paper.

The Superheroes

> "Orphans make the best recruits."
> (M in *Skyfall*)

All this, of course, changes in the superhero comics and graphic novels. Even though juvenile audiences are also part of the intended readership, the atmosphere is darker, and pain, grief and suffering are integral elements of the stories. First among the typical characteristics of the superhero, as enumerated by Romagnoli and Pagnucci, is the problematic background: "His/her origins are, in some way, informed by tragedy" (2013, 8). Similarly, in Richard Reynolds's *Super Heroes: A Modern Mythology* the first item on a list of defining features states that the superhero "often reaches maturity without having a relationship with his parents" (1992, 16), orphanhood being a fairly common reason for this separation. The absent father of divine nature, a stock item in mythology, of course, does not translate well into our social and cultural environment—even though by now there are a few superheroes with divine ancestry or even divine nature, e.g. Thor and the Asgard gang—and so it is most often death that intervenes and provides the necessary background for the abandoned hero. In consequence, the protagonists are frequently troubled and occasionally even mentally unbalanced, motivated by a hopeless desire to undo the trauma that usually originated in the violent loss of their parents or other loved ones. In this respect, the biographies of the superheroes are often closely modelled on Campbell's monomyth (Campbell 1993, 245 and passim), in which the hero usually grows up as an orphan or in the absence of at least one parent—mostly the father, who may be a deity—, has special abilities, receives a call to adventure, and has to accomplish various tasks, occasionally with the support of a helper—the best examples are probably Heracles, Perseus and Bellerophon. The mythical hero then proceeds to an apotheosis and a possibly sacred marriage, gains an elixir, a tool, or the power to heal the land, and returns to his place of origin to take up the position of the ruler together with his queen. This pattern resurfaces throughout history in various guises; we can detect it in the Arthurian romances, the *bildungsroman*, and all kinds of adventure genres, in particular picaresque tales and, not least, the Western.

An important aspect the superhero shares with the Western as a fundamentally American genre is the reluctance or inability to enter a mature sexual relationship. As Leslie Fiedler suggested: "The mythic America is boyhood" (Fiedler 1966, 144), and the prototypical American hero leaves society and the threat of the civilizing domestic woman for a predominantly male in-group and the perpetual brawls between peers. Hence, in superhero comics the pattern of the monomyth necessarily appears in an abbreviated form, as the superhero, who in his disguise as a caped crusader has left the norms and confines of respectable society, is stuck in an eternal narrative loop, an endless reiteration of adventures that promise, but ultimately fail to offer a solution to the never-ending quest. The structure of the stories never passes beyond the sequences that can be found between the hero's departure from his original home and the return which would include apotheosis, marriage, and rulership. The stories are, as Umberto Eco wrote in the context of Superman, a closed form:

> Superman happens to live in an imaginary universe in which, as opposed to ours, causal chains are not open (A provokes B, B provokes C, C provokes D and so on ad infinitum), but closed (A provokes B, B provokes C, C provokes D and D provokes A), and it no longer makes sense to talk about temporal progression on the basis of which we usually describe the happenings of the macrocosm. (Eco 1979, 115-16)

This has consequences for the concept of the traumatized orphan. While the mythical hero can complete the finite number of tasks and symbolically overcome his troubled past, achieve a form of redemption and thus end the quest, the superhero's endless cycle of tasks and duties, which need to be fulfilled only to be replaced by new versions of the same, indicate that the trauma cannot be resolved. In consequence, the originally heroic actions eventually begin to appear as compulsive behaviour, the adventures as repetitions of incomplete initiations, and the superhero as a neurotic or psychotic who is unable to escape the clutches of his past. This matches the development from the fairly optimistic and frequently humorous superheroes in the earlier comic books for chiefly juvenile audiences to the increasingly darker protagonists of recent graphic novels that touch upon more mature topics including a psychological depth that frequently resembles an abyss.

In discussing superheroes, one faces a serious problem. Some of them have been re-written so often that the biographies are no longer coherent, and incompatible elements have been introduced by different artists; in consequence there are now different earths and universes in the DC and Marvel Multiverses with alternative stories and backgrounds to the characters (e.g. in *The Wedding Album*, December 1996, Superman actually marries Lois Lane, but the marriage is "annulled" in 2011 in the course of *The New 52* relaunch and Superman is once more a bachelor). It is not possible to take up all the variants and occasionally weird extensions to the sagas in this essay, and so I will keep to the traditional tales and stories of origin and only include alternatives if needed.

In some cases, e.g. Superman, Batman or Spider-Man, the story of origins is frequently retold or alluded to.

> Even more than "death" stories, crossovers, event stories, and attire changes, origin stories are the core of superheroes' existences. Origins not only reflect the sociohistorical contexts in which heroes were created, but they also reflect a culture's understanding of what makes superheroes unique storytelling vehicles. [...] The sheer number of repeated tellings of origin stories per character is astounding as well, but the redundancy also represents the importance of these origins. (Romagnoli and Pagnucci 2013, 109-10)

One might add here that the redundancy of the re-tellings is also symptomatic of a trauma, and the hero has to experience his original catastrophe over and over again. While reading the whole Superman or Batman series—and also those of various other superheroes—along such lines would not be particularly convincing, as audience demands and commercial interests are more relevant for the endless repetitions than post-traumatic re-enactment, more recent works have focused on trauma and compulsion in the hero as well as in the villains, and here the assessment certainly carries some interpretive persuasion (Vanderbeke 2014, 313). In the course of the many revisions mentioned above, however, the usually rather sparse original story is also expanded with changing elements or nuances, occasionally also with new figures, motivations, a widening context and increasing significance. I will return to such changes in the discussion of Batman's story of origin. To begin with the beginning, however, it is necessary to look at the first famed superhero orphan, Superman.

Superman, or: A Stranger in a Strange World

Superman, created in 1938 by Jerry Siegel and Joe Shuster, is the paradigmatic superhero. Of course, there had already been various masked crime fighters, e.g. The Scarlet Pimpernel, Zorro, The Shadow, The Green Hornet or The Phantom, and also masked villains, e.g. Fantomas, but Superman started a new era in comics, usually referred to as the Golden Age. The first issue opened with his story of origin, a story that would later be expanded and altered, but never radically changed. The caption of the first panel tells the reader that: "As a distant planet was destroyed by old age, a scientist placed his infant son within a hastily devised space-ship, launching it towards earth" (Siegel and Shuster 1938, 1). Superman thus closely fits the "powerful and perennial" foundling plot as described by Bowlby: "A baby is abandoned by parents who cannot or will not give it a life; by good fortune it is rescued; eventually, it goes on to achieve great things" (2013, 87). In the first Superman story, the wreck of the rocket is found by a passing motorist and the baby is put into an orphanage. About a year later the Kents were first introduced (their names varied in the first years until they became fixed as Jonathan and Martha), and since then it has become part of the Superman myth that he grew up with loving foster parents in Smallville, Kansas.

As Bowlby points out, the foundling plot is usually at odds with the social reality of the cultures in which it appears (2013, 87), and Superman is no exception. Kansas in the late 1930s was not a particularly inviting place. Farms were suffering from droughts and often faced foreclosure. Immigrants posed a threat because they were regarded as a new cheap labour force endangering employment on a limited job market. In the cotemporary movie *The Wizard of Oz* (1939), Kansas may have been a place Dorothy longs to return to, turning the tale into a "metaphor for the plight of the dispossessed American farmer" (Packer 2010, 94), but for an alien immigrant baby it was certainly "no place like home." But then the location of little Kal-El's touchdown on Earth may have been part of the creators' agenda, the rural landscape of the Midwest serving as the heartland of America and its people as the proverbial salt of the earth. The second panel of *Action Comics* #1 shows him as a toddler in nappies single-handedly lifting a heavy armchair to the astonishment of his attendants. His story thus draws on aspects of the traditional 'strong boy', who from birth shows extraordinary physical strength—in the case of Superman in consequence of evolutionary perfection as "the child's physical structure was millions of years advanced" (Siegel and Shuster 1938, 1). The "strong boy" is a stock figure in myths and fairy tales all over the world (Aarne-Thompson-Uther type 650A). Most famous, of course, is Heracles, who strangles two giant snakes in his cradle; in America this type appears in the tall tales about the lumberjack Paul Bunyan or the folk tradition of the steel-driving John Henry. The strong boys frequently develop into working heroes, and one of the recurrent patterns is that they take up work with exploitive masters who will then be punished for the maltreatment of their labourers. The strong boys are thus redressing social injustice with their enormous strength. Siegel once suggested that the difference between Superman and his later clones was that they lacked the "Man of Steel's empathy for the downtrodden" (Kaplan 2008, 20), and this is, indeed, an important element of the early Superman stories. As Roger Sabin points out:

> In his earliest outings, he had been a kind of super social worker, in the comic's words, a "Champion of the Oppressed", reflecting the liberal idealism of Franklin Roosevelt's New Deal. Drunks, wife-batterers and gamblers received his attention, while in one famous tale a mine owner who obliges miners to labour in dangerous conditions is compelled by Superman to experience those conditions himself. (2001, 61)

In addition, various elements from Jewish scripture and mythology can be detected in Superman's origins—both Jerry Siegel and Joe Shuster were Jews, and so were many other creators of superheroes like Bob Kane and Bill Fingers (Batman), Will Eisner (The Spirit), Jack Kirby and Joe Simon (Captain America) or Stan Lee (almost all Marvel superheroes of the Silver Age). In Jewish tradition, the 'strong boy' is Samson, who is actually mentioned variously in the comic (Weinstein 2006, 28)—and it is a recurrent element in the Superman stories that scissors break in the attempt to cut his hair, e.g. in *Superman Takes a Wife* (*Action Comics* #484, 1978) when Lois Lane thus realizes that her new husband Clark Kent is Superman. As in the story of Samson, women and extraordinary strength don't mix well, and in *Superman II* (1980), the man of steel voluntarily removes his powers before spending a night with Lois Lane, indicating that superpowers and sexuality are mutually exclusive.

In addition, Superman's birth name Kal-El may have a Hebrew etymology, El being one of the ancient names for God in the Bible and Kal "the root of several Hebrew words meaning 'with lightness,' 'swiftness,' 'vessel' and 'voice'" (Weinstein 2006, 25). In consequence, Larry Tye writes that Superman is "the ultimate foreigner escaping to America from his intergalactic shtetl and shedding his Jewish name for Clark Kent, a pseudonym as transparently WASPish as the ones Jerry [Siegel] had chosen for himself" (Tye, 66). Alternatively, in a 1972 story, "The Greatest Green Lantern of All", Superman's mother reveals that the name Kal-El means "Star Child" in Kryptonese (*Superman* #257, 4). "The Star Child", however, is also the title of a Jewish legend as retold for children by Aunt Naomi (Landa 1919, 87-98), about the birth and youth of Abraham, who left the land of his ancestors to go into exile, i.e. the Promised Land. According to the tale, Abraham's birth was announced by a star and perceived as a threat to King Nimrod. Predictably the king wanted to kill the new born baby, but the parents deceived him, and Abraham was hidden and brought up in a cave—the story obviously merges elements from the Bible with the myth of Zeus, who as an infant needed protection against Cronus.

More important than Samson or Abraham are Noah, the sole survivor of a destroyed world, and Moses, sent as a baby in a tiny boat down the Nile to save him from the Pharaoh's mass slaughter of Hebrew children. Both saviour figures have to escape mass death, and in 1938, the year of the November pogroms in Germany, the topicality of such tales was evident. "Just as the baby Superman was sent away from Krypton to avoid the mass destruction of his people, many Jewish children were sent on the Kindertransport to seek safety with families in England" (Weinstein 2006, 22). The motif of the Jewish refugee orphan was taken up again in a very different kind of comic, Will Eisner's *A Contract with God* (1978), in which a young boy is sent to America to escape the anti-Semitic pogroms in Tsarist Russia—I will discuss this graphic novel later.

It is improbable that Siegel and Shuster were aware of all the possible readings of their hero's origins and name, but it is highly probable that they had some of them in mind when they created the orphan from a doomed world seeking refuge in the proverbial land of the free. A year before America rejected the Jewish refugees who came with the MS St Louis, Superman's story of origin not only presented an idealized version of the immigrant orphan but also suggested that the host country would profit immensely from the new refugees, from their unwavering loyalty to a welcoming nation and from their extraordinary abilities. In the new environment, the orphan becomes an iconic saviour figure, the immigrant the epitome of American values.

Baby Kal-El would probably have been too young to experience the loss of his parents and his home planet, but in his case the trauma is also physically embodied in two reminders of Krypton: Kryptonite and the city of Kandor. Kryptonite is a collective term for various radiating materials from Superman's home planet, which either have reached our world after the planet's destruction or are harvested by supervillains operating on a galactic scale. It comes in several colours and with different detrimental effects on the hero, ranging from a weakening of the superpowers to various forms of transformation or mutation and occasionally bizarre symptoms. In the comics' fictional universe, Superman's powers result from the absorption and storage of high energy solar radiation, but Kryptonite blocks these processes and replaces solar energy with its own harmful radiation. Ultimately it can cause the death of a Kryptonian. Kryptonite thus serves as the hero's weakness akin to Achilles' heel or Siegfried's vulnerable spot between his shoulder blades. Of course, the physics and chemistry of Kryptonite is pseudo-scientific patter, but on a psychological level it indicates a return of the repressed, a materialized memory that embodies the harmful and occasionally disastrous effects of unresolved trauma. The orphan immigrant thrives in his new benevolent environment, empowered by our source of life, but always threatened by the fragments from his past that will paralyse him or evoke strange alterations in his behaviour and physique. As such, the past becomes a weapon that can be used against him, an instrument for the villains to turn the hero's pain, grief and suffering to their own advantage, while the most effective protection against the debilitating effects is the hero's insulation from the source of the radiation, which is, in fact, also the source of his own origin.

Kandor shares some of these aspects of Kryptonite, even though it has no harmful effects as such. Originally a city of Krypton, it was miniaturized and "stolen" by the supervillain Brainiac some years prior to Krypton's destruction. He keeps the city in a glass container resembling a bottle until it is retrieved by Superman and brought to his Fortress of Solitude in the Arctic. After many unsuccessful attempts, in "Let My People Grow" (Superman #338, 1979), Superman finally manages to restore Kandor and its population of several million inhabitants to normal size on another planet, but in various later stories the bottle city is again located in his retreat. Like Kryptonite, Kandor is a material memory of Superman's past, and his efforts to restore it to normalcy can be seen as attempts to overcome the trauma and to return to his place of origin. As indicated above, Superman is predominantly well-adjusted and content in his new world, but the Fortress of Solitude serves as an externalized symptom of occasional feelings of isolation and estrangement. Mike Kelley, an artist who recreated various versions of Kandor, suggested that for Superman the city is a "perpetual reminder of his inability to escape the past, and his alienated relationship to his present world" (qtd. from Heins 2015). But Kandor is not only a reminder of a lost past. The orphan now has to protect the 'toy' version of his parent world, which suggests that he has to protect his traumatic memories in the secrecy of his hidden retreat. As guardian of Kandor, Superman becomes responsible for the survivors of his home planet, an enormous duty that can be turned against him. In Frank Miller's *The Dark Knight Strikes Again* (2002), Lex Luthor, one of Superman's arch-enemies, with the help of Brainiac takes the city as a hostage and thus forces Superman to comply with his wishes. Once more, the orphan can be subdued by villains who take control of remnants of his past and turn them into a weapon against him. In Miller's latest sequel, *The Master Race* (2015-2017), the Kandorians are returned to human size. Led by a religious fanatic, they demand to be worshipped like gods or else Earth will be destroyed. But as this graphic novel can well be read as one more example of Miller's Islamophobia, I prefer not to analyse it in the context of orphanhood and trauma.

Batman: Weird Figure of the Dark

If Superman is the paradigmatic superhero, Batman, created by Bob Kane and Bill Fingers in 1939, is the epitome of the deeply traumatized orphan. He witnessed his parents' murder as a young boy, and this experience became decisive for the rest of his life. The story was first told on two pages in November 1939: When the Wayne family are walking home from a movie they are held up by a small-time criminal who wants to steal Martha Wayne's necklace. Thomas Wayne tries to stop him and is shot, and so is Martha when she calls for help and the police. The robber escapes and young Bruce Wayne takes a crucial decision: "I swear by the spirits of my parents to avenge their deaths by spending the rest of my life warring on all criminals" (Various 2004, 17). He studies to become a master scientist, trains his body to athletic perfection and then, on an evening when he contemplates a future disguise, a huge bat flies in the window and settles the question: "'It's an omen. I shall become a <u>Bat</u>!' And thus is born this weird figure of the dark. This avenger of evil, 'The Batman'" (17, emphasis in the original).

This iconic scene has been retold over and over again, turning Thomas and Martha Wayne into the probably most often murdered figures in popular culture, and while other stories of superhero origins are occasionally revised and the previously dead resurrected by some ingenious narrative trick, Bruce Wayne's parents "are the ultimate deaths in comics. With utmost certainty, it can be guaranteed that these two characters will never come back from the dead. Batman exists because they were murdered in front of Bruce's eyes when he was a child" (Romagnoli and Pagnucci 2013, 161). Nevertheless, as we shall see, comics—like life—are full of surprises.

In the course of time some items were added to this scenario. In "The Origin of Batman" (*Batman* #47, 1948), after the murders the killer is terrified by the boy's eyes: "Something about young Bruce's eyes made the killer retreat … They were accusing eyes that memorized his every feature … Eyes that would never forget" (Various 2004, 46). And they don't, as Batman in this story after many years recognizes the killer, Joe Chill, on a photograph. Chill has by then become a racketeer, smuggling criminals across state borders, and Batman reveals his identity to him and tells him that he will eventually get him. The murderer is then killed by his own people when he incautiously tells them that he killed Batman's parents and is thus responsible for the existence of their nemesis.

In another twist (in *Detective Comics* #235, 1956), Batman finds out that his parents had not simply been in the wrong place at the wrong time, but that Joe Chill had been hired to kill his father as revenge because Thomas Wayne had, in a bat costume at a Masquerade Ball, been abducted to treat a wounded criminal but managed to turn him and his gang over to the police. The background of the murders later grew into more and more complex, and occasionally absurd, tales—in Andrew Vachss' novel *Batman. The Ultimate Evil* (1995), Martha Wayne is revealed to have been a social worker fighting child abuse; in "The New 52" universe (2011), Martha had another son, born prematurely and put in an asylum, who may or may not become one of Batman's future enemies.

More interesting are some details that were later added to the traumatic scene. In Frank Miller's *Batman: Year One* (1987), the movie the Wayne family watched prior to the assault is revealed to have been *The Mark of Zorro*, and indeed, Zorro, another masked and caped vigilante, seems to have been an inspiration for Bob Kane when he invented his superhero (Misiroglu 2012, 422). In Miller's *The Dark Knight Returns* (1986) the necklace which originally was the objective of the killer's assault is specified as a pearl necklace—the falling pearls of the ripped necklace have since become iconic themselves—and in Jeph Loeb's *The Long*

Halloween (1997) it is Bruce who persuades his mother to wear the pearls on that fatal day. He is thus burdened with the feeling that he is responsible for his parents' deaths. As Reynolds argues, Batman turns detective "out of an obsessive need to expunge his sense of guilt and failure towards his parents" (1992, 67).

In consequence, Batman is far more troubled than the usually more cheerful Superman, and the comics are atmospherically far darker. To some extent, the figure is an inversion of Superman. While the man of iron is introverted, shy and slightly melancholic in his role as the reporter Clark Kent and sparkling and humorous whenever he becomes Superman, Batman is an extroverted playboy and philanthropist at day but turns into the Dark Knight whenever he puts on his costume and roams the streets of Gotham City. The resulting psychological depth and the underlying motif of the vigilante in search for revenge and retribution allow for a far larger scope of revision and re-interpretation. Therefore, Batman is probably the most malleable figure in the superhero genre, and he has been rewritten from ever new perspectives. His personality ranges from a fairly humorous and self-assured masked detective (predominantly in the stories from the 40s to the 60s) to an obsessed and haunted victim of trauma (e.g. Jeph Loeb's *The Long Halloween*), a self-righteous crusader who in Tim Burton's movie *Batman Returns* transgresses the rules he pretends to maintain (Hassler-Forest 2015, 105), and ultimately to the *alter ego* of his psychopathic enemies who tumbles on the brink of insanity himself (e.g. Grant Morrison's and Dave McKean's *Arkham Asylum: A Serious House on Serious Earth*). In fact, madness is occasionally presented as a solution, a way to overcome the trauma, at least as seen by the antagonists. In Alan Moore's and Brian Bolland's *The Killing Joke*, the Joker suggests an ingenious way to escape the endless quest for revenge: "If you hurt inside, get certified, and if life should treat you bad, don't get ee-ee-even, get mad" (1988, 26), and in *Arkham Asylum* the Joker parts from Batman with the words: "Enjoy yourself out there in the Asylum. Just don't forget—If it ever gets too tough ... There's always a place for you here" (n. pag.; Script, 65-66).

Some of this darkness already informed Batman's first appearances—it was mellowed later and then increasingly returned in the course of the general remake of the superhero genre in the 1980s. In fact, quite possibly the very conception of the original Bat-Man already drew on contemporary medial re-workings of gothic horror. While bats may be eerie or creepy, most are rather small and harmless and thus not necessarily scary to hardened criminals. In 1939, however, when Batman was first created, the most famous bat of popular culture was probably

Dracula; the movie by Tod Browning, starring Bela Lugosi in his iconic role, had just been released in 1931. It may thus be assumed that the man-sized bat drew some of his impact and the atmosphere of dread from associations with the vampire. In more recent revisions of both tales the figures may occasionally tend to cross over. In Francis Ford Coppola's *Bram Stoker's Dracula* (1992), the vampire may walk in bright daylight and behave like a playboy while in Frank Miller's *The Dark Knight Returns* (1986) Bruce Wayne is haunted by a demon bat with pronounced canines, and during the day he rests in his vault—it seems as if he only leaves his cave in the dark when his wounds from the fights of the previous night have been provisionally patched up (Vanderbeke 1994, *passim*).

Not only is Bruce Wayne an orphan, but also Dick Grayson, the first Robin, who served as Batman's sidekick until 1984 and later temporarily even became Batman when Bruce Wayne equally temporarily died in one of the storylines. The juvenile side-kick was introduced because Bob Kane felt that the masked and mysterious Batman was possibly not a quite suitable figure of identification for the younger readers (Fingeroth 2004, 68). Like his mentor, Dick Grayson, the youngest member of the aerialists "The Flying Graysons", witnesses the death of his parents who are murdered by a mafia boss in the attempt to extort protection money from the owner of the circus. In his case, however, retribution comes swiftly: Batman immediately takes him as a legal ward without any procedure over custody; his training and the subsequent discovery and defeat of the villain then all take place in the first story ("Robin the Boy Wonder", *Detective Comics* #38, April 1940). Guided by Batman, Dick Grayson seems to recover from the trauma far more quickly, and in his role as an identification figure for the juvenile audience he remained generally light-hearted, occasionally reckless, but always loyal and devoted to his mentor and the common cause. Therefore, while the death of his parents is not forgotten, it is far less momentous for the series and the hero's psyche than the murder of the Waynes. Dick Grayson later left Batman to embark on an independent career as Nightwing; his role was taken over by various subsequent Robins.

In the Batman series as well as in other superhero comics some of the villains also turn out to be orphans. The Penguin, for example, experienced a rather traumatic childhood. Rejected already as a baby by his father because of his ugliness, he remained an outcast in his own family and was also constantly bullied and abused by his peers. His mother, though, doted on him, and after the death of his father from pneumonia forced him always to carry an umbrella—later, as a criminal, umbrellas serve him as all kinds of weapons from blades to flame throwers or guns. The orphan can thus take different paths, and the versions as already outlined at the beginning of this chapter all appear on the pages of Batman. He represents the troubled child that has to fend for himself but manages to fulfil its potential as a boon to society, Robin is adopted into a wealthy new home where he develops into a paragon of domestic virtues, while the villains show the orphan as their counterpart, i.e. moral failures and epitomes of depravity. Mentally unstable or openly sociopathic, they are taking revenge on society, and within the torn and corrupt society of Gotham City they become the trauma they originally suffered from.

In some versions, the war between good and evil, the superheroes and the supervillains, which is played out nightly in the dark cityscape, collapses and is now enacted within the Wayne family. Similar to many other superheroes, Batman's biography was considerably extended and altered in later versions and timelines. In one of the spin-offs, *The World of Flashpoint Featuring Batman* (2011), the story of origin is, *pace* Romagnoli and Pagnucci (2013, see above), indeed changed, and now it is Bruce who is killed—in consequence his father Thomas becomes Batman and his mother Martha declines into insanity and turns into the Joker. More interestingly, in other versions Batman may have an elder or younger brother Thomas Jr. On the so-called Earth One, he is born prematurely after his pregnant mother was involved in a car crash. Suffering from head injuries, he is put into a clinic where he is abused. Later he escapes and becomes Boomerang Killer. In another storyline, on antimatter Earth, he witnesses the death of Martha and Bruce and later develops into Owlman, an evil version of Batman. Thomas Jr. is, of course, another orphan; however, he does not respond to the trauma by devoting his life to the war against crime but rather turns to the dark side and becomes a supervillain. The troubled psyche and split personality that we can find in later Batman stories is now externalized and played out in a fraternal conflict, which is again reminiscent of warring brothers in mythology. The brothers—or, in the Flashpoint story, Thomas and Martha—become complementary; alter egos which, like matter and antimatter, cancel each other out in a zero-sum game.

The Rest of the Superhero Multiverse

The formulas that were outlined for Superman and Batman were repeated and adapted to new contexts at the beginning of the Silver Age of Comics, the early 1960s, when Marvel Comics launched a new set of superheroes with tremendous success. Most often, however, the traumatic past of the orphan is revealed only later in the course of the series—the first introduction of a new superhero is frequently a test run within another series, and only after the new figure has been sufficiently successful and sales figures promise to remain profitable for a while are the biographical facts fleshed out or adapted to the present requirements. But in the case of Peter Parker, a.k.a. Spider-Man, created by Stan Lee and Steve Ditko in 1962, the story of origin is almost as famous as Batman's—to some extent he seems to be derivative of the Dark Knight. But now it is his uncle who is killed by a criminal, and he serves not only as the embodiment of the trauma but also as a call to action. The death of Peter Parker's parents was only revealed several years later. In *The Amazing Spider-Man Annual* #5 (1968) Spider-Man learns that his parents died in a plane crash under the suspicion of being traitors to their country. Of course, he can clear their reputation and prove that they were murdered by Red Skull (actually also an orphan who was mistreated as a child but taken up by the Nazis and turned into a supervillain; Coogan 2006, 78). The death of the uncle, told in the very first Spider-Man story (*Amazing Tales* #15, August 1962), is far more momentous, as Peter has to bear at least some of the blame. Bullied and rejected by his peers, he does not feel that he has any obligations towards the society he lives in. Having gained his superpowers from the bite of a radioactive spider, he first tries to make some money in the wrestling ring. One evening he lets a thief who is being chased by a guard escape, claiming that catching criminals is not his responsibility, only to learn after a few days that this thief has later murdered his beloved uncle Ben. The story then ends with the famous line "And a lean, silent figure slowly fades into the gathering darkness, aware at last that in this world, with great power must also come—great responsibility!" Peter Parker is thus orphaned twice, and Fingeroth suggests that

> Spider-Man's quest is the most difficult and perilous of all the orphan quests.
> Because Spider-Man is seeking revenge on *himself.*
> No matter how many symbolic stand-ins for the burglar he defeats, it will never be enough for him. Indeed, Peter Parker's internalization of his guilt over his perceived culpability in his uncle's death can be defined as classic neurotic behavior. (2004, 74-75)

But then Spider-Man is not as fully traumatized as Bruce Wayne. Instead, his moods change with the momentary role he plays. As Spider-Man he is "probably the wittiest and drollest of superheroes" (75), but as Peter Parker he is generally gloomy, lonely, and depressed, and he seems to have been so even before his uncle was killed. Moreover, for a long time he was not able to start any relationship with a girl, a predicament he shares with various other superheroes. On the first full page panel in the first Spider-Man story he is introduced—and dismissed as "Midtown High's only professional wallflower"—by the girl he adores. Stan Lee, his creator, described him as "a teenager with all the problems, hang-ups, and angst of any teenager" (qtd. from Bainbridge 2009, 69), i.e. as the perfect identification figure for the nerdy adolescent comic-book reader. Bagge writes in ironic anger about this side of the protagonist:

> What's really annoying about Peter Parker, however, is the relentless POUTING he indulges in. Except for when he's in costume, he rarely gloats or even expresses a single moment of joy over his superheroic exploits. Instead all he can do is dwell on the downside of his chosen profession. He's a real glass-half-empty kind of guy, totally in need of a serious bitchslapping. He was at his worst whenever he was around one of his beautiful girlfriends, at which point his pout-o-meter would go through the roof. (2010, 119-20)

In Spider-Man, his creators Stan Lee and Steve Ditko thus merged Superman's split personality—the shy Clark Kent vs. the outgoing superhero—with Batman's trauma and the obsession to heal the past.

Occasionally, the origin of the superpowers is directly linked to the loss of a parent. In the rather short-lived comic *Brain Boy* (1962), the future superhero's fate "is determined when his parents, Matt Price and his pregnant wife, Mary, collide with an electrical tower after their car loses a tyre. Dad perishes in the accident, but mother and foetus survive, and two months later young Matt Junior is born, speaking fluent English" (Morris 2015, 130)—the superpowers then include intellectual and parapsychological abilities like telepathy, telekinesis, levitation and mind-control. As the series only lasted six issues, in which Brain Boy fights a mad dictator, a T Rex, a millionaire's time machine, an army of metal people, and an invasion of microscopic aliens (Internet Archive), the impact of the trauma was never really explored.

In many comics of the golden and silver ages, the supervillains are or seem to be older than the superheroes. In such cases, they may thus appear as versions of "evil dad", and the older generation strives to overcome and defeat the younger or even adolescent heroes who threaten their position of power. In a reversal of the Oedipal complex, it is the fathers who now try to kill their sons. This idea has been formulated variously, e.g. by Pier Paolo Pasolini in his play *Affabulazione* (1966) or by Thomas Pynchon in *Gravity's Rainbow* where "Pernicious Pop" launches random attacks on his son Slothrop. In works of popular culture, the battle of Darth Vader against his son Luke Skywalker has become iconic. In the Spider-Man series, the original Green Goblin (created July 1964), one of Parker's archenemies and murderer of Gwen Stacy, one of his love interests, was in August 1966 revealed to be Norman Osborne, the emotionally cold father of Peter Parker's best friend Harry Osborne. Harry, whose mother died subsequent to his birth, later becomes the second Green Goblin as he blames Spider-Man for his father's death. Once more, we get the image of conflicting orphans who turn from friends to enemies and thus demonstrate the alternative options and courses the orphan can take.

The reversal of the Oedipus complex can also be found at the root of the childhood trauma. In *The Incredible Hulk*, created by Stan Lee and Jack Kirby in 1962, Dr. Brian Banner is an alcoholic and abusive father who hates Bruce and kills his wife when she tries to intervene and protect her son. The split personality of the bright mind fighting with repressed rage and fear seems to have developed already in Bruce's childhood, either as an inheritance from his father or as the result of the traumatic experiences, and so the gamma-ray accident that turns him into the raging Hulk externalizes the internal struggles and allows for a return of the repressed.

A quite different variant of the orphan motif can be found in series that depict not the individual superhero but groups of superheroes, especially in *X-Men*, created 1963 by Stan Lee and Jack Kirby. The X-Men team, which includes girls, was brought together by Charles Francis Xavier, a.k.a. Prof. X, under the cover of his School for Gifted Youngsters, i.e. for adolescent mutants with supernatural powers. Xavier himself is gifted with various psychic powers. Several members of the X-Men team are orphaned or functional orphans, and Prof. Xavier's school almost feels like an orphanage. Originally, the series followed the usual battles between a team of superheroes and various teams of supervillains, chiefly Magneto's Brotherhood of Evil Mutants. But over time and with new editors and artists, especially Chris Claremont, who started to write for the series in 1975, the perspective changed and new topics were explored using the guise of the superhero comic. It will not be possible to outline the developing biographies of the main characters chronologically and with respect to the publication history, therefore I will simply present the most important elements without regard to when they were introduced.

Xavier lost his father early in his life and was brought up by his mother and an abusive stepfather. Xavier's mother also died, and he then learned that his stepfather was involved in his father's death. The crucial moment in his life takes place in Haifa in a clinic for Holocaust victims where he meets the Auschwitz-Birkenau survivor Magnus, whose real name is Max

Eisenhardt and who lost his family in the holocaust; he will later become Magneto. He is, thus, another refugee orphan coming to America, but he is quite different from Superman and certainly no epitome of the American ideology. Instead he will come to question the promises of liberty and equality.

Max Eisenhardt's traumatic past is told in a particularly impressive work, *X-Men: Magneto Testament* by Greg Pak and Carmine Di Giandomenico, published from November 2008 to March 2009. It is a holocaust narrative without any superhero action—the only reference to Max's future life as Magneto can be found on the covers of the first two issues where the figure of the supervillain appears as his mirror image in a puddle or as a shadowy presence in the clouds over the concentration camp. In many ways, *Testament* is far closer to graphic novels like Spiegelman's *Maus* than to the superhero genre, and like *Maus* it seems to have been taken up in school curricula. The story is interspersed with historical facts and some pages read like a history book in graphic format; the one-volume issue comes with endnotes and a teacher's guide, and it is supplemented with another comic, *The Last Outrage* by Rafael Medoff, Neal Adams and Joe Kubert, about the artist Dina Babbit and her fight to have the portraits returned to her which she was forced to paint while she was imprisoned in Auschwitz.

Magneto Testament ends with the words: "Tell everyone who will listen. Tell everyone who won't. Please. Don't let this ever happen again", and the determination to prevent discrimination against and oppression of those who are regarded as different, deviant or "other", i.e. the mutants, motivates Magneto after he has acquired his superpowers. In Haifa, Magnus and Xavier start out as friends, but later become archenemies over their disagreement about possible future relations between normal humans and mutants. Xavier is a radical pacifist, arguing for coexistence and mutual support, while Magnus, in consequence of his traumatic experiences under Nazism and the atrocities of Auschwitz, distrusts mankind and fears a new racism directed against mutants. In an interview with CNN, Stan Lee suggested that "They were meant to emphasize the conflict between people who felt that we've got to all work together and find a way to get along, and people who feel 'we're not treated well, therefore we're going to strike back with force!'" (Hoevel 2010). Significantly, it is now the orphaned child of wealthy American parents who leads the forces of good and non-violence in an increasingly violent battle against the evil mutants led by a refugee from Nazi Germany. The immigrant is no longer a promise to his new host country but poses a threat; neither is he embraced in the way Superman was. Instead, the world of the X-Men is marked by discrimination and by people who hate and despise born mutants (Fingeroth 2004, 105).

In consequence, the conflict in the X-Men series has been read in the light of the civil rights movement; Xavier and Magneto have been compared to Martin Luther King and Malcolm X as representatives of the different strategies within the struggle for equal rights (Romagnoli and Pagnucci 2013, 25). It seems as if the analogy, which is also quite controversial as both figures are decidedly white, developed over time, and Claremont said in an interview about his work in the 1970s:

> It was too close. It had only been a few years since the assassinations. In a way, it seemed like that would be too raw. My resonance to Magneto and Xavier was borne more out of the Holocaust. It was coming face to face with evil, and how do you respond to it? In Magneto's case it was violence begets violence. In Xavier's it was the constant attempt to find a better way. As we got distance from the '60s, the Malcolm X-Martin Luther King-Mandela resonance came into things. It just fit. (Hanks 2011)

But then, as Reynolds points out,

> the whole theme of the X-Men—the isolation of mutants and their alienation from 'normal' society—can be read as a parable of the alienation of any minority. The original Magneto and his Brotherhood of Evil Mutants, who disdained to cooperate with homo sapiens, could be read as an example of a minority grouping determined to force its own place within society. (1992, 79)

The conflict that supposedly reflects the civil rights movement and the struggle for equal rights is, however, not fought between the dispossessed and the racist society but between different perspectives on how this battle should be fought—open resistance or endlessly turning the other cheek. In this situation, Xavier's agenda ties in with the treatment of discrimination in a multitude of works of popular culture that address racism in American history: in an intolerant environment the rejected minority has to prove its virtues and acceptability—possibly by some great service that deserves the gratitude of the prejudiced majority—and then the previously excluded will be granted entry to respectable society and the history of racial strife and oppression will simply be forgiven and forgotten. The service that is repeatedly offered is the fight against those mutants who chose more direct forms of resistance—it is a new version of the Western motive of the good Indian helping the white man against the belligerent and violent bad Indians, with the difference that now, as mutants, the members of the despised minority are far more powerful than the normal humans. Active resistance thus poses a real threat to society, and the help from the benevolent mutants is an essential, if never quite officially recognised, necessity.

In the figure of Magneto, on the other hand, the experiences of the past have led to a complete disillusionment with visions of integration and cooperation; the response to racism has triggered an alternative racism and the firm belief in the mutants' superiority (Romagnoli and Pagnucci 2013, 25). Evolutionary concepts are employed—and abused—to argue that evolution may occasionally quicken its pace and move in jumps. The basis is probably Stephen Jay Gould and Niles Eldredge's concept of the punctuated equilibrium from 1977, according to which evolution may in specific times of environmental change or the migration into very different environments speed up in contrast to the very slow change of phyletic gradualism—however, even in those times evolutionary developments would take a very long time (hundreds of thousands of years instead of millions of years), an aspect which is dismissed when, in the movie *X-Men 2*, Prof. X claims that occasionally evolution takes leaps and new forms arise instantaneously. In the case of Magneto, the orphan would thus be the member and herald of a new species (*homo superior*) that is bound to conquer and dominate—the disinherited will inherit the Earth.

The recruits in this battle are the members of different mutant communities, which, as mentioned above, very much feel like orphanages, even though only some of the members are actually orphans. Some of the others were rejected by their hostile peer groups (e.g. the Beast or Iceman) or even by their parents (e.g. Toad) when their difference first became manifest, and so they appear as functional orphans. In their histories and stories of origin, the members of the groups are quite similar, and this may be the reason why in this series the protagonists occasionally change sides, i.e. superheroes may temporarily or permanently become supervillains and vice versa.

In the course of the publication history, superhero comics became increasingly cruel and occasionally bizarre. With the rise of graphic novels and longer narratives the texts catered to new audiences—or rather tried to retain the readers who had grown up with comics and continued reading them after their adolescence. The stories became more violent, and sexuality was also no longer banned from the superhero tales. Many comics published since the mid-1980s would not have been "Approved by the Comics Code Authority" in the 1950s and 60s, and with the coming of the new millennium, publishers (Marvel in 2001, DC Comics in 2011) replaced the stamp by their own rating systems, e.g. T for teens or A for adults. More mature themes became part of the stories, and in consequence

the origin stories have in some cases become excessively violent and the
traumata heightened to almost absurd levels.

The next examples are once more taken from the X-Men series.
Wolverine, created by Roy Thomas, Len Wein and John Romita Sr. in
1974, is one of the on-and-off members of the team and has over the
decades acquired an increasingly wild and violent origin story. He grew up
as James Howlett, son of John and Elizabeth Howlett, but his biological
father was the alcoholic and violent groundkeeper Thomas Logan. In
consequence of complicated circumstances, Thomas Logan broke into the
house of his employer and killed John Howlett; this led to the first
manifestation of Wolverine's claws, with which he killed the intruder, his
real father. His mother, already partly deranged after the death of another
son, committed suicide. Wolverine thus killed his father in the attempt to
avenge his alleged father and, in consequence, also lost his mother.

But even this scenario can still be exceeded. One of the original X-Men
in 1963 was Scott Summers, a.k.a. Cyclops, who as a boy witnessed the
death of his parents in a plane crash. In 1969 the story was extended and
his brother Alex, a.k.a. Havok, was introduced. The story now ran that
with only one parachute on the plane, the parents forced Scott and his
brother Alex to use it together—the boys were later separated. Alex
eventually also became an on-and-off member of the X-Men, but
occasionally his mind was taken over by evil forces and he unwillingly
joined the opponents in battles against the X-Men. Later it was revealed
that the parents were, in fact, kidnapped by aliens and that the mother was
raped and then killed by the mad and evil Shi'ar Emperor. In 2006 finally
(maybe), another brother, Gabriel, a.k.a. Vulcan, made his appearance.
Apparently, the mother was pregnant at the time of her death, the baby
was harvested from her body, and after being enslaved by the Shi'ar,
Gabriel made his way back to Earth, was eventually taken up by the X-
Men (cf. Kaveney 2008, 31), but ultimately became a rather ambiguous
supervillain and ruler of the Shi'ar Empire. Over time we thus find three
orphaned brothers, one of which is an epitome of the superhero, the second
a superhero who is occasionally manipulated to join the forces of evil, and
the third turns out to be a supervillain. All possibilities are played out
within one family.

It will have become clear that with the extension of the origin stories—
not only those of the superheroes but also their opponents'—the
dichotomy between good and evil is problematized. Within one family we
find a superhero, a supervillain and an ambivalent figure, in alternative
universes a superhero may turn out to be a supervillain, the superheroes
and supervillains have similar pasts, and so the members of both groups

are traumatized and psychologically damaged. This may serve in some cases to blur the strict division between good and evil that usually informs the basic dichotomies of popular literature and culture. Similar stories of origin may, however, also indicate that there is always the choice to do well, which is not the one taken by the villains. If some traumatized orphans—Batman and Spider-Man are the obvious examples—decide not merely to work through their trauma by taking revenge for the death of their loved ones but to fight crime for the rest of their lives, a different decision can be regarded as a moral failure. In his book *Mindhunter*, John Douglas, profiler for the FBI and possibly the model for Jack Crawford in Richard Harris's *The Silence of the Lambs*, admitted that the serial killers he investigated were not psychologically normal, but he insisted that they were still responsible, as they knew the difference between right or wrong. And in an interview, Andrew Vachss, advocate for child protection and attorney representing only children and youths, but also writer of crime fiction about child abuse, argued that there is always a choice. He claims that if we do not insist that behaviour is the result of free choice we disrespect those who have been badly mistreated and abused but still managed to live a decent life (Vachss and Leggewie 1994, 32). The ideology of the superhero comics subscribes to this perspective which ultimately claims that everyone is capable of molding his or her own fortune: the villains may have suffered from the trauma of being orphaned—and more—but ultimately they have taken the decision to commit crimes while the superheroes have decided for pro-sociality and the war on crime. In recent comics, the psychologically damaged hero occasionally trembles on the line between normality and psychosis, between good and evil, but he or she will ultimately end up on the right side, demonstrating that the internal battle can be won and that we are thus permitted to condemn those who fail to follow their suit. Thus, the superhero comic on the one hand offers some compassion and understanding for the victims of trauma who turn against society but on the other hand stresses the role of choice and allows the reader to pass verdict on them.

As mentioned above, it will not be possible to address all orphaned superheroes and all issues related to orphanhood in superhero comics in this chapter—even though some of the characters, e.g. Daredevil or the Punisher, would deserve closer attention. One fairly new series however, ought to be briefly mentioned, because it actually has orphans it its title. In *Protocol: Orphans*, created by Michael Alan Nelson and Mariano Navarro, the US government has taken parentless children and trained them to become superspies. They are not really superheroes, but dressed in costumes that resemble those of superheroes, and their fighting abilities are certainly far above average. Led by a mostly invisible "Dad" and under the supervision of some "Grandparents," they follow orders for the benefit of the public—e.g. disable a bomb that threatens a packed stadium in the first issue—in a pattern that resembles *Mission Impossible* or *Charlie's Angels*.

Will Eisner: *A Contract with God*[3]

Most of the texts discussed in this chapter have been comic series, but the orphan is, of course, also an important ingredient in independent graphic novels. As it is impossible to offer a complete survey of the medium, I want, instead, to discuss one particularly important work. It is part of a cycle of stories, *A Contract with God and Other Tenement Stories*, first published in 1978. The paperback edition was marketed as a "graphic novel", it "did much to popularize the term and to jump-start the re-branding of comics as an art form for grown-ups" (Mazur and Danner 2014, 181). It is the tale of another Jewish refugee coming to America, not from Nazi Germany but from Tsarist Russia. Quite possibly the story was at least partly written as a more realistic alternative to Superman's immigration tale. Already in the 1940s, Eisner's 'superhero' The Spirit could well have been conceptualized as a counter-image to Superman: he is "an all-too-human detective inhabiting the gritty nourish [*sic*] Central City" (Greg Smith 2010, 184), looks very much like Clark Kent in his trench coat and fedora and usually travels by tram or subway rather than flight. Furthermore, he is decidedly not the persistently cheerful and victorious type—and he seems to be drenched by every rain shower that happens to pour down on the Bronx. It may thus be argued that in *A Contract with God* Eisner also wanted to offer a very different perspective on the orphaned refugee from racism and persecution.

In this story, America does not welcome the new orphaned arrival. Hence, it is not a place of peace and goodwill in which an immigrant superhero embraces the host country's ideology and enduringly re-establishes the equilibrium whenever a criminal disrupts the social order. Instead, the young Frimme Hersh comes from a Russian shtetl where he has lived as the "child of the childless" (18). As a boy, he is an epitome of virtue and helpfulness, and he is repeatedly told that God will reward his good deeds. In gratitude for his kindness, the inhabitants of the village pool all their money and send him off to America to protect him from the Tsarist pogroms. On his way one night in the forest, he decides to make 'A Contract with God' and writes it on a flat stone. The exact conditions of this agreement remain rather vague, but Frimme seems to promise to fulfil all religious duties and serve his community to his best ability in expectation that God will not send any harm his way, but protect him from all evil.

After his arrival in America, he becomes a member of the Hassidic community of the Bronx, devoting his life to good works, and, as his kindness becomes well known, one day a baby girl is left on his doorstep. He adopts the child, names her Rachele after his mother, and gives her all his love, but then she falls ill and dies. In his grief, Frimme takes this as a violation of the contract and rages against God, who seems to respond in a thunderstorm, "and the old tenement trembled under the fury of the dialogue" (28). In his rebellion against God, Frimme resigns from all his religious and altruistic obligations. He turns into the caricature of the Jewish capitalist and property shark—and he takes "a mistress, a 'shikseh' from Scranton, Pa" (42). His financial success, however, does not bring any happiness, and so after some time he asks the elders of the Jewish community to draw up another contract with God, this time in the right language and binding for both sides—in return he will donate his first property, the tenement at 55 Dropsie Avenue, to the synagogue. After long discussions whether such a contract is permissible, the elders comply and Frimme happily signs the new agreement—and shortly afterwards dies of a heart attack.

> At the exact moment of Hersh's last earthly breath ... a mighty bolt of lightning struck the city ... Not a drop of rain fell ... Only an angry wind swirled about the tenements. On Dropsie Avenue the old tenements seemed to tremble in the storm. It reminded the tenants of that day long ago when Frimme Hersh argued with God and terminated their contract. (53-54, ellipses in the original)

Once more God seems to speak in thunder and lightning, a fire starts and quickly consumes all the old buildings on the street, except for the house at 55 Dropsie Avenue, which is miraculously spared. A young boy selflessly helps to fight the fire and saves the lives of several inhabitants, and like the young Frimme he is told that God will reward him. Racism, however, is also part of American life, and while there are no pogroms, he is bullied by three boys but fights back valiantly—and then he finds the stone with the contract that Frimme had thrown away in his rebellion against God, and he puts his name under Frimme's, "thereby entering into A Contract with God" (61).

A Contract with God is a tale of orphans. Frimme is an orphan who adopts another orphan—the motif of the baby on the doorstep is reminiscent of *Gasoline Alley* and *Popeye*, but now the setting is more realistic, and the baby is taken in by the bachelor "since no-one wanted a child born of God-knows-what kind of parents" (25). Most importantly, however, Frimme feels that he has been cheated and abandoned by God, and he is, thus, a spiritual orphan. The image of God that is evoked by Eisner is very much that of the deity in the Old Testament, who unleashes the forces of nature in his wrath, even though, of course, there is no direct indication that the thunder is really the voice of God. There are references to Noah and Moses—"The tenement at 55 Dropsie Avenue seemed ready to rise and float away on the swirling tie 'like the ark of Noah'" (9)—when Frimme returns in the pouring rain after Rachele's funeral, and the very first panel shows a stone table hanging over Frimme's head which is reminiscent of the tables Moses brings back from Mount Sinai. Later some more stone tablets are used for captions, and, of course, the stone with the contract also looks like a miniature version of Moses' tables.

These references to Biblical tales of God's covenants indicate that the story can be read allegorically and Frimme as representative of the Jewish people who had to leave their home and, despite being God's chosen nation, face chiefly pain and suffering, contempt and persecution. The contract with God appears as a private version of the Biblical covenants, and the old problem, why the chosen people have to suffer persecution and diaspora, is repeated on a smaller, but certainly not less tragic scale. Virtue, faith, and the fulfilment of all religious obligations are not rewarded, the economic exchange at the root of the covenant is violated, and God, of course, cannot be held accountable. In contrast to Noah's tale, however, it is not God who saves the exemplary Frimme from the pogroms, but the people in his village who tell him that "The next attack may wipe us out, so we have selected you to save, for we believe that you are favoured by God" (20). Like Noah—or Superman—Frimme may thus be the sole survivor of his people.

But then it is Job, the "blameless and upright man, who fears God and turns away from evil" (Job 1:8) that Frimme most resembles, and like Job he is also bereft of his hope and happiness as "the Lord gave and the Lord has taken away" (1:21). Of course, Frimme enters the contract without any kind of agreement with God, and his terms are similar to an insurance policy in which good deeds serve as payment; but then the death of the innocent girl does not fit a religious framework in which God's ways are more than just arbitrary or downright vicious. So, unlike Job, Frimme rebels against God when the divine grace seems to have been withdrawn, but strangely it appears as if now his questionable financial operations are favoured by "uncanny luck" (41). If the previous pages ask why God does not reward virtue, the following sequence of events poses the problem why the ungodly and selfish flourish at the expense of the poor.

In the 2006 preface to a reprint Eisner wrote: "The creation of this story was an exercise in personal agony. My only daughter, Alice, had died of leukaemia eight years before the publication of this book. My grief was still raw. My heart still bled. In fact, I could not bring myself to discuss the loss. […] This is the first time in thirty-four years that I have openly discussed it" (xvi).

As the graphic expression of Eisner's personal struggle and pain, *A Contract with God* carefully avoids any answer to the questions it poses about the relationship between God and man. It remains strictly ambiguous, on the one hand suggesting divine interference, on the other hand steering clear of any confirmation. The ambiguity can also be found in the execution of the comic and in Eisner's style of drawing. Eisner had always been fond of splash panels and bleeds, e.g. the issues of *The Spirit* often opened with a full-page panel. In *A Contract with God* there are hardly any frames and only rarely anything resembling a grid. Many pages only have one panel, and if there are two or more they frequently blend into each other. On the other hand, elements within the pictures occasionally substitute as frames, and the wall between the windows in the following picture emphasizes the emotional distance between Hersh and his mistress.

(Eisner 41, Copyright © 1978, 1985, 1989, 1995, 1996 by Will Eisner.
Used by permission of W. W. Norton & Company, Inc.)

Additionally, in this image the hatching appears like an indoor version of the rain, which dominates the first pages depicting Frimme's mourning after the funeral. Rain has always played an important part in Eisner's works, and this specific rain, a "thick, persistent drizzle, much heavier than normal water, that bounces off whatever it hits [...], reflecting the doom in bad men's hearts" is even called "Eisnershpritz" (Wolk 2007, 166). In *A Contract with God* is seems to be impossible to escape the rain that indicates not only despair, but possibly also God's displeasure.

The orphan in *A Contract with God* is ultimately a metaphor for the human condition in a world in which God may or may not have abandoned mankind to a life of uncertainty and suffering, of assumed promises that are not kept, and of hopes that are shattered. The last segment of the story indicates that these questions will resurface over and over again, that a new contract will always be made and, probably, also violated in an endless cycle of hope and despair.

The motif of the Jewish orphan was taken up again in Eisner's *Fagin the Jew*. Similar to other revisions of canonical works, most famously *Wide Sargasso Sea* by Jean Rhys, Eisner changes the perspective and now Fagin, the villain of the strongly anti-Semitic *Oliver Twist*, tells Charles Dickens his life shortly before he will be executed. Moses Fagin's father, who fled to the "tolerant" England from an unspecified middle European country, was murdered by a group of Englishmen who refused to pay a gambling debt when the boy was just 13; the mother died soon afterwards. The subsequent life of Fagin is described as an inevitable life of crime— honest work is almost impossible to find or to maintain—, discrimination and punishment. Fagin's motivation is quite different from the evil intentions as narrated in Dickens's novel as he tries to protect his boys from the "bitter refuge of workhouses" (52), and he actually helps Oliver to regain a place in respectable society and re-join his family. Indeed, it is Sikes who commits the most heinous crimes. In the end, Dickens promises to treat Fagin's "race more evenly" (114) in his later books.

Life Writing

"Life writing" is an umbrella term which covers a variety of genres, ranging from biography and autobiography to diary, memoir, confession or, more recently, internet blogs, and it may even blend into documentary or journalism. In comics, it probably first appeared in the 1960s with the rise of underground comix and thus a turn to more mature topics. With the rejection of the Comics Code, previously tabooed topics like sexuality could be explored, and several authors began to introduce autobiographical elements into their stories, among them famously Robert Crumb, Justin Green, and Harvey Pekar. This was also the time when the near absolute male dominance of the terrain was challenged and "we first see women using comics as a form of personal expression" (Chute 2010, 14). Important female authors included, among many others, Aline Kominsky (after 1978 Kominsky-Crumb), Trina Robbins, and Linda Barry, soon to be joined by Alison Bechdel who started her comic strip *Dykes to Watch Out For* in 1983.

Life writing in underground comix was marked by a mixture of honesty and graphic explicitness that was frequently regarded as offensive. Chute writes about the work of Kominsky-Crumb that it combines "enjoyment and shame" and not merely celebrates transgression (2010, 30), an aspect that is also present in many of the other "autographics" (Whitlock 2006, 966). Comics being what they are, graphic life writing frequently involves at least some degree of fictionalization. Linda Barry calls her work *One! Hundred! Demons!* "autobifictionalography" (Barry 2002, 5; see also Böger, forthcoming), other authors show their awareness of the problematic status of their works between realist autobiography and fiction in their subtitles—Alison Bechdel's *Fun Home* is *A Family Tragicomic*, Chester Brown's *I Never Liked You* announces itself as *A Comic Strip Narrative* and G. Neri's and Randy DuBurke's *Yummy: The Last Days of a Southside Shorty* suggests elements of the documentary. The graphic style usually also shows a distinct departure from aspirations to realism as many of the narratives are not presented in glossy or realistic colours but rather in black and white or washed-out greens, greys, or blues; in others works (e.g. by Linda Barry or Aline Kominsky-Crumb) vivid colours or unrealistic and occasionally hallucinogenic or surrealist elements serve to defamiliarize the imagery and add to the graphic expression of mental states.

As these works are, indeed, autobiographic in the widest sense, they deal with real experiences, including various forms of trauma and grief— (sexual) abuse, illness, catastrophes like 9/11 or Hurricane Katrina, depressions and frustrations, discrimination, gang wars, religious oppression, crises of faith, etc.—but orphans now hardly play any significant role. In this the texts resemble realist literature and autobiographical writing in the 20th century in which the orphan is no longer a common figure, if only because the death of parents is no longer a frequent occurrence.

Instead of the story of the juvenile orphan, however, some of the comics deal with the experience of being orphaned, i.e. the loss of a parent at a later stage of life. Most famously, Alison Bechdel's *Fun Home* describes the death—possibly suicide—of her father when she already went to college and had just revealed to her parents that she is a lesbian. The graphic novel is then an exploration of her relationship with her father who was a carefully closeted homosexual, director of a funeral home, and teacher of English literature. This is merged with the realization of her own sexual orientation and identity in the course of her adolescence. The story weaves back and forth between childhood memories and the narrator's response to her father's death and her subsequent life. The death itself, as it usually happens in real life, is not witnessed but conveyed via telephone, and it appears to be almost banal, as the focus is less of the loss but rather on the narrator's ambivalent reactions and her strategies to cope with a kind of emotional numbness. It seems as if she is constantly monitoring her responses from a detached distance, "marveling at the dissonance between this apparently carefree activity [of bicycling home] and my new tragic circumstances" (Bechdel 2007, 46), crying in the arms of her girlfriend but exchanging "ghastly, uncontrollable grins" (46) with her brother when they first meet before the funeral. The ambivalence is expressed graphically in two panels, showing the narrator as a split personality while she is facing her father's corpse in the funeral home.

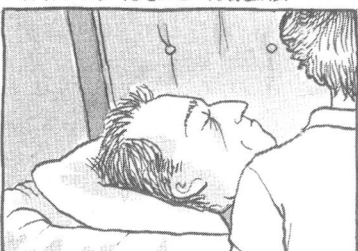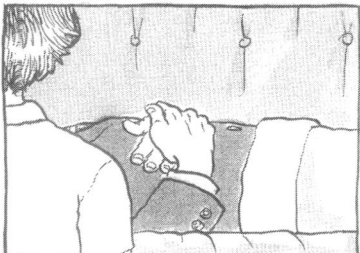

(Bechdel, 52, © 2006 by Alison Bechdel: Used with permission.)

The narrator, however, does not directly address the issue of orphanhood. The death of the father is perceived less as the loss of a protective parent than as a trigger to revisit childhood and adolescent memories and, in consequence of the father's homosexuality and creativity, also as an investigation into her own sexual and artistic identity, with her father serving as a troubling guide and occasionally also as a doubtful mirror image.

The death of a parent is also a topic in two autographics by Chester
Brown, but while it is certainly an important aspect, its presence on the
pages is reduced to an absolute minimum, marked by conspicuous evasion
rather than by exploration. The graphic novel *I Never Liked You* (1994)
consists of short, if not fragmentary, episodes—the subtitle *A Comic Strip
Narrative* is quite fitting as most episodes contain only five or six panels.
The narrator appears to be an emotionally inhibited adolescent who, being
rather good looking, is very attractive to girls but unable to respond
adequately to their advances. The emotional numbness seems to be an
inherent element in this family, and while the narrator at different times
wishes that he could express his affections towards his mother or one or
the other of the girls, he either does not manage to speak out or, in one
case, fails to follow up on a sudden and unexpected declaration of love.
The mother first appears as deeply religious—possibly a fanatic—rigidly
forbidding any kind of vulgarity or taking the Lord's name in vain. She
then shows up on and off throughout the narrative, and some of the short
episodes are rather bewildering, e.g. when she tells her quite young and
not particularly interested sons that "most men expect women to look a
certain way and not all of them look that way" (26), and that, in
consequence of having rather small breasts, she wears a padded brassiere.
She later declares quite suddenly that she had mental problems in the past,
that once more she is not feeling well and that she is going to have herself
hospitalized because she needs to get herself sorted out. The responses of
her sons to this news, "Okay" and "Alright" (146), once more emphasize
the lack of any affectionate behaviour in the family. Her condition
deteriorates, and during a visit of her sons—probably the only one—she is
completely contorted and inarticulate. Once more the narrator, who had
planned to express his love to her, does not manage to do so. The
information about her death is presented rather casually while we see the
narrator climbing a staircase: "So one day while we were on vacation at
our grandmother's, our father told Gordon and me that our mother was
gone" (175). Trying to cry, he manages to shed only a single tear. The
episode concludes with the statement: "My father caught a flight to
Montreal that day and arranged the funeral. Neither Gordon nor I attended
it. We weren't asked if we wanted to" (177). Brown was 17 years old
when his mother died, and thus again the concept of literal orphanhood
does not really apply. But then the narrator seems to be orphaned from the
very beginning, living in a family of recluses who lack not only affection
but even minimal courtesy and compassion—when the mother buys a wig
because her hair is thinning, her sons bluntly tell her that it is "ugly" and
"awful" (77). The mother's behaviour and ailment remain ambivalent,

they can be read as a cause or a symptom, and her death as a conclusion or as a signpost for the narrator's future life.

Brown once more, albeit only implicitly, addressed his mother's illness and death in the rather short comic "My Mom was a Schizophrenic" (1998). The comic itself does not refer to his mother's death after it has been announced in the first three words of the title—only in the notes does Brown state somewhat dismissively: "My mother died in an institution in 1976 (See my book *I never liked you* for more on this, though not much more.)" (215). Instead, the narrator discusses the medical assessment of schizophrenia with recourse to many traditional or dissident psychological authorities like Kraepelin, Bleuler, Szasz, Farber, Grof or Laing, who appear as 'talking heads'. The graphic form is minimalistic, and throughout the comic the narrator is presented with hardly any variation in his pose while he suggests that schizophrenia may not be a psychological illness at all but rather an apt response to the "sterile barrenness of modern cities" (213), a psychological condition that shows similarities with shamans' trances or psychedelic drug trips.

Again, the dead mother is chiefly present in her absence, her death seemingly only the trigger for a semi-academic discussion. The very blandness of the comic, however, matches the content of the text, the monotonous rhythms and repetitive tasks of modern life, and the isolation and loneliness of the solitary figure of the narrator in front of a sterile barren wall. This self-reflexivity is a fundamental element of the "story" as well as the artistic expression:

> The images without the text would be pure redundancy, the text without the drawings merely a dry lecture. Together they become a very personal account. Even though the mother is only mentioned in the title, her presence and death can be felt throughout the story, and the factual discourse on schizophrenia is ultimately a memoir. (Vanderbeke 2014, 319)

As indicated, in these graphic narratives the loss of a parent does not result in "orphanhood" except in a purely literal sense. They are, ultimately, very similar to other tales about the death of loved ones, e.g. Alicia Torres' *American Widow*, which tells about the death of the narrator's husband, who was one of the victims of the terror attacks of September 11, 2001. A common element seems to be that death is numbing rather than shocking—even in Art Spiegelman's highly expressive "Prisoner on the Hell Planet", a four-page section of *Maus* rendered in woodcut style, the narrator's first response to his mother's suicide is: "I felt confused; I felt angry; I felt numb! ... I didn't exactly feel like crying, but figured I should!" (103). The actual moment when the narrators learn about the death of loved ones is usually embedded in a normality that does not allow for dramatic ruptures and offers itself as a default mode that facilitates evasion and detachment. The actual loss only confirms what had already been felt before, an existential distance that cannot be bridged. The treatment of parental death is, ultimately, very similar to Virginia Woolf's *To the Lighthouse*, in which the death of the parent is a central element of the narrative, but within the narration it actually takes place in a subordinate clause within a parenthesis (Woolf 1985, 120).

In addition to these narratives, there are again tales of functional orphans. G. Neri's and Randy DuBurke's *Yummy: The Last Days of a Southside Shorty* tells the story of Robert Sandifier who at the age of eleven killed a 14-year-old girl, Shavon Dean, in what may have been an initiation for the Black Disciples, a Chicago street gang. After a 77-hour 'manhunt', he was found dead, murdered by two gang members to prevent him from turning informant for the police in case of his capture (Newafrican77, all information about Yummy's life is taken from this website, which is in agreement with the other sources I have found and also with the graphic novel, in which many of the sources are quoted verbatim). Robert Sandifier grew up in a dysfunctional family, and even this term may be too positive. His father had been sent to jail before his birth on a felony gun charge and remained permanently absent throughout Yummy's life. His mother was a drug addict and prostitute; at the time of his death she had been arrested 41 times. Yummy was severely abused— according to a report of the Department of Children and Family Services he suffered not only from general neglect but also from cigarette burns and beatings with electric cords. According to Cook County public guardian Patrick Murphy, he was "a kid who was made and turned into a sociopath by the time he was three years old" (Gibbs, qtd. in Neri and DuBurke 2010, 61). He was handed over to his grandmother, but his situation did not really improve, and by the age of eight he had dropped out of school and started to build his own criminal record, including shoplifting, residential burglary, armed robbery, and auto theft. The graphic novel, told by a fictitious narrator whose brother Gary is also a member of the Black Disciples, then presents Yummy's enlistment in the gang, and once more it seems that orphans are the best recruits. The leader of the gang, aptly called Monster, appeals to the boy's search for a home, but also makes it clear that there is a price to be paid: "Now we family. You work for us" (37). The point is later driven home once more when one of the locals suggest: "The Disciples ain't stupid. They got this endless supply of young ones with no daddy, just looking for attention. So they use these kids for hit men while they sit back and reap the rewards" (59). While Yummy is not literally an orphan, he seems to be orphaned not only by his parents, but also by his environment, his surrogate family, and ultimately the authorities and institutions.

Yummy focuses on the origins of street violence and presents the juvenile killer as a bully, an already hardened criminal at the age of eleven, but also as a child in need of comfort and protection that craves sweets, hugs his teddy bear, and fails to comprehend the consequences of his action, claiming that the murder wasn't his fault as he didn't intend to kill Shavon: "I didn't do nothing wrong. She got in the way" (49). An eleven-page sequence (53-63) presents the narrator's attempts to understand Yummy, the contradictory answers he receives from the people who knew him, official statements from journalists, members of the police, lawyers, academics, and politicians, including President Clinton, and it ends in the question: "I wondered if I grew up like him, would I have turned out the same" (63).

The imagery of the graphic novel is rendered in black and white with strong contrasts of light and shade in a style that occasionally bears a certain resemblance to woodcuts—it was brought to perfection in Frank Miller's *Sin City*, which may well be an intended association. Moreover, as in Bechdel's *Fun Home*, panel divisions are used to split larger images into fragments, now indicating disruption, anxiety, and a world that has turned to pieces (e.g. Neri and DuBurke 2010, 48).

The graphic novel ends with a "solution" that emphasizes traditional family values as a remedy against the lure of street gangs and the concomitant violence. After a visit to Shavon's house where they leave some flowers and pray for her family, the narrator's mother declares, "Now let's go home and be a family" (91). Finally, Gary also shows up, subdued, disillusioned with the gang, and longing for his family home. The last page then shows the family driving home, and the captions run: "I don't know which was worse, the way Yummy lived or the way he died. But if we can live through all this craziness and stay a family --- maybe that's worth fighting for" (94).

In addition to such tales of children being orphaned or becoming functional orphans, the concept of the orphan also, occasionally, appears to be in the eyes of the academic beholder. In a paper on *Maus*, Hamida Bosmajidan distinguishes between the narrator Artie Spiegelman and the author Art Spiegelman and argues that trauma, grief, and the feeling of guilt often prevent holocaust survivors from connecting to their children. This may result in a form of erasure: "The children feel at times as if they did not exist for the parents, for the controlling event—the master narrative, uttered or unuttered—all but consumes the parent" (Bosmajian 1998, 5). The narrator Artie, then, gives voice to his father's traumatic experiences, but simultaneously silences his own voice in the process.

> By appropriating his father's story within the frame of his own story, he writes and draws Vladek's ordeal into permanent existence, but he himself is at the end psychologically and literally unacknowledged and orphaned. (Bosmajian 1998, 5)

The metaphor is awkward, as this kind of self-effacement reverses the concept of the orphan. The son is not bereft of his parents but of his own voice and thus identity. Thus, while Artie is literally orphaned by his mother's suicide when he is 20 years old (Spiegelman, 102), his real orphanhood is caused by his father's inability to see beyond his own grief and to recognize his son's own suffering. It seems as if the orphan has turned into an open—or even empty—metaphor, indicating any kind of solitude and grief, be it bereavement or abandonment, loss or effacement, psychological trauma or existential despair.

In lieu of a conclusion

In this chapter I have tried to offer a survey of the diversity and multiplicity of motifs and narrative patterns to be found on the pages of the allegedly trivial genre or medium. All the topics, types, and treatments of orphanhood in mainstream literature can also be found in comics. The early years still present the dichotomy of innocence versus depravity that was common in the 18th and 19th centuries, replacing the panoramic view of the sprawling narratives with mini-tales that fit the format of the comic strip and add up to a sometimes literally endless chain of interchangeable events. Only in rare cases like *Gasoline Alley* does a narration in real time surpass the repetitive structure of the usual strips and thus allow for developments in characters and the socio-political environment. The fictional comic books and in particular the superhero comics return to even earlier patterns and draw on motifs from myths and fairy tales. In this respect, they are rather similar to present day High Fantasy, which also has recourse to pre-modern and pre-enlightenment traditions in the construction of social environments for narratives that regularly follow the basic outline of Joseph Campbell's monomyth, including the almost ubiquitous orphan as hero. Life writing, then, transforms realistic experiences into artistic formats that could possibly be described as graphic understatement or hyperbole, as minimalized or overblown expression. In particular narratives dealing with catastrophes and tragic events—at least those that I am aware of—have a tendency to verge towards reduced colour schemes and imagery, quite possibly as an intended contrast to the high-gloss pages of recent superhero comics and thus as an implicit suggestion of authenticity. But then it is often the muted voices and constrained expressions that have the strongest impact and make the deepest impression—and so it may well be in comics and graphic narratives.

At the beginning of this chapter I suggested that the comic may itself be a kind of functional orphan, rejected and abandoned by its more respectable "parents", literature and the visual arts. As such it also shows all the diverse features of the orphan, including the dichotomy between the innocence and purity of the *Rousseauian* child and the depravity of the incorrigible rascal, the aspiration to be accepted into respectable society as well as anarchic rebellion against all possible conventions and taboos. Over the last decades, it seems as if the comic has, albeit slowly and with strong reservations from the more conservative sectors of traditional Culture, been admitted into schools, feuilletons, museums, and the halls of higher learning. Hopefully it will also follow the firmly established course of narrative patterns and, like the orphan in fiction, invigorate its new environment.

Notes

[1] I would like to thank Sebastian Domsch, Oliver Moisich, and Marie Vanderbeke, who acted as first readers and offered very perceptive and helpful comments and suggestions.

[2] Similar views and agendas can be found in other comics as well, and hypocritical politicians, social servants and reformers are occasionally among the criminals hunted by masked vigilantes. Wright suggests, for example, that the "Green Lantern reserved some of his greatest moral outrage not for the straightforward crooks that he routinely nabbed but for those self-styled local reformers and public servants who had only their own selfish interests at heart. In ["The Adventure of the Underfed Orphans;" *All-American Comics* 31 (DC Comics, October 1941); D.V.], the Green Lantern exposes "Honest" John Logan, who claims to be a progressive reformer and sponsor of a municipal orphanage when, in fact, he is a crook who has conspired with the superintendent of the orphanage to pocket the public funds while the orphans starve" (Wright 2001, 24).

[3] Some of the ideas presented in this subchapter have already been discussed in my paper on *Graphic Grief* (2014) and are quoted from there.

Works Cited

Askeland, Lori. 2001. "Orphans and Orphanages." In *Girlhood in America: An Encyclopedia* 2 vol., edited by Miriam Forman-Brunell, 483-89. Santa Barbara, Denver and Oxford: ABC-CLIO.

Auerbach, Nina. 1975. "Incarnations of the Orphan." *English Literary History* 42 (3): 395-419.

Bagge, Peter. 2010. "Spiderman Sucks." In *The Best American Comics Criticism*, edited by Ben Schwartz, 117-21. Seattle: Fantagraphics Books.

Bainbridge, Jason. 2009. "'Worlds Within Worlds': The Role of Superheroes in the Marvel and DC Universes." In *The Contemporary Comic Book Superhero*, edited by Angela Ndalianis, 64-85. New York: Routledge.

Balzer, Jens, and Lambert Wiesing. 2010. *Outcault: Die Erfindung des Comic*. Bochum and Essen: Christian A. Bachmann Verlag.

Banta, Martha. 2003. *Barbaric Intercourse: Caricature and the Culture of Conduct, 1841-1936*. Chicago and London: University of Chicago Press.

Barker, Martin. 1984. *A Haunt of Fears: The Strange History of the British Horror Comics Campaign*. London and Sydney: Pluto Press.

Barry, Lynda. 2002. *One! Hundred! Demons!* Seattle: Sasquatch Books.

Bave, Radhika M. 2013. "Orphan Annie-Eye Nuclei." *Journal of Oral and Maxillofacial Pathology* 17, no. 2 (May-August): 154-55. http://www.ncbi.nlm.nih.gov/pmc/articles/PMC3830218/.

Bechdel, Alison. 2007. *Fun Home: A Family Tragicomic*. Boston and New York: A Mariner Book.

Blackbeard, Bill. 1995. "The Yellow Kid the Yellow Decade." In Richard F. Outcault. *The Yellow Kid. A Centennial Celebration of the Kid Who Started Comics*, 16-136. Northampton, MA: Kitchen Sink Press.

Blakemore, Erin. 2014. "Our Obsession with Orphans: A Short History from Jane Eyre to Annie." *JSTOR Daily*, December 17, 2014. http://daily.jstor.org/our-obsession-with-orphans/.

Bosmajian, Hamida. 1998. "The Orphaned Voice in Art Spiegelman's *Maus* I & II." *Literature and Psychology* 44 (1-2): 1-22. Repr. http://www.oswego.edu/~jayaward/Bosmajian.pdf.

Bowlby, Rachel. 2013. *A Child of One's Own: Parental Stories*. Oxford: Oxford University Press.

Böger, Astrid. Forthcoming. "Life Writing." In *Handbook of Comics and Graphic Narratives*, edited by Dan Hassler-Forest, Sebastian Domsch, and Dirk Vanderbeke. Berlin and Boston: De Gruyter.

Brown, Chester. 2014. *I Never Liked You: A Comic Strip Narrative* [1994]. Montreal: Drawn & Quarterly.

—. 2006. "My Mom Was a Schizophrenic." In *An Anthology of Graphic Fiction, Cartoons & True Stories*. Vol. II, edited by Ivan Brunetti, 209-16. New Haven and London: Yale University Press.

Busch, Wilhelm. 1962. *Eins zwei drei im Sauseschritt*. Berlin: Eulenspiegel Verlag.

—. 1967. *Dieses war der erste Streich*. Berlin: Eulenspiegel Verlag.

Campbell, Joseph. 1993. *The Hero with a Thousand Faces* [1949]. London: Fontana Press.

Carver, Stephen. "More Weird Tales from the Vault of Fear: The EC Legacy." *Ainsworth and Friends. Essays in 19th Century Literature and the Gothic*. https://ainsworthandfriends.wordpress.com/2016/02/16/more-weird-tales-from-the-vault-of-fear-the-ec-legacy/.

Chute, Hillary L. 2010. *Graphic Women: Live Narrative and Contemporary Comics*. New York: Columbia University Press.

Coogan, Peter. 2006. *Superhero: The Secret Origin of a Genre*. Austin, TX: MonkeyBrain Books.

Douglas, John, and Mark Olshanker. 1995. *Mindhunter: Inside the FBI's Elite Serial Crime Unit*. New York et al.: Pocket Star Books.

Duggan, Jennifer. 2016. "Traumatic Origins: Orphanhood and the Superhero." In *Good Grief. Children and Comics*, edited by Michelle Ann Abate and Joe Sutcliff Sanders, 47-67. Columbus, OH: Billy Ireland Cartoon Library & Museum.

Eco, Umberto. 1979. "The Myth of Superman." In *The Role of the Reader: Explorations in the Semiotics of Texts*, 107-24. Bloomington, IN: Indiana University Press.

Eisner, Will. 2006. *A Contract with God and Other Tenement Stories* [1978]. New York: DC Comics.

—. 2003. *Fagin the Jew*. New York et al.: Doubleday.

Feldstein, Al, and Jack Kamen. 1954. "The Orphan." *Shock SuspenStories* #14 (April-May): 1-8.

Fiedler, Leslie. 1966. *Life and Death in the American Novel*, revised edition. New York: Stein and Day.

Fingeroth, Danny. 2004. *Superman on the Couch*. New York and London: Continuum.

Gaiman, Neil. 1996. *Sandman*, vol. 9: *The Kindly Ones*. New York: Vertigo.

Gaines, William. "Testimony of William M. Gaines, Publisher, Entertaining Comics Group, New York, N.Y." (The 1954 Senate Subcommittee Hearings into Juvenile Delinquency). Reprinted at http://www.thecomicbooks.com/gaines.html.

—. 1983. "An Interview with William Gaines." *The Comics Journal* #81 (May). Reprinted at http://classic.tcj.com/interviews/an-interview-with-william-m-gaines-part-one-of-three/.

Gans, Grobian. 1972. *Die Ducks: Psychogramm einer Sippe*. Reinbek bei Hamburg: Rowohlt.

Gavin, Adrienne E. 2012. "The Child in British Literature: An Introduction." In *The Child in British Literature: Literary Constructions of Childhood*, edited by A.E. Gavin, 1-18. Basingstoke: Palgrave Macmillan.

Gibbs, Nancy R. 2001. "Murder in Miniature." *Time Magazine* June 24. http://content.time.com/time/magazine/article/0,9171,165100,00.html.

Gordon, Ian. 1998. *Comic Strips and Consumer Culture, 1890-1945*. Washington and London: Smithsonian Institution Press.

Gould, Stephen Jay, and Niles Eldredge. 1977. "Punctuated Equilibria: The Tempo and Mode of Evolution Reconsidered." *Paleobiology* 3 (2): 115-51.

Grandinetti, Fred M. 2004. *Popeye: An Illustrated Cultural History*. Jefferson, N.C. and London: McFarland.

Gray, Harold. 1974. *Little Orphan Annie and Little Orphan Annie in Cosmic City*. New York: Dover Publications.

—. 2008. *The Complete Little Orphan Annie*, vol. 1: *Will Tomorrow Ever Come—Daily Comic Strips 1924-1927*, edited by Dean Mullaney. San Diego: IDW Publishing.

Hanks, Henry. 2011. "The Secret to 'X-Men's' Success." CNN. June 3. http://www.cnn.com/2011/SHOWBIZ/Movies/06/03/xmen.legacy.go/.

Harvey, Robert C. 1994. *The Art of the Funnies: An Aesthetic History*. Jackson: University Press of Mississippi.

—. 2013. "The Orphan's Epic." *The Comics Journal* May 20. http://www.tcj.com/the-orphans-epic/.

Hassler-Forest, Dan. 2015. "Superheroes and the Law—Batman, Superman, and the 'big Other'." In *Zizek and the Law*, edited by Laurent de Sutter, 101-17. London: Routledge.

Heer, Jeet. 2006. "Introduction." In Frank King. *Walt & Skeezix 1923 & 1924*, edited by Chris Ware, Jeet Heer, and Chris Oliveros, 9-89. Montreal: Drawn and Quarterly.

—. 2008. "Dream Big and Work Hard." In Harold Gray. *The Complete Little Orphan Annie*, vol. 1: *Will Tomorrow Ever Come*, edited by Dean Mullaney, 11-27. San Diego: IDW Publishing.

—. 2010. "Drawn from Life." In *Best American Comics Criticism*, edited by Ben Schwartz, 133-43. Seattle: Fantagraphics Books.

—. 2014. "Harold Gray and the Limits of Conservative Anti-Racism." *The Comics Journal* July 7, 2014. Adapted from the introduction to *The Complete Little Orphan Annie*, vol. 10. http://www.tcj.com/harold-gray-and-the-limits-of-conservative-anti-racism/.

Heins, Scott. 2015. "Be Transported to Krypton with Mike Kelley's Dazzling Superman-Inspired Sculptures." *Gothamist—Arts and Entertainment*. Sept. 11, 2015. http://gothamist.com/2015/09/11/mike_kelley_superman_kandor.php#photo-1.

Hoevel, Ann. 2010. "How to succeed in comics: Why Stan is 'The Man'." CNN, September 9, 2010. http://www.cnn.com/2010/LIVING/09/09/stan.the.man.lee/.

Honeyman, Susan. 2005. *Elusive Childhood: Impossible Representations in Modern Fiction*. Columbus, OH: Ohio State University Press.

Internet Archives. "Brain Boy 6". https://web.archive.org/web/20070311100358/http://-www.challengersoftheunknown.com:80/BB06.html.

Jenks, Chris. 2005. *Childhood*. 2nd edn. London and New York: Routledge.

Kaplan, Arie. 2008. *From Krakow to Krypton: Jews and Comic Books*. Philadelphia, PA: The Jewish Publication Society.

Kaveney, Roz. 2008. *Superheroes: Capes and Crusaders in Comics and Films*. London and New York: I.B. Tauris.

Kimball, Melanie A. 1999. "From Folktales to Fiction: Orphan Characters in Children's Literature." *Library Trends* 47 (3): 558-78.

King, Frank. 2005. *Walt & Skeezix. 1921 & 1922* (reprint of *Gasoline Alley*), edited by Chris Ware. Montreal: Drawn & Quarterly.

—. 1927. *Gasoline Alley Daily*. Strip from November 23, 1927. Reprinted http://www.comicartfans.com/gallerypiece.asp?piece=922235.

Landa, Gertrude (Aunt Naomi). 1919. *Jewish Fairy Tales and Legends*. New York: Bloch Publishing.

Lewis, R.W.B. 1955. *The American Adam: Innocence, Tragedy, and Tradition in the Nineteenth Century*. Chicago: University of Chicago Press.

Loudon, Irvine. 1986. "Deaths in Childbirth from the Eighteenth Century to 1935." *Medical History* 30: 1-41.

Mazur, Dan, and Alexander Danner. 2014. *Comics: A Global History, 1968 to the Present*. London: Thames and Hudson.

McCloud, Scott. 1994. *Understanding Comics*. New York: HarperCollins.

Meyer, Christina. 2012. "Urban America in the Newspaper Comic Strips of the Nineteenth Century: Introducing the Yellow Kid." *ImageTexT: Interdisciplinary Comics Studies* 6 (2). http://www.english.ufl.edu/imagetext/archives/v6_2/meyer/index.shtml.

Miller, Frank, Klaus Jansen, Lynn Varley, and John Costanza. 1986. *The Dark Knight Returns*. New York: DC Comics.

Miller, Frank, David Mazzuchelli, Todd Klein, and Richmond Lewis. 1987. *Batman: Year One*. New York: DC Comics.

Miller, Frank, and Lynn Varley. 2002. *The Dark Knight Strikes Again*. New York: DC Comics.

Misiroglu, Gina. 2012. *The Superhero Book: The Ultimate Encyclopedia of Comic-Book Icons and Hollywood Heroes*. Detroit: Visible Ink Press.

Moore, Alan, and Brian Bolland. 1988. *Batman: The Killing Joke*. New York: DC Comics.

Morris, Jon. 2015. *The League of Regrettable Superheroes*. Philadelphia, PA: Quirk Books.

Morrison, Grant, and Dave McKean. 2004. *Batman: Arkham Asylum: A Serious House on Serious Earth* [1989], 15th Anniversary Edition. New York: DC Comics.

Neri, G., and Randy DuBurke. 2010. *Yummy: The Last Days of a Southside Shorty*. New York: Lee & Low Books.

Newafrican77. "The Forgotten Story of Robert 'Yummy' Sandifer." March 9, 2014. https://newafrikan77.wordpress.com/2014/03/09/the-forgotten-story-of-robert-yummy-sandifer/.

Nikolajeva, Maria. 2002. *The Rhetoric of Character in Children's Literature*. Lanhan, MA, and London: The Scarecrow Press.

Nixon, Cheryl L. 2011. *The Orphan in Eighteenth-Century Law and Literature: Estate, Blood, and Body*. Farnham and Burlington: Ashgate.

Nyberg, Amy Kiste. 2005. "'No Harm in Horror': Ethical Dimensions of the Postwar Comic Book Controversy." In *Comics as Philosophy*, edited by Jeff MacLoughlin, 27-45. Jackson: University Press of Mississippi.

Outcault, Richard F. 1995. *R.F. Outcault's The Yellow Kid: A Centennial Celebration of the Kid Who Started Comics*. Introduction by Bill Blackbeard. Northampton, MA: Kitchen Sink Press.

Packer, Sharon. 2010. *Superheroes and Superegos: Analyzing the Minds behind the Masks*. Santa Barbara, CA.: Praeger.

Pak, Greg, and Carmine Di Giandomenico. 2009. *X-Men: Magneto Testament*. New York: Marvel.

Petersen, Robert S. 2011. *Comics, Manga, and Graphic Novels: A History of Graphic Narratives*. Santa Barbara, CA, et al.: Praeger.

Puschmann-Nalenz, Barbara. 2014. "The Figure of the Orphan in Contemporary Fiction." In *Narrating Loss: Representations of Mourning, Nostalgia and Melancholia in Contemporary Anglophone Fiction*, edited by Brigitte Johanna Glaser and Barbara Puschmann-Nalenz, 179-202. Trier: WVT.

Reynolds, Richard. 1992. *Superheroes: A Modern Mythology*. Jackson: University Press of Mississippi.

Riley, James Whitcomb. 1994. *Little Orphant Annie and Other Poems*. New York: Dover Publications.

Romagnoli, Alex S., and Gian S. Pagnucci. 2013. *Enter the Superheroes: American Values, Culture, and the Canon of Superhero Literature*. Plymouth et al.: Scarecrow Press.

Rowson, Martin. 2013. "Towards a Theory of Literary Adaptation in Comic Book Format: A Graphic Response." In *Anglistentag 2012 Potsdam*, edited by Karin Röder and Ilse Wischer, 237-43. Trier: WVT.

Sabin, Roger. 2001. *Comics, Comix and Graphic Novels: A History of Comic Art*. New York: Phaidon.

Santod, Avi. 2015. *Selling the Silver Bullet: The Lone Ranger and Transmedia Brand Licensing*. Austin, TX: University of Texas Press.

Schwartz, Ben. 2010. "Like a Prairie Fire, even Hotter: Harold Gray, Politics, and the Not-So-Funny Funnies." In *Best American Comics Criticism*, edited by Ben Schwartz, 129-32. Seattle: Fantagraphics Books.

Siegel, Jerry, and Joe Shuster. 1998. "Superman." *Action Comics* #1, June 1938, 1-13. New York: DC Comics.

Smith, Bruce. 1982. *The History of Little Orphan Annie*. New York: Ballantine Books.

Smith, Greg M. 2010. "Will Eisner, Vaudevillian of the Cityscape." In *Comics and the City: Urban Space in Print, Picture and Sequence*, edited by Jörn Ahrens, and Arno Meteling, 183-98. New York: Continuum.

Spiegelman, Art. (1986/1992) 2003. *The Complete Maus*. London: Penguin.

Torres, Alicia, and Sungyoon Choi. 2008. *American Widow*. New York: Random House.

Twain, Mark. 2004. *The Adventures of Huckleberry Finn*, edited by Gerald Graff and James Phelan. Boston and New York: Bedford/St Martins.

Tye, Larry. 2012. *Superman: The High-Flying History of America's Most Enduring Hero*. New York: Random House.

Vachss, Andrew, and Claus Leggewie. 1994. *Über das Böse*. Frankfurt: Eichborn.

Vanderbeke, Dirk. 1994. "Von Menschen und Fledermäusen: Francis Ford Coppolas *Dracula* und Frank Millers *Batman*." *Neue Rundschau* 105 (2): 33-42.

—. 2014. "Graphic Grief." In *Narrating Loss: Representations of Mourning, Nostalgia and Melancholia in Contemporary Anglophone Fictions*, edited by Brigitte Glaser and Barbara Puschmann-Nalenz, 309-26. Trier: WVT.

Various. 2004. *Batman in the Forties*. New York: DC.

Watson, James, and Anne Hill. 2012. *Dictionary of Media and Communication Studies*, 8th edn. London: Bloomsbury Academic.

Weinstein, Simcha. 2006. *Up, Up, and Oy Vey! How Jewish History, Culture and Values Shaped the Comic Book Superhero*. Fort Lee, NJ: Barricade Books.

Whitlock, Gillian. 2006. "Autographics. The Seeing 'I' of the Comics." *Modern Fiction Studies* 52 (4): 965-79.

Wiacek, Win. "E.C. Segar's Popeye volume 6: 'Me Li'l Swee'Pea'." (Review). http://www.comicsreview.co.uk/nowreadthis/2014/01/29/e-c-segars-popeye-volume-6-me-lil-sweepea/.

Wolk, Douglas. 2007. *Reading Comics*. Philadelphia, PA: Da Capo Press.

Wood, Mary. 2014a. "Yellow Kid Readership." In *The Yellow Kid on the Paper Stage*. 2 February 2014. American Studies at the University of Virginia. http://xroads.virginia.edu/~ma04/wood/ykid/readership.htm.

—. 2014b. "Commodifying the Kid." In *The Yellow Kid on the Paper Stage*. 2 February 2014. American Studies at the University of Virginia. http://xroads.virginia.edu/~ma04/wood/ykid/commodify.htm.

Woolf, Virginia. (1927) 1985. *To The Lighthouse*. London: Grafton.

Wright, Bradford W. 2001. *Comic Book Nation: The Transformation of Youth Culture in America*. Baltimore and London: The Johns Hopkins University Press.

INDEX